Teach

Yourself

Java

Joseph O'Neil

Osborne/**McGraw-Hill**

Berkeley New York St. Louis San Francisco Auckland Bogotá Hamburg London Madrid Mexico City
Milan Montreal New Delhi Panama City Paris São Paulo Singapore Sydney Tokyo Toronto

PUBLISHER
Brandon A. Nordin

EDITOR IN CHIEF
Scott Rogers

ACQUISITIONS EDITOR
Wendy Rinaldi

PROJECT EDITOR
Heidi Poulin

EDITORIAL ASSISTANT
Debbie Escobedo

TECHNICAL EDITOR
Thomas Feng

COPY EDITOR
Gary Morris

PROOFREADER
Rhonda Holmes

INDEXER
Sheryl Schildt

COMPUTER DESIGNERS
Jani Beckwith
Ann Sellers

ILLUSTRATOR
Brian Wells

Osborne/**McGraw-Hill**
2600 Tenth Street
Berkeley, California 94710
U.S.A.

For information on translations or book distributors outside
the U.S.A., or to arrange bulk purchase discounts for sales
promotions, premiums, or fund-raisers, please contact
Osborne/**McGraw-Hill** at the above address.

Teach Yourself Java

17 18 19 20 DOC/DOC 1 5 4 3 2 1

ISBN 0-07-882570-9

This book is dedicated to Jennifer Casto,
John Casto, and Matthew Mitchell.

Contents at a Glance

▼
▼

Contents

Foreword

*F*OREWORD BY HERBERT SCHILDT

Several years ago, I designed and created the first of Osborne's *Teach Yourself* series of books when I wrote *Teach Yourself C*. This was quickly followed by my book *Teach Yourself C++*. These books are based on a unique, hands-on approach that builds and reinforces a thorough understanding of the material, allowing a reader to master topics as quickly as possible. Given the success of the original *Teach Yourself* books, I was pleased to learn that a Java book would be added to this series. I was even more pleased when Joe O'Neil asked if I would edit it!

Joe O'Neil, a world-class Java programmer and author, follows the format and organization used by my original books. This approach presents each topic, shows examples, and then offers exercises to check your understanding. This methodology is especially well suited to someone working on his or her own. You can work at your own pace, in your own time.

One of the greatest strengths of Joe's book is found in its examples. Joe has a gift for presenting interesting, practical programs that clearly illustrate salient points of each discussion. Many of the examples include code that you can easily adapt for your own use.

Whether you're just starting out in programming or moving your programming expertise to Java, I'm sure that you will find Joe's book to be an excellent introduction.

HS
August 22, 1998

Acknowledgments

Megg Bonar was the acquisitions editor for this project. Scott Rogers, Heidi Poulin, Gary Morris, Debbie Escobedo, and many other people at Osborne/McGraw-Hill also played essential roles in producing this book. Thanks are due to all of them.

Herb Schildt and I have worked together on several projects during the past few years. His experience and guidance have been invaluable. Sheryl Schildt indexed the book and also prevented some errors.

Thomas Feng did an outstanding job as technical reviewer. He provided significant comments that improved the book.

Finally, congratulations to the team at Sun Microsystems for inventing and developing Java software technology.

Introduction

Java is an important and exciting advance in software technology. It enables you to build platform-independent programs that execute in a wide variety of hardware and software environments. Developers around the world are now using Java to build software for consumer devices, personal computers, minicomputers, and mainframes. They are constructing mission-critical applications for many different industries.

One of the important environments in which Java is found is the Internet. Web pages can include references to small Java programs known as applets that are dynamically retrieved from a Web server and downloaded to a user's machine. Applets execute within the environment provided by the Web browser. They provide powerful ways for a user to interact with a Web page.

The Java language includes several significant features. It is object-oriented and, therefore, enables substantial code reuse. Exception handling is provided. This allows you to handle run-time problems in an organized manner. Garbage collection is used to automatically reclaim the memory resources of objects that are no longer used. The Java syntax is very straightforward. Some of the more troublesome features of other languages were deliberately omitted. Support for multithreaded programming is available. These and other features make it much easier to write robust programs in Java.

The Java class libraries provide a wealth of functionality. This book covers only a small fraction of their capabilities. You will see how to perform file input and output, build distributed applications, provide animations with multithreaded applets, construct graphical user interfaces, and much more.

WHO IS THE AUDIENCE FOR THIS BOOK?

This book is intended for anyone who wants to design and develop Java applications and applets.

It will be helpful if you have already done some computer programming. However, this is not absolutely required. The book begins with the basics and provides step-by-step instructions for creating simple applications.

The topics of object-oriented programming, multithreading, and networking are covered. These are central to any discussion of Java. Even if you are not familiar with these subjects, the book includes the information you need.

There is not sufficient space in this book to cover all aspects of the Java class libraries. For more information, I recommend *Java 1.1: The Complete Reference, Second Edition,* by Herbert Schildt and Patrick Naughton. It is a valuable resource for any Java programmer and is also available from Osborne/McGraw-Hill.

HOW THIS BOOK IS ORGANIZED

This book uses a unique approach to teach the basics of Java programming. It describes a topic and then uses many examples and exercises to help you understand and apply that information. An appendix at the end of the book contains answers for the exercises.

Each chapter begins with a Review Skills Check. This contains exercises that test your knowledge of the preceding chapter. Each chapter ends with a Mastery Skills Check and Cumulative Skills Check. The former contains exercises that test your understanding of the material in that chapter. The latter contains exercises that require proficiency with any of the material that has previously been covered in the book.

Each chapter builds upon the previous ones. Therefore, it is best to work through the book in sequence.

WHAT'S IN THIS BOOK?

The book contains the sixteen chapters summarized here:

Chapter 1, "Fundamentals," describes how Java allows you to build platform-independent software. You will learn to build simple applications by using the tools and class libraries in the Java Development Kit (JDK). Strings, characters, and simple types are demonstrated. You will also learn about expressions, assignments, and arrays. A list of the Java keywords is also provided.

Chapter 2, "Using Classes and Methods," begins by outlining the structure of a method. It then demonstrates static and instance methods and variables. The wrapper classes that encapsulate simple types are demonstrated. Garbage collection is explained. Finally, you will see how to use command-line arguments provided to an application.

Chapter 3, "Introducing Java's Control Statements," explains the **if**, **if-else**, and **for** statements. These are used in virtually every Java program. The increment, decrement, relational, logical, and ternary operators are also discussed.

Chapter 4, "More About Control Statements and Operators," provides additional information about the **if** and **for** statements. The **while**, **do**, **break**, **continue**, and **switch** statements are also explained. Finally, the bitwise operators are demonstrated.

Chapter 5, "Creating Classes," explains how to create simple classes. You will learn about constructors, instance variables and methods, static variables and methods, local variables and variable scope, method overloading, and argument passing.

Chapter 6, "Inheritance," considers how to define a class that extends another class. You will see how method overriding enables code reuse. The modifiers that can be used for class, variable, constructor, and method declarations are considered. Finally, the classes **Object** and **Class** are examined.

Chapter 7, "Interfaces and Packages," considers two important features of the Java language. An *interface* is a group of constants and method declarations. It is an abstract description of functionality. A *package* is a group of classes and interfaces. It is a mechanism for organizing the name space.

Chapter 8, "Exceptions", shows how to handle errors that occur during the execution of a Java program. You will learn about the classes, keywords, and statements that are used for exception handling.

Chapter 9, "Multithreaded Programming," studies how to create and use threads. You may think of a thread as a sequence of execution in a process. They are invaluable when building many types of Java programs. The chapter explains thread synchronization, deadlock, and communication.

Chapter 10, "Introducing the Java Class Libraries," begins our study of the most commonly used classes and interfaces. Classes allow you to work with random numbers, dates, calendars, vectors, stacks, and hash tables. You can also parse strings into tokens.

Chapter 11, "Input and Output," introduces streams. These are abstractions for either a source or destination of data. You will learn the distinction between character and byte streams. These provide sequential access to data. Random access files allow non-sequential access to data. A class is available that allows you to tokenize input from a stream. Serialization and deserialization can be used to save and restore the state of a set of objects.

Chapter 12, "Networking," demonstrates one way that programs on different machines can communicate with each other. You will see how to use the Transmission Control Protocol (TCP) or User Datagram Protocol (UDP) for this purpose.

Chapter 13, "Applets," describes applets. These are small programs that are executed by using a Web browser or a JDK tool. Applets are the most common type of Java program in use today. You will see how to build applets that draw shapes, present text, display images, and use threads to provide animations.

Chapter 14, "An Introduction to Event Handling," begins with an explanation of the delegation event model. This is the foundation for our study of this topic. You will see how an applet can receive and process mouse input. Adapter, inner, and anonymous inner classes are also described. They provide mechanisms that make it easier to construct event handling code.

Chapter 15, "The Abstract Window Toolkit," shows how to build graphical user interfaces for applets and applications. You will see how to use buttons, check boxes, lists, scroll bars, and other components. Windows, frames, menu bars, menus, dialogs, and file dialogs are examined. The different types of events generated by these elements are handled by the delegation event model. You will be able to build very attractive and powerful applets and applications after you master this material.

Chapter 16, "Topics for Further Investigation," briefly mentions some of the other Java technologies that you can investigate. These include Swing, Servlets, Java Database Connectivity (JDBC), Remote Method Invocation (RMI), Java Beans, Enterprise Java Beans, Enterprise Services, Java Media and Communication API, Security, PersonalJava, and EmbeddedJava.

WHAT YOU'LL NEED

The instructions and examples in this book use the Java Developer Kit
(JDK) from Sun Microsystems. The JDK is available free-of-charge on
the Web at **java.sun.com**. Several vendors provide development
environments for working with Java software. It should be
straightforward to apply the information in this book to those
environments.

CODE ON THE WEB

The source code for all of the programs in this book is available
free-of-charge on the Web at **www.osborne.com**. In addition, all
supporting files such as image files and HTML files are available on
that site. The code for each example is held in a separate subdirectory.
This is consistent with the conventions used for naming Java packages.

1

Fundamentals

THERE has been an exponential growth of interest in the Java programming language in recent years. This chapter provides some background that is needed to understand how this technology began and why it is particularly well-suited to creating dynamic content for the World Wide Web. Key concepts of Java and object-oriented programming are then introduced. You will see how to build a simple application by using the class libraries and tools supplied in the Java Development Kit (JDK).

The eight simple types provided by the Java language are introduced. Strings and characters are also described. Arithmetic operators are used to perform calculations with variables. Type conversions in expressions and assignments are illustrated. The three types of program comments are demonstrated.

You will then see how to create and use one-dimension and multidimensional arrays. Finally, the Java keywords are listed.

1.1 *B*ACKGROUND

Java was created by a team of programmers at Sun Microsystems in 1991. Their original goal was to develop a language that could be used to write software for different consumer electronic devices. The main challenge such devices presented was that they were all different. Thus, the defining aspect of their job was to create a computer language that could be used to build programs that would run in fundamentally different execution environments. Because these machines provided a wide variety of hardware and software environments, it was necessary that Java be *platform-independent*. This would allow the same software to execute without change on a heterogeneous set of devices.

However, Java did not become a success because of its intended use in consumer electronic devices. Instead, it was the explosive growth of the World Wide Web and the Internet that caused Java to receive so much attention. What the Internet has in common with consumer electronic devices is its diversity of hardware. The Internet allows many different types of computers to be connected together, including computers that use fundamentally different CPUs and operating systems. Therefore, the ability to write a portable program is as beneficial to the Internet as it is to consumer electronic devices. Java's "write once, run anywhere" philosophy provided a tremendous advantage.

The inventors of Java examined many different programming languages and adopted their best features. As you progress through this book, you will see how Java's clean and thorough approach to object-oriented programming makes it much easier to reuse and maintain software.

1.2 *B*YTECODES AND THE JAVA VIRTUAL MACHINE (JVM)

Since platform-independence is a defining characteristic of Java, it is important to understand how it is achieved. Programs exist in two forms: *source code* and *object code*. Source code is the textual version of the program that you write using a text editor. The programs printed in this book are shown as source code. The executable form of a program is object code. Object code can be executed by the computer. Typically, object code is specific to a particular CPU. Therefore, it cannot be executed on a different platform. Java removes this restriction in a very elegant manner.

Like all computer languages, a Java program begins with its source code. The difference is what happens when a Java program is compiled. Instead of producing executable code, the Java compiler produces an object file that contains *bytecodes*. Bytecodes are instructions that are not for any specific CPU. Instead, they are designed to be interpreted by a *Java Virtual Machine* (JVM). The key to Java's platform-independence comes from the fact that the same bytecodes can be executed by any JVM on any platform. As long as there is a JVM implemented for a given environment, it can run any Java program. For example, Java programs can execute under Windows 98, Solaris, IRIX, or any other platform for which a JVM has been implemented. If you design and build a new type of computer, a JVM can be implemented for that platform. This would then allow any Java program to execute in that new environment.

Although bytecodes are typically interpreted by a JVM, it is also possible to build computer hardware that can execute the bytecode instructions directly. Sun Microsystems and its partners are producing silicon chips for this purpose. See their Web site for more information.

1.3 **A**PPLICATIONS AND APPLETS

There are two types of programs that can be built in Java: *applications* and *applets*. Applications can be directly executed by a JVM. Applets require a Web browser to execute. The browser includes a JVM and also provides an execution environment for the applet. You will see later in this book that an applet can interact with the browser. It is also possible to use a tool called the applet viewer to run an applet. This utility is included in the Java Development Kit (JDK) and is used to test applets.

Applets are typically downloaded from a Web server to a user's machine. This is done automatically when a Web page includes a reference to an applet. In this manner, an applet written by any developer in the world may be dynamically downloaded from a Web server and executed on a client PC or workstation.

One of the significant challenges faced by the inventors of Java was security. It was necessary to ensure that applets downloaded to a user's computer did not cause harm. Later chapters of this book describe Java's security model in detail, and you will see how applets can be restricted from accessing resources on a user's machine. But in the most general sense, Java achieves security through the same mechanism by which it achieves portability: the bytecodes and the Java Virtual Machine. Since the JVM is in control of the execution of a Java program, it can prevent unauthorized activities. This design is often called the *sandbox model*.

1.4 **C**LASSES AND OBJECTS

Classes and objects form the building blocks of any Java program. Therefore, a basic understanding of them is necessary.

An *object* is a region of storage that defines both *state* and *behavior*. The storage can be either memory or disk. State is represented by a set of variables and the values they contain. Behavior is represented by a set of methods and the logic they implement. Thus, an object is a combination of data and the code that acts upon it.

A *class* is a template from which objects are created. That is, objects are instances of a class. The mechanism to create a new object is called *instantiation*.

Let us consider an example to clarify these concepts. Assume that a software system controls a set of mobile robots that store and retrieve materials from shelves in a large warehouse. A separate object represents each robot. Its state includes variables such as current position and velocity. Another variable indicates if that robot is currently busy or idle. The behavior of a robot is defined by methods that cause it to change position or velocity.

1.5 THE THREE PRINCIPLES OF OBJECT-ORIENTED PROGRAMMING

Three language features are fundamental to object-oriented programming. These are encapsulation, inheritance, and polymorphism. They are briefly introduced in the following sections and addressed more fully in later chapters.

ENCAPSULATION

Encapsulation is the mechanism that associates data with the code that manipulates it. You may think of the code as providing a protective capsule around the data. Direct access to the data from other software is not permitted.

Encapsulation provides significant benefits. First, it allows you to more easily modify the form of the data that is used to store information. For example, you may be using a linked list to store some information and wish to change this to a hash table to obtain improved performance. If all access to this data structure is done through a set of well-defined access methods, this change can be done without requiring any modification to other software that invokes these methods. Second, it becomes much easier to coordinate access to sensitive information. For example, you may want to require a login and password as arguments to the methods that modify certain pieces of data. Third, it is much easier to synchronize access to data by multiple threads. You will learn about threads later.

INHERITANCE

Inheritance is a mechanism that allows a class to be defined as a specialization of another class. This facilitates software reuse because the structure and behavior already implemented by one class may be used as a starting point to define other classes. When a class **Y** inherits from a class **X**, it is said that **Y** is a *subclass* of **X** and **X** is the *superclass* of **Y**. It can also be said that **Y** *extends* **X**. Other classes may extend **Y**. In this manner, a hierarchy of inheritance relationships may be established for a set of classes.

A given class may have multiple subclasses. However, Java permits a class to have only one immediate superclass. There is a class named **Object** at the root of the inheritance hierarchy. Therefore, all Java classes inherit directly or indirectly from **Object**.

To clarify these points, consider the class hierarchy shown in Figure 1-1. **Object** is at the root of the tree. Some of its subclasses are named **A**, **B**, and **C**. Class **A** has subclasses named **D**, **E**, and **F**. Class **C** is the superclass of **G**. Assume that **A** has methods named **a1**, **a2**, and **a3**. These are inherited by all of the subclasses of **A**.

In later chapters you will see that there are mechanisms to control which variables and methods can be accessed by a subclass.

POLYMORPHISM

Polymorphism is a mechanism that is often summarized as "one interface, multiple implementations." Consider the class hierarchy shown in Figure 1-2. This shows that **Shape** has multiple subclasses named **Ellipse**, **Rectangle**, and **Triangle**. Each of these represents various types of shapes.

The class **Shape** defines a method called **getArea( )** that returns the area of a shape. However, this method is not implemented by that class. Therefore, it is an *abstract* method and **Shape** is an *abstract* class.

FIGURE 1-1

A class inheritance hierarchy

▼

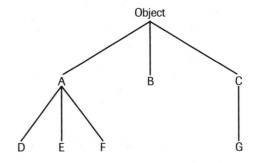

FIGURE 1-2

A class inheritance hierarchy
▼

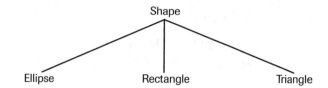

This means that no objects of class **Shape** can be created. However, the functionality of that class can be inherited by its subclasses.

The various subclasses of **Shape** *do* implement the **getArea( )** method. However, the manner in which the area is calculated is completely different for **Ellipse**, **Rectangle**, and **Triangle** objects. Therefore, if you have several **Shape** objects and need to compute their total area, this can be done by invoking the **getArea( )** method on each of these objects. Java ensures that the correct implementation is invoked for each object. This is done at run time and shows polymorphism in action.

One of the key benefits of object-oriented programming can now be seen. Assume that one million lines of Java code already exist to manage a set of shapes. Now you want to accommodate a new subclass of **Shape** called **Trapezoid**. It, too, provides an implementation of **getArea( )**. It is not necessary to laboriously search through the one million lines of existing code and update this software. It will work correctly because **Trapezoid** implements the methods that are expected of any **Shape**.

1.6 ▮ *THE JAVA CLASS LIBRARIES*

In addition to the language itself, Java defines a rich set of *class libraries*. These provide a large number of standard classes and methods that any Java program can use. These libraries provide for I/O, mathematical operations, networking, event handling, and many other capabilities. Table 1-1 lists some of the most commonly used class libraries and summarizes their primary functions. This functionality is grouped into various *packages*. A package is a collection of classes. You can see that a package is named as a sequence of identifiers separated by periods. For example, the package that contains the I/O library is **java.io**. Chapter 7 discusses packages.

Package	Description
java.applet	Allows you to build applets.
java.awt	Provides an Abstract Window Toolkit (AWT) so graphical user interfaces can be constructed.
java.awt.event	Handles events from AWT components.
java.awt.image	Performs image processing.
java.beans	Forms the basis for Java software components.
java.io	Supports input and output.
java.lang	Provides core Java functionality.
java.net	Enables networking.
java.util	Offers utility functionality.

TABLE 1-1 *Some Java Packages* ▼

The Java class libraries are frequently expanded to provide additional functionality. You should periodically check the Sun Microsystems Web site to keep informed about developments in this area.

1.7 ▮ *THE JAVA DEVELOPMENT KIT (JDK)*

The Java Development Kit (JDK) contains what you need to start building and executing Java applications and applets. It can be downloaded for free from the Sun Microsystems Web site.

There are different versions of the JDK. For example, one version is for a Windows environment. Another is for a Solaris platform. Be careful to download the correct version for your computer.

Follow the instructions to install the JDK on your machine. It contains a Java Virtual Machine (JVM) for your platform and the Java class libraries. Also included are a set of tools including a compiler, an interpreter, and an applet viewer.

Several vendors sell integrated development environments for Java programmers. You may wish to investigate and purchase these products.

1.8   **Y**OUR FIRST JAVA APPLICATION

Before discussing any more theory, it will be helpful to examine a Java program. This section provides step-by-step instructions that lead you through the process of building and executing a simple Java application. Along the way, several key concepts are introduced that apply to all Java programs.

It is assumed that you downloaded and installed the JDK from Sun Microsystems or an Integrated Development Environment (IDE) from another vendor. The specific commands shown here are for a Windows environment. However, you should have little difficulty applying the concepts to other platforms.

First, use your favorite text editor to create a file that contains the following program. Call this file **Example1.java.** The prefix of the filename must match the class it declares. Java is case sensitive; so be certain to enter both the name of the file and its contents exactly as shown here:

```
class Example1 {
  public static void main(String args[]) {
    System.out.println("This is the output from Example1");
  }
}
```

Let us consider each of the lines in this program. The first line begins with the keyword **class**. In a Java program all action takes place within one or more classes. Thus, every program contains at least one class specification. Here, a new class called **Example1** is being declared.

The second line declares a method named **main( )** in that class. All Java applications begin execution at **main( )**. It accepts one argument called **args** that is an array of **String** objects. These are not used in this example. However, you will see later in this book how they can provide command-line arguments to an application. There are three keywords before the token **main**. The **public** keyword is an access specifier that indicates this method can be called by code outside the

Example1 class. Other types of access specifiers are also defined by Java. The **static** keyword indicates that this method is associated with the **Example1** class, not an instance of that class. The distinction between static and instance forms of variables and methods is described in Chapter 2. The **void** keyword indicates that this method does not return a value.

The third line displays a string on the standard output, usually the screen. This is done by calling a method named **println**. You can see that the string is enclosed in double quotes and passed as an argument to that method. Remember that all code in Java must be part of some method in a class. A complete explanation of the syntax **System.out.println( )** is beyond the scope of this chapter. At this point it is sufficient to say that the **println( )** method outputs the string that is supplied as its argument and then outputs a newline character. A semicolon terminates the statement.

The fourth and fifth lines provide closing braces that match the braces at the end of the second and first lines, respectively.

Before you can execute the program, you must compile it. Open a command prompt window by selecting Start | Programs | Command Prompt. Change to the directory containing your source file. Then enter the following command:

```
javac Example1.java
```

This command should return without error. Check that a file named **Example1.class** has been created in the directory. This contains the bytecodes for your application.

You may now invoke the Java interpreter to run your program. Enter the following command:

```
java Example1
```

You should see the following output:

```
This is the output from Example1
```

EXAMPLES

1. Program statements are executed in sequence from the first statement to the last. For example, try the following program:

```
class Example2 {
  public static void main(String args[]) {
    System.out.println("This is on the first line.");
    System.out.println("This is on the second line.");
  }
}
```

When you run this version of the program, you will see the following output:

```
This is on the first line.
This is on the second line.
```

Later in this book, you will learn how control statements can alter the flow of control.

2. As explained, Java is case sensitive. For example, the following line is not valid because the keyword **class** is capitalized.

```
Class Example1 {
```

EXERCISE

1. Enter and compile the example programs. Make sure you have correctly installed your Java development environment and everything is working correctly. From this point forward you will be entering and compiling many examples and exercises. Now is the time to make sure that everything is operating smoothly.

1.9   *VARIABLES AND ASSIGNMENTS*

Perhaps the most fundamental concept in programming is the variable. A *variable* is a named memory location that can hold a value. Only the most trivial programs do not include variables. In Java, unlike some computer languages, all variables must be declared before they can be used. A variable declaration serves one important purpose: It tells the compiler what *type* of variable is being used. Java supports eight different basic data types, as shown in Table 1-2 along with the Java keywords that represent them.

A variable of type **char** is 16 bits long and is most commonly used to hold a single Unicode character.

A **boolean** variable may be either **true** or **false**.

Signed whole number values can be assigned to variables of types **byte**, **short**, **int**, and **long**.

Variables of types **float** and **double** hold signed floating-point values, which may have fractional components. The difference between **float** and **double** is that **double** provides about twice the precision (number of significant digits) as does **float**.

To declare a variable, use this form:

type varName;

Type	Description	Keyword
character	16-bit Unicode character data	char
boolean	true/false values	boolean
byte	8-bit signed integer numbers	byte
short	16-bit signed integer numbers	short
integer	32-bit signed integer numbers	int
long	64-bit signed integer numbers	long
float	32-bit signed floating-point numbers	float
double	64-bit signed floating-point numbers	double

TABLE 1-2   *Java's Eight Basic Data Types* ▼

Here, *type* is the type of the variable and *varName* is its name. For example, the following statement declares **counter** to be of type **int**.

```
int counter;
```

A variable declaration is a statement and must end in a semicolon.

You will learn in Chapters 2 and 5 about the different kinds of variables. For the moment, let us concern ourselves only with variables declared inside a method. These are called *local variables*. A local variable is known to—and may be accessed by—only the method in which it is declared. It is common practice to declare all local variables used by a method at the start of the method, after the opening curly brace. There are two important points you need to know about local variables at this time. First, the local variables in one method have no relationship to the local variables in another method. That is, if a variable named **count** is declared in one method, another variable named **count** may also be declared in a second method—the two variables are completely separate from and unrelated to each other. Second, local variables are created when a method is called and are destroyed when it returns. Therefore local variables do not maintain their values between method calls.

You can declare more than one variable of the same type by using a comma-separated list. For example, the following statement declares three floating-point variables named **x**, **y**, and **z**:

```
float x, y, z;
```

Variable names in Java can consist of the letters of the alphabet, the digits 0 through 9, and the underscore. However, a digit may not start a variable name. Java is case sensitive. This means that the upper- and lowercase letters are treated as entirely different letters. For example, **count** and **COUNT** are two completely different variable names.

To assign a value to a variable, put its name to the left of an equal sign. Put the value you want to give the variable to the right of the equal sign. An assignment operation is a statement; therefore, it must be terminated by a semicolon. The general form of an assignment statement is shown here:

varName = value;

Here, the name of the variable is *varName* and its value is *value*. You will see that the right side of the assignment statement can be either a constant or an expression.

The compiler generates an error message if you attempt to use a variable that has not been initialized.

For example, to assign an integer variable named **num** the value 100, you can use this statement:

```
num = 100;
```

In the preceding assignment, 100 is a constant. Just as there are different types of variables, there are different types of constants. A *constant* is a fixed value used in your program. Constants are often used to initialize variables at the beginning of a program's execution.

It is possible to assign a value to a variable when it is declared. This is called *variable initialization*. It essentially combines the variable's declaration with an assignment statement. For example,

```
int num = 100;
```

creates the variable **num** and assigns it the value 100. If you attempt to use an uninitialized variable, the Java compiler generates an error message.

A character constant is specified by placing the character between single quotes. For example, you may specify a character such as '**A**'. Integers are specified as whole numbers.

An integer literal is assumed to be of type **int**. The maximum integer literal is $2^{31} - 1$, which equals 2147483647. The minimum integer literal is -2^{31} which equals –2147483648.

To express a **long** value, you must use either 'L' or 'l' as a suffix. For example, the following statement declares and initializes a **long** variable:

```
long m = 2147483648L;
```

Integer literals may also be expressed in octal or hexadecimal forms. An octal number must begin with the digit 0 and be followed by the digits 0 through 7. A hexadecimal number must begin with the character sequence 0x or 0X. The allowed hexadecimal digits include 0 through 9, a through f, and A through F.

A numeric literal that includes a decimal point or exponent is assumed to be of type **double**. The following are some examples of **double** literals:

```
.5   0.8   9e-2   -8.7e-5
```

To express a **float** value, you must use either 'F' or 'f' as a suffix. For example, the following statement initializes a **float** variable:

```
float f = 1.5e-3f;
```

Literals that are **float** or **double** can only be expressed in decimal form. Octal or hexadecimal forms cannot be used.

You can use **Sytem.out.println( )** to display values of characters, booleans, integers, and floating-point values. To do so, however, you must know more about the **println( )** method. To see how this is done, let's look first at an example. The statements:

```
int i = 50;
System.out.println("The value of i is " + i);
```

display **The value of i is 50** on the screen. The value of the **int** variable **i** is converted to a string. The concatenation operator then combines these two strings to form one string that is the argument to the **println( )** method. This technique can be generalized to the other built-in data types.

EXAMPLES

1. The program shown here illustrates the three new concepts introduced in this section. First, it declares a **float** variable named **price**. Second, it assigns this variable the value 45.35. Finally, it displays the price. The **print( )** method sends output to the console. The difference between the **println( )** and **print( )** methods is that the former automatically appends a newline to its string argument and the latter does not. Examine this program closely.

```
class DisplayFloat {
  public static void main(String args[]) {
    float price;
    price = 45.35f;
    System.out.print("The price is ");
    System.out.println(price);
  }
}
```

Output from this application is shown here:

```
The price is 45.35
```

2. This program creates variables of types **char**, **short**, and **double**. Each is initialized when declared and their values are displayed.

```
public class OutputVariables {
  public static void main(String args[]) {
    char ch = 'X';
    short s = 456;
    double d = 123.009;
    System.out.println("ch is " + ch);
    System.out.println("s is " + s);
    System.out.println("d is " + d);
  }
}
```

Output from this application is shown here:

```
ch is X
s is 456
d is 123.009
```

EXERCISES

1. Write a program that declares one integer variable called **num**. Give this variable the value 1000 and then, using one **println( )** statement, display the value on the screen like this:

```
1000 is the value of num
```

2. What happens if you try to compile the following program?

```
class UninitializedVariables {
  public static void main(String args[]) {
    char c;
    boolean flag;
    System.out.println(c);
    System.out.println(flag);
  }
}
```

1.10 STRINGS AND CHARACTERS

Since strings and characters are used by nearly every Java program, let's take a closer look at them.

Strings are easily defined by enclosing a series of characters between double quotes. This is how you provide an argument to the **println( )** method. Strings may be of any length, but they cannot include a line break.

To include a double quote within a string, precede the double quote by a backslash character. In this context, the backslash prevents the compiler from treating the double quote as a termination for the string.

Java provides an operator to append one string to another. This is the concatenation operator, and it is represented by a '+' symbol. The result of a string concatenation can be used anywhere that a quoted string can be used.

You may declare a variable of type **String** and initialize it with a string. For example,

```
String s = "Enter an integer value: ";
```

After this statement executes, **s** contains the string "Enter an integer value: ". You can use it anywhere you can use a string. There is much more to learn about **String** objects, and we will revisit the topic in the next chapter.

Finally, it is important to note that Java strings are not null-terminated as they are in some other computer languages, such as C++.

A character literal is enclosed by single quotes. For example, the following line assigns a value to a **char** variable:

```
char c = 'A';
```

Java characters are 16-bit Unicode characters. Unicode is a character set that can accommodate many different human languages. The Java designers did this so character sets for different languages could also be accommodated. This enables developers to write Java applications that can work for international audiences. Since Unicode includes the standard ASCII character set with which you are probably familiar, the fact that Java uses Unicode will be of little consequence. For more information about Unicode, see the Web site at **www.unicode.org**.

EXAMPLES

1. This example illustrates the use of the backslash character. Notice that there are two embedded double quotes in the string.

```java
class LincolnQuote {
  public static void main(String args[]) {
    String s = "Lincoln said: " +
      "\"Four score and seven years ago\"";
    System.out.println(s);
  }
}
```

Output from this application is shown here:

```
Lincoln said: "Four score and seven years ago"
```

2. The following program illustrates how the + operator can be used to concatenate three strings. In this case, the resulting string provides an argument for the **println( )** method. Notice that the argument to the method may span several lines. However, the double quotes that enclose a string must appear on the same line. Otherwise, a compiler error is generated.

```java
class Concatenation {
  public static void main(String args[]) {
    System.out.println("My book " +
      "will teach you " +
      "about Java programming");
  }
}
```

Output from this application is shown here:

```
My book will teach you about Java programming
```

3. The following program shows an example of string initialization.

```java
class StringVariables {
  public static void main(String args[]) {
    String s1 = "My book teaches ";
    String s2 = "you how to ";
```

```
        String s3 = "use Java";
        System.out.println(s1 + s2 + s3);
    }
}
```

Output from this application is as follows:

```
My book teaches you how to use Java
```

Here, the string variables **s1**, **s2**, and **s3** are initialized as shown. Then they are concatenated in the **println( )** statement.

EXERCISES

1. Write a program that displays a string with an embedded quote. For example: Juliet said: "Romeo, where art thou?"

2. Write a program that creates a string variable called **myName**. Using concatenation, assign the variable your first and last names. Use one string literal for your first name and another for your last name. Then display your name.

1.11 ARITHMETIC OPERATORS AND EXPRESSIONS

An expression is a combination of operators and operands. It follows the rules of algebra and should be familiar. Java allows several types of expressions. In this section we will look only at arithmetic expressions.

Table 1-3 lists the arithmetic operators.

These operators cannot be used with **boolean** operands.

The **–** has two meanings. First, it is the subtraction operator. Second, it can be used as a unary minus to reverse the sign of a number. A unary operator uses only one operand.

An expression may appear on the right side of an assignment statement. For example, this program fragment assigns the variable **answer** a value of 3100.

```
int answer;
answer = 100 * 31;
```

Operator	Meaning
+	addition
-	subtraction (also unary minus)
*	multiplication
/	division
%	modulus
+=	addition assignment
-=	subtraction assignment
*=	multiplication assignment
/=	division assignment
%=	modulus assignment
++	increment
—	decrement

TABLE 1-3 *The Arithmetic Operators* ▼

The *, /, and % are higher in precedence than the + and the -. However, you can use parentheses to alter the order of evaluation. For example, this expression produces the value zero:

10 - 2 * 5

but this one produces the value 40:

(10 - 2) * 5

A Java expression may contain variables, constants, or both. For example, assuming that **answer** and **count** are variables, this expression is perfectly valid.

```
answer = count - 100;
```

Finally, you may use spaces liberally within an expression.

The addition, subtraction, multiplication, and division assignment operators can be used to write abbreviated forms of assignment statements. For example, the following statement:

```
j = j + 6;
```

can also be expressed as:

```
j += 6;
```

Here, the value on the right side of the addition assignment operator is added to the variable on the left side of the statement.

The increment and decrement operators are discussed in Chapter 3.

EXAMPLES

1. The modulus operator returns the remainder of a division. For example, the remainder of 10 % 3 equals 1. This program shows the outcome of some arithmetic operations.

```java
public class Arithmetic {
  public static void main(String args[]) {
    System.out.print(5/2);
    System.out.print(" " + 5%2);
    System.out.print(" " + 4/2);
    System.out.println(" " + 4%2);
  }
}
```

Output from this application is shown here:

```
2 1 2 0
```

2. In long expressions, the use of parentheses and spaces can add clarity, even if they are not necessary. For example, examine this expression:

```
count*num+88/val-19%count
```

The following expression produces the same result, but is much easier to read.

```
(count * num) + (88 / val) - (19 % count)
```

3. As stated earlier, the – can be used as a unary operator to reverse the sign of its operand. To see how this works, try this program:

```java
class Unary {
  public static void main(String args[]) {
    int i = 10;
    i = -1;
    System.out.println("This is " + i);
  }
}
```

1. What are the values of the following expressions?

```
5 % 3 + 1
5 / 3 + 1
5 * 3 + 1
```

2. Write a program that calculates how long it takes to drive from New York to Los Angeles at 75 mile per hour. (Use 3,000 miles as the approximate distance between the two cities.)

3. Is the following expression valid?

((10) + (((5))) / 9)

4. What are the values of the following expressions?

```
-5.6 % 3.3
5.6 % -3.3
```

1.12 *T*YPE CONVERSION IN EXPRESSIONS

Unlike many other computer languages, Java lets you mix different types of data together in one expression. For example, this is valid Java code:

```
char ch;
int i;
float f;
double outcome;

ch = '0';
i = 10;
f = 10.2f;

outcome = ch * i / f;
```

Java allows the mixing of types within an expression because it has a strict set of conversion rules that dictate how type differences are resolved. Let's look closely at them in this section.

One portion of Java's conversion rules is called *integral* promotion. In Java, whenever a **char**, a **byte**, or a **short** is used in an expression, its value is automatically elevated to **int** during the evaluation of that expression. Keep in mind that the integral promotion is only in effect during the evaluation of an expression. The variable does not become physically larger. (In essence, the compiler just uses a temporary copy of its value.)

After the automatic integral promotions are applied, the Java compiler converts all operands "up" to the type of the largest operand. This is called *type promotion* and is done on an operation-by-operation basis, as described in the following type-conversion algorithm.

IF either operand is a double
THEN the other operand is converted to double
ELSE IF either operand is a float
THEN the other operand is converted to float
ELSE IF either operand is long
THEN the other operand is converted to long

Once these conversion rules have been applied, each pair of operands will be of the same type and the result of each operation will be the same as the type of both operands.

EXAMPLES

1. In the following program, **i** is elevated to a **float** during the evaluation of the expression **i * f**. Thus, the program prints 232.5.

```
class TypePromotion {
   public static void main(String args[]) {
      int i;
      float f;
      i = 10;
      f = 23.25f;
      System.out.println(i * f);
   }
}
```

2. Even though the final outcome of an expression will be of the largest type, the type conversion rules are applied on an operation-by-operation basis. For example, in the expression

```
100.0f/(10/3)
```

the division of 10 by 3 produces an integer result, since both are integers. Then this value is elevated to 3.0f to divide 100.0f.

1. Given these variables,

```
char ch;
short s;
long l;
float f;
```

what is the overall type of the following expression?

```
f/ch - (i * l)
```

2. What is the type of the subexpression i * l in the preceding exercise?

1.13   *T*YPE CONVERSION IN ASSIGNMENTS

In an assignment statement where the type of the right side differs from that of the left, the type of the right side is converted into that of the left. When the type of the left side is larger than the type of the right side, this process causes no problems. This is known as a *widening conversion* and is illustrated in the following program:

```
class WideningConversion {
  public static void main(String args[]) {
    byte b = 127;
    int i;
    i = b;
    System.out.println(i);
  }
}
```

Here, since an **int** is larger than a **byte**, the assignment of **b** to **i** causes no trouble.

However, when the type of the left side is smaller than the type of the right, a compiler error results. Consider the following program. The compiler issues an error message about the assignment of **i** to **b**. It complains that the types are incompatible for assignment.

```
class BadAssignment {
  public static void main(String args[]) {
    byte b;
```

```
    int i = 127;
    b = i;
    System.out.println(b);
  }
}
```

The way to fix this problem is by using a *type cast*. A type cast takes this general form:

(*type*) *value*

where type is the name of a valid Java data type. For example, the correct version of the previous program is shown in the following listing. This program outputs the value 127.

```
class GoodAssignment {
  public static void main(String args[]) {
    byte b;
    int i = 127;
    b = (byte)i;
    System.out.println(b);
  }
}
```

Here, the type cast causes the value of **i** to be converted to a byte.

The preceding assignment illustrates a *narrowing conversion*. This is because the size of the type on the left side of the assignment can be insufficient to contain the value on the right side. Consider the following program. It outputs the value 2. Only the least significant 8 bits of variable **i** are assigned into **b**.

```
class NarrowingConversion {
  public static void main(String args[]) {
    byte b;
    int i = 258;
    b = (byte)i;
    System.out.println(b); // displays 2
  }
}
```

When a **float** or **double** is assigned to an integer type, *truncation* may occur. Consider the following program. Its output is 23. This is because the fractional component of **f** is discarded.

```
class Truncation {
  public static void main(String args[]) {
    float f = 23.9999f;
    int i = (int)f;
    System.out.println(i);
  }
}
```

EXAMPLES

1. It is possible to assign **char** values to **int** or **long** variables. The following program outputs the value 65.

```
class CharAssignment {
  public static void main(String args[]) {
    char ch = 'A';
    int i = ch;
    System.out.println(i);
  }
}
```

2. You must understand how automatic type conversion in expressions and type conversion in assignments interact. Consider the following program. It does not compile. The problem is with the statement **byte b3 = b1 * b2;**. This occurs because the right side of the assignment statement is automatically promoted to an **int**. This resulting value must be type cast to a **byte** in order for the statement to compile.

```
class AssignmentProblem {
  public static void main(String args[]) {
    byte b1 = 1;
    byte b2 = 2;
    byte b3 = b1 * b2;
    System.out.println(b3);
  }
}
```

3. You cannot cast a variable that is on the left side of an assignment statement. For example, this is an invalid statement in Java:

```
int num;
(float) num = 123.23; /* this is incorrect */
```

1. Does the following program compile?

```
class AssignmentQuestion {
  public static void main(String args[]) {
    short s1 = 1;
    short s2 = s1 + 1;
    System.out.println(s2);
  }
}
```

2. In your own words, explain why a narrowing conversion might be a source of problems.

1.14 COMMENTS

A comment is a note to yourself (or others) that you put into your source code. All comments are ignored by the compiler. They exist solely for your benefit. Comments are used primarily to document the meaning and purpose of your source code, so that you can remember later how it functions and how to use it.

There are three forms of comments in Java. The first is the single-line comment. This begins with the two-character sequence // and includes the rest of the characters on the same line. The following example shows one way to include a comment immediately after a statement.

```
int i = 10; // i is used as a counter
```

The second form of Java comment is the multiline comment. It begins with the two-character sequence /* and ends with the two-character sequence */. Here is a simple example of its use:

```
/* This is a comment. */
```

This form of comment may also extend over several lines as shown here:

```
/*
  This is a longer comment
  that extends over
  five lines.
*/
```

The third form of Java comment is documentation comment. It begins with the three-character sequence /** and ends with the two-character sequence */. Here is a simple example of its use:

```
/**
   This is a Java
   documentation
   comment
*/
```

The advantage of documentation comments is that tools can extract them from source files and automatically generate documentation for your programs. The JDK has a tool named **javadoc** that performs this function.

In Java, a comment can go anywhere except in the middle of a keyword or class, method, or variable name.

You can use a comment to temporarily remove a line of code. Simply surround the line with the comment symbols.

Comments may not be nested. For example, Java will not accept this:

```
/* this is a comment /* this is another comment
   nested inside the first — which will cause
   a syntax error */ with a nested comment
*/
```

EXAMPLE

1. You cannot place a comment inside the name of a method or variable name. For example, this is an incorrect statement:

   ```
   pri/* wrong */nt("this won't work");
   ```

EXERCISES

1. Is this comment correct?

   ```
   /**/
   ```

2. Is this comment correct?

   ```
   /* System.out.println("this is a test"); */
   ```

3. Go back and add comments to the programs developed in previous sections.

1.15 ◯*NE-DIMENSIONAL ARRAYS*

A *one-dimensional array* is a list of variables of the same type that are accessed through a common name. An individual variable in the array is called an *array element.* Arrays form a convenient way to handle groups of related data. For example, you might use an array to hold the average daily temperature over a 30-day period. Using an array to represent this data allows you to easily manipulate it. Because Java makes extensive use of arrays, they are introduced here.

To create an array, you need to perform two steps: (1) declare the array and (2) allocate space for its elements. These steps are now discussed in detail.

First, to declare a one-dimensional array, use this general form:

type varName[ ];

Here, *type* is a valid Java data type and *varName* is the name of the array.

For example, consider the declaration shown here:

```
int ia[];
```

This creates a variable named **ia** that refers to an integer array. But it does not actually create storage for the array.

Second, to allocate space for a one-dimensional array, use this general form:

varName = new *type*[*size*];

Here, *varName* is the name of the array, *type* is a valid Java type, and *size* specifies the number of elements in the array. You can see that the **new** operator is used here to allocate memory for the array.

For example, consider the allocation shown here:

```
ia = new int[10];
```

This creates an integer array with ten elements that may be accessed via **ia**.

These two steps may be combined into one Java statement as shown here:

type varName = new *type*[*size*];

For example, consider this declaration and allocation:

```
int ia = new int[10];
```

Figure 1-3 represents the structure of a one-dimensional array that has ten elements.

Once an array has been created, an individual element is accessed by indexing the array. This is done by specifying the number of the desired element inside square brackets. Array indexes begin at zero. This means that if you want to access the first element in an array, use zero for the index.

For example, consider this assignment:

ia[2] = 10;

This assigns the value 10 to the third element of **ia**. Remember, array indexes begin at zero, so **ia[2]** refers to the third element.

In Java, the number of elements in an array may be obtained via the following expression:

varName.length

Here, *varName* is the name of the array.

Java performs bounds checking on array indexes at run time. This means that it is not possible to overrun the end of an array. For example, if an array is declared as having five elements, you cannot access the (nonexistent) tenth element. Doing so generates an exception, which is essentially a run-time error. (Exceptions are discussed in Chapter 8.)

FIGURE 1-3	int ia[ ]=new int[10];
A one-dimension array ▼	ia[0] ia[1] ia[2] ia[3] ia[4] ia[5] ia[6] ia[7] ia[8] ia[9]

Java also allows you to use an abbreviated syntax to declare, allocate, and initialize the elements of an array. This can be done with an array initializer of the following form:

type varName[ ] = { *e0 ... en* };

Here, *varName* is the name of the array and *type* is a valid Java type. The elements of the array are *e0* through *en*. (Obviously, *e0* through *en* must be of the correct type; otherwise, a compiler error occurs.) In this case, **new** is not used and sufficient memory for the array is automatically provided.

You may assign one array variable to another. However, the array itself is not physically copied. Instead, the variable on the left side of the assignment will simply refer to the same array as the variable on the right side of the assignment.

For example, consider the following statements:

```
int j[] = { 0, 1, 2, 3, 4, 5 };
int k[];
k = j;
```

After these statements execute, variables **j** and **k** refer to the same array.

EXAMPLES

1. The following program creates and initializes a one-dimensional array named **myarray** that has four elements. The first statement in the **main( )** method declares and allocates space for the array. The elements of the array are then initialized. The total number of elements is obtained via **myarray.length** and displayed. Finally, the values of the array elements are displayed.

```
class OneDimensionArray {

  public static void main(String args[]) {

    // Declare and allocate space
    int myarray[] = new int[4];

    // Initialize elements
    myarray[0] = 33;
    myarray[1] = 71;
```

```
      myarray[2] = -16;
      myarray[3] = 45;

      // Display length
      System.out.println("myarray.length = " +
        myarray.length);

      // Display elements
      System.out.println(myarray[0]);
      System.out.println(myarray[1]);
      System.out.println(myarray[2]);
      System.out.println(myarray[3]);
    }
  }
```

Output from this application is shown here:

```
myarray.length = 4
33
71
-16
45
```

2. The following program illustrates how to use an array initializer. The output from this program is identical to that of the previous example.

```
class ArrayInitializer {

  public static void main(String args[]) {

    // Declare, allocate, initialize
    int myarray[] = { 33, 71, -16, 45 };

    // Display length
    System.out.println("myarray.length = " +
      myarray.length);

    // Display elements
    System.out.println(myarray[0]);
    System.out.println(myarray[1]);
    System.out.println(myarray[2]);
    System.out.println(myarray[3]);
    }
  }
```

3. You may assign one array variable to another, but be careful. Doing so causes both variables to refer to the same instance of the array; the array itself is not copied. The following program demonstrates this effect. Notice that variables **array1** and **array2** refer to the same array. Therefore, any change to those array elements affects both variables.

```
class ArrayReference {

  public static void main(String args[]) {

    // Declare and allocate space for array1
    float array1[] = new float[3];

    // Initialize array1
    array1[0] = -3.45f;
    array1[1] = 7.7f;
    array1[2] = 101.56f;

    // Declare and allocate space for array2
    float array2[] = new float[3];

    // Make array2 refer to the same array as array1
    array2 = array1;

    // Display the elements of array2
    System.out.println("array2:");
    System.out.println(array2[0]);
    System.out.println(array2[1]);
    System.out.println(array2[2]);

    // Change an element
    array2[1] = 100;

    // Display the elements of array1
    System.out.println("array1:");
    System.out.println(array1[0]);
    System.out.println(array1[1]);
    System.out.println(array1[2]);

    // Display the elements of array2
    System.out.println("array2:");
    System.out.println(array2[0]);
    System.out.println(array2[1]);
```

```
        System.out.println(array2[2]);
    }
}
```

Output from this application is shown here:

```
array2:
-3.45
7.7
101.56
array1:
-3.45
100.0
101.56
array2:
-3.45
100.0
101.56
```

EXERCISES

1. Can you declare a one-dimensional array that includes both **double** and **float** elements?

2. Write a program that creates and initializes a four-element **byte** array. Display its elements.

3. Write a program that creates and initializes a four-element **double** array. Calculate and display the average of its values.

1.16   *M*ULTIDIMENSIONAL ARRAYS

In addition to one-dimensional arrays, you can create arrays of two or more dimensions. In Java, multidimensional arrays are implemented as arrays of arrays. You need to perform two steps to work with multidimensional arrays: (1) declare the array and (2) allocate space for its elements. These are the same two steps seen for one-dimension arrays, but the details are different. Let us look at how to work with a two-dimension array.

First, to declare a two-dimensional array, use the general form shown here:

type varName[ ][ ];

Here, *type* is a valid Java data type and *varName* is the name of the array. Notice that the two sets of brackets indicate there are two dimensions for this array.

For example, consider the declaration shown here:

```
float fa[][];
```

This creates a variable that refers to a two-dimension floating-point array, but it does not actually create storage for the array.

Second, to allocate space for a two-dimension array, you may use this general form:

varName = new *type*[*size1*][*size2*];

Here, *varName* is the name of the array and *type* is a valid Java type. The dimensions of the array are specified by *size1* and *size2*.

For example, consider the allocation shown here:

```
fa = new float[2][3];
```

This creates a 2x3-element array of floating-point values that may be accessed via **fa**.

These two steps may be combined into one Java statement as shown here:

type varName = new *type*[*size1*][*size2*];

For example, consider the declaration and allocation shown here:

```
float fa[][] = new float[2][3];
```

Figure 1-4 represents the structure of a two-dimensional array.

Once a multidimensional array has been created, an individual element is accessed by indexing the array. A separate index

FIGURE 1-4

A multidimensional array

▼

float fa[ ][ ]=new float[2][3],

fa[0][0]	fa[0][1]	fa[0][2]
fa[1][0]	fa[1][1]	fa[1][2]

must be provided for each dimension. Array indexes begin at zero for each dimension.

For example, consider the initialization shown here:

fa[0][1] = 10;

This assigns the value 10 to the element with indexes 0 and 1.

The size of a multidimensional array can be obtained via the expression:

varName.length

Here, *varName* is the name of the array.

The value that is returned is the length of the first dimension.

You may use the following syntax to obtain the length of an individual array element:

varName[index].length

Here, *varName* is the name of the array and *index* identifies a specific element of that array.

You may also use array initializers for multidimensional arrays. For an array with three elements, this is done with the following form:

type varName[ ][ ] = { { e00 ... e0x }, { e10 ... e1y}, { e20 .. e2z} };

Here, *varName* is the name of the array and *type* is a valid Java type. This form more clearly shows that multidimensional arrays in Java are really arrays of arrays. That is, the first element of *varName* is an array whose elements are *e00* through *e0x*. The second element of *varName* is an array whose elements are *e10* through *e1y*. The third element of *varName* is an array whose elements are *e20* through *e2z*.

EXAMPLES

1. The following program creates and initializes a 3×2 matrix. The first statement in the **main( )** method declares and allocates space for the array elements. The elements of the array are then initialized. Finally, the values of the array elements are displayed.

```
class TwoDimensionArray {

  public static void main(String args[]) {

    // Declare and allocate space
    int myarray[][] = new int[3][2];

    // Initialize elements
    myarray[0][0] = 33;
    myarray[0][1] = 71;
    myarray[1][0] = -16;
    myarray[1][1] = 45;
    myarray[2][0] = 99;
    myarray[2][1] = 27;

    // Display length
    System.out.println("myarray.length = " +
      myarray.length);

    // Display elements
    System.out.println(myarray[0][0]);
    System.out.println(myarray[0][1]);
    System.out.println(myarray[1][0]);
    System.out.println(myarray[1][1]);
    System.out.println(myarray[2][0]);
    System.out.println(myarray[2][1]);
  }
}
```

Output from this application is shown here:

```
myarray.length = 3
33
71
-16
45
99
27
```

2. The following program shows how an array initializer is used with a two-dimension array. The first element of **myarray** is an array that contains the values 33 and 71. The second element of **myarray** is an array that contains the values –16 and 45. The last element of **myarray** is an array that contains the values 99 and 27. The expression **myarray.length** is equal to three in this example. Output from this example is identical to that seen from the previous example.

```
class TwoDimensionArrayInitializer {

  public static void main(String args[]) {

    // Declare, allocate, initialize
    int myarray[][] = {
      { 33, 71 },
      { -16, 45 },
      { 99, 27 }
    };

    // Display length
    System.out.println("myarray.length = " +
      myarray.length);

    // Display elements
    System.out.println(myarray[0][0]);
    System.out.println(myarray[0][1]);
    System.out.println(myarray[1][0]);
    System.out.println(myarray[1][1]);
    System.out.println(myarray[2][0]);
    System.out.println(myarray[2][1]);
  }
}
```

3. Multidimensional arrays in Java are implemented as arrays of arrays. Therefore, unlike some other computer languages, it is not necessary for arrays to be square matrices. For example, the following program shows how to create a two-dimension array that is not a square matrix. The first element in **myarray** is an array with two elements. The second element in **myarray** is an array with four elements. The third element in **myarray** is an array with one element.

```
class UnevenTwoDimensionArrayInitializer {

  public static void main(String args[]) {

    // Declare, allocate, initialize
    int myarray[][] = {
      { 33, 71 },
      { -16, 45, 50, -7 },
      { 99 }
    };

    // Display lengths of the array and its elements
```

```
    System.out.println("myarray.length = " +
        myarray.length);
    System.out.println("myarray[0].length = " +
        myarray[0].length);
    System.out.println("myarray[1].length = " +
        myarray[1].length);
    System.out.println("myarray[2].length = " +
        myarray[2].length);

    // Display elements
    System.out.println(myarray[0][0]);
    System.out.println(myarray[0][1]);
    System.out.println(myarray[1][0]);
    System.out.println(myarray[1][1]);
    System.out.println(myarray[1][2]);
    System.out.println(myarray[1][3]);
    System.out.println(myarray[2][0]);
  }
}
```

Output from this application is shown here:

```
myarray.length = 3
myarray[0].length = 2
myarray[1].length = 4
myarray[2].length = 1
33
71
-16
45
50
-7
99
```

1. Write an application that creates a two-dimension array with **float** values. The first element should be an array containing –56.7f. The second element should be an array containing 500.1f and 70.70f. The third element should be an array containing 100.9f, 0.5f, and 20.20f. Declare, allocate, and initialize the array. Display its length and elements.

2. Write an application that creates a two-dimension array with **int** values. The first, second, and third elements should be arrays with one, two, and three numbers, respectively. Display the length of each dimension.

3. Write an application that creates a three-dimension array with **byte** values. The index of each dimension ranges from zero to two. Display the values of this array.

1.17 *T*HE JAVA KEYWORDS

Before concluding this chapter, you should familiarize yourself with the keywords of the Java language. They are listed in Table 1-4.

The lowercase lettering of the keywords is significant. Java requires that all keywords be in lowercase form. For example, **RETURN** will not be recognized as the keyword **return**. Also, no keyword may be used as a variable or method name.

abstract	const	finally	int	public	throw
boolean	continue	float	interface	return	throws
break	default	for	long	short	transient
byte	do	goto	native	static	try
cast	double	if	new	super	void
catch	else	implements	package	switch	volatile
char	extends	import	private	synchronized	while
class	final	instanceof	protected	this	

TABLE 1-4 *The Java Keywords* ▼

**Mastery
Skills Check**

1. What is the difference between applications and applets?

2. What are bytecodes?

3. What is an object?

4. What is a class?

5. What is encapsulation?

6. What is inheritance?

7. What is polymorphism?

8. What is the first method executed in an application?

9. What are the eight basic data types in Java?

10. What is a type cast and when is it necessary?

11. What two steps are needed to create an array?

12. How do you determine the length of an array?

13. What are the three types of Java comments?

14. Is **CLASS** a keyword?

2

Using Classes and Methods

A s explained in Chapter 1, all program activity takes place within a class. Thus, classes and their objects are fundamental to Java. Although you will learn much more about classes as you progress through this book, there are some important issues that you must understand now. We will be making extensive use of the Java class libraries in the examples throughout this book, and you will need to understand how to use them. In the course of this chapter, several of these classes are described. They include **Math**, which supports mathematical operations; **String**, which provides string handling; and **System**, which encapsulates the run-time environment.

This chapter begins by describing the basic structure of methods. Methods contain the code for a Java program. Next, the difference between static and instance forms of methods and variables is discussed. Since both are used by the Java class libraries, an understanding of this topic is required.

The Java "wrapper" classes are described. These encapsulate the simple types and allow you to deal with them as objects. This is valuable for several reasons. For example, the wrapper classes provide a way to convert between the simple types and their string equivalents.

Next, the creation of objects via the **new** operator is explained and arrays of objects are discussed. You will then see how to read and process command-line arguments. Finally, a brief introduction to the **System** class is provided.

Review
Skills Check

Before proceeding, you should be able to answer these questions and perform these exercises.

1. Why is Java platform-independent?

2. Name five packages in the Java class libraries and briefly describe their function.

3. What is a narrowing conversion?

4. What methods allow you to output strings and simple types to the console?

5. What is integral promotion?

6. Which of these variable names are invalid in Java?

    a. _count

    b. 123count

    c. $test

    d. This_is_a_long_name

    e. new-word

2.1 *THE STRUCTURE OF A METHOD*

A method is essentially a set of program statements. It forms the fundamental unit of execution in Java. Each method exists as part of a class. You may view a Java program as a set of one or more classes that each contain one or more methods. During the execution of a program, methods may invoke other methods in the same or a different class.

No program code can exist outside a method, and no method can exist outside a class. This is the reason the examples used in Chapter 1 always declared the **main( )** method to be part of a class.

Although we will look more closely at methods later, a general understanding is required now.

A simplified form of a method is shown here:

```
retType mthName(paramList) {   // body of method
}
```

Here, *retType* specifies the return type. This is the type of the value that the method returns to its caller. You must specify a return type for each method. If a method does not return a value, its return type must be declared as **void**. The name of the method itself is *mthName*. The optional list of parameters for a method is shown in *paramList*. The parameters to a method receive the values of the arguments when a method is called.

The general form of a parameter list is as follows:

```
pType0 p0, pType1 p1, pType2, ... pTypeN pN
```

Here, the parameters are *p0* through *pN* and the types of these parameters are *pType0* through *pTypeN*, respectively.

This book uses the convention that method names begin with lowercase letters and class names begin with uppercase letters.

Although this is not required by the Java language, it is a helpful technique to follow.

As a method executes, it may encounter a run-time error. The Java language provides a feature called exception handling that allows you to deal with such problems. An exception is an object that is generated when a run-time error occurs. You will learn more about this topic in Chapter 8.

However, at this point, you should be aware that a method declaration can include a clause that indicates the types of exceptions that can be generated by that method. The general form of such a declaration is as follows:

retType mthName(paramList) throws *exceptionList* {   // body of method
}

Here, *exceptionList* is a list that indicates the types of exceptions that can be generated by this method. For example, a method that parses a string and returns its integer equivalent may generate a **NumberFormatException** if the string is not correctly formatted. You will see examples of such methods later in this chapter. Many of the Java library methods can throw exceptions.

A method is invoked by using its name and passing it an optional set of arguments as shown here:

mthName(args);

Here, *mthName* is the name of the method and *args* is the optional list of arguments. The arguments are separated by commas.

EXAMPLES

1. Here is the declaration of a method that accepts **int** and **String** parameters and returns a **boolean** type.

```
boolean process(int i, String s) {
  // body of method
}
```

2. Here is the declaration of a method that accepts an array of **int** objects as its parameter but does not return a value.

```
void displayInts(int array[]) {
  // body of method
}
```

3. This method accepts one string parameter and returns an **int**. It can generate an exception of class **ExceptionX**.

```
int parse(String s) throws ExceptionX {
  // body of method
}
```

4. Some methods have no parameters. This is illustrated by the following declaration:

```
void displayCurrentTime() {
.. // body of method
}
```

5. When library methods are described in this book, they are shown using their prototype form, which consists of their return type, name, and parameter list. For example, the prototype for the standard method **toLowerCase( )** is shown here:

```
char toLowerCase(char c);
```

As indicated, this method accepts one parameter that is a **char** and returns a **char**.

EXERCISES

1. What is a method?
2. If a method returns a string, what is its return type?
3. If a method returns no value, what is its return type?
4. What is an exception?
5. What does a **throws** clause in a method declaration indicate?

2.2   *I*NTRODUCING STATIC METHODS AND VARIABLES

There are two ways that an item can be a member of a class. First, it can be a *static member*. A static member is defined for the class itself and exists independently of any object of that class. Second, it can be an *instance member*. An instance member is defined for objects of the class; thus it is bound to an instance (i.e., object) of its class. Since several of Java's library classes make extensive use of both static and instance members, it is necessary for you to understand the distinction between them. This section discusses static members, and the following section describes instance members.

A static method is associated with a class. Therefore, it is not necessary to create an instance of that class in order to invoke such a method. To call a static method, use the following syntax:

    clsName.mthName(args);

Here, *clsName* is the name of the class and *mthName* is the name of the static method. The optional arguments to the method are *args*.

The **Math** class provides several good examples of static methods. These are summarized in Table 2-1.

Notice that some of the methods in this table have the same name but take different types of arguments. This feature of Java is called *method overloading* and is discussed in Chapter 5.

Like a static method, a static variable is also associated with a class. It is not necessary to create an instance of that class in order to read or write such a variable. It is accessed through its class name, as follows:

    clsName.varName

Here, *clsName* is the name of the class and *varName* is the name of the static variable. Since a static variable is associated with a class, there is only one copy of the variable and it is shared by all objects of that class.

The **Math** class provides two constants named **E** and **PI** that are static variables. These are **double** values. Static variables are frequently constant values that apply for all instances of a class.

Method	Description
static double abs(double *d*)	Returns the absolute value of *d*
static float abs(float *f*)	Returns the absolute value of *f*
static int abs(int *i*)	Returns absolute value of *i*
static long abs(long *l*)	Returns absolute value of *l*
static double acos(double *d*)	Returns the arc cosine of *d*
static double asin(double *d*)	Returns the arc sine of *d*
static double atan(double *d*)	Returns the arc tan of *d*
static double atan2(double *a*, double *b*)	Returns the arc tan of *a/b*
static double ceil(double *d*)	Returns the smallest integer that is greater than or equal to *d*
static double cos(double *radians*)	Returns the cosine of *radians*
static double exp(double *d*)	Returns e raised to the power *d*
static double floor(double *d*)	Returns the largest integer that is less than or equal to *d*
static double log(double *d*)	Returns the natural logarithm of *d*
static double max(double *d*, double *e*)	Returns the maximum of *d* and *e*
static float max(float *f*, float *g*)	Returns the maximum of *f* and *g*
static int max(int *i*, int *j*)	Returns the maximum of *i* and *j*
static long max(long *l*, long *m*)	Returns the maximum of *l* and *m*
static double min(double *d*, double *e*)	Returns the minimum of *d* and *e*
static float min(float *f*, float *g*)	Returns the minimum of *f* and *g*
static int min(int *i*, int *j*)	Returns the minimum of *i* and *j*
static long min(long *l*, long *m*)	Returns the minimum of *l* and *m*
static double pow(double *x*, double *y*)	Returns *x* raised to the power *y*
static double random( )	Returns a random number
static double rint(double *d*)	Returns the integer nearest to *d*
static long round(double *d*)	Returns the **long** integer closest to *d*
static int round(float *f*)	Returns the integer closest to *f*
static double sin(double *radians*)	Returns the sin of *radians*
static double sqrt(double *d*)	Returns the square root of *d*
static double tan(double *radians*)	Returns the tan of *radians*

TABLE 2-1 *Static Methods Defined by **Math*** ▼

EXAMPLES

1. The following program illustrates how to use some of the static methods of the **Math** class.

```
class MathDemo {
  public static void main(String args[]) {
    System.out.println("Max of -8 and -4 is " +
      Math.max(-8, -4));
    System.out.println("Min of -8 and -4 is " +
      Math.min(-8, -4));
    System.out.println("Absolute value of -18 is " +
      Math.abs(-18));
    System.out.println("The ceiling of 45.7 is " +
      Math.ceil(45.7));
    System.out.println("The floor of 45.7 is " +
      Math.floor(45.7));
  }
}
```

Notice how the **Math** static methods are called. Also, notice how the return values of these methods are used with the **println( )** statements. A value returned by a method can be used any place that a value is required.

Output from this application is shown here:

```
Max of -8 and -4 is -4
Min of -8 and -4 is -8
Absolute value of -18 is 18
The ceiling of 45.7 is 46.0
The floor of 45.7 is 45.0
```

2. The following program shows how the static variables of the **Math** class may be accessed.

```
class EPI {
  public static void main(String args[]) {
    System.out.println("E = " + Math.E);
    System.out.println("PI = " + Math.PI);
  }
}
```

Output from this application is shown here:

```
E = 2.718281828459045
PI = 3.141592653589793
```

3. The following program shows how to use the static variable named **Math.PI** to compute the area and circumference of a circle with radius 5.

```
class AreaCircumference {
  public static void main(String args[]) {
    double radius = 5;
    double area = Math.PI * radius * radius;
    double circumference = 2 * Math.PI * radius;
    System.out.println("Radius is " + radius);
    System.out.println("Area is " + area);
    System.out.println("Circumference is " +
        circumference);
  }
}
```

Output from this application is shown here:

```
Radius is 5.0
Area is 78.53981633974483
Circumference is 31.41592653589793
```

EXERCISES

1. Write a program that displays the square root of 23.45.

2. Write a program that displays the value of 2 raised to the power 12.

3. Write a program to compute the hypotenuse of a right triangle whose sides are 4.5 and 8.9 units long.

2.3 *INTRODUCING INSTANCE METHODS AND VARIABLES*

An instance method is associated with and operates upon an object. Therefore, it is necessary to create an instance of that class in order to invoke such a method. To call an instance method, use the syntax shown here:

objRef.mthName(args);

Here, *objRef* is an object reference variable and *mthName* is the name of the method. The optional arguments to the method are *args*.

The **String** class provides several good examples of instance methods. Some of these were introduced in the previous chapter. Table 2-2 summarizes some of the more commonly used instance methods provided by this class.

An instance variable is also associated with an object. It is necessary to create an instance of a class in order to read or write it. The syntax to access such a variable is as follows:

objRef.varName

Here, *objRef* is an object reference variable and *varName* is the name of the instance variable. Each object has its own copy of an instance variable. Examples of instance variables are provided in Chapter 5.

EXAMPLES

1. The following program displays the substring formed by the first ten characters of a string.

```
class First10Chars {
  public static void main(String args[]) {
    String s = "One Two Three Four Five Six Seven";
    String substring = s.substring(0, 10);
    System.out.println(substring);
  }
}
```

Output from this application is shown here:

```
One Two Th
```

2. The following program searches a string for a currency value that starts with the character '$'. The dollar amount is then displayed.

```
class DollarAmount {
  public static void main(String args[]) {
    String s1 = "The total cost is $45.67";
    int i1 = s1.indexOf('$');
    String s2 = s1.substring(i1);
    System.out.println(s2);
  }
}
```

Output from this application is shown here:

```
$45.67
```

Method	Description
char charAt(int *i*)	Returns the character at index *i*.
boolean endsWith(String *s*)	Returns **true** if the current object ends with the same sequence of characters as *s*. Otherwise, returns **false**.
boolean equals(Object *s*)	Returns **true** if the current object and *s* have the same sequence of characters. Otherwise, returns **false**.
boolean equalsIgnoreCase(String *s*)	Same as **equals( )**. However, the case of the characters is ignored.
byte[ ] getBytes( )	Returns a byte array containing the characters in the current object.
int indexOf(int *ch*)	Returns the index of the first instance of character *ch* in the current object. Returns –1 if *ch* is not in the current object.
int indexOf(String *s*)	Searches the current object for *s*. If found, returns the index of the first character. Otherwise, returns –1.
int lastIndexOf(int *ch*)	Returns the index of the last instance of the character *ch* in the current object. Returns –1 if *ch* is not in the current object.
int length( )	Returns the number of characters in the current object.
boolean startsWith(String *s*)	Returns **true** if the current object starts with the same sequence of characters as *s*. Otherwise, returns **false**.
String substring(int *start*)	Returns a **String** object that is a substring of the current object. The substring begins at index *start* in the current object and contains all of its remaining characters.
String substring(int *start*, int *end*)	Returns a **String** object that is a substring of the current object. The substring begins at index *start* in the current object and contains all of its characters up to (but not including) index *end*.
String toLowerCase( )	Returns a **String** object whose characters are the lowercase equivalents of those in the current object.
String toUpperCase( )	Returns a **String** object whose characters are the uppercase equivalents of those in the current object.

TABLE 2-2 *Some Instance Methods Defined by **String*** ▼

EXERCISES

1. Write a program that displays the substring formed by the last ten characters of a string. Hint: Use the **length( )** method.

2. A string contains five numbers separated by commas. Write a program that displays the last number.

T *HE INTEGER CLASS*

Integer is one of the commonly used classes in the Java class libraries. An **Integer** object encapsulates a simple **int** value. In other words, **Integer** is a wrapper class for **int**. **Integer** is an excellent example of a class that provides both static and instance methods. We will use its functionality often throughout this book.

The **Integer** class defines **MAX_VALUE** and **MIN_VALUE** as two of its static variables. These contain the maximum and minimum values that can be accommodated by the 32 bits of a simple **int** type.

Table 2-3 summarizes some of the most commonly used static methods of this class. Notice that some of these methods can generate an exception if their string argument is not correctly formatted. Table 2-4 summarizes some of the most commonly used instance methods of this class.

Note that there is no way to change the value encapsulated by an **Integer** object. In other words, the object is *immutable* after it has been created.

Method	Description
static Integer decode(String *s*) throws NumberFormatException	Returns an **Integer** object whose value is equivalent to *s* in radix 10.
static int parseInt(String *s*) throws NumberFormatException	Returns an **int** whose value is equivalent to *s* in radix 10.
static int parseInt(String *s*, int *r*) throws NumberFormatException	Returns an **int** whose value is equivalent to *s* in radix *r*.
static String toBinaryString(int *i*)	Returns a **String** object containing the binary equivalent of *i*.
static String toHexString(int *i*)	Returns a **String** object containing the hex equivalent of *i*.
static String toOctalString(int *i*)	Returns a **String** object containing the octal equivalent of *i*.
static Integer valueOf(String *s*) throws NumberFormatException	Returns an **Integer** object whose value is equivalent to *s* in radix 10.
static Integer valueOf(String *s*, int *r*) throws NumberFormatException	Returns an **Integer** object whose value is equivalent to *s* in radix *r*.

TABLE 2-3 *Some Static Methods Defined by* **Integer** ▼

Method	Description
byte byteValue( )	Returns the **byte** equivalent of the current object.
double doubleValue( )	Returns the **double** equivalent of the current object.
boolean equals(Object *obj*)	Returns **true** if *obj* and the current object have the same value.
float floatValue( )	Returns the **float** equivalent of the current object.
int intValue( )	Returns the **int** equivalent of the current object.
long longValue( )	Returns the **long** equivalent of the current object.
short shortValue( )	Returns the **short** equivalent of the current object.
String toString( )	Returns the string equivalent of the current object.

TABLE 2-4 *Some Instance Methods Defined by **Integer*** ▼

EXAMPLES

1. The following program illustrates how some of the **Integer** static and instance methods can be used. The **main( )** method begins by assigning a string literal to variable **s**. The static method **valueOf( )** accepts this **String** object as an argument. It creates a new **Integer** object that encapsulates the value represented by **s** and returns this object. This object is assigned to the variable **obj**.

   The instance method named **intValue( )** is then used to obtain a simple **int** equivalent to the value encapsulated by **obj**. The value returned by this method is assigned to the variable **i**.

   The variable **i** is incremented by 10 and displayed by **println( )**.

```
class StringToInt {
  public static void main(String args[]) {
    String s = "125";
    Integer obj = Integer.valueOf(s);
    int i = obj.intValue();
    i += 10;
    System.out.println(i);
  }
}
```

Output from this application is shown here:

135

The preceding program can be rewritten as shown in the following listing. Notice that the second and third lines of the **main( )** method in **StringToInt** have been combined to form the second line of the **main( )** method in **StringToInt2**.

```java
class StringToInt2 {
  public static void main(String args[]) {
    String s = "125";
    int i = Integer.valueOf(s).intValue();
    i += 10;
    System.out.println(i);
  }
}
```

The key points of these two examples are: (1) The static method **valueOf( )** accepts a **String** argument and returns an **Integer** object. (2) The instance method **intValue( )** returns the **int** equivalent of the value encapsulated by an **Integer** object.

Study the preceding program very carefully. Make sure you understand the expression "Integer.valueOf(s).intValue( )". It is used very frequently in the examples of this book.

2. The following program outputs the binary, hex, and octal forms of an **int** value.

```java
class BinaryHexOctal {
  public static void main(String args[]) {
    int i = 11;
    System.out.println("Binary is " +
      Integer.toBinaryString(i));
    System.out.println("Hex is " +
      Integer.toHexString(i));
    System.out.println("Octal is " +
      Integer.toOctalString(i));
  }
}
```

Output from this application is shown here:

```
Binary is 1011
Hex is b
Octal is 13
```

1. Write a program that displays the hex equivalent of an **int**.
2. Rewrite the **StringToInt2** example so it uses the **parseInt( )** method.

2.5 *T*HE new *OPERATOR*

Up to this point, you have been creating objects indirectly, such as through the use of some of Java's static methods. It is now time to learn how to create an object directly. Objects are created using the **new** operator. Or, put differently, the **new** operator creates an instance of a class. It is invoked as follows:

clsName objRef = new *clsName*(*args*);

Here, *clsName* is the name of the class to be instantiated. (*Instantiated* means to create an instance.) A reference to the new object is assigned to a variable named *objRef*. Notice the expression immediately to the right of the keyword **new**. This is known as a *constructor*. A constructor creates an instance of a class. It has the same name as the class and may optionally have an argument list *args*.

Figure 2-1 illustrates the relationship between objects and object reference variables. In the diagram, the variable named **varA** refers to one object. Variables named **varB** and **varC** both refer to a second object. The third object is referred to by the variable named **varD**.

A key point to understand is that the variable is distinct from the object. In effect, a variable that serves as an object reference has an implicit pointer to the object. However, a Java programmer cannot directly access the pointer. Also note that multiple variables may refer to the same object.

The symbol **null** has a special meaning in Java. It represents the value of an object reference variable when that variable does not reference any object

The **Integer** class used in the previous section has two constructors, as follows:

Integer(int *i*)
Integer(String *s*) throws NumberFormatException

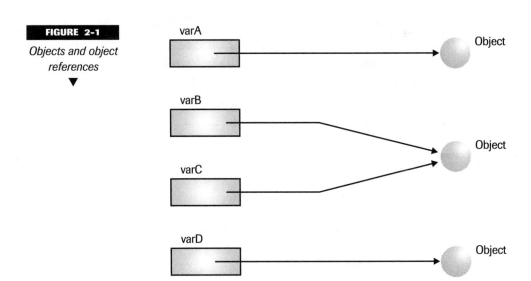

varA

Object

varB

Object

varC

varD

Object

Here, *i* is a simple **int** value and *s* is a **String** object. Notice that the second form of the constructor can throw an exception if the constructor argument is not correctly formatted. The first form of the constructor cannot throw such an exception because any **int** can be used to create an **Integer** object.

EXAMPLES

1. The following program illustrates how to use both **Integer** constructors.

```
class IntegerConstructors {
  public static void main(String args[]) {
    Integer iobj1 = new Integer(5);
    Integer iobj2 = new Integer("6");
    int i1 = iobj1.intValue();
    int i2 = iobj2.intValue();
    int sum = i1 + i2;
    System.out.println("i1 = " + i1);
    System.out.println("i2 = " + i2);
    System.out.println("sum = " + sum);
  }
}
```

Output from this application is shown here:

```
i1 = 5
i2 = 6
sum = 11
```

2. The following example illustrates that multiple variables can reference a single object.

```
class MultipleReferences {
  public static void main(String args[]) {
    Integer obj1 = new Integer(5);
    Integer obj2 = obj1;
    Integer obj3 = obj1;
    System.out.println(obj1);
    System.out.println(obj2);
    System.out.println(obj3);
  }
}
```

Output from this application is shown here:

```
5
5
5
```

3. The following example illustrates that a variable may refer to one object and later refer to a different object.

```
class MultipleObjects {
  public static void main(String args[]) {
    Integer obj = new Integer(5);
    System.out.println(obj);
    obj = new Integer(6);
    System.out.println(obj);
    obj = new Integer(7);
    System.out.println(obj);
  }
}
```

Output from this application is shown here:

```
5
6
7
```

EXERCISES

1. Write a program that creates two **Integer** objects by using the different constructors. Use the instance method named **equals( )** to test if they represent the same value.

2. What is the meaning of **null**?

2.6 **G**ARBAGE COLLECTION

The previous section described how to create an object and reference it from a variable. When an object is no longer referenced by any variable, it then becomes eligible for *garbage collection*. This is a feature of the Java language that automatically reclaims the memory resources used by an object.

It is not possible for you to explicitly delete an object in Java. This is one of the major benefits of the language because it eliminates one common source of programming errors. In some other languages, it is the responsibility of the programmer to explicitly delete objects that are no longer used. If this is not done correctly, memory may be exhausted when a program runs for a long time. Alternatively, objects may be accidentally deleted when some variables still hold references to them. This causes other run-time errors. Both of these problems can be very difficult to debug.

There are several different algorithms that can be used in the JVM to implement garbage collection. This selection is made by the JVM developer. Different vendors employ different strategies.

Finally, you should not assume that an object is immediately garbage-collected when it is no longer referenced by a variable. Garbage collection is a task that is controlled by the JVM. The JVM determines when it should be scheduled for execution.

EXAMPLE

1. The following example illustrates some of the concepts of garbage collection. An **Integer** variable is created and assigned to variable **i**. The object is used in the next statement. Another **Integer** variable is created and assigned to variable **i**. The result is that the first object is no longer referenced by any variable and therefore becomes eligible for garbage collection. Note, however,

that the JVM determines when its memory resources are actually reclaimed.

```
class GarbageCollectionDemo {
  public static void main(String args[]) {
    Integer i = new Integer(5);
    System.out.println(i);
    i = new Integer(6);
    System.out.println("Integer(5) can be recycled.");
    System.out.println(i);
  }
}
```

Output from this program is shown here:

```
5
Integer(5) can be recycled.
6
```

As the output suggests, once **i** has been assigned a reference to the object created by **Integer(6)**, the **Integer(5)** object can be recycled.

EXERCISES

1. What is garbage collection?

2. Why is garbage collection a major advantage of the Java language?

3. When is an object garbage collected?

2.7 *OTHER WRAPPER CLASSES*

There are wrapper classes for each of the eight simple types defined by Java. These are **Boolean, Character, Byte, Short, Integer, Long, Float**, and **Double**. They encapsulate **boolean, char, byte, short, int, long, float**, and **double** values. One of the primary benefits of the wrapper classes is that they provide methods to convert strings to simple types. This is very useful because it gives us a mechanism by which to process user input. Note that the simple value encapsulated by a wrapper object is *immutable* and cannot be changed after that object has been created.

You have already seen the **Integer** class. Let us briefly examine the functionality provided by the other wrapper classes.

The **Boolean** class encapsulates a **boolean** value. It defines the following constants: **FALSE** and **TRUE**. This class provides these constructors:

Boolean(boolean *b*)
Boolean(String *s*)

Here, *b* is a **boolean** value and *s* is the string equivalent of a **boolean** value (e.g., "true," "false"). There are two static methods as follows:

boolean getBoolean(String *s*)
Boolean valueOf(String *s*)

Here, *s* represents the string equivalent of a **boolean** value. The first form returns the corresponding **boolean** value. The second form returns a **Boolean** object that encapsulates the value represented by *s*.

A commonly used instance method is **booleanValue( )**, whose signature is shown here:

boolean booleanValue( )

Method	Description
boolean isDigit(char *c*)	Returns **true** if *c* is a digit. Otherwise, returns **false**.
boolean isLetter(char *c*)	Returns **true** if *c* is a letter. Otherwise, returns **false**.
boolean isLetterOrDigit(char *c*)	Returns **true** if *c* is a letter or digit. Otherwise, returns **false**.
boolean isLowerCase(char *c*)	Returns **true** if *c* is a lowercase character. Otherwise, returns **false**.
boolean isSpaceChar(char *c*)	Returns **true** if *c* is a space. Otherwise, returns **false**.
boolean isUpperCase(char *c*)	Returns **true** if *c* is an uppercase character. Otherwise, returns **false**.
boolean isWhitespace(char *c*)	Returns **true** if *c* is a white space character. Otherwise, returns **false**.
char toLowerCase(char *c*)	Returns the lowercase equivalent of *c*.
char toUpperCase(char *c*)	Returns the uppercase equivalent of *c*.

TABLE 2-5 *Some Static Methods Defined by **Character*** ▼

This method returns the **boolean** value encapsulated by the current object.

The **Character** class encapsulates a **char** value. We will take only a brief look at its functionality.

This class provides the following constructor:

Character(char *c*)

Here, *c* is a **char** value.

Table 2-5 summarizes some static methods provided by this class.

One of the instance methods provided by this class is **charValue( )**. This method returns the **char** value that is encapsulated by a **Character** object and has the following form:

char charValue( )

The **Byte** class encapsulates a **byte** value. It defines the constants **MAX_VALUE** and **MIN_VALUE** and provides these constructors:

Byte(byte *b*)

Byte(String *s*) throws NumberFormatException

Here, *b* is a **byte** value and *s* is the string equivalent of a **byte** value.

The following table summarizes some static methods provided by this class.

Method	Description
Byte decode(String *s*) throws NumberFormatException	Returns a **Byte** object encapsulating the value represented by *s*
byte parseByte(String *s*) throws NumberFormatException	Returns a **byte** value equivalent to *s* in radix 10
byte parseByte(String *s*, int *radix*) throws NumberFormatException	Returns a **byte** value equivalent to *s* in *radix*
String toString( )	Returns the string equivalent of the current object
Byte valueOf(String *s*) throws NumberFormatException	Returns a **Byte** object encapsulating the value represented by *s*
Byte valueOf(String *s*, int *radix*) throws NumberFormatException	Returns a **Byte** object encapsulating the value represented by *s* in *radix*

The following table summarizes some instance methods provided by the **Byte** class.

Method	Description
byte byteValue( )	Returns the **byte** equivalent of the current object
double doubleValue( )	Returns the **double** equivalent of the current object
float floatValue( )	Returns the **float** equivalent of the current object
int intValue( )	Returns the **int** equivalent of the current object
long longValue( )	Returns the **long** equivalent of the current object
short shortValue( )	Returns the **short** equivalent of the current object
String toString( )	Returns the string equivalent of the current object

The **Short** class encapsulates a **short** value. It defines the constants **MAX_VALUE** and **MIN_VALUE** and provides the following constructors:

Short(short *s*)

Short(String *str*) throws NumberFormatException

Here, *s* is a **short** value and *str* is the string equivalent of a **short** value. The following table summarizes some static methods provided by this class.

Method	Description
Short decode(String *s*) throws NumberFormatException	Returns a **Short** object encapsulating the value represented by *s*.
short parseShort(String *s*) throws NumberFormatException	Returns a **short** value equivalent to *s*.
short parseShort(String *s*, int *radix*) throws NumberFormatException	Returns a **short** value equivalent to *s* in *radix*.
String toString( )	Returns the string equivalent of the current object.
Short valueOf(String *s*) throws NumberFormatException	Returns a **Short** object encapsulating the value represented by *s*.
Short valueOf(String *s*, int *radix*) throws NumberFormatException	Returns a **Short** object encapsulating the value represented by *s* in *radix*.

The following table summarizes some instance methods provided by this class.

Method	Description
byte byteValue( )	Returns the **byte** equivalent of the current object.
double doubleValue( )	Returns the **double** equivalent of the current object.

Method	Description
float floatValue( )	Returns the **float** equivalent of the current object.
int intValue( )	Returns the **int** equivalent of the current object.
long longValue( )	Returns the **long** equivalent of the current object.
short shortValue( )	Returns the **short** equivalent of the current object.
String toString( )	Returns the string equivalent of the current object.

The **Long** class encapsulates a **long** value. It defines the constants **MAX_VALUE** and **MIN_VALUE** and provides the following constructors:

Long(long *l*)
Long(String *str*) throws NumberFormatException

Here, *l* is a **long** value and *str* is the string equivalent of a **long** value.
Table 2-6 summarizes some static methods provided by this class.
Table 2-7 summarizes some instance methods provided by this class.
The **Float** class encapsulates a **float** value. It defines several constants: The largest and smallest float values are saved in **MAX_VALUE** and **MIN_VALUE**. There are also special constants that represent infinite values. These are **NEGATIVE_INFINITY** and **POSITIVE_INFINITY**. Finally, the constant **NaN** indicates that a value

Method	Description
long parseLong(String *s*) throws NumberFormatException	Returns a **long** value equivalent to *s*
long parseLong(String *s*, int *radix*) throws NumberFormatException	Returns a **long** value equivalent to *s* in *radix*
String toBinaryString(long *l*)	Returns a binary representation of *l*
String toHexString(long *l*)	Returns a hex representation of *l*
String toOctalString(long *l*)	Returns an octal representation of *l*
String toString(long *l*)	Returns the string equivalent of *l*
Long valueOf(String *s*) throws NumberFormatException	Returns a **Long** object encapsulating the value represented by *s*
Long valueOf(String *s*, int *radix*) throws NumberFormatException	Returns a **Long** object encapsulating the value represented by *s* in *radix*

TABLE 2-6 *Some Static Methods Defined by* ***Long*** ▼

Method	Description
byte byteValue( )	Returns the **byte** equivalent of the current object.
double doubleValue( )	Returns the **double** equivalent of the current object.
float floatValue( )	Returns the **float** equivalent of the current object.
int intValue( )	Returns the **int** equivalent of the current object.
long longValue( )	Returns the **long** equivalent of the current object.
short shortValue( )	Returns the **short** equivalent of the current object.
String toString( )	Returns the string equivalent of the current object.

TABLE 2-7   *Some Instance Methods Defined by **Long*** ▼

is not a number. If you divide a floating-point number by zero, the result is **NaN**.

The **Float** class provides these constructors:

```
Float(float f)
Float(double d)
Float(String s) throws NumberFormatException
```

Here, f and d are **float** and **double** types to be encapsulated in a **Float** object. In the last form, s is the string representation of a **float** value.

The following table summarizes some static methods provided by this class.

Method	Description
boolean isInfinite(float f)	Returns **true** if f represents an infinite value. Otherwise, returns **false**.
boolean isNaN(float f)	Returns **true** if f does not represent a number. Otherwise, returns **false**.
String toString(float f)	Returns the string equivalent of f.
Float valueOf(String s) throws NumberFormatException	Returns a **Float** object that encapsulates the float value represented by s.

Table 2-8 summarizes some instance methods provided by this class.

The **Double** class encapsulates a **double** value. It defines several constants. The largest and smallest float values are saved in **MAX_VALUE** and **MIN_VALUE**. There are also special constants that represent infinite values. These are **NEGATIVE_INFINITY** and

Method	Description
byte byteValue()	Returns the **byte** equivalent of the current object.
double doubleValue()	Returns the **double** equivalent of the current object.
float floatValue()	Returns the **float** equivalent of the current object.
int intValue()	Returns the **int** equivalent of the current object.
boolean isInfinite()	Returns **true** if the value is **NEGATIVE_INFINITY** or **POSITIVE_INFINITY**. Otherwise, returns **false**.
boolean isNaN()	Returns **true** if the value is **NaN**. Otherwise, returns **false**.
long longValue()	Returns the **long** equivalent of the current object.
short shortValue()	Returns the **short** equivalent of the current object.
String toString()	Returns the string equivalent of the current object.

TABLE 2-8 *Some Instance Methods Defined by **Float*** ▼

POSITIVE_INFINITY. Finally, the constant **NaN** indicates that a value is not a number. If you divide a floating-point number by zero, the result is **NaN**.

This class provides these constructors:

```
Double(double d)
Double(String s) throws NumberFormatException
```

Here, *d* is a **double** value to be encapsulated in a **Double** object. In the last form, *s* is the string representation of a **double** value.

The following table summarizes some static methods provided by this class.

Method	Description
boolean isInfinite(double *d*)	Returns **true** if *d* represents an infinite value. Otherwise, returns **false**.
boolean isNaN(double *d*)	Returns **true** if *d* does not represent a number. Otherwise, returns **false**.
String toString(double *d*)	Returns the string equivalent of *d*.
Double valueOf(String *s*) throws NumberFormatException	Returns a **Double** object that encapsulates the float represented by *s*.

Table 2-9 summarizes some instance methods provided by this class.

Method	Description
byte byteValue( )	Returns the **byte** equivalent of the current object.
double doubleValue( )	Returns the **double** value of the current object.
float floatValue( )	Returns the **float** equivalent of the current object.
int intValue( )	Returns the **int** equivalent of the current object.
boolean isInfinite( )	Returns **true** if the value is NEGATIVE_INFINITY on POSITIVE_INFINITY. Otherwise, returns **false**.
boolean isNaN( )	Returns **true** if the value is NaN. Otherwise, returns **false**.
long longValue( )	Returns the **long** equivalent of the current object.
short shortValue( )	Returns the **short** equivalent of the current object.
String toString( )	Returns the string equivalent of the current object.

TABLE 2-9   *Some Instance Methods Defined by **Double** ▼*

EXAMPLE

1. The following application initializes two **double** variables to zero, and then divides one by the other. The static **isInfinite( )** and **isNaN( )** methods are used to test the result. (**NaN** represents an attempt to divide 0 by 0.) The constants defined by the **Double** class are then displayed.

```
class DoubleDemo {

  public static void main(String args[]) {

    // Declare and initialize variables
    double d1 = 0;
    double d2 = 0;

    // Divide these values
    double d3 = d1/d2;
    System.out.println(d3);

    // Test for infinity and NaN
    System.out.println(Double.isInfinite(d3));
    System.out.println(Double.isNaN(d3));

    // Display max, min, and infinity values
    System.out.println(Double.MAX_VALUE);
    System.out.println(Double.MIN_VALUE);
    System.out.println(Double.POSITIVE_INFINITY);
```

```
        System.out.println(Double.NEGATIVE_INFINITY);
    }
}
```

Output from this program is shown here:

```
NaN
false
true
1.7976931348623157E308
4.9E-324
Infinity
-Infinity
```

EXERCISES

1. Write an application that demonstrates some static methods of the **Character** class.

2. Write an application that demonstrates how to parse strings that contain hex, octal, and decimal forms of **short** numbers. Use methods provided by the **Short** class. Add these values together and display their sum.

2.8   *T*HE STRINGBUFFER CLASS

A previous section of this chapter discussed some instance methods of the **String** class. However, there is no way to change the character sequence encapsulated by a **String** object after it is created. The **StringBuffer** class also encapsulates a sequence of characters. However, it does provide methods to append or insert characters. You will see objects of this class used in examples in later chapters of this book.

Its constructor has the following forms:

StringBuffer( )
StringBuffer(int *size*)
StringBuffer(String *s*)

The first form of the constructor initializes the buffer size to 16 characters. The second form explicitly sets the buffer capacity to *size* characters. The final form initializes the buffer with the contents of *s* and also reserves another 16 characters for expansion.

The internal buffer used by a **StringBuffer** object is automatically increased if necessary. However, this takes additional processing. Therefore, some extra space is automatically allocated by the constructors.

Table 2-10 summarizes some instance methods provided by this class.

Method	Description
StringBuffer append(boolean *b*)	Appends the string equivalent of *b*
StringBuffer append(char *ch*)	Appends *ch*
StringBuffer append(double *d*)	Appends the string equivalent of *d*
StringBuffer append(float *f*)	Appends the string equivalent of *f*
StringBuffer append(int *i*)	Appends the string equivalent of *i*
StringBuffer append(long *l*)	Appends the string equivalent of *l*
StringBuffer append(Object *obj*)	Appends the string equivalent of *obj*
StringBuffer append(String *str*)	Appends the string equivalent of *str*
int capacity( )	Returns the current capacity of the string buffer
char charAt(int *i*)	Returns the character at index *i*
StringBuffer insert(int *i*, boolean *b*)	Inserts the string equivalent of *b* before index *i*
StringBuffer insert(int *i*, char *ch*)	Inserts *ch* before index *i*
StringBuffer insert(int *i*, int *j*)	Inserts the string equivalent of *j* before index *i*
StringBuffer insert(int *i*, long *l*)	Inserts the string equivalent of *l* before index *i*
StringBuffer insert(int *i*, Object *obj*)	Inserts the string equivalent of *obj* before index *i*
StringBuffer insert(int *i*, String *str*)	Inserts *str* before index *i*
int length( )	Returns the number of characters in the buffer
StringBuffer reverse( )	Reverses the character sequence
void setCharAt(int *i*, char *ch*)	Sets the character at index *i* to *ch*
void setLength(int *len*)	Sets the buffer capacity to *len*
String toString( )	Returns a **String** object that contains the character sequence

TABLE 2-10 *Some Instance Methods Defined by **StringBuffer*** ▼

EXAMPLE

1. This example creates **StringBuffer** objects by using the three forms of constructors and displays their current capacity and sizes.

```
class StringBufferDemo {
  public static void main(String args[]) {
    StringBuffer sb1 = new StringBuffer();
    StringBuffer sb2 = new StringBuffer(30);
    StringBuffer sb3 = new StringBuffer("abcde");
    System.out.println("sb1.capacity = " +
      sb1.capacity());
    System.out.println("sb1.length = " + sb1.length());
    System.out.println("sb2.capacity = " +
      sb2.capacity());
    System.out.println("sb2.length = " + sb2.length());
    System.out.println("sb3.capacity = " +
      sb3.capacity());
    System.out.println("sb3.length = " + sb3.length());
  }
}
```

Output from this application is shown here:

```
sb1.capacity = 16
sb1.length = 0
sb2.capacity = 30
sb2.length = 0
sb3.capacity = 21
sb3.length = 5
```

EXERCISES

1. Create a **StringBuffer** object and illustrate how to append characters. Display the capacity and length of the string buffer.

2. Create a **StringBuffer** object and illustrate how to insert characters at its beginning.

3. Create a **StringBuffer** object and illustrate the operation of the **append( )** and **reverse( )** methods.

2.9 **A**RRAYS OF OBJECTS

In the previous chapter, you saw how to create arrays of simple types. It is also possible to create arrays of objects. These may have one or multiple dimensions. The steps to accomplish this are the same as for arrays of simple types. In particular: (1) declare the array and (2) allocate space for the array elements. The elements can then be initialized.

EXAMPLES

1. This example shows how to create an array of five strings.

```
class StringArray {
  public static void main(String args[]) {
    String array[] = new String[5];
    array[0] = "String 0";
    array[1] = "String 1";
    array[2] = "String 2";
    array[4] = "String 4";
    System.out.println(array.length);
    System.out.println(array[0]);
    System.out.println(array[1]);
    System.out.println(array[2]);
    System.out.println(array[3]);
    System.out.println(array[4]);
  }
}
```

Output from this application is shown here:

```
5
String 0
String 1
String 2
null
String 4
```

Notice that the array element at index 3 was not explicitly initialized to reference an object. Therefore, it is equal to **null** as seen in the output. The **null** value indicates that the variable does not currently refer to any object.

2. This example creates an array of five strings, calculates their average size, and displays this value.

```
class StringAverage {
  public static void main(String args[]) {
    String array[] = new String[5];
    array[0] = "Short string";
    array[1] = "A much longer string";
    array[2] = "This is a complete sentence!";
    array[3] = "Token";
    array[4] = "This is the longest element in the " +
      "array";
    int total = array[0].length();
    total += array[1].length();
    total += array[2].length();
    total += array[3].length();
    total += array[4].length();
    System.out.println("The average string size is " +
      total/5);
  }
}
```

Output from this application is shown here:

```
The average string size is 21
```

EXERCISES

1. Write an application that creates an array with five **Float** arguments and display the length of the array and its elements.

2. Create an array to store five objects that are of class **Integer**, **String**, **Boolean**, **Character**, and **Double**. Display the elements.

2.10 *C*OMMAND-LINE ARGUMENTS

As you know, all Java applications contain a static method named **main( )**. This method takes one argument that is an array of **String** objects. These objects represent any arguments that may have been entered by the user on the command line. This section examines how you may read and use these command-line arguments.

The number of command-line arguments is obtained via the expression **args.length**. This is an **int** type. The individual arguments are accessed as **args[0]**, **args[1]**, **args[2]**, and so forth.

EXAMPLES

1. The following example reads and displays three command-line arguments.

```
class CommandLineArguments {
  public static void main(String args[]) {
    System.out.println("args.length = " + args.length);
    System.out.println("args[0] = " + args[0]);
    System.out.println("args[1] = " + args[1]);
    System.out.println("args[2] = " + args[2]);
  }
}
```

You may invoke this application from the command line as follows:

```
java CommandLineArguments 1 2 abcde
```

The output from this application is shown here:

```
args.length = 3
args[0] = 1
args[1] = 2
args[2] = abcde
```

2. The following application accepts two command-line arguments, converts them to integers, and displays their sum.

```
class Add2Integers {

  public static void main(String args[]) {

    // Get first integer
    int i = Integer.parseInt(args[0]);

    // Get second integer
    int j = Integer.parseInt(args[1]);

    // Display their sum
```

```
        int sum = i + j;
        System.out.print("Sum is " + sum);
    }
}
```

You may invoke this application from the command line as shown here:

```
java Add2Integers 3 4
```

With these command-line arguments, the output from the application is:

```
Sum is 7
```

If you execute this program without supplying two arguments, an **ArrayIndexOutOfBoundsException** is generated and displayed. If an argument is not correctly formatted as a number, a **NumberFormatException** occurs.

EXERCISES

1. Write an application that accepts two **double**s as its command-line arguments, multiplies these together, and displays the product.

2. Write a program that accepts the radius of a circle as its command-line argument and displays the area of this shape.

2.11 *T*HE SYSTEM CLASS

The **System** class defines several attributes related to the run-time environment. You have already seen one use of the **System** class. It has a static variable named **out** that contains a reference to a **PrintStream** object. The **print( )** and **println( )** methods of that object display their string arguments on the standard output. The static variable **err** also holds a reference to a **PrintStream** object. This is the standard error stream. The static variable **in** contains a reference to an **InputStream** object. **PrintStream** and **InputStream** are classes that provide support for I/O.

Another static method of the **System** class is **exit( )**. It terminates the current application and has this form:

void exit(int *code*)

Here, *code* is the exit code. By convention, a value of zero indicates normal termination. Other values can be used to report some problem.

The static **currentTimeMillis( )** method returns the number of milliseconds between the current time and midnight, January 1, 1970, Greenwich Mean Time. Its form is shown here:

long currentTimeMillis( )

The static **arraycopy( )** method copies elements from a source array to a destination array. Its general form is:

void arraycopy(Object *source*, int *sourceIndex*, Object *destination*,
　　　　　int *destinationIndex*, int *size*)

Here, *source* is the array from which *size* elements should be read starting at *sourceIndex*. The elements should be written to *destination* starting at *destinationIndex*.

EXAMPLE

1. This example illustrates the use of the **arraycopy( )** method. Five elements are copied from **array1** to **array2**. The ten elements in **array2** are then displayed.

```
class ArrayCopy {
  public static void main(String args[]) {
    int array1[] = { 0, 1, 2, 3, 4, 5, 6, 7, 8, 9 };
    int array2[] = { 0, 0, 0, 0, 0, 0, 0, 0, 0, 0 };
    System.arraycopy(array1, 0, array2, 0, 5);
    System.out.print("array2: ");
    System.out.print(array2[0] + " ");
    System.out.print(array2[1] + " ");
    System.out.print(array2[2] + " ");
    System.out.print(array2[3] + " ");
    System.out.print(array2[4] + " ");
    System.out.print(array2[5] + " ");
    System.out.print(array2[6] + " ");
    System.out.print(array2[7] + " ");
    System.out.print(array2[8] + " ");
```

```
        System.out.println(array2[9]);
    }
}
```

Output from this application is shown here:

```
array2: 0 1 2 3 4 0 0 0 0 0
```

---

1. Write an application that displays the number of milliseconds between the current time and midnight, January 1, 1970, Greenwich
Mean Time.

Mastery

Skills Check

Before continuing, you should be able to answer these questions and complete these exercises:

1. What are static variables and methods? How are they accessed?

2. What are instance variables and methods? How are they accessed?

3. Explain the syntax for using the **new** operator.

4. Name the eight wrapper classes.

5. What is the result if you divide a floating-point number by zero?

6. The moon's gravity is about 17 percent of Earth's. Write a program that accepts your Earth weight as a command-line argument and displays your effective weight on the moon.

7. Write a program that accepts an angle in degrees as a command-line argument and displays the cosine, sine, and tangent of that angle.

**Cumulative
Skills Check**

This section checks how well you have integrated material in this chapter with that from the preceding chapters.

1. Name the Java keywords that you have used in the first two chapters. Explain each of their meanings.

2. Write a program that creates **Boolean**, **Character**, **Byte**, **Short**, **Integer**, **Long**, **Float**, and **Double** objects to encapsulate eight values supplied as command-line arguments. Display the string equivalent of each object.

3. Build an application that creates and initializes an array with five **Character** objects. Then, create a **StringBuffer** object and append the array elements to the string buffer. Finally, display the string buffer.

3

Introducing Java's Control Statements

chapter objectives

P ROGRAM control statements determine your program's flow of execution. In this chapter you will learn about two of Java's most important program control statements: **if** and **for**. In addition, you will learn about blocks of code, the increment and decrement operators, the backslash operators, the relational and logical operators, and the ternary operator.

Review

Skills Check

Before proceeding, you should be able to correctly answer these questions and do these exercises.

1. What is the lifetime of static, instance, and local variables?

2. Give an example of a static method and static variable.

3. Name six instance methods that are provided by the **Byte**, **Short**, **Integer**, **Long**, **Float**, and **Double** classes.

4. Write a program that displays the natural logarithm of its command-line argument.

3.1 ▰ *T HE if STATEMENT*

The **if** statement is one of Java's *selection statements* (sometimes called *conditional statements*). Its operation is governed by the outcome of a conditional test that evaluates to either **true** or **false**. Simply put, selection statements make decisions based upon the outcome of some condition.

In its simplest form, the **if** statement allows your program to conditionally execute a statement. This form of the **if** is shown here:

if(*expr*) *statement*;

Here, *expr* is any expression that evaluates to a **boolean** value. If the expression evaluates as **true**, the statement will be executed. Otherwise, the statement is bypassed, and the line of code following the **if** is executed. The statement that follows an **if** is usually referred to as the target of the **if** statement.

The expression inside **if** typically compares one value with another by using a relational operator. Java uses > as its *greater than* operator. The outcome of this comparison is either **true** or **false**. For example, 10 > 9 is **true**, but 9 > 10 is **false**. Therefore, this **if** will cause the message **true** to be displayed.

```
if(10 > 9) System.out.println("true");
```

However, because the expression in the following statement is **false**, the **if** does not execute its target statement as shown here:

```
if(5 > 9) System.out.println("this will not print");
```

Java uses < as its *less than* operator. For example, 10 < 11 is **true**. To test for equality, Java provides the = = operator. (There can be no space between the two equal signs.) Therefore, 10 = = 10 is **true**, but 10 = = 11 is **false**.

The following table summarizes the Java relational operators. These test the relationship between two operands. The operands may be expressions or values. The outcome of a relational operation is a **boolean** value.

Operator	Meaning	Example
==	Equals	i == j
!=	Not equals	i != j
>	Greater than	i > j
<	Less than	i < j
>=	Greater than or equals	i >= j
<=	Less than or equals	i <= j

The following application shows how an **if** statement is used with an expression containing a relational operator. It displays a message if there are no command-line arguments.

```
class IfDemo {
  public static void main(String args[]) {
    if(args.length == 0)
      System.out.println("You must have command line arguments");
  }
}
```

Remember, a number is not a **boolean**. Therefore, it is not valid to have an **if** statement such as the one shown here:

```
if(count + 1) System.out.println("Not Zero");
```

Such a line generates a compiler error.

EXAMPLE

1. Write an application that accepts one command-line argument. Convert this to a **double** and display the square root of that number. Note that if the number is negative, its square root is a pure imaginary number.

```
class SquareRoot {
  public static void main(String args[]) {
    double d = Double.valueOf(args[0]).doubleValue();
    if(d < 0)
      System.out.print(Math.sqrt(-d) + "i");
    if(d >= 0)
      System.out.print(Math.sqrt(d));
  }
}
```

EXERCISES

1. Write an application that accepts one command-line argument. Convert this to an **int** and display a line reporting if that number is even or odd. (Hint: Use Java's modulus operator %.)

2. Write an application that converts between meters and feet. Its first command-line argument is a number. Its second command-line argument is either "feet" or "meters." If this argument equals "feet," display a string reporting the equivalent number of meters. If this argument equals "meters," display a string reporting the equivalent number of feet. Otherwise, report that the unit system is not recognized. (Note: One meter is equal to 3.28 feet.)

3.2 **T**HE *if-else* STATEMENT

You can add an **else** statement to the **if**. When this is done, the **if** statement looks like this:

   if(expression)
      statement 1;
   else
      statement 2;

If the expression is **true**, the target of the **if** will execute and the **else** portion will be skipped. However, if the expression is **false**, the target of the **if** is bypassed and the target of the **else** will execute. Under no circumstances will both statements execute. Thus, the addition of the **else** provides a two-way decision path.

EXAMPLE

1. You can use the **else** to create more efficient code in some cases. For example, the **else** is used in place of a second **if** in the program from the preceding section.

```
class SquareRoot2 {
  public static void main(String args[]) {
    double d = Double.valueOf(args[0]).doubleValue();
    if(d < 0)
      System.out.print(Math.sqrt(-d) + "i");
    else
      System.out.print(Math.sqrt(d));
  }
}
```

Recall that the original version of this program explicitly tested for nonnegative numbers by comparing **d** to 0 using a second **if** statement. But since there are only two possibilities-**d** is either negative or non-negative-there is no reason for this second test.

EXERCISE

1. Write an application that accepts two command-line arguments. Convert these to **double** values and divide the first number by the second number. Use an **if-else** statement to prevent division by zero from occurring.

BLOCKS OF CODE

In Java, you can group two or more statements together. This is called a *block of code* or a *code block*. To create a block of code, you surround the statements in the block with opening and closing curly braces. Once this is done, the statements form one logical unit, which may be used instead of a single statement.

For example, the general form of the **if** using blocks of code is:

```
if(expression) {
  statement1;
  statement2;
    .
    .
    .
  statement M;
}
else {
  statement1;
  statement2;
    .
    .
    .
  statement N;
}
```

If the expression evaluates to **true**, then all the statements in the block of code associated with the **if** will be executed. If the expression is **false**, then all the statements in the **else** block will be executed. (Remember, the **else** is optional and need not be present.) For example, this fragment prints a message if the variable **num** is positive.

```
if(num > 0) {
  System.out.println("This is ");
  System.out.println("an example of ");
  System.out.println("a code block.");
}
```

Keep in mind that a block of code represents one indivisible logical unit. This means that under no circumstances could one of the **println( )** statements in this fragment execute without the others also executing.

The statements that appear within the block of code are usually indented. Although Java does not care where a statement appears on a line, it is common practice to indent one level at the start of a block. Indenting makes the structure of a program easier to understand. Also, the placement of the curly braces is arbitrary. However, the way they are shown in the example is a common technique and will be used by the examples in this book.

EXAMPLE

1. The following application displays the cosine, sine, and tangent of its command-line argument. However, it displays an error message if no command-line argument has been provided.

```java
class Angle {
  public static void main(String args[]) {
    if(args.length > 0) {
      double angle =
        Double.valueOf(args[0]).doubleValue();
      double radians = angle * Math.PI/180;
      System.out.println("cosine: " + Math.cos(radians));
      System.out.println("sine: " + Math.sin(radians));
      System.out.println("tangent: " +
        Math.tan(radians));
    }
    else {
      System.out.println("Provide an angle in degrees " +
        "as command line argument");
    }
  }
}
```

EXERCISE

1. Is this fragment correct?

```java
if(count < 100)
  System.out.println("Number is less than 100.");
  System.out.println("Its square is " + count * count);
}
```

*T*HE *for* STATEMENT

The **for** loop is one of Java's three loop statements. It allows one or more statements to be repeated and is considered by many Java programmers to be its most flexible loop. Although the **for** loop allows a large number of variations, we will examine only its most common form in this section.

The **for** loop is used to repeat a statement or block of statements a specified number of times. Its general form for repeating a single statement is shown here.

for(initialization; test; increment) *statement*;

The initialization section typically gives an initial value to the variable that controls the loop. This variable is usually referred to as the *loop-control variable.* The initialization section is executed only once, before the loop begins.

The test section of the loop typically tests the loop-control variable against a target value. If the test evaluates **true**, the loop repeats. If it is **false**, the loop stops, and program execution picks up with the next line of code that follows the loop. The test is performed at the start or top of the loop each time the loop is repeated.

The increment section of the **for** is executed at the bottom of the loop. That is, the increment portion is executed after the statement or block that forms its body has been executed. The purpose of the increment portion is typically to increase (or decrease) the loop-control variable by a certain amount.

This program uses a **for** loop to print the numbers **1** through **10** on the screen.

```
public class ForDemo {
  public static void main(String args[]) {
    for(int num = 1; num < 11; num = num + 1)
      System.out.print(num + " ");
    System.out.println("terminating");
  }
}
```

Output from this application is shown here:

1 2 3 4 5 6 7 8 9 10 terminating

First, the loop control variable **num** is initialized to 1. Next, the expression **num < 11** is evaluated. Since it is **true**, the **for** loop begins running. After the number is printed, **num** is incremented by one and the conditional test is evaluated again. This process continues until **num** equals 11. When this happens, the **for** loop stops, and "terminating" is displayed. Keep in mind that the initialization portion of the **for** loop is only executed once, when the loop is first entered.

As stated earlier, the conditional test is performed at the start of each iteration. This means that if the test is initially **false**, the loop will not execute even once. For example, the following program only displays "terminating" because **num** is initialized to 11, causing the conditional test to fail.

```
public class ForDemo2 {
  public static void main(String args[]) {
    for(int num = 11; num < 11; num = num + 1)
      System.out.print(num + " ");
    System.out.println("terminating");
  }
}
```

To repeat several statements, use a block of code as the target of the **for** loop. For example, the following program computes the product and sum of the numbers from 1 to 5.

```
public class ProductAndSum {
  public static void main(String args[]) {
    int sum = 0;
    int prod = 1;
    for(int num = 1; num < 6; num = num + 1) {
      sum = sum + num;
      prod = prod * num;
    }
    System.out.print("product and sum: " + prod + " " + sum);
  }
}
```

Output from this application is shown here:

```
Product and sum: 120 15
```

A **for** loop can run negatively. For example, this fragment decrements the loop-control variable.

```
for(int num = 20; num > 0; num = num - 1) . . .
```

Further, the loop-control variable may be incremented or decremented by more than one. For example, this program counts to 100 by fives.

```
public class CountTo100By5 {
  public static void main(String args[]) {
    for(int i = 0; i < 101; i = i + 5)
      System.out.print(i + " ");
  }
}
```

Output from this application is shown here:

```
0 5 10 15 20 25 30 35 40 45 50 55 60 65 70 75 80 85 90 95 100
```

EXAMPLES

1. The following application accepts one command-line argument. It counts the number of digits and letters in that string and displays these values.

```
class CountLettersDigits {
  public static void main(String args[]) {
    int digits = 0;
    int letters = 0;
    for(int i = 0; i < args[0].length(); i = i + 1) {
      char ch = args[0].charAt(i);
      if(Character.isDigit(ch))
        digits += 1;
      else if(Character.isLetter(ch))
        letters += 1;
    }
    System.out.println("There are " + digits + " digits");
    System.out.println("There are " + letters + " letters");
  }
}
```

2. The following application accepts one command-line argument and tests if it is a prime number.

```
class PrimeTest {

  public static void main(String args[]) {

    // Convert command line argument
    int num = Integer.parseInt(args[0]);

    // Test for factors
    boolean prime = true;
    for(int i = 2; i <= num/2; i = i + 1)
      if((num % i) == 0) prime = false;

    // Display results
    if(prime == true)
      System.out.print("The number is prime.");
    else
      System.out.print("The number is not prime.");
  }
}
```

EXERCISES

1. Create a program that displays the numbers from 1 to 100.

2. Write a program that prints the numbers between 17 and 100 that can be evenly divided by 17.

3. Write a program that displays all the factors of a number entered by the user. For example, if the user entered 8, it would respond with 2 and 4.

3.5 INCREMENT AND DECREMENT OPERATORS

When you learned about the **for** in the preceding section, the increment portion of the loop looked more or less like the one shown here:

```
for(num = 0; num < some_value; num = num + 1) . . .
```

Although not incorrect, you will almost never see a statement like **num = num + 1** in professionally written programs because Java provides a special operator that increments a variable by one. The increment operator is **+ +** (two pluses with no intervening space). Using the increment operator, you can change this line of code:

```
i = i + 1;
```

into

```
i++;
```

Therefore, the **for** shown earlier will normally be written like this:

```
for(num = 0; num < some_value; num++) . . .
```

In a similar fashion, to decrease a variable by one, you can use the decrement operator: --. (There must be no space between the two minus signs.) Therefore,

```
count = count - 1;
```

can be rewritten as

```
count--;
```

The increment and decrement operators do not need to follow the variable; they can precede it. Although the effect on the variable is the same, the position of the operator does affect when the operation is performed. To see how, examine this program.

```
class IncrementTest {
  public static void main(String args[]) {
    int i, j;
    i = 10;
    j = i++;
    /* this will print 11 10 */
    System.out.println("i and j: " +  i + " " + j);
  }
}
```

Don't let the **j = i+ +** statement trouble you. The increment operator may be used as part of any valid Java expression. This statement works like this. First, the current value of **i** is assigned to **j**.

Then **i** is incremented. This is why **j** has the value 10, not 11. When the increment or decrement operator follows the variable, the operation is performed after its value has been obtained for use in the expression. Therefore, assuming that **max** has the value 1, an expression such as

```
count = 10 * max++;
```

assigns the value 10 to **count** and increases **max** by one.

If the variable is preceded by the increment or decrement operator, the operation is performed *before* its value has been obtained for use in the expression. For example, rewriting the previous program as follows causes **j** to be 11.

```
class IncrementTest2 {
  public static void main(String args[]) {
    int i, j;
    i = 10;
    j = ++i;
    /* this will print 11 11 */
    System.out.println("i and j: " +  i + " " + j);
  }
}
```

If you are simply using the increment or decrement operators to replace equivalent assignment statements, it doesn't matter if the operator precedes or follows the variable. This is a matter of your own personal style.

EXAMPLES

1. This is a revised version of an application shown in the previous section. It counts the number of digits and letters in the command-line argument. The increment operator is used in this version.

```
class CountLettersDigits2 {
  public static void main(String args[]) {
    int digits = 0;
    int letters = 0;
    for(int i = 0; i < args[0].length(); i++) {
      char ch = args[0].charAt(i);
      if(Character.isDigit(ch))
```

```
            ++digits;
          else if(Character.isLetter(ch))
            ++letters;
        }
      System.out.println("There are " + digits +
        " digits");
      System.out.println("There are " + letters +
        " letters");
    }
  }
```

2. This program illustrates the use of the increment and decrement operators.

```
class IncrementDecrement {
  public static void main(String args[]) {
    int i;
    i = 0;
    System.out.println(++i);   // prints 1
    System.out.println(i++);   // prints 1
    System.out.println(i);     // prints 2
    System.out.println(-i);    // prints 1
    System.out.println(i-);    // prints 1
    System.out.println(i);     // prints 0
  }
}
```

Output from this program is shown here:
1
1
2
1
1
0

EXERCISES

1. Write an application that displays all numbers between 20 and 30. Use a **for** loop and the increment operator.

2. Change all appropriate assignment statements in this program to increment or decrement statements.

```
class BeforeIncrementDecrement {
  public static void main(String args[]) {
```

```
        int a, b;
        a = 1;
        a = a + 1;
        b = a;
        b = b - 1;
        System.out.println(a + " " + b);
    }
}
```

3.6 BACKSLASH CODES

So far, we have used **println( )** to output strings and numbers. The Java language also defines several special character codes, shown in Table 3-1, that represent characters that cannot be entered from the keyboard, are nonprinting characters, may not be found in all character sets, or serve other unique needs. You can use the backslash codes anywhere you can use a normal character. The backslash constants are also referred to as *escape sequences*.

Perhaps the single most important backslash code is **\n**, which is often referred to as a *newline* character. Its use is illustrated in the following program:

```
class NewlineDemo {
  public static void main(String args[]) {
    System.out.print("This is line one\n");
    System.out.print("This is line two\n");
    System.out.print("This is line three");
  }
}
```

Output from this program appears on the screen as shown here:

```
This is line one.
This is line two.
This is line three.
```

Remember, the backslash codes are character constants. Therefore, to assign one to a character variable, you must enclose the backslash code within single quotes, as shown in this fragment:

```
char ch;
ch = '\t'; /* assign ch the tab character */
```

Code	Meaning
\b	Backspace
\n	Newline
\r	Carriage return
\f	Form feed
\t	Horizontal tab
\"	Double quote
\'	Single-quote character
\0	Null
\\	Backslash
\N	Octal constant (where N is 0 to 7)
\NN	Octal constant (where N is 0 to 7)
\MNN	Octal constant (where M is 0 to 3 and N is 0 to 7)
\uxxxx	Unicode character (where xxxx are four hexadecimal constants)

TABLE 3-1 *The Backslash Codes* ▼

EXAMPLES

1. You can enter any special character by specifying it as an octal or hexadecimal value following the backslash. The octal number system is based on 8 and uses the digits 0 through 7. In octal, the number 010 is the same as 8 in decimal. The hexadecimal number system is based on 16 and uses the digits 0 through 9 plus the letters A through F, which stand for 10, 11, 12, 13, 14, and 15. For example, the hexadecimal number 10 is 16 in decimal.

   The ASCII character set is defined from 0 to 127. However, many computers, including most PCs, use the values 128 to 255 for special and graphics characters. If your computer supports these extra characters, the following program will display a few of them on the screen. The following program outputs four Unicode characters:

```
class SpecialCharacters {
  public static void main(String args[]) {
    System.out.print("\u00a0 \u00a1 \u00a2 \u00a3");
  }
}
```

2. The \n newline character does not have to go at the end of the string that is being output by **println( )**. It can go anywhere in the string. Further, there can be as many newline characters in a string as you desire. The point is that there is no connection between a newline and the end of a string. For example, the program

```
class EmbeddedNewlines {
  public static void main(String args[]) {
    System.out.print("one\ntwo\nthree\nfour");
  }
}
```

displays

```
one
two
three
four
```

on the screen.

EXERCISE

---

1. Experiment on your own with the backslash codes.

3.7 **R**ELATIONAL AND BOOLEAN LOGICAL OPERATORS

The first part of this chapter listed the relational operators. These have been frequently used in the samples presented so far. Some further information about these operators is presented in this section. In addition, you will learn about the boolean logical operators. These work with **boolean** operands. Since the outcome of the relational operators is a **boolean** value, the relational operators are frequently used in conjunction with the boolean logical operators. The following table summarizes these operators

Operator	**Action**
&	AND
|	OR
^	Exclusive OR
!	NOT
&&	AND (short circuit)
||	OR (short circuit)
==	Equals
!=	Not equals

According to this truth table, the Boolean logical operators support the basic logical operations of AND, OR, Exclusive OR, and NOT.

p	**q**	**p & q**	**p | q**	**p ^ q**	**!p**
false	false	false	false	false	true
false	true	false	true	true	true
true	false	false	true	true	false
true	true	true	true	false	false

The *&&* and || operators are known as the *short circuit* operators. They function slightly differently than the *&* and | operators. The difference is that the *&* and | operators always evaluate both of their operands. However, the *&&* and || operators first evaluate their left operand and only evaluate their right operand if necessary. For example, both operands of the *&* operator are always evaluated in the following expression:

```
((a >= 0) & (c > b/a))
```

Now consider this expression:

```
((a >= 0) && (c > b/a))
```

Here, the right operand is not evaluated if **a** is negative because the result is **false** no matter what the right-hand operand is. That is, since both operands of an AND must be **true** for the result to be **true**, the first **false** operand determines the outcome. A similar condition applies to an OR operation. The first **true** operand determines the outcome. In cases involving ANDs and ORs, the short circuit operators can be used to create more efficient code by avoiding the unnecessary processing of meaningless statements.

The relational and logical operators are both lower in precedence than the arithmetic operators. This means that an expression like

```
10 + count > a + 12
```

is evaluated as if it were written

```
(10 + count) > (a + 12)
```

You may link any number of relational operations together using logical operators. For example, this expression joins three relational operations:

```
var > max || !(max == 100) && 0 <= item
```

The table below shows the relative precedence of the relational and Boolean logical operators.

Highest	!
	> >= < <=
	== !=
	&
	^
	|
	&&
Lowest	||

There is one important fact to remember about the values produced by the relational and logical operators: the result is either **true** or **false**. Your programs may make use of this fact.

You can use the relational and logical operators in both the **if** and **for** statements. For example, the following statement reports when both **a** and **b** are positive.

```
if(a > 0 && b > 0) System.out.println("Both are positive.");
```

EXAMPLES

1. The following application illustrates how to use the relational operators. This program accepts two command-line arguments, converts them to **int** values, and exercises each of the relational operators.

```java
class RelationalOperatorDemo {
  public static void main(String args[]) {
    int i = Integer.parseInt(args[0]);
    int j = Integer.parseInt(args[1]);
    System.out.println("i = " + i);
    System.out.println("j = " + j);
    System.out.println("Relational operators:");
    System.out.println("i < j " + (i < j));
    System.out.println("i <= j " + (i <= j));
    System.out.println("i == j " + (i == j));
    System.out.println("i > j " + (i > j));
    System.out.println("i >= j " + (i >= j));
    System.out.println("i != j " + (i != j));
  }
}
```

2. The following application illustrates how to use the boolean logical operators. This program accepts two command-line arguments, converts them to **boolean** values, and exercises each of the operators. (For example, you may enter "java LogicalOperatorDemo true false" on the command line to execute this program.)

```java
class LogicalOperatorDemo {
  public static void main(String args[]) {
    boolean i = Boolean.valueOf(args[0]).booleanValue();
    boolean j = Boolean.valueOf(args[1]).booleanValue();
    System.out.println("i = " + i);
    System.out.println("j = " + j);
    System.out.println("Logical operators:");
    System.out.println("i & j " + (i & j));
    System.out.println("i | j " + (i | j));
    System.out.println("i ^ j " + (i ^ j));
    System.out.println("!i " + !i);
    System.out.println("i && j " + (i && j));
    System.out.println("i || j " + (i || j));
    System.out.println("i == j " + (i == j));
    System.out.println("i != j " + (i != j));
  }
}
```

EXERCISES

1. What does this loop do?

   ```
   for(x = 0; x < 100; x++) System.out.println(x);
   ```

2. Is this expression true?

   ```
   !(10 == 9)
   ```

3. Under what conditions will the right-hand operand of the following expression be evaluated?

   ```
   ((a >=0) || (c > b/c))
   ```

4. On your own, experiment with the relational and logical operators.

3.8 *T*ERNARY OPERATOR

Java contains a ternary operator that acts as an abbreviated form of an if-then-else statement. Its format is shown here:

expr1 ? expr2 : expr3

Here, *expr1* can be any **boolean** expression. If *expr1* is **true**, then *expr2* is evaluated. Otherwise, *expr3* is evaluated. The value returned by the ternary operator is either the value of *expr2* or *expr3*. The types of *expr2* and *expr3* must be the same.

EXAMPLE

1. This example illustrates how to use the ternary operators. If **i** is greater than **j**, the operator returns the value of **i**. Otherwise, it returns the value of **j**.

```
class TernaryOperatorDemo {
  public static void main(String args[]) {
    int i = 10;
    int j = 5;
    System.out.println((i > j) ? i : j);
  }
}
```

The output from this program is shown below:

10

EXERCISE

---

1. Write a program that uses a ternary operator to test if a number is even or odd. Return either "Even" or "Odd" from the ternary operator. Display the value.

Mastery
Skills Check

Before continuing, you should be able to answer these questions and complete these exercises.

1. Describe the syntax of an **if-else** statement.

2. Describe the syntax of a **for** statement.

3. What are the relational operators, and what operations do they perform?

4. What are the Boolean logical operators and their meanings?

5. Write an application that creates an **int** array with ten elements. Use a **for** loop to initialize the array elements with the values -1 through -10. Then use another **for** loop to display the array elements.

Cumulative
Skills Check

This section checks how well you have integrated material in this chapter with that from the preceding chapters.

1. Write a program that outputs a table of numbers. Each line in the table contains three entries: the number, its square, and its cube. Begin with 1 and end with 10. Also, use a **for** loop to generate the numbers

2. What are the increment and decrement operators, and what do they do?

3. Write a program that prints the numbers 1 to 100 using five columns. Have each number separated from the next by a tab.

4. Contrast the behavior of the *&* and *&&* operators.

4

More About Control Statements and Operators

T HIS chapter continues the discussion of program control in Java. Some additional information is provided about the **if** and **for** statements. You will then learn how to establish loops with the **while** and **do** statements. Nested loops are demonstrated. These are valuable in many programming situations. The **break**, **continue**, and **switch** statements can also be used to direct the flow of your program. Finally, the bitwise operators are discussed.

Review

Skills Check

Before proceeding, you should be able to answer these questions and perform these exercises.

1. What is a block of code? How do you make one?

2. How do you output a tab using **print( )**?

3. How can this statement be rewritten?

```
count = count + 1;
```

4. The expression that controls the **if** and the test section of the **for** must be of what type?

4.1 NESTED if STATEMENTS

When an **if** statement is the target of another **if** or an **else**, it is said to be nested within the outer **if**. Here is a simple example of a nested **if**.

```
if(count > max) // outer if
  if(error) System.out.println("Error, try again."); // nested if
```

Here, the **println( )** statement will only execute if **count** is greater than **max** and if **error** is true. Notice how the nested **if** is indented. This is common practice. It enables anyone reading your program to know quickly that the **if** is nested and what actions are nested. A nested **if** may also appear inside a block of statements that are the target of the outer **if**.

One confusing aspect of nested **if**s is illustrated by the following fragment.

```
if(p)
  if(q) System.out.println("p and q are true");
else System.out.println("To which statement does this else apply?");
```

Which **if** is associated with the **else**? Fortunately, the answer is quite easy: an **else** always associates with the nearest **if** within the same block that does not already have an **else** associated with it. In this example, the **else** is associated with the second **if**, even though the indentation suggests the contrary.

EXAMPLES

1. It is possible to string together several **if**s and **else**s into what is sometimes called an **if-else-if** ladder or **if-else-if** staircase because of its visual appearance. In this situation a nested **if** has as its target another **if**. The general form of the **if-else-if** ladder is shown here.

```
if(expression) statement;
else
  if(expression) statement;
  else
    if(expression) statement;
            .
            .
            .
          else statement;
```

The conditions are evaluated from the top downward. As soon as a **true** condition is found, the statement associated with it is executed and the rest of the ladder is bypassed. If none of the conditions is **true**, the final **else** will be executed. That is, if all other conditional tests fail, the last **else** statement is performed. If the final **else** is not present, no action will take place if all other conditions are false.

Although the indentation of the general form of the **if-else-if** ladder just shown is technically correct, it can lead to overly deep indentation. Because of this, the **if-else-if** ladder is generally written like this:

```
if(expression) statement;
else if(expression) statement;
```

```
else if(expression) statement;
     .
     .
     .
else statement;
```

The following program illustrates the operation of an **if-else-if** ladder. It accepts one command-line argument, converts this to an **int**, and displays a string reporting if the value is negative, zero, one, two, three, or greater than three.

```java
class IfElseLadder {
  public static void main(String args[]) {
    int i = Integer.valueOf(args[0]).intValue();
    if(i < 0)
      System.out.print("Negative number");
    else if(i == 0)
      System.out.print("Zero");
    else if(i == 1)
      System.out.print("One");
    else if(i == 2)
      System.out.print("Two");
    else if(i == 3)
      System.out.print("Three");
    else
      System.out.print("Greater than three");
  }
}
```

Once a match is found, any remaining **if** statements are skipped. This means that the program isn't wasting time on needless operations. While this is not too important in this example, you will encounter situations where it will be significant.

2. Remember, an **else** associates with the nearest **if** that is within *its same block*. Consider the following fragment.

```java
if(x) {
  if(y) {
    if(z) // ...
  }
  else // ...
}
```

Here, **else** associates with **if(y)** because it is the nearest **if** within its block. It does not associate with **if(z)** because it is not within **if(z)**'s scope.

EXERCISES

1. To which **if** do the **else** statements relate in this example? Execute this program with different values for the command-line argument.

```
class IfElse {
  public static void main(String args[]) {
    int i = Integer.parseInt(args[0]);
    if(i > 0)
      if(i > 3)
        System.out.println("i > 0 and i > 3");
      else
        System.out.println("i > 0 and i <= 3");
    else
      System.out.println("i <= 0");
  }
}
```

2. In the following fragment, to which **if** does the **else** associate?

```
if(count < 10) {
  if(!done)
    System.out.println("running...");
  if(count == 5) {
    System.out.println("half way");
    x = y * 2;
  }
  else count ++;
}
```

4.2 *V**ARIATIONS OF THE* for *LOOP*

The initialization, test, and increment portions of the **for** loop are not limited to these narrow roles. The **for** loop places no limits on the types of expressions that occur inside it. For example, you do not have to use the initialization section to initialize a loop-control variable. Further, a loop-control variable is not necessary because the conditional test expression may use some other means of stopping the loop. Finally, the increment portion is technically just an expression that is evaluated each time the loop iterates. It does not have to increment or decrement a variable.

Another important reason the **for** is so flexible is that one or more of the expressions inside it may be empty. For example, if the loop-control variable has already been initialized outside the **for**, there is no need for an initialization expression.

EXAMPLES

1. As explained, it is possible to leave an expression in a loop empty. For example, this program accepts one command-line argument. It converts this string to an **int** and counts down to zero from this number. Here, the loop-control variable is initialized outside the loop, so the initialization portion of the loop is empty.

```java
class ExpressionLoop {
  public static void main(String args[]) {
    int i = Integer.parseInt(args[0]);
    for( ; i > 0; i-) System.out.print(i + " ");
  }
}
```

2. Using the **for**, it is possible to create a loop that never stops. This type of loop is usually called an *infinite* loop. Although accidentally creating an infinite loop is a bug, you will sometimes want to create one on purpose. (Later in this chapter, you will see that there are ways to exit even an infinite loop!) To create an infinite loop, use a **for** construct like this:

```java
for( ; ; ) {
  .
  .
  .
}
```

As you can see, there are no expressions in the **for**. When there is no expression in the conditional portion, the compiler assumes that it is **true**. Therefore, the loop continues to run.

3. It is perfectly valid for the loop-control variable to be altered outside the increment section. For example, the following program manually increments **i** at the bottom of the loop.

```
class EmptyForIncrement {
  public static void main(String args[]) {
    int i;
    for(i = 0; i < 10; ) {
      System.out.println(i);
      i++;
    }
  }
}
```

Output from this application is shown here:

```
0
1
2
3
4
5
6
7
8
9
```

EXERCISES

1. To create time-delay loops, **for** loops with empty targets are sometimes used. Create a program that accepts one command-line argument. Convert that string to an **int** and decrement its value in a loop. Sound the bell when the value reaches zero. (Note that the bell character is \u0007.)

2. Even if a **for** loop uses a loop-control variable, it need not be incremented or decremented by a fixed amount. Instead, the amount added or subtracted may vary. Write a program that

begins at 1 and runs to 1000. Have the program add the loop-control variable to itself inside the increment expression. This is an easy way to produce the arithmetic progression 1 2 4 8 16, and so on.

*T*HE while *LOOP*

The **while** statement provides another form of loop. It has the syntax shown here:

while(*expression*) statement;

Of course, the target of **while** may also be a block of code. The **while** loop works by repeating its target as long as the expression is **true**. When it becomes **false**, the loop stops. The value of the expression is checked at the top of the loop. This means that if the expression is initially **false**, the loop will not execute even once.

EXAMPLES

1. The following application illustrates the behavior of a **while** loop. A command-line argument is converted to an **int** value, and the program counts down from this number.

```
class WhileDemo {
  public static void main(String args[]) {
    int i = Integer.parseInt(args[0]);
    while(i > 0) {
      System.out.print(i + " ");
      i--;
    }
  }
}
```

2. Here is an example that uses a **while** to count the number of vowels in the string specified as a command-line argument.

```
class VowelCounter {
  public static void main(String args[]) {
    int vowels = 0;
    int i = args[0].length() - 1;
    while(i >= 0) {
```

```
char c = args[0].charAt(i);
if(c == 'A' || c == 'a')
   ++vowels;
else if(c == 'e' || c == 'E')
   ++vowels;
else if(c == 'i' || c == 'I')
   ++vowels;
else if(c == 'o' || c == 'O')
   ++vowels;
else if(c == 'u' || c == 'U')
   ++vowels;
—i;
        }
   System.out.println("The number of vowels is " +
   vowels);
     }
   }
```

EXERCISES

1. Write an application that accepts several command-line arguments, converts each of these to a number, and adds these numbers together. Use a **while** loop to iterate through the command-line arguments. (Hint: Recall that **args.length** contains the number of command-line arguments.)

2. Use a **while** loop to generate random numbers and maintain a running sum of these values. Terminate when the sum exceeds 20. (Hint: Use the **Math.random( )** method to obtain random numbers.)

4.4 *THE do LOOP*

The **do** statement provides another form of loop. It has the following syntax:

```
do{
  statements
} while(expression);
```

If only one statement is being repeated, the curly braces are not necessary. Most programmers include them, however, so that they can easily recognize that the **while** that ends the **do** is part of a **do** loop, not the beginning of a **while** loop.

The **do** loop repeats the statement or statements while the expression is **true**. It stops when the expression becomes **false**. The **do** loop is unique because it will always execute the code within the loop at least once, since the expression controlling the loop is tested at the bottom of the loop.

EXAMPLE

1. The following application uses a **do** loop to generate 15 prime numbers.

```java
class PrimeNumbers {

    public static void main(String args[]) {
        int count = 0;
        int number = 1;

        do {

            // Test for factors
            boolean prime = true;
            for(int i = 2; i <= number/2; i++)
                if((number % i) == 0) prime = false;

            // Display if prime
            if(prime == true) {
                System.out.print(number + " ");
                ++count;
            }

            // Increment number
            ++number;
        } while(count < 15);
    }
}
```

Output from this application is shown here:

```
1 2 3 5 7 11 13 17 19 23 29 31 37 41 43
```

1. Write an application that generates the first 15 numbers in the Fibonacci series (i.e., 1 1 2 3 5 8 13 21 . . .). A number in this series is calculated by adding together the two numbers that precede it. Use a **do** loop to control the computations.

2. Show how to replace this **for** loop with a **while**.

```
for(i = 0; i < 10; i += 2) // ...
```

4.5   NESTED LOOPS

When the body of one loop contains another, the second is said to be nested inside the first. Any of Java's loops may be nested within any other loop. As a simple example of nested **for** statements, this fragment prints the numbers 1 to 10 on the screen ten times.

```
for(i = 0; i < 10; i++) {
  for(j = 1; j < 11; j++) System.out.print(j + " "); /* nested loop */
System.out.println("");
}
```

EXAMPLE

1. This program uses three **for** loops to print the alphabet three times, each time printing each letter twice.

```
class Alphabet3 {
  public static void main(String args[]) {
    int i, j, k;
    for(i = 0; i < 3; i++)
      for(j = 0; j < 26; j++)
        for(k = 0; k < 2; k++)
          System.out.print((char)('A' + j));
  }
}
```

The statement

```
System.out.print((char)('A' + j));
```

works because ASCII codes for the letters of the alphabet are strictly ascending: each one is greater than the letter that precedes it.

1. Write an application that counts the total number of characters in all of its command-line arguments.

2. Write a program that finds all the prime numbers between 100 and 200.

*T*HE break *STATEMENT*

The **break** statement allows you to exit a loop from any point within its body, bypassing its normal termination expression. When the **break** statement is encountered inside a loop, the loop is immediately stopped, and program control resumes at the next statement following the loop. For example, this loop prints only the numbers 1 to 10.

```
class BreakDemo {
  public static void main(String args[]) {
    int i;
    for(i = 1; i < 100; i++) {
      System.out.println(i);
      if(i == 10) break;
    }
  }
}
```

The **break** statement can be used with all three of Java's loops.

1. The following application searches through its command-line arguments for a string that begins with the character '$'. If this is located, that string is displayed and the loop terminates.

```
class DollarArgument {
  public static void main(String args[]) {
    for(int i = 0; i < args.length; i++) {
```

```
            if(args[i].startsWith("$")) {
              System.out.print(args[i]);
              break;
            }
          }
        }
      }
```

2. A **break** only exits its immediately enclosing loop. For example:

```
class BreakNestedLoop {
  public static void main(String args[]) {
    for(int i = 0; i < 10; i++) {
      for(int j = 0; j < 10; j++) {
        System.out.println(j);
        if(j == 4) break;
      }
    }
  }
}
```

Here, the digits 0 through 4 are printed ten times. The **break** only affects the nested loop; the outer loop runs to completion.

EXERCISES

1. Write an application that searches through its command-line arguments. If an argument is found that does not begin with an uppercase letter, display an error message and terminate.

2. On your own, write several short programs that use **break** to exit a loop. Be sure to try all three loop statements.

4.7 *THE* continue *STATEMENT*

The **continue** statement is somewhat the opposite of the **break** statement. It forces the next iteration of the loop to take place, skipping any code in between itself and the test condition of the loop. For example, this program displays output only for the last five iterations of the loop.

```
class ContinueDemo {
  public static void main(String args[]) {
    for(int x = 0; x < 100; x++) {
      if(x < 95) continue;
      System.out.println(x);
    }
  }
}
```

Each time the **continue** statement is reached, it causes the loop to repeat, skipping the **println( )** statement.

In **while** and **do-while** loops, a **continue** statement will cause control to go directly to the test condition and then continue the looping process. In the case of **for**, the increment part of the loop is performed, the conditional test is executed, and the loop continues.

EXAMPLE

1. The following application displays ten random numbers whose values are between 0.2 and 0.8. Notice that a **continue** statement is used to ignore values that lie outside this range. A **break** statement stops the **while** loop.

```
class RandomNumbers {
  public static void main(String args[]) {
    int i = 0;
    while(i < 10) {
      double d = Math.random();
      if(d < .2 || d > .8)
        continue;
      System.out.println(d);
      ++i;
    }
  }
}
```

EXERCISE

1. Write a program that prints only the odd numbers between 1 and 100. Use a **for** loop that looks like this:

```
for(i = 1; i < 101; i++) . . .
```

Use a **continue** statement to avoid printing even numbers.

| 4.8 | *T*HE switch *STATEMENT* |

Although **if** is good for choosing between two alternatives, it quickly becomes cumbersome when several alternatives are needed. Java's solution to this problem is the **switch** statement. The **switch** statement is Java's multiple selection statement. It is used to select one of several alternative paths in program execution and works like this: An expression is successively tested against a list of **char**, **byte**, **short**, or **int** constants. When a match is found, the statement sequence associated with that match is executed. The general form of the **switch** statement is

```
switch(expression) {
    case constant1:
        statement sequence
        break;
    case constant2:
        statement sequence
        break;
    case constant3:
        statement sequence
        break;
        .
        .
        .

    default:
        statement sequence
        break;
}
```

where the default statement sequence is performed if no matches are found. The default is optional. If all matches fail and default is absent, no action takes place. When a match is found, the statements associated with that case are executed until **break** is encountered or, in the case of default or the last case, the end of the **switch** is reached.

The **switch** statement differs from an **if** statement. The former can only test for equality. However, the **if** conditional expression can be of any type. Also, **switch** will work only with **char**, **byte**, **short**, or **int** types. You cannot, for example, use floating-point numbers. Also, no two case constants in the same **switch** can have identical values.

The statement sequences associated with each case are not blocks; they are not enclosed by curly braces.

EXAMPLES

1. As a very simple example, this program recognizes its command-line arguments and prints the name of the one you enter. That is, if you enter **2**, the program displays **two**.

```java
class SwitchDemo {
  public static void main(String args[]) {
    int i = Integer.parseInt(args[0]);
    switch(i) {
      case 1:
        System.out.println("one");
        break;
      case 2:
        System.out.println("two");
        break;
      case 3:
        System.out.println("three");
        break;
      case 4:
        System.out.println("four");
        break;
      default:
        System.out.println("Unrecognized Number");
    }
  }
}
```

2. It is possible to have a **switch** as part of the statement sequence of an outer **switch**. This is called a *nested* **switch**. If the case constants of the inner and outer **switch** contain common values, no conflicts will arise. For example, the following code fragment is perfectly acceptable.

```java
switch(a) {
  case 1:
    switch(b) {
      case 0: System.out.println("b is false");
              break;
```

```
      case 1: System.out.println("b is true");
    }
   break;
 case 2:
    .
    .
    .
```

3. The **break** statement is optional. When encountered within a **switch**, it causes the program flow to exit from the entire **switch** statement and continue on to the next statement outside the **switch**. This is much the way it works when breaking out of a loop. However, if a **break** statement is omitted, execution continues into the following case or default statement (if either exists). That is, when a **break** statement is missing, execution "falls through" into the next case and stops only when a **break** statement or the end of the **switch** is encountered. For example, study this program carefully. Once execution begins inside a case, it continues until a **break** statement or the end of the **switch** is encountered.

```
class MissingBreaks {
  public static void main(String args[]) {
    int i = 3;
    switch(i) {
    case 5:
      System.out.println("Greater than 4");
    case 4:
      System.out.println("Greater than 3");
    case 3:
      System.out.println("Greater than 2");
    case 2:
      System.out.println("Greater than 1");
    case 1:
      System.out.println("Greater than 0");
      break;
    default:
      System.out.println("Greater than 5" +
        " or negative");
    }
  }
}
```

Output from this program is shown next:

```
Greater than 2
Greater than 1
Greater than 0
```

4. The statement sequence associated with a case may also
   be empty. This allows two or more cases to share a common
   statement sequence without duplication of code. For
   example, here is a program that categorizes a letter as a vowel
   or consonant.

```java
class EmptyCase {

  public static void main(String args[]) {

    // Get first character of argument
    char ch = args[0].charAt(0);

    // Determine if it is a vowel or consonant
    switch(ch) {
      case 'a':
      case 'e':
      case 'i':
      case 'o':
      case 'u':
      case 'y':
        System.out.println("Vowel");
        break;
      default:
        System.out.println("Consonant");
    }
  }
}
```

EXERCISES

1. What compile errors occur with the following program?

```java
class BadSwitch {
  public static void main(String args[]) {
    int i = 1;
    int j = 2;
    switch(Integer.parseInt(args[0])) {
      case i:
        System.out.println("1");
```

```
        break;
    case j:
        System.out.println("2");
        break;
    default:
        System.out.println("Default");
    }
  }
}
```

2. On your own, write a program that uses a **switch** statement.

---

*T*HE BITWISE OPERATORS

Java is a language rich with operators. Indeed, Java performs with operators many things that other languages perform with methods. Earlier you learned about its arithmetic operators. Here we will examine Java's bitwise operators. These are operators that can manipulate the individual bits of a character or integer.

Java provides three categories of bitwise operators: logical, shift, and assignment. These operators may be applied only to Java's integer types: **char**, **byte**, **short**, **int**, and **long**. Java's bitwise logical operators are listed in the following table:

Operator	Meaning
&	AND
		OR
^	eXclusive OR (XOR)
~	Bitwise complement

These perform their logical operation on a bit-by-bit basis. For example,

0010 0011 & 1010 0101

yields

0010 0001

As you can see, the logical AND was applied to corresponding bits in each operand.

There are three operators that can shift the bits of a character or integer. They are listed here:

Operator	**Meaning**
>>	Shift right with sign extension
>>>	Shift right with zero fill
<<	Shift left with zero fill

The shift operators have this general form:

value << *num*
value >> *num*
value >>> *num*

Here, *value* is the value being shifted and *num* is the number of bit positions to shift. For example:

16 >> 2

yields a result of 4. Here's why. The binary bit pattern for 16 is

0001 0000

After right shifting two places, the bit pattern becomes

0000 0100

which is the number 4. The difference between > > and > > > is that > > fills in the leftmost bit with its previous value. Thus, it preserves the sign of the number. The > > > operator fills the leftmost bit with zero.

There are several operators that combine a bitwise operation with an assignment:

Operator	**Meaning**
&=	AND and assignment
|=	OR and assignment
^=	eXclusive OR (XOR) and assignment

<u>Operator</u>	<u>Meaning</u>
>>=	Shift right with sign extension and assignment
>>>=	Shift right with zero fill and assignment
<<=	Shift left with zero fill and assignment

These are used to replace a statement such as

```
x = x << 2;
```

with

```
x <<= 2;
```

The bitwise operators are a powerful addition to the Java language that help give you detailed control of the contents of an integer value.

EXAMPLES

1. This example illustrates how to use various bitwise operators. Notice that a right shift of one bit is equivalent to division by two and a left shift of one bit is equivalent to multiplication by two.

```
class BitwiseOperators {
  public static void main(String args[]) {
    char c = 'A';
    byte b = 100;
    short s = 100;
    int i = -100;
    long lo = 100;
    System.out.println(c & 0xf);
    System.out.println(b | 1);
    System.out.println(s ^ 1);
    System.out.println(~i);
    System.out.println(lo | 1);
    System.out.println(i >> 2);
    System.out.println(s >>> 2);
    System.out.println(i << 2);
  }
}
```

Output from this application is shown next:

```
1
101
101
99
101
-25
25
-400
```

2. The following program displays the individual bits of a **byte**
   value. It illustrates how to use the AND operator and the left
   shift with an assignment operator. Note that negative numbers
   are represented by a twos-complement value in Java.

```
class ShowBits {
  public static void main(String args[]) {
    byte b = -5;
    for(int i = 7; i >= 0; i—) {
      if((b & 0x80) == 0)
        System.out.println("Bit " + i + " is 0");
      else
        System.out.println("Bit " + i + " is 1");
      b <<= 1;
    }
  }
}
```

Output from this application is shown here:

```
Bit 7 is 1
Bit 6 is 1
Bit 5 is 1
Bit 4 is 1
Bit 3 is 1
Bit 2 is 0
Bit 1 is 1
Bit 0 is 1
```

EXERCISES

1. What is the output from this program?

```
class BitwiseOperators2 {
  public static void main(String args[]) {
    short s = 0xff;
    System.out.println(s);
```

```
        System.out.println(s & 0xf);
        System.out.println(s | 1);
        System.out.println(s ^ 1);
        System.out.println(~s);
        System.out.println(s >> 2);
        System.out.println(s >>> 2);
        System.out.println(s << 2);
    }
}
```

2. Write an application that accepts an integer as its argument and reports the number of bits that are set in that value.

Mastery

Skills Check

At this point, you should be able to answer these questions and perform these exercises.

1. Show three ways to create an infinite loop in Java.

2. Explain the behavior of the **break** statement.

3. Explain the behavior of the **continue** statement.

4. Is this **switch** statement correct?

```
switch(i) {
  case 1: System.out.println("nickel");
    break;
  case 2: System.out.println("dime");
    break;
  case 3: System.out.println("quarter");
}
```

5. Because of the **for** loop's flexibility, you can use it to construct loops that are the equivalent of both the **while** and the **do**. Show the **for** equivalent of the following loop.

```
i = 10;
while(i > 0) {
  // ...
  i—;
}
```

6. Explain what makes the **do** loop unique.

7. What is the difference between > > and > > >?

Cumulative
Skills Check

This section checks how well you have integrated the material in this chapter with that from earlier chapters.

1. Write an application that can process a sequence of command-line arguments that describe the quantities and types of coins held by a person. This sequence of arguments might be similar to the following: 5 nickels 4 quarters 2 dimes. In this case, the program would display a message indicating that the total value of these coins is $1.45.

2. Write a program that accepts one command-line argument and displays its Spanish equivalent. For example, the tokens "One," "Two," "Three," "Four," and "Five" are translated to "Uno," "Dos," "Tres," "Quatro," and "Cinco."

5

Creating Classes

chapter objectives

THIS chapter describes how to create classes. The possible members of a class include variables, constructors, and methods. Each of these is discussed. Both constructors and methods may be overloaded. Examples are provided to demonstrate both of these features. Chapter 2 described how to use static and instance forms of variables and methods. This chapter demonstrates how these may be declared. Local variables and variable scope are discussed. Finally, you will see how simple values, arrays, and objects are passed as arguments to a method.

Review

Skills Check

Before proceeding, you should be able to answer these questions and perform these exercises.

1. What are the three parts of a **for** loop?

2. What is one important difference between a **do** loop and a **while** loop?

3. Write a program that generates and displays random numbers between 1 and 10. Also maintain and display a running total of these values. Terminate the program after the total exceeds 100.

4. Write a program that accepts a set of arguments, converts them to numbers, and displays the numbers in ascending order.

5. List and describe the bitwise operators.

5.1 *T*HE GENERAL FORM OF A CLASS

So far we have been using classes, but without much explanation. Now it is time to begin their formal examination. As explained, all program activity in a Java program occurs within a class. But beyond that, the class is the means by which you define objects. Thus, an understanding of the class is critical to successful Java programming.

A class may contain three types of items: variables, methods, and constructors. Variables represent its state. Methods provide the logic that constitutes the behavior defined by a class. As you saw earlier, there can be both static and instance variables and methods. Constructors initialize the state of a new instance of a class.

A simplified form of a class declaration is shown here:

```
class clsName {
   // instance variable declarations
   type1 varName1 = value1;
   type2 varName2 = value2;
   ...
   typeN varNameN = valueN;

   // constructors
   clsName(cparams1) {
     // body of constructor
   }
   clsName(cparams2) {
     // body of constructor
   }
   ...
   clsName(cparamsN) {
     // body of constructor
   }

   // methods
   rtype1 mthName1(mparams1) {
     // body of method
   }
   rtype2 mthName2(mparams2) {
     // body of method
   }
   ...
   rtypeN mthNameN(mparamsN) {
     // body of method
   }
}
```

The keyword **class** indicates that a class named *clsName* is being declared. This name must follow the Java naming conventions for identifiers. The instance variables named *varName1* through *varNameN* are included using the normal variable declaration syntax. Each variable must be assigned a type shown as *type1* through *typeN* and may be initialized to a value shown as *value1* through *valueN*. The initialization is optional. More detail about instance variable declaration and initialization is provided later in this chapter.

Constructors always have the same name as the class. They do not have return values. Their optional parameter lists are *cparams1* through *cparamsN*.

Methods named *mthName1* through *mthNameN* can be included. The return types of the methods are *rtype1* through *rtypeN*, and their optional parameter lists are *mparams1* through *mparamsN*.

Throughout this chapter we will examine the constituents of a class and various issues surrounding them.

5.2 CREATING SIMPLE CLASSES

We will begin our study of the class with its simplest form: a class that contains only variables. In essence, such a class defines a compound data type that consists of its individual data members. Consider the following listing:

```
class Sample {
   int a;
   int b;
   int c;
}
```

This declaration defines a class called **Sample** that consists of three integer members: **a**, **b**, and **c**. It is important to understand that this declaration does not actually create any objects. It simply defines the form of an object. An object is created via the **new** operator.

To create objects of type **Sample**, use statements such as the following:

```
Sample one = new Sample();
Sample two = new Sample();
```

After these statements execute, there are two objects that have the form described by **Sample**. The variable **one** holds a reference to one of these objects. The variable **two** holds a reference to the other. Each object has its own copies of variables **a**, **b**, and **c**.

EXAMPLES

1. The following example declares a simple class named **Point3D**. Instances of this class encapsulate the three coordinates of a point in space. This class has three **double** instance variables named **x**, **y**, and **z**.

    The class named **Point3DExample** defines one **static** method named **main( )**. It begins by using the **new** operator to create an instance of the **Point3D** class. A reference to this new object is assigned to the local variable named **p**. The instance variables of that object are assigned values in the next three statements. These values are then displayed via the **println( )** method.

    ```
    class Point3D {
      double x;
      double y;
      double z;
    }

    class Point3DExample {
      public static void main(String args[]) {
        Point3D p = new Point3D();
        p.x = 1.1;
        p.y = 3.4;
        p.z = -2.8;
        System.out.println("p.x = " + p.x);
        System.out.println("p.y = " + p.y);
        System.out.println("p.z = " + p.z);
      }
    }
    ```

    Output from this application is shown here:

    ```
    p.x = 1.1
    p.y = 3.4
    p.z = -2.8
    ```

2. It is important to understand that each object has its own copy of the instance variables defined for its class. Consider the following program. Two **Point3D** objects are created. References to these objects are assigned to variables **p1** and **p2**. The variables are initialized and displayed. The key point is that the values of **x**, **y**, and **z** associated with **p1** are separate and distinct from the values associated with **p2**.

```
class Point3D {
   double x;
   double y;
   double z;
}

class TwoPoint3DExample {

   public static void main(String args[]) {

      Point3D p1 = new Point3D();
      Point3D p2 = new Point3D();

      // point p1
      p1.x = 1.1;
      p1.y = 3.4;
      p1.z = -2.8;

      // point p2
      p2.x = 100.1;
      p2.y = 103.4;
      p2.z = -202.8;

      System.out.println("p1.x = " + p1.x);
      System.out.println("p1.y = " + p1.y);
      System.out.println("p1.z = " + p1.z);
      System.out.println("p2.x = " + p2.x);
      System.out.println("p2.y = " + p2.y);
      System.out.println("p2.z = " + p2.z);

   }
}
```

The output from this example is shown here:

```
p1.x = 1.1
p1.y = 3.4
p1.z = -2.8
p2.x = 100.1
p2.y = 103.4
p2.z = -202.8
```

3. This application declares a class named **Circle**. It has instance variables for the center and radius of the circle. The **new** operator is used to create a **Circle** object. Its instance variables are initialized and displayed.

```
class Circle {
  double x;
  double y;
  double radius;
}

class CircleExample {
  public static void main(String args[]) {
    Circle c = new Circle();
    c.x = 12.1;
    c.y = 24.5;
    c.radius = 4;
    System.out.println("c.x = " + c.x);
    System.out.println("c.y = " + c.y);
    System.out.println("c.radius = " + c.radius);
  }
}
```

Output from this application is shown here:

```
c.x = 12.1
c.y = 24.5
c.radius = 4.0
```

EXERCISES

1. Write an application that declares a class named **Person**. It should have instance variables to record name, age, and salary. These should be of types **String**, **int**, and **float**. Use the **new** operator to create a **Person** object. Set and display its instance variables.

2. Write an application that declares a class named **Sphere**. It should have instance variables to record its radius and the coordinates of its center. These should be of type **double**. Use the **new** operator to create a **Sphere** object. Set and display its instance variables.

3. A class declaration is sometimes likened to a cookie cutter. Can you explain why?

5.3	# *A*DDING CONSTRUCTORS

Often an object will require some form of initialization when it is created. To accommodate this, Java allows you to define constructors for your classes. A *constructor* is a special method that creates and initializes an object of a particular class. It has the same name as its class and may accept arguments. In this respect, it is similar to any other method. However, a constructor does not have a return type. Instead, a constructor returns a reference to the object that it creates. If you do not explicitly declare a constructor for a class, the Java compiler automatically generates a default constructor that has no arguments. This is why the examples in the preceding section did not need to include an explicit constructor.

A constructor is never called directly. Instead, it is invoked via the **new** operator.

EXAMPLES

1. Let us enhance the **Point3D** class by creating a constructor that accepts three **double** arguments and uses them to initialize its instance variables. The arguments are the coordinates of the point.

```java
class Point3D {
  double x;
  double y;
  double z;

  Point3D(double ax, double ay, double az) {
    x = ax;
    y = ay;
    z = az;
  }
}

class Point3DConstructor {
  public static void main(String args[]) {
    Point3D p = new Point3D(1.1, 3.4, -2.8);
    System.out.println("p.x = " + p.x);
    System.out.println("p.y = " + p.y);
```

```
            System.out.println("p.z = " + p.z);
    }
}
```

Output from this application is shown here:

```
p.x = 1.1
p.y = 3.4
p.z = -2.8
```

2. This application illustrates how a constructor may be added to
   the **Circle** class that was developed in the preceding section. The
   constructor accepts three arguments that are the coordinates of
   the center and the radius. These arguments are used to initialize
   the instance variables.

```
class Circle {
   double x;
   double y;
   double radius;

   Circle(double ax, double ay, double aradius) {
      x = ax;
      y = ay;
      radius = aradius;
   }
}

class CircleConstructor {

   public static void main(String args[]) {

      Circle c = new Circle(17.5, 18.4, 6);
      System.out.println("c.x = " + c.x);
      System.out.println("c.y = " + c.y);
      System.out.println("c.radius = " + c.radius);
   }
}
```

Output from this application is shown here:

```
c.x = 17.5
c.y = 18.4
c.radius = 6
```

1. Add a constructor to the **Person** class developed in the Section 5-2 exercises.

2. Add a constructor to the **Sphere** class developed in the Section 5-2 exercises.

5.4 *C*ONSTRUCTOR OVERLOADING

A class may have several constructors. This feature is called *constructor overloading*. When constructors are overloaded, each is still called by the name of its class. However, it must have a different parameter list. In more precise terms, the *signature* of each constructor must differ.

The signature of a constructor is a combination of its name and the sequence of its parameter types. If two constructors in the same class have the same signature, this represents an ambiguity. The Java compiler issues an error message because it is unable to determine which form to use. Thus, overloaded constructors must differ in their signatures.

Overloaded constructors are very common in Java programming because they provide several ways to create an object of a particular class. Consider an object that has multiple instance variables. In some situations, you need to assign default values to all of these variables. Other situations require that specific values be assigned to some variables and defaults be assigned to the remaining variables. This can be done by providing multiple constructors for the class.

Overloaded constructors also allow you to create and initialize an object by using different types of data. This is convenient for a programmer because he or she does not need to convert data to one type. Instead, this work is done by the constructors.

1. In the following listing, there are three constructors for the **Point3D** class. The first form accepts one **double** argument. This value is used to initialize the **x** instance variable. The **y** and **z** instance variables are initialized to one. The second form accepts two **double** arguments. These values are used to

initialize the **x** and **y** instance variables. The **z** instance variable is initialized to one. The third form has three **double** arguments. These are used to initialize all of the instance variables. Observe that a programmer can use the constructor that is most appropriate for his or her requirements.

```
class Point3D {
  double x;
  double y;
  double z;

  Point3D(double ax) {
    x = ax;
    y = 1;
    z = 1;
  }

  Point3D(double ax, double ay) {
    x = ax;
    y = ay;
    z = 1;
  }

  Point3D(double ax, double ay, double az) {
    x = ax;
    y = ay;
    z = az;
  }
}

class Point3DOverloadConstructors {

  public static void main(String args[]) {

    Point3D p1 = new Point3D(1.1);
    System.out.println("p1.x = " + p1.x);
    System.out.println("p1.y = " + p1.y);
    System.out.println("p1.z = " + p1.z);
    Point3D p2 = new Point3D(1.1, 3.4);
    System.out.println("p2.x = " + p2.x);
    System.out.println("p2.y = " + p2.y);
    System.out.println("p2.z = " + p2.z);
    Point3D p3 = new Point3D(1.1, 3.4, -2.8);
    System.out.println("p3.x = " + p3.x);
    System.out.println("p3.y = " + p3.y);
```

```
      System.out.println("p3.z = " + p3.z);
    }
}
```

Output from this program is shown here:

```
p1.x = 1.1
p1.y = 1.0
p1.z = 1.0
p2.x = 1.1
p2.y = 3.4
p2.z = 1.0
p3.x = 1.1
p3.y = 3.4
p3.z = -2.8
```

2. The following example illustrates how overloaded constructors can initialize an object by using different types of data. The **Widget** class provides three constructors that each accept one argument of type **String**, **StringBuffer**, or **double**. Notice that any necessary data conversion is done by the constructor.

```
class Widget {
  double w;

  Widget(String s) {
    w = Double.valueOf(s).doubleValue();
  }

  Widget(StringBuffer sb) {
    String s = sb.toString();
    w = Double.valueOf(s).doubleValue();
  }

  Widget(double d) {
    w = d;
  }
}

class WidgetConstructors {

  public static void main(String args[])   {

    Widget w1 = new Widget("5.5");
    System.out.println(w1.w);

    StringBuffer sb = new StringBuffer("-17.8");
```

```
      Widget w2 = new Widget(sb);
      System.out.println(w2.w);

      Widget w3 = new Widget(2.5e-17);
      System.out.println(w3.w);
   }
}
```

Output from this program is shown here:

```
3.5
-17.8
2.5E-17
```

EXERCISES

1. Write an application that defines a **Circle** class with two constructors. The first form accepts a **double** value that represents the radius of the circle. This constructor assumes that the circle is centered at the origin. The second form accepts three **double** values. The first two arguments define the coordinates of the center, and the third argument defines the radius.

2. Write an application that defines a **Sphere** class with three constructors. The first form accepts no arguments. It assumes the sphere is centered at the origin and has a radius of one unit. The second form accepts one **double** value that represents the radius of the sphere. It assumes the sphere is centered at the origin. The third form accepts four **double** arguments. These specify the coordinates of the center and the radius.

5.5 *T*HE *this* KEYWORD

The **this** keyword refers to the object that is currently executing. You will see that it is sometimes useful for a method to reference instance variables relative to the **this** keyword, as follows:

this.*varName*

Here, *varName* is the name of an instance variable.

There is also another use of the **this** keyword. It allows one constructor to explicitly invoke another constructor in the same class. This is done with the following syntax:

this(*args*);

Here, *args* is an optional set of arguments that may be passed to a constructor. The sequence of types in this argument list determines which form of the constructor is invoked.

You can only use this syntax as the first line in a constructor. Otherwise, a compiler error is generated.

EXAMPLES

1. This example illustrates how the **this** keyword can be used to refer to the current object. Notice that the three lines inside the constructor reference the instance variables in this manner. Compare this program with the version shown in a previous section. Here, the names of the constructor parameters are identical to the names of the instance variables that are being initialized. It is not necessary to use different names for the parameters. This provides a cleaner coding style and makes it easier for a reader to understand the logic of a constructor.

```java
class Point3D {
   double x;
   double y;
   double z;

   Point3D(double x, double y, double z) {
     this.x = x;
     this.y = y;
     this.z = z;
   }
}

class ThisKeywordDemo {
  public static void main(String args[]) {
    Point3D p = new Point3D(1.1, 3.4, -2.8);
    System.out.println("p.x = " + p.x);
    System.out.println("p.y = " + p.y);
```

```
      System.out.println("p.z = " + p.z);
  }
}
```

Output from this program is shown here:

```
p.x = 1.1
p.y = 3.4
p.z = -2.8
```

2. This example illustrates how the **this** keyword can be used by one constructor to explicitly invoke another constructor in its same class. Notice that the first two constructors use the **this** keyword to explicitly invoke the third constructor.

```
class Circle {
  double x;
  double y;
  double radius;

  Circle(double x) {
    this(x, 0, 1);
  }

  Circle(double x, double y) {
    this(x, y, 1);
  }

  Circle(double x, double y, double radius) {
    this.x = x;
    this.y = y;
    this.radius = radius;
  }
}

class CircleThis {

  public static void main(String args[]) {

    Circle c = new Circle(1.1, 3.4, 10);
    System.out.println("c.x = " + c.x);
    System.out.println("c.y = " + c.y);
    System.out.println("c.radius = " + c.radius);
  }
}
```

Output from this application is shown here:

```
c.x = 1.1
c.y = 3.4
c.radius = 10
```

One constructor using **this** to invoke another constructor is common in professionally written Java programs. It prevents the unnecessary duplication of code.

1. Modify the overloaded constructors to the **Sphere** class that was developed in the Section 5.4 exercises to use the **this** keyword.

5.6 *INSTANCE VARIABLES AND METHODS*

Each object has its own copy of all instance variables defined by its class. Thus, an instance variable relates to an instance (object) of its class. We have been using instance variables since the start of this chapter. For example, **x**, **y**, and **z** are instance variables of the **Point3D** class. An instance variable may be declared by using the following form:

type varName1;

Here, the name of the variable is *varName1* and the required type is *type*.

It is also possible to declare several instance variables on the same line, as follows:

type varName1, varName2, ... varNameN;

Here, the names of the variables are *varName1*, *varName2*, and *varNameN*.

Instance variables are initialized to default values during the creation of an object. Variables of type **boolean** are set to **false**. Numbers are set to zero. Any variable that acts as an object reference is set to **null**.

However, you can assign a value to a variable at its declaration, as follows:

type varName1 = expr1;

Here, the name of the variable is *varName1* and its type is *type*. An expression *expr1* appears on the right side of the assignment.

It is also possible to combine the declaration and initialization of several variables onto one line, as follows:

type varName1, varName2 = expr2, ... varNameN;

Here, the variable named *varName2* is initialized to the value of the expression *expr2*. The other variables on that line are initialized to default values.

An instance method acts upon an object and can be declared, as follows:

```
rtype mthName(mparams) {
   // body of method
}
```

Here, *mthName* is the name of the method and *rtype* is its return type. An optional list of parameter types shown as *mparams* may be supplied.

EXAMPLES

1. This example illustrates instance variable declaration and initialization. A class **Bag** has instance variables of various types. Some of these are initialized to default values when an object of that class is created. Others are explicitly initialized.

   The class **BagTest** creates a **Bag** object. The instance variables for that object are then displayed. Observe that the variables **flag, i, l, m,** and **s1** have default values of **false, 0, 0, 0,** and **null**, respectively.

```
class Bag {
   boolean flag;
   int i, j = 2, k = 3, l, m;
   double array[] = { -3.4, 8.8e100, -9.2e-100 };
   String s1, s2 = new String("Hello");
}
```

```
class BagTest {
  public static void main(String args[]) {
    Bag bag = new Bag();
    System.out.println(bag.flag);
    System.out.println(bag.i);
    System.out.println(bag.j);
    System.out.println(bag.k);
    System.out.println(bag.l);
    System.out.println(bag.m);
    for(int i = 0; i < bag.array.length; i++)
      System.out.println(bag.array[i]);
    System.out.println(bag.s1);
    System.out.println(bag.s2);
  }
}
```

Output from this application is shown here:

```
false
0
2
3
0
0
-3.4
8.8E100
-9.2E-100
null
Hello
```

2. Let's enhance the **Point3D** class by creating an instance method named **move( )** that changes the position of the point. Its three arguments are the new coordinates. The **main( )** method of the **Point3DMethod** class creates a **Point3D** object, displays its coordinates, moves it, and displays its new coordinates.

```
class Point3D {
  double x;
  double y;
  double z;

  Point3D(double x) {
    this(x, 0, 0);
  }

  Point3D(double x, double y) {
```

```
      this(x, y, 0);
  }

  Point3D(double x, double y, double z) {
    this.x = x;
    this.y = y;
    this.z = z;
  }

  // An instance method.
  void move(double x, double y, double z) {
    this.x = x;
    this.y = y;
    this.z = z;
  }
}

class Point3DMethod {

  public static void main(String args[]) {

    Point3D p = new Point3D(1.1, 3.4, -2.8);
    System.out.println("p.x = " + p.x);
    System.out.println("p.y = " + p.y);
    System.out.println("p.z = " + p.z);
    p.move(5, 5, 5);
    System.out.println("p.x = " + p.x);
    System.out.println("p.y = " + p.y);
    System.out.println("p.z = " + p.z);
  }
}
```

Output from this application is shown here:

```
p.x = 1.1
p.y = 3.4
p.z = -2.8
p.x = 5.0
p.y = 5.0
p.z = 5.0
```

3. A key point to understand about **move( )** is that it acts on an individual object of type **Point3D**. Thus, changes made to one object do not affect any other object. For example, this version of **main( )** creates two objects. As the output shows, moving one does not affect the other.

```
class Point3D {
  double x;
  double y;
  double z;

  Point3D(double x) {
    this(x, 0, 0);
  }

  Point3D(double x, double y) {
    this(x, y, 0);
  }

  Point3D(double x, double y, double z) {
    this.x = x;
    this.y = y;
    this.z = z;
  }

  // An instance method.
  void move(double x, double y, double z) {
    this.x = x;
    this.y = y;
    this.z = z;
  }
}

class TwoPoints {

  public static void main(String args[]) {

    Point3D p = new Point3D(1.1, 3.4, -2.8);
    Point3D p2 = new Point3D(9.6, 8.8, 100.2);
    System.out.println("p.x = " + p.x);
    System.out.println("p.y = " + p.y);
    System.out.println("p.z = " + p.z);
    System.out.println("p2.x = " + p2.x);
    System.out.println("p2.y = " + p2.y);
    System.out.println("p2.z = " + p2.z);
    p.move(5, 5, 5);
    System.out.println("p.x = " + p.x);
    System.out.println("p.y = " + p.y);
    System.out.println("p.z = " + p.z);
    System.out.println("p2.x = " + p2.x);
    System.out.println("p2.y = " + p2.y);
```

```
        System.out.println("p2.z = " + p2.z);
    }
}
```

The output is shown here:

```
p.x = 1.1
p.y = 3.4
p.z = -2.8
p2.x = 9.6
p2.y = 8.8
p2.z = 100.2
p.x = 5.0
p.y = 5.0
p.z = 5.0
p2.x = 9.6
p2.y = 8.8
p2.z = 100.2
```

4. Let us add two instance methods to the **Circle** class. The first is named **move( )**. This takes two **double** parameters that are new values for the coordinates of the center. The second is named **scale( )**. This takes one **double** parameter that is used to scale the radius.

```
class Circle {
  double x;
  double y;
  double radius;

  Circle(double radius) {
    this.radius = radius;
  }

  Circle(double x, double y, double radius) {
    this.x = x;
    this.y = y;
    this.radius = radius;
  }

  void move(double x, double y) {
    this.x = x;
    this.y = y;
  }

  void scale(double a) {
    radius *= a;
```

```
      }
    }

    class CircleMethods {

      public static void main(String args[]) {

        Circle c = new Circle(4);
        c.move(2, 2);
        c.scale(0.5);
        System.out.println("c.x = " + c.x);
        System.out.println("c.y = " + c.y);
        System.out.println("c.radius = " + c.radius);
      }
    }
```

Output from this application is shown here:

```
c.x = 2.0
c.y = 2.0
c.radius = 2.0
```

---

1. Add two instance methods to the **Sphere** class that was developed in the Section 5.5 exercises. The first is named **move( )**. This takes three **double** parameters that are new values for the coordinates of the center. The second is named **scale( )**. This takes one **double** parameter that is used to scale the radius. Demonstrate these two methods.

5.7 **S***TATIC VARIABLES AND METHODS*

A static variable is shared by all objects of its class and thus relates to the class itself. A static variable may be declared by using the **static** keyword as a modifier, as follows:

static *type varName1*;

Here, the name of the variable is *varName1* and its type is *type*.

It is also possible to declare several static variables on the same line, as follows:

static *type varName1, varName2, ... varNameN*;

Here, the names of the variables are *varName1, varName2,* and *varNameN.*

Static variables are initialized to default values when the class is loaded into memory. Variables of type **boolean** are set to **false.** Numbers are set to zero. Any variable that acts as an object reference is set to **null.**

However, you can assign a value to a variable at its declaration, as follows:

static *type varName1 = expr1*;

Here, the name of the variable is *varName1* and the required type is *type.* An expression *expr1* appears on the right side of the assignment.

It is also possible to combine the declaration and initialization of several variables onto one line, as follows:

static *type varName1, varName2 = expr2, ... varNameN*;

Here, the variable named *varName2* is initialized to the value of *expr2.* The other variables on that line are initialized to default values.

You may define a block of statements to be executed when a class is loaded into memory. This is known as a *static initialization block.* Its syntax is shown here:

```
class clsName {
  ...
  static {
    // statement block
  }
}
  ...
}
```

A static method may be declared by using the **static** keyword as a modifier. A static method acts relative to a class. It does not act on specific objects of its class. To declare a method as static, precede its declaration with the **static** keyword, as follows:

```
static rtype mthName(mparams) {
  // body of method
}
```

Here, *mthName* is the name of the method and *rtype* is its return type. An optional list of parameter types shown as *mparams* may be specified. (In Chapter 6, you will learn about other modifiers that may be used in a method declaration.)

EXAMPLES

1. This example illustrates static variable declaration and initialization. A class **StaticBag** has static variables of various types. Some of these are initialized to default values when the class is loaded into memory. Others are explicitly initialized. The class **StaticBagTest** creates a **StaticBag** object. The static variables for that class are then displayed. Observe that the variables **flag**, **i**, **l**, **m**, and **s1** have default values of **false**, **0, 0, 0,** and **null**.

```
class StaticBag {
  static boolean flag;
  static int i, j = 2, k = 3, l, m;
  static double array[] = { -3.4, 8.8e100, -9.2e-100 };
  static String s1, s2 = new String("Hello");
}

class StaticBagTest {
  public static void main(String args[]) {
    System.out.println(StaticBag.flag);
    System.out.println(StaticBag.i);
    System.out.println(StaticBag.j);
    System.out.println(StaticBag.k);
    System.out.println(StaticBag.l);
    System.out.println(StaticBag.m);
    for(int i = 0; i < StaticBag.array.length; i++)
      System.out.println(StaticBag.array[i]);
    System.out.println(StaticBag.s1);
    System.out.println(StaticBag.s2);
  }
}
```

Output from this application is shown here:

```
false
0
2
3
0
0
-3.4
8.8E100
-9.2E-100
null
Hello
```

2. This application illustrates how to declare and use static and instance variables in a class. The class **Thing** declares a static variable **count** and an instance variable **name**. One copy of the former variable is shared by all instances of the class. It is incremented each time the constructor is invoked. A separate copy of the latter variable exists for each object. These contain references to strings.

The **main( )** method creates three objects and illustrates how the **count** variable is incremented each time the constructor is called.

```
class Thing {
   static int count;
   String name;

   Thing(String name) {
     this.name = name;
     ++count;
   }
}

class StaticVariable {

   public static void main(String args[]) {

     Thing t1 = new Thing("Bowling Ball");
     System.out.println(t1.name + " " + t1.count);
     Thing t2 = new Thing("Ping Pong Ball");
     System.out.println(t2.name + " " + t2.count);
     Thing t3 = new Thing("Football");
     System.out.println(t3.name + " " + t3.count);
   }
}
```

Output from this application is shown here:

```
Bowling Ball 1
Ping Pong Ball 2
Football 3
```

3. This example illustrates how to declare and use a static initialization block. The static variable named **array** references a one-dimensional array of six **int** elements. The static initialization block sets the values for these entries. They are then displayed by the **main( )** method.

```java
class X {
  static int array[];

  static {
    array = new int[6];
    for(int i = 0; i < 6; i++)
      array[i] = i;
  }
}


class StaticInitializationBlock {

  public static void main(String args[]) {

    for(int i = 0; i < 6; i++)
      System.out.println(X.array[i]);
  }
}
```

Output from this application is shown here:

```
0
1
2
3
4
5
```

As this example shows, the static initialization block executes at program start-up.

4. This example illustrates how to declare and use a static method in a class. The class **LinearEquation** has one static method that determines the root of the equation $y(x) = ax + b = 0$.

```
class LinearEquation {
  static double solve(double a, double b) {
    return -b/a;
  }
}

class StaticMethod {
  public static void main(String args[]) {
    System.out.println(LinearEquation.solve(2, 2));
  }
}
```

Output from this application is shown here:

```
-1.0
```

EXERCISE

1. Write an application that accepts one command-line argument and displays its Spanish equivalent. For example, the tokens "uno," "dos," "tres," "quatro," and "cinco" are the Spanish tokens for the numbers "one" through "five." Create a class with a static method to accomplish this task.

5.8 LOCAL VARIABLES AND VARIABLE SCOPE

So far we have been using mostly static and instance variables. However, Java has another kind: the *local* variable. Local variables are declared inside a method and exist only during its execution. Several different methods may use the same name for a local variable. However, the variables have no relationship with each other.

Default values are not assigned to local variables. In this respect, they are unlike static and instance variables. Instead, you must explicitly assign a value to each local variable. Until this happens, its contents are indeterminate.

Unlike static and instance variables, which are available from anywhere in a class, local variables are only available within their scope. The *scope* of a variable is the region of a program in which it may be directly accessed. In Java, a block defines a scope. Thus, each time you start a new block (i.e., use an opening curly brace), you begin a new scope. This scope continues until the end of the block. The most common scope for a local variable is that defined by a method. For a variable declared within a method, the scope of that variable extends from its declaration until the end of its method.

Local variables are created upon entry into their block and destroyed upon exit. Thus, local variables do not hold their values between activations. This means that local variables do not maintain their values from one method call to the next. Also, although parameters receive the arguments passed to the method, they otherwise act as local variables.

A local variable may be declared with the same name as a static or instance variable. In that case, the local variable *hides* the static or instance variable. Therefore, any reference to that name accesses the local variable.

Variables can also be defined inside statement blocks. For example, variables can be defined inside **do**, **for**, or **while** loops. These are not visible outside that block.

EXAMPLES

1. This example illustrates how to declare and use local variables. The class **MyObject** has a static variable **s** and an instance variable **i**. These are declared and initialized at the beginning of the class. The **f( )** method begins by displaying the values of these variables. Its next three lines declare three local variables. The local variables **s** and **i** hide the static and instance variables that also have those same names. This occurs for the remainder of **f( )**. The values of the local variables are then displayed.

```java
class MyObject {
  static short s = 400;  // Static variable
  int i = 200;  // Instance variable

  void f() {
    System.out.println("s = " + s);
    System.out.println("i = " + i);
    short s = 300;  // Local variable
```

```
      int i = 100;   // Local variable
      double d = 1E100;   // Local variable
      System.out.println("s = " + s);
      System.out.println("i = " + i);
      System.out.println("d = " + d);
  }
}

class LocalVariables {
  public static void main(String args[]) {
    MyObject myObject = new MyObject();
    myObject.f();
  }
}
```

Output from this application is shown here:

```
s = 400
i = 200
s = 300
i = 100
d = 1.0E100
```

2. This example illustrates the scope of a variable. A class **X** has a method **f( )** that contains a **for** loop. The loop-control variable is **j**. The variable **k** is declared and initialized inside the loop. Both of these values are displayed on each iteration of the loop. The scope of variable **j** covers the entire loop. The scope of variable **k** extends from its declaration to the end of the loop. The Java compiler issues an error message if you attempt to access **j** or **k** outside the **for** loop.

```
class X {
  void f() {
    for(int j = 0; j < 5; j++) {
      int k = 100;
      System.out.println("j = " + j + "; k = " + k);
    }
  }
}

class VariableScope {
  public static void main(String args[]) {
    X x = new X();
    x.f();
```

```
    }
}
```

Output from this application is shown here:

```
j = 0; k = 100
j = 1; k = 100
j = 2; k = 100
j = 3; k = 100
j = 4; k = 100
```

Observe that the variable **j** is the loop-control variable and it is incremented on each loop iteration. The variable **k** is local to the **for** loop and is always initialized to 100 immediately prior to the invocation of **println( )**.

EXERCISES

1. What is the output from the following program?

```java
class Class1 {
    int i = 1000;

    void f() {
        int i = 100;
        System.out.println(i);
        g();
    }

    void g() {
        System.out.println(i);
    }
}

class VariableHidingDemo1 {
    public static void main(String args[]) {
        Class1 class1 = new Class1();
        class1.f();
    }
}
```

2. What is the output from the following program?

```java
class Class2 {
    int i = 1000;
```

```
void f() {
  System.out.println(i);
  for(int i = 0; i < 5; i++) {
    System.out.print(i + " ");
  }
  System.out.println("");
  System.out.println(i);
}
}

class VariableHidingDemo2 {
  public static void main(String args[]) {
    Class2 class2 = new Class2();
    class2.f();
  }
}
```

| 5.9 | # *M*ETHOD OVERLOADING |

Like constructors, methods can also be overloaded. This occurs when two or more methods have the same name but a different signature. Recall that the *signature* of a method is a combination of its name and the sequence of its parameter types. If two methods in the same class have the same signature, this represents an ambiguity. The Java compiler issues an error message because it is unable to determine which form to use.

Method overloading is frequently used in Java programming because it allows you to use the same name for a group of methods that basically have the same purpose. The **println( )** method is a good example of this concept. It has several overloaded forms. Each of these accepts one argument of a different type. The type may be a **boolean, char, int, long, float, double, char[ ], String,** or **Object**. It is much more convenient for programmers to remember one method name rather than several different ones.

Another advantage of method overloading is that it provides an easy way to handle default parameter values. Assume that a method has one required parameter and two optional parameters. Three overloaded forms of this method can be defined. These accept one, two, or three parameters. If an optional argument is not provided, the programmer can simply ignore it. The method itself can be designed to use a default value for that parameter. Again, you can use the same name for a group of methods that basically have the same purpose.

1. The following application contains three forms of the **move( )** method. The first form translates the point along the x-axis. The second form updates the x and y coordinates. The last form modifies all coordinates.

```java
class Point3D {
  double x;
  double y;
  double z;

  Point3D(double x) {
    this(x, 0, 0);
  }

  Point3D(double x, double y) {
    this(x, y, 0);
  }

  Point3D(double x, double y, double z) {
    this.x = x;
    this.y = y;
    this.z = z;
  }

  void move(double x) {
    this.x = x;
  }

  void move(double x, double y) {
    this.x = x;
    this.y = y;
  }

  void move(double x, double y, double z) {
    this.x = x;
    this.y = y;
    this.z = z;
  }
}
```

```
class Point3DOverloadMethods {

  public static void main(String args[]) {

    Point3D p = new Point3D(1.1, 3.4, -2.8);
    p.move(5);
    System.out.println("p.x = " + p.x);
    System.out.println("p.y = " + p.y);
    System.out.println("p.z = " + p.z);
    p.move(6, 6);
    System.out.println("p.x = " + p.x);
    System.out.println("p.y = " + p.y);
    System.out.println("p.z = " + p.z);
    p.move(7, 7, 7);
    System.out.println("p.x = " + p.x);
    System.out.println("p.y = " + p.y);
    System.out.println("p.z = " + p.z);
  }
}
```

Output from this application is shown here:

```
p.x = 5.0
p.y = 3.4
p.z = -2.8
p.x = 6.0
p.y = 6.0
p.z = -2.8
p.x = 7.0
p.y = 7.0
p.z = 7.0
```

2. The following application illustrates how the **move( )** method
   of **Circle** may be overloaded. The first form translates the circle
   along the x-axis. The second form modifies both coordinates of
   the center. Note that it is not possible to write a third form of
   the constructor that accepts only one **double** argument and
   translates the circle along its y-axis. The Java compiler would
   issue an error message because two constructors would have
   the same signature.

```
class Circle {
  double x;
  double y;
  double radius;
```

```
    Circle(double radius) {
      this.radius = radius;
    }

    Circle(double x, double y, double radius) {
      this.x = x;
      this.y = y;
      this.radius = radius;
    }

    void move(double x) {
      this.x = x;
    }

    void move(double x, double y) {
      this.x = x;
      this.y = y;
    }

    void scale(double a) {
      radius *= a;
    }
}

class CircleOverloadMethod {

  public static void main(String args[]) {

    Circle c = new Circle(4);
    c.move(2);
    c.scale(0.5);
    System.out.println("c.x = " + c.x);
    System.out.println("c.y = " + c.y);
    System.out.println("c.radius = " + c.radius);
    c.move(-2, -2);
    c.scale(2);
    System.out.println("c.x = " + c.x);
    System.out.println("c.y = " + c.y);
    System.out.println("c.radius = " + c.radius);
  }
}
```

Output from this application is shown here:

```
c.x = 2.0
c.y = 0.0
c.radius = 2.0
c.x =   -2.0
```

```
c.y = -2.0
c.radius = 4.0
```

EXERCISE

1. Overload the **move( )** method of the **Sphere** class that was developed in the Section 5.6 exercise.

5.10 *A RGUMENT PASSING*

All method arguments are passed by value. This means that copies of the arguments are provided to a method. Any changes to those copies are not visible outside the method. This is easy to understand for simple types.

The situation changes when an array or object is passed as an argument. In this case the entire array or object is not actually copied. Instead, only a copy of the reference is provided. Therefore, any changes to the array or object are visible outside the method. However, the reference itself is passed by value.

As a point of interest, arguments are passed on the stack. They are pushed on the stack when a method is called and popped off the stack when it returns.

EXAMPLES

1. This example illustrates the effects of Java's call-by-value argument passing. Method **a( )** accepts three arguments: an **int**, an **int** array, and an object reference. The values of these arguments are displayed before and after the method call. The key points to note are: (1) The change to the first argument is not visible to the **main( )** method. (2) The changes to the array and object are visible to the **main( )** method.

```
class CallByValue {

  public static void main(String args[]) {

    // Initialize variables
```

```
    int i = 5;
    int j[]  = { 1, 2, 3, 4 };
    StringBuffer sb = new StringBuffer("abcde");

    // Display variables
    display(i, j, sb);

    // Call method
    a(i, j, sb);

    // Display variables again
    display(i, j, sb);
  }

  static void a(int i, int j[], StringBuffer sb) {
    i = 7;
    j[0] = 11;
    sb.append("fghij");
  }

  static void display(int i, int j[], StringBuffer sb) {
    System.out.println(i);
    for(int index = 0; index < j.length; index++)
      System.out.print(j[index] + " ");
    System.out.println("");
    System.out.println(sb);
  }
}
```

Output from this application is shown here:

```
5
1 2 3 4
abcde
5
11 2 3 4
abcdefghij
```

2. The following program illustrates that references to arrays are passed by value. An **int** array named **x** is created in the **main( )** method and passed as an argument to the **change( )** method. The **change( )** method modifies its copy of the argument. However, this modification is not visible to the caller. The **display( )** method is called immediately before and after the **change( )** method is invoked. As expected, its output is the same in both cases.

```
class ArrayArgument {

  public static void main(String args[]) {

    // Initialize variables
    int x[] = { 11, 12, 13, 14, 15 };

    // Display variables
    display(x);

    // Call method
    change(x);

    // Display variables
    display(x);
  }

  public static void change(int x[]) {
    int y[] = { 21, 22, 23, 24, 25 };
    x = y;
  }

  public static void display(int x[]) {
    for(int i = 0; i < x.length; i++)
      System.out.print(x[i] + " ");
    System.out.println("");
  }
}
```

Output from this program is shown here:

```
11 12 13 14 15
11 12 13 14 15
```

EXERCISES

1. What is the output from this program?

```
class CallByValue2 {

  public static void main(String args[]) {
```

```
      // Initialize variables
      StringBuffer sb = new StringBuffer("abcde");

      // Display variable
      System.out.println(sb);

      // Call method
      a(sb);

      // Display variable again
      System.out.println(sb);
    }

  public static void a(StringBuffer sb) {
    sb = new StringBuffer("wxyz");
    }
  }
```

2. What is the output from this program?

```
  class Arguments {

  public static void main(String args[]) {

    StringBuffer sba = new StringBuffer("aaaaa");
    StringBuffer sbb = new StringBuffer("bbbbb");

    System.out.println("sba = " + sba);
    System.out.println("sbb = " + sbb);

    f(sba, sbb);

    System.out.println("sba = " + sba);
    System.out.println("sbb = " + sbb);
    }

  public static void f(StringBuffer sb1, StringBuffer sb2) {
    sb1 = new StringBuffer("ccccc");
    sb2.append("ddddd");
    }
  }
```

Mastery
Skills Check

At this point you should be able to answer these questions and perform these exercises:

1. What is a simple form of a class declaration?

2. What is a constructor?

3. What is a type signature?

4. What is the scope of a variable?

5. What is variable hiding?

6. What is method overloading?

7. How are simple types, arrays, and objects passed as arguments to a method?

8. How does a local variable differ from an instance variable?

9. What is wrong with the following fragment?

```
for(int i = 0; i < 10; i++) {
  // ...
}
i = 20;
```

Cumulative
Skills Check

This section checks how well you have integrated the material in this chapter with that of the earlier chapters.

1. Write an application that creates ten **Rock** objects and saves these in an array. Randomly select a mass between 1 and 10 kilograms for each rock as it is created. After all rocks have been created, display their individual masses and the total mass of all rocks.

2. A trapezoid is a geometric shape that has four sides. Two of these are parallel and are called the bases of the trapezoid. The height is the distance between the bases. Define a **Trapezoid** class that encapsulates the height and the length of each base. Provide a constructor that initializes these instance variables. Provide one instance method that calculates the area of the shape. The area equals 0.5 * height * (base1 + base2). Instantiate an object of this class and invoke its method.

3. What is the output from the following program?

```java
class AnotherObject {
  int i;
  String s;
  double d;

  AnotherObject(int i, String s, double d) {
    this.i = i;
    this.s = s;
    this.d = d;
  }

  void display() {
    System.out.println("i = " + i + "; s = " + s + "; d =
      " + d);
  }
}

class Test {
  public static void main(String args[]) {
    AnotherObject ao1 = new AnotherObject(5, "Hello",
      3.4E100);
    AnotherObject ao2 = ao1;
    ao1.i = 3;
    ao1.s = "New string";
    ao1.d = 6.02E23;
    ao2.display();
  }
}
```

6

Inheritance

C HAPTER 1 introduced the concept of inheritance. This feature allows one class to specialize the state and behavior of another class. Significant code reuse can be achieved by this technique, which is one of the primary advantages of object-oriented programming.

This chapter describes how to establish inheritance relationships among classes. The **extends** keyword is used for this purpose.

A discussion of variables and inheritance is provided. Variable hiding occurs when a variable in one class has the same name as a variable in a superclass. You will see how to access hidden variables from a subclass.

Method overriding occurs when a method in one class has the same type signature as a method in a superclass. This is one of the most important features of Java because it forms the basis for run-time polymorphism.

Both methods and constructors can be overridden. The **super** keyword is used to invoke a superclass method or constructor.

The modifiers that may be used with class, variable, constructor, and method declarations are discussed. This material is introduced here because certain modifiers can be explained only after the fundamentals of class inheritance are understood.

Finally, the class **Object** is at the root of the class hierarchy. Its functionality is inherited by all classes. The class **Class** provides valuable information about a class itself. This chapter concludes by briefly looking at these two classes.

Review

Skills Check

Before proceeding, you should be able to answer these questions and perform these exercises.

1. Describe two uses of the **this** keyword.

2. How are arguments passed in Java?

3. What is the signature of a method?

4. Write an application that uses objects to model the solar system. Create a class named **Planet** to encapsulate the name of a planet and the number of its moons. Another class named **SolarSystem** holds references to the nine planets. Both of these classes provide a method named **display( )** that outputs the encapsulated information. Instantiate the **SolarSystem** class and invoke its **display( )** method.

SUBCLASSES

One of the foundations of object-oriented programming (OOP) is *inheritance.* This feature was briefly introduced in Chapter 1. It allows one class to reuse the functionality provided by its superclasses.

The **extends** clause in a class declaration establishes an inheritance relationship between two classes. It has the following syntax:

```
class clsName2 extends clsName1 {
  // class body
}
```

Here, *clsName2* is a subclass of *clsName1*. It can also be said that *clsName1* is the superclass of *clsName2*. If the **extends** clause is omitted from the declaration of a class, the Java compiler assumes that **Object** is its superclass. You will see later in this chapter that **Object** is at the root of the Java class hierarchy.

A class may directly extend only one superclass. However, it may have several subclasses. Each of those subclasses may itself have several subclasses. In this manner, an inheritance hierarchy is established.

There is an important feature of Java that relates to class hierarchies and reference variables. As you know, to declare a variable that references an object, you use the following syntax:

clsName varName;

Here, *varName* is the name of the variable and *clsName* is the name of its class. Thus, *varName* can reference any object of class *clsName*. However, it can also reference any object whose class is a subclass of *clsName*. For example, assume that class **X** is the superclass of class **X1** and class **X1** is the superclass of class **X11**. In this case, a variable of class **X** can reference any object of class **X**, **X1**, or **X11**.

To summarize: A superclass reference can refer to an object of its class or any object derived from that class. This is an important feature of Java and is used extensively when implementing run-time polymorphism.

EXAMPLE

1. This example shows how to declare a simple class inheritance hierarchy. Class **X** implicitly extends **Object**. Classes **X1** and **X2** extend **X**. Classes **X11** and **X12** extend **X1**. Classes **X21** and **X22** extend **X2**. Observe that the **main( )** method declares a variable **x** of class **X**. It then instantiates an object of each class and assigns an object reference to **x**.

```
class X {
}

class X1 extends X {
}

class X2 extends X {
}

class X11 extends X1 {
}

class X12 extends X1 {
}

class X21 extends X2 {
}

class X22 extends X2 {
}

class InheritanceHierarchy {
  public static void main(String args[]) {
    X x;
    System.out.println("Instantiating X");
    x = new X();
    System.out.println("Instantiating X1");
    x = new X1();
    System.out.println("Instantiating X11");
    x = new X11();
    System.out.println("Instantiating X12");
    x = new X12();
    System.out.println("Instantiating X2");
    x = new X2();
    System.out.println("Instantiating X21");
    x = new X21();
    System.out.println("Instantiating X22");
    x = new X22();
  }
}
```

Output from this application is shown here:

```
Instantiating X
Instantiating X1
Instantiating X11
Instantiating X12
```

```
Instantiating X2
Instantiating X21
Instantiating X22
```

EXERCISE

1. What compilation error occurs with the following
   program? Why?

```
class Parent {
}

class Child extends Parent {
}

class ObjectReferenceVariable {
  public static void main(String args[]) {
    Parent p;
    p = new Parent();
    p = new Child();
    Child c;
    c = new Child();
    c = new Parent();
  }
}
```

6.2 **INHERITANCE AND VARIABLES**

A class inherits the state and behavior defined by all of its superclasses.
State is determined by variables; behavior is determined by methods.
Therefore, an object has one copy of every instance variable defined
not only by its class but also by every superclass of its class.

A static or instance variable in a subclass may have the same
name as a superclass variable. In that case, the variable *hides* the
superclass variable. These two variables may have the same type or
different types.

It is possible to access a hidden variable by using the **super**
keyword, as follows:

super.*varName*

Here, *varName* is the name of the variable in the superclass. This syntax may be used to read or write the hidden variable.

This use of **super** can be very useful in some situations. Assume that one person has already developed and tested a class. You need to extend that class but wish to use the same name given to a variable in the superclass for a variable in your subclass because it most clearly represents a quantity or concept. The **super** keyword enables you to access the superclass variable and construct a subclass by using the same variable name.

You may not use expressions such as "super.super.varName" to access a hidden variable two levels up in the inheritance hierarchy.

EXAMPLES

1. The following application demonstrates a class inheritance hierarchy. Class **W** extends **Object** and has one instance variable of type **float**. Class **X** extends **W** and has one instance variable of type **StringBuffer**. Class **Y** extends **X** and has one instance variable of type **String**. Class **Z** extends **Y** and has one instance variable of type **Integer**.

An object of class **Z** has the instance variables that are defined in all of the superclasses. The **main( )** method instantiates class **Z** with the **new** operator, initializes the instance variables, and displays their values.

```
class W {
   float f;
}

class X extends W {
   StringBuffer sb;
}

class Y extends X {
   String s;
}

class Z extends Y {
   Integer i;
```

```
  }

class Wxyz {
  public static void main(String args[]) {
    Z z = new Z();
    z.f = 4.567f;
    z.sb = new StringBuffer("abcde");
    z.s = "Teach Yourself Java";
    z.i = new Integer(41);
    System.out.println("z.f = " + z.f);
    System.out.println("z.sb = " + z.sb);
    System.out.println("z.s = " + z.s);
    System.out.println("z.i = " + z.i);
  }
}
```

Output from this application is shown here:

```
z.f = 4.567
z.sb = abcde
x.s = Teach Yourself Java
z.i = 41
```

2. This example illustrates variable hiding. Here, class **E** declares an instance variable named **x** of type **int**. Class **F** is a subclass of **E** and also declares an instance variable named **x** of type **String**.

   The **main( )** method first creates an object of class **F**. A reference to this object is assigned to a local variable named **f** of type **F**. The expression **f.x** is, therefore, of type **String**.

   Next, an object of class **E** is created. A reference to this object is assigned to a local variable named **e** of type **E**. The expression **e.x** is, therefore, of type **int**.

*The declaration of **x** in class **F** hides the declaration of **x** in class **E**.*

```
class E {
  int x;
}

class F extends E {
  String x;
}
```

```
class Ef {
  public static void main(String args[]) {
    F f = new F();
    f.x = "This is a string";
    System.out.println("f.x = " + f.x);
    E e = new E();
    e.x = 45;
    System.out.println("e.x = " + e.x);
  }
}
```

Output from this application is shown here:

```
f.x = This is a string
e.x = 45
```

3. Variable hiding also applies for static variables. The following listing shows how classes **P** and **Q** each define a variable named **x** of type **int** and **String**, respectively.

   Key point: The declaration of **x** in class **Q** hides the declaration of **x** in class **P**.

```
class P {
  static int x;
}

class Q extends P {
  static String x;
}

class Pq {
  public static void main(String args[]) {
    P p = new P();
    p.x = 55;
    System.out.println("p.x = " + p.x);
    Q q = new Q();
    q.x = "This is a string";
    System.out.println("q.x = " + q.x);
  }
}
```

Output from this application is shown here:

```
p.x = 55
q.x = "This is a string";
```

4. This example illustrates how to access hidden variables via the **super** keyword. Class **M100** declares and initializes an **int**

variable **i**. Class **M200** extends **M100** and also declares and initializes an **int** variable **i**. The **display( )** method in **M200** displays both the **i** variable declared in **M200** and the **i** variable declared in **M100**. Observe how the **super** keyword is used to obtain the value of the hidden variable.

```
class M100 {
  int i = 100;
}

class M200 extends M100 {
  int i = 200;
  void display() {
    System.out.println("i = " + i);
    System.out.println("super.i = " + super.i);
  }
}

class SuperKeyword {
  public static void main(String args[]) {
    M200 m200 = new M200();
    m200.display();
  }
}
```

Output from this application is shown here:

```
i = 200
super.i = 100
```

EXERCISES

1. Write an application that demonstrates a class inheritance hierarchy. Class **M** extends **Object** and has two instance variables of type **float** and **String**. Class **N** extends **M** and has one instance variable of type **Double**. Instantiate class **N**. Initialize and display its variables.

2. Write an application that illustrates variable hiding. Class **S** declares an instance variable named **x** of type **Integer**. Class **T** extends **S** and declares an instance variable named **x** of type **StringBuffer**. Instantiate both of these classes. Initialize and display the variable named **x** in each of these objects.

3. Write an application that illustrates how to access a hidden variable. Class **G** declares a static variable **x**. Class **H** extends **G** and declares an instance variable **x**. A **display( )** method in **H** displays both of these variables.

6.3   *M*ETHOD OVERRIDING

Method overriding occurs when a class declares a method that has the same type signature as a method declared by one of its superclasses. Recall that a type signature is a combination of a method name and the sequence of its parameter types. When a method in a subclass overrides a method in a superclass, the method in the superclass is hidden relative to the subclass object.

Method overriding is a very important capability because it forms the basis for run-time polymorphism. Recall from Chapter 1 that polymorphism means "one interface, multiple implementations." The signature of the method defines the interface, and each overridden version provides a unique implementation.

As explained, a superclass reference can be used to refer to a subclass object. The dynamic method dispatch mechanism in Java selects the appropriate version of an overridden method to execute based on the class of the executing object, not the type of a variable that references that object. Thus, the actual version of an overridden method that is executed is determined at run-time, not compile time.

Remember that dynamic method dispatch resolves calls to overridden methods at run-time.

The Java compiler issues an error message if a method overrides another method but has a different return type.

EXAMPLES

---

1. This example illustrates method overriding. Here, three classes form an inheritance hierarchy. Each class declares a method named **hello( )** with the same type signature. Therefore, the **hello( )** method in a subclass overrides that of its superclass.

```
class A1 {
  void hello() {
    System.out.println("Hello from A1");
  }
}

class B1 extends A1 {
  void hello() {
    System.out.println("Hello from B1");
  }
}

class C1 extends B1 {
  void hello() {
    System.out.println("Hello from C1");
  }
}

class MethodOverriding1 {
  public static void main(String args[]) {
    C1 obj = new C1();
    obj.hello();
  }
}
```

Output from this application is shown here:

```
Hello from C1
```

This is expected because the object referenced by variable **obj** is of class **C1**.

2. Let us consider a similar version of the previous example. The important difference is in the first line of the **main( )** method. Variable **obj** is now of type **A2**. However, the object itself is of type **C2**. What will the program output?

```
class A2 {
  void hello() {
    System.out.println("Hello from A2");
  }
}

class B2 extends A2 {
  void hello() {
    System.out.println("Hello from B2");
  }
}
```

```
  }

class C2 extends B2 {
  void hello() {
    System.out.println("Hello from C2");
  }
}

class MethodOverriding2 {
  public static void main(String args[]) {
    A2 obj = new C2();
    obj.hello();
  }
}
```

Output from this application is shown here:

```
Hello from C2
```

It is the type of the object itself, not the type of the variable **obj,** that determines which **hello( )** method is executed. An object of class **C2** can be referenced by a variable of class **A2** because **C2** is a subclass of **A2**. (Remember that a superclass reference can refer to objects of its class or any of its subclasses.)

This feature of Java that allows it to dynamically select the correct version of an overridden method to execute is called *dynamic method dispatch*. It is a very important capability because it allows Java to provide run-time polymorphism. You will see other examples of this feature later in this chapter.

EXERCISES

1. What is the output from the following program?

```
class A3 {
  void hello() {
    System.out.println("Hello from A3");
  }
  void hello(int i) {
    System.out.println("Hello from A3 " + i);
  }
}

class B3 extends A3 {
```

```
    void hello() {
      System.out.println("Hello from B3");
    }
  }

  class C3 extends B3 {
    void hello(String s) {
      System.out.println("Hello from C3 " + s);
    }
  }

  class MethodOverriding3 {
    public static void main(String args[]) {
      A3 obj = new C3();
      obj.hello();
    }
  }
```

2. Write a program that illustrates method overriding. Class **Bond** is extended by **ConvertibleBond**. Each of these classes defines a **display( )** method that outputs the string "Bond" or "ConvertibleBond", respectively. Declare an array to hold six **Bond** objects. Initialize the elements of the array with a mix of **Bond** and **ConvertibleBond** objects. Execute a program loop to invoke the **display( )** method of each object.

6.4 *I*NHERITANCE AND METHODS

The previous section described how method overriding operates in an inheritance hierarchy. The dynamic dispatch mechanism in Java automatically selects the correct version of a method for execution based upon the type of object being referred to at the time the method is executed. Thus, an overriding method masks the one defined by the superclass. But this raises an interesting question: What if you want to access the functionality present in the superclass version of an overridden method? Fortunately, Java provides a mechanism to allow this.

To access a superclass method use the **super** keyword, as follows:

super.mthName(args)

Here, *mthName* is the name of the superclass method and *args* is its optional argument list.

The ability to invoke the superclass version of an overridden method is very important. It is often the case that a subclass extends the functionality of a superclass by overriding a method. To gain access to the functionality supplied by the superclass, the subclass needs to call the overridden method in its superclass either before or after completing its own processing. This is how significant code reuse is achieved.

EXAMPLE

1. This example declares three classes that are related in an inheritance hierarchy. Each provides a method named **hello( )** with the same type signature. The **hello( )** method of **K1** invokes the **hello( )** method of its superclass. The **hello( )** method of **J1** also invokes the **hello( )** method of its superclass. Each overridden version of this method displays a string for the user. Observe that the string is also passed as an argument to the superclass method.

```java
class I1 {
  void hello(String s) {
    System.out.println("I1: " + s);
  }
}

class J1 extends I1 {
  void hello(String s) {
    super.hello(s);
    System.out.println("J1: " + s);
  }
}

class K1 extends J1 {
  void hello(String s) {
    super.hello(s);
    System.out.println("K1: " + s);
  }
}
```

```
class SuperForMethods1 {

  public static void main(String args[]) {

    System.out.println("Instantiating I1");
    I1 obj = new I1();
    obj.hello("Good morning");

    System.out.println("Instantiating J1");
    obj = new J1();
    obj.hello("Good afternoon");

    System.out.println("Instantiating K1");
    obj = new K1();
    obj.hello("Good evening");
  }
}
```

Output from this application is shown here:

```
Instantiating I1
I1: Good morning
Instantiating J1
I1: Good afternoon
J1: Good afternoon
Instantiating K1
I1: Good evening
J1: Good evening
K1: Good evening
```

Study this output carefully, and make certain you can explain it.

EXERCISE

1. Write an application that illustrates how a method can invoke a
   superclass method. Class **I2** is extended by **J2**. Class **J2** is
   extended by **K2**. Each of these classes defines a
   getDescription( ) method that returns a string. That string
   includes a description of the class plus descriptions of each
   superclass. Instantiate each of these classes and invoke the
   getDescription( ) method.

| 6.5 | *INHERITANCE AND CONSTRUCTORS* |

The state and behavior of a class are defined not only by that class but also by each of its superclasses. Therefore, in order to correctly initialize an object, it is not sufficient to execute a constructor only for one class. A constructor for each superclass must also be executed.

Furthermore, a superclass constructor must execute before a subclass constructor. This is necessary so the state and behavior defined by the superclass may be correctly and completely initialized before a subclass constructor executes. In fact, this may be a prerequisite in order for the subclass constructor to execute properly.

The **super** keyword is used to explicitly invoke a superclass constructor. It has the following form:

```
super(args);
```

Here, *args* is the optional list of arguments for the superclass constructor. The sequence of types in *args* determines which form of the superclass constructor is selected by the Java compiler. If you use this form, it must appear as the first statement of the constructor. This is how the Java compiler ensures that the superclass constructor executes before the subclass constructor.

Recall that Chapter 5 described how a constructor can invoke another constructor in the same class. This is done by using the form shown below:

```
this(args);
```

If you use this form, it must appear as the first statement of the constructor. Therefore, a given constructor cannot use both **super( )** and **this( )**.

However, if you write a constructor that does not use either **super( )** or **this( )** to explicitly invoke another constructor, the Java compiler automatically calls **super( )** to invoke the default superclass constructor. Recall that a default constructor has no arguments.

In other words, the Java compiler assumes that the first line of every constructor is an implicit call to the default superclass constructor unless you explicitly use **super( )** or **this( )** to request different behavior.

EXAMPLES

1. Consider the following application. Class **S1** declares an instance variable named **s1** of type **int**. Class **T1** extends **S1** and declares an instance variable named **t1** of type **int**. Class **U1** extends **T1** and declares an instance variable named **u1** of type **int**. These variables are initialized by the constructor for that class. Each constructor also displays a string to indicate that it has started execution.

   The **main( )** method begins by instantiating class **U1**. The default constructor for **U1** is used with the **new** operator. The instance variables for the object are then displayed.

```
class S1 {
  int s1;
  S1() {
    System.out.println("S1 Constructor");
    s1 = 1;
  }
}

class T1 extends S1 {
  int t1;
  T1() {
    System.out.println("T1 Constructor");
    t1 = 2;
  }
}

class U1 extends T1 {
  int u1;
  U1() {
    System.out.println("U1 Constructor");
    u1 = 3;
  }
}

class InheritanceAndConstructors1 {
  public static void main(String args[]) {
    U1 u1 = new U1();
    System.out.println("u1.s1 = " + u1.s1);
    System.out.println("u1.t1 = " + u1.t1);
    System.out.println("u1.u1 = " + u1.u1);
  }
}
```

Output from this application is shown here:

```
S1 Constructor
T1 Constructor
U1 Constructor
u.s1 = 1
u.t1 = 2
u.u1 = 3
```

Observe that the superclass constructor executes before the subclass constructor.

2. The following application illustrates the explicit use of **super( )** in an inheritance hierarchy. Class **U2** extends **T2**. The **U2** constructor accepts three arguments. Its first statement calls **super( )** to invoke the **T2** constructor. Class **T2** extends **S2**. The **T2** constructor accepts two arguments. The first statement in that constructor calls **super( )** to invoke the **S2** constructor.

```
class S2 {
  int s2;
  S2(int s2) {
    this.s2 = s2;
  }
}

class T2 extends S2 {
  int t2;
  T2(int s2, int t2) {
    super(s2);
    this.t2 = t2;
  }
}

class U2 extends T2 {
  int u2;
  U2(int s2, int t2, int u2) {
    super(s2, t2);
    this.u2 = u2;
  }
}

class InheritanceAndConstructors2 {
  public static void main(String args[]) {
    U2 u2 = new U2(1, 2, 3);
    System.out.println("u2.s2 = " + u2.s2);
    System.out.println("u2.t2 = " + u2.t2);
```

```
        System.out.println("u2.u2 = " + u2.u2);
    }
}
```

The output from this program is shown here:

```
u2.s2 = 1
u2.t2 = 2
u2.u2 = 3
```

Note that all of the constructors have been executed.

EXERCISES

1. Modify the previous example by inserting **println( )** statements to monitor the execution order of the constructors.

2. Why must **super( )** or **this( )** be the first statement in a constructor?

6.6 CLASS MODIFIERS

There are three possible modifiers that may precede the **class** keyword. These are summarized in the following table:

Keyword	Meaning
abstract	Cannot be instantiated
final	Cannot be extended
public	Can be accessed by any other class. If this keyword is missing, access to the class is limited to the current package.

Let's discuss each of these modifiers in more detail.

Abstract classes are very important in object-oriented programming. They are typically used to declare functionality that is implemented by one or more subclasses. The advantage of such a design is that the **abstract** class specifies *what* functionality is provided but not *how* that functionality is provided. Therefore, the subclasses may use different implementations to achieve the same objective.

For example, assume that there is an **abstract** class **Shape**. It declares a **display( )** method that displays the shape on a monitor. The implementation of this method cannot be provided by **Shape**. Instead, it must be provided by the individual subclasses of **Shape**. For example, subclasses such as **Circle**, **Rectangle**, and **Triangle** each contain a **display( )** method that does the required work.

Abstract classes cannot be instantiated. The compiler issues an error message if this is attempted. The methods in an **abstract** class often have empty bodies. Some of the methods themselves may be declared as **abstract**. These consist of a declaration without any body. (Section 6-9 discusses **abstract** methods.)

You may encounter the term *concrete class* in the literature. This is a class that can be instantiated. Typically, there are multiple subclasses of an **abstract** class. These are often concrete classes that implement the functionality declared by the **abstract** class.

A **final** class cannot be extended. Classes are sometimes declared in this manner so the methods implemented by that class cannot be overridden. For example, the **Math** class is **final**. If a class is **final**, all of its methods are also **final**. (Section 6-9 discusses **final** methods.) The compiler issues an error message if you attempt to extend a **final** class. The **abstract** and **final** modifiers are mutually exclusive.

A **public** class can be accessed by any other class in an application. If this modifier is missing, the class may only be accessed by code in the same package. Chapter 7 discusses packages in more detail. For the moment, simply think of a package as a set of classes. Each class is a member of one package. All of the classes developed so far in this book have been members of a default package.

If none of these modifiers is specified, the class is assumed to be neither **abstract** nor **final**. It may be accessed only by code in the same package.

EXAMPLES

1. This example demonstrates an **abstract** class. The class **Shape** is declared **abstract** in this situation because it should never be instantiated. (Notice that its **display( )** method is empty.) Instead, only its subclasses should be instantiated. There are three subclasses of **Shape**. Each provides a different implementation of the **display( )** method. This is the essence of polymorphism!

The **main( )** method declares a variable named **s** of class **Shape** and initializes this to reference a new **Circle** object. The **display( )** method of this object is then called. A **Rectangle** object is then instantiated. Variable **s** is assigned a reference to this object. Its **display( )** method is invoked. Finally, a new **Triangle** object is created. Variable **s** is assigned a reference to this object. Its **display( )** method is invoked.

In all cases, the dynamic method dispatch mechanism of Java invokes the correct implementation of the **display( )** method.

```
abstract class Shape {
  void display() {
  }
}

class Circle extends Shape {
  void display() {
    System.out.println("Circle");
  }
}

class Rectangle extends Shape {
  void display() {
    System.out.println("Rectangle");
  }
}

class Triangle extends Shape {
  void display() {
    System.out.println("Triangle");
  }
}

class AbstractClassDemo {
  public static void main(String args[]) {
    Shape s = new Circle();
    s.display();
    s = new Rectangle();
    s.display();
    s = new Triangle();
    s.display();
  }
}
```

Output from this application is shown next:

```
Circle
Rectangle
Triangle
```

2. The following application illustrates how the **final** keyword can be used in a class modifier. This program does not compile because the declaration of class **V2** attempts to extend **V1**, which is declared as a **final** class.

```
final class V1 {
}

class V2 extends V1 {
}

class FinalClass {
  public static void main(String args[]) {
    V1 obj = new V1();
  }
}
```

EXERCISES

1. Can a class declaration include both the **abstract** and **final** modifiers?

2. What is the difference between abstract and concrete classes?

3. Enhance the first example in this section by adding **Trapezoid** and **Rhombus** as two more subclasses of **Shape**. Demonstrate how they can be instantiated and displayed.

6.7 **V**ARIABLE MODIFIERS

There are seven possible modifiers that may precede the declaration of a variable. These are summarized in the following table:

Keyword	Meaning
final	Is a constant
private	Can be accessed only by code in the same class
protected	Can be accessed only by code in a subclass or the same package
public	Can be accessed by any other class
static	Is not an instance variable
transient	Is not part of the persistent state of this class
volatile	Can change unexpectedly

Some of these modifiers are mutually exclusive. For example, only one of the **public**, **protected**, and **private** keywords may be used.

A discussion of the **transient** and **volatile** modifiers is beyond the scope of this chapter. The next example illustrates a **final** variable. The other modifiers are demonstrated in Chapter 7.

If none of these modifiers are specified, the variable is assumed to be a non-**final**, non-**transient**, non-**volatile** instance variable. It may be accessed only by code in the same package.

EXAMPLE

1. One of the common uses of **final** is to create named constants. For example, the following application illustrates this use of **final.** It creates a variable **x** whose value cannot be changed.

```
class L {
  static final int x = 5;
}

class FinalVariable {
  public static void main(String args[]) {
    System.out.println(L.x);
  }
}
```

Output from this application is shown here:

5

1. Write an application that shows how to combine the **static** and **final** keywords in a variable modifier to define a constant.

2. Attempt to set the value of **x** in the sample program shown in the example. What happens?

6.8   *C*ONSTRUCTOR MODIFIERS

There are three possible modifiers that may precede the declaration of a constructor. These are summarized in the following table:

Keyword	Meaning
private	Can be invoked only by code in the same class
protected	Can be invoked only by code in a subclass or the same package
public	Can be invoked by any other class

These modifiers are mutually exclusive. If none is specified, the default is that only code in the same package may access that constructor.

1. This example defines a class with two constructors. The default constructor should not be invoked by other classes because there are no reasonable defaults for the **name** and **age** variables. Therefore, it is declared as **private** to prevent access by another class. The other constructor requires that two arguments be supplied to initialize the instance variables.

```
class Person {
  String name;
  int age;

  public Person(String name, int age) {
    this.name = name;
    this.age = age;
  }
```

```
    private Person() {
    }
}

class PrivateConstructor {

    public static void main(String args[]) {

        // Public constructor may be invoked
        Person p1 = new Person("John", 30);
        System.out.println(p1.name);
        System.out.println(p1.age);

        // Private constructor may not be invoked
        // Person p2 = new Person();
    }
}
```

Output from this application is shown here:

```
John
30
```

EXERCISE

1. Modify the preceding example and attempt to use the default constructor of the **Person** class. Observe the compiler error that occurs.

6.9

M ETHOD MODIFIERS

There are eight possible modifiers that may precede the declaration of a method. These are summarized in the following table:

Keyword	Meaning
abstract	Is not implemented by this class
final	May not be overridden
native	The method is implemented in the machine code used by the host CPU, not using Java bytecodes

Keyword	Meaning
private	Can be invoked only by code in the same class
protected	Can be invoked only by code in a subclass or the same package
public	Can be invoked by any other class
static	Is not an instance variable
synchronized	Acquires a lock when it begins execution

If a class contains an **abstract** method, that class itself must also be declared **abstract**. Otherwise, the Java compiler issues an error message.

The **public**, **protected**, and **private** modifiers are mutually exclusive. These are discussed in Chapter 7.

The **synchronized** modifier is described in Chapter 8. It is very important in multithreaded programming.

The **native** modifier is beyond the scope of this book.

If none of these modifiers are specified, the method is assumed to be a non-**abstract**, non-**final**, non-**native**, non-**synchronized** method. It may be accessed only by code in the same package.

EXAMPLES

1. The class **JetPlane** declares one **abstract** method named **numEngines( )**. Therefore, the class itself must also be declared **abstract**. There are two concrete subclasses named **DC8** and **DC10**. Each of these provides a different implementation of the **numEngines( )** method. The **main( )** method instantiates each of these classes and invokes its **numEngines( )** method.

This is an excellent example of run-time polymorphism. Each subclass provides a different form of the method.

```
abstract class JetPlane {
   abstract int numEngines();
}

class DC8 extends JetPlane {
   int numEngines() {
```

```
        return 4;
    }
}

class DC10 extends JetPlane  {
    int numEngines() {
        return 3;
    }
}

class JetPlanes {
    public static void main(String args[]) {
        System.out.println(new DC8().numEngines());
        System.out.println(new DC10().numEngines());
    }
}
```

Output from this application is shown here:

```
4
3
```

2. It is sometimes useful to limit the number of instances of a class to one. The following example shows how this can be accomplished. The default constructor is declared as **private**. This ensures that it cannot be invoked from outside the class. The static **getInstance( )** method must be used to obtain a **Singleton** object. When this method is first called, the static **singleton** variable is **null**. In that case, the constructor is invoked to create an instance of this class and initialize the variable. Subsequent invocations of **getInstance( )** return a reference to the one object that was created. The constructor is not called again.

   The **main( )** method of **SingletonDemo** calls **getInstance( )** twice. The return values from these invocations are compared. These refer to the same object.

```
class Singleton {
    static Singleton singleton;

    private Singleton() {
    }

    public static Singleton getInstance() {
        if(singleton == null)
```

```
            singleton = new Singleton();
          return singleton;
        }
    }

    class SingletonDemo {

      public static void main(String args[]) {
        Singleton s1 = Singleton.getInstance();
        Singleton s2 = Singleton.getInstance();
        if(s1 == s2)
          System.out.println("Equal");
        else
          System.out.println("Not equal");
      }
    }
```

Output from this application is shown here:

```
Equal
```

This indicates that **s1** and **s2** refer to the same object.

EXERCISES

1. Explain the meanings of all modifiers for the **main( )** method in an application.

2. Declare an abstract class **Vehicle** with an abstract method named **numWheels( )**. Provide subclasses **Car** and **Truck** that each implement this method. Create instances of these subclasses and demonstrate the use of this method.

6.10 *T*HE OBJECT AND CLASS CLASSES

The **Object** class is at the top of the Java class hierarchy, and all objects-even those that you create-descend from **Object**. Therefore, the state and behavior defined by this class are inherited by all other classes. At this point, we will examine only a subset of its methods.

The **equals( )** method tests if two variables refer to the same object. Its signature is shown next:

```
boolean equals(Object obj)
```

This method returns **true** if the current object and *obj* are the same object. Otherwise, it returns **false**.

The **getClass( )** method returns a **Class** object for the current object. Its signature is shown here:

```
Class getClass()
```

The **toString( )** method returns a string equivalent of the current object. Its signature is shown here:

```
String toString()
```

It is common for classes to override this method so useful information may be provided via the **print( )** and **println( )** methods you have seen since Chapter 1.

The **Class** class encapsulates information about a class or interface in an executing program. (Chapter 7 discusses interfaces.) These **Class** objects are automatically created by the Java Virtual Machine (JVM) when the class is first loaded into memory. In addition, a **Class** object exists for each simple type and **void**. A separate **Class** object also exists for each array of a given type with specific dimensions.

In this book, only three of the methods defined by **Class** are used. The **getName( )** method returns the name of the type. Its signature is shown here:

```
String getName()
```

The **getSuperclass( )** method returns the **Class** object for the superclass of this class. Its signature is shown here:

```
Class getSuperclass()
```

The **forName( )** method returns the **Class** object for a named class. Its signature is shown here:

```
static Class forName (String clsName) throws ClassNotFoundException
```

Here, cIsName is the name of the class.

1. This example illustrates how some of the methods of the **Object** and **Class** classes can be used. An **Integer** object is created, and the **getClass( )** method inherited from **Object** is called to obtain the **Class** object for that object. Because **Class** overrides the **toString( )** method, useful information about that object can be presented via the **println( )** method.

```
class ClassDemo {

  public static void main(String args[]) {

    Integer obj = new Integer(8);
    Class cls = obj.getClass();
    System.out.println(cls);
  }
}
```

Output from this application is shown here:

```
class java.lang.Integer
```

1. Many classes override the **toString( )** method, so useful information may be presented via the **print( )** or **println( )** method. Create a class that has static and instance variables. Provide a **toString( )** method that returns useful information about an object of that type.

2. Write a program that creates an **Integer** object. Then obtain the associated **Class** object. Invoke the **getSuperclass( )** method to get the **Class** object for the superclass of **Integer**. Invoke the **getName( )** method to obtain the name of the superclass. Display that name.

Mastery
Skills Check

Before continuing, you should be able to answer these questions and complete these exercises:

1. What is run-time polymorphism?

2. What is dynamic method dispatch, and how does it form the basis for run-time polymorphism?

3. The abstract **Fruit** class has four subclasses named **Apple**, **Banana**, **Orange**, and **Strawberry**. Write an application that demonstrates how to establish this class hierarchy. Declare one instance variable of type **String** that indicates the color of a fruit. Create and display instances of these objects. Override the **toString( )** method of **Object** to return a string with the name of the fruit and its color.

4. The abstract **Airplane** class has three subclasses named **B747**, **B757**, and **B767**. Each airplane type can transport a different number of passengers. Each airplane object has a unique serial number. Write an application that declares this class hierarchy. Instantiate several types of airplanes and display them. Override the **toString( )** method of **Object** to return a string with the type, serial number, and capacity.

Cumulative
Skills Check

This section checks how well you have integrated material in this chapter with that from the preceding chapters.

1. Contrast method overloading and method overriding.

2. What are three uses for the keyword **super**?

3. The abstract **Monster** class has three concrete subclasses named **Vampire**, **Werewolf**, and **Zombie**. Create six different monsters

of various types, and store them in a one-dimension array. Create a loop that displays the type of each monster.

4. The abstract **Widget** class has four concrete subclasses named **WidgetA**, **WidgetB**, **WidgetC**, and **WidgetD**. Each of these four classes has a different mass in kilograms. The mass of any **WidgetA** object is 4 kilograms. The masses for the **WidgetB**, **WidgetC**, and **WidgetD** classes are 1, 5, and 17 kilograms, respectively. Each **Widget** object has a string that identifies its color. Create six different widgets, and store them in a one-dimension array. Display the entries in the array and their total mass.

7

Interfaces and Packages

N *interface* is a group of constants and method declarations. You may view it as an abstract description of functionality. This chapter begins by describing the syntax for creating interfaces. An interface may be implemented by different classes. The developers of those classes can do this in different ways. In addition, a class may implement several interfaces.

An interface name can be used as the type of a variable. The variable can then reference any object that implements that interface. It is possible for an interface to extend another interface. In fact, an interface may extend several other interfaces.

The **instanceof** operator tests if an object is of a particular class or implements a particular interface. It is very useful in some situations.

A *package* is a group of classes and interfaces. It provides a mechanism for organizing the name space. In other words, this ensures that the names selected for use in one package do not conflict with those in another package.

The CLASSPATH environment variable determines where the JDK tools search for packages. Therefore, it is important that you understand how to use this variable.

The **import** statement allows you to use abbreviated names for classes and interfaces that are located in packages. Several examples illustrate its use.

Finally, you will see that the developer of a package can restrict access to its contents.

Review
Skills Check

Before proceeding, you should be able to answer these questions and perform these exercises.

1. What is variable hiding?

2. Name the optional class modifiers.

3. Name the optional variable modifiers.

4. Name the optional constructor modifiers.

5. Name the optional method modifiers.

6. Describe the sequence in which constructors are invoked.

7. Create a class named **Water** that encapsulates some frequently used constants about that molecule such as its boiling and freezing points and density. Display this data.

7.1 *I*NTERFACES

An *interface* is a group of constants and method declarations that define the form of a class. However, it provides no implementation for its methods. In essence, an interface allows you to specify what a class must do, but not how it will get done. Other classes that you create can implement an interface. Thus, interfaces are another means by which polymorphism is supported by Java.

Here is a simplified form of an interface declaration:

```
intfModifier interface intfName {
  varModifier1 type1 varName1 = value1;
  varModifier2 type2 varName2 = value2;
  varModifier3 type3 varName3 = value3;

  ...
  varModifierN typeN varNameN = valueN;
  mthModifier1 rtype1 mthName1(params1);
  mthModifier2 rtype2 mthName2(params2);

  ...
  mthModifierN rtypeN mthNameN(paramsN);
}
```

Here, *intfModifier* is an optional modifier that establishes the access permissions for this interface. If this modifier equals **public**, code in any other package may use the interface. If the modifier is omitted, access to this interface is limited to code in the same package.

The keyword **interface** indicates that an interface named *intfName* is being declared. This name must follow the Java naming conventions for identifiers.

Variables named *varName1* through *varNameN* can be included as shown. These are of types *type1* through *typeN*, respectively. Each must be assigned a constant value in the interface definition. Each variable may have an optional modifier shown as *varModifier1* through *varModifierN*. However, every interface variable is implicitly **public**, **static**, and **final**. Therefore, variable modifiers are generally not used. Recall from the previous chapter that any variable whose modifiers are **public**, **static**, and **final** is a constant.

You may combine the declaration of several variables onto one line as shown here:

varModifier type varName1 = value1, ... varNameN = valueN;

Each of the tokens in this line has the same meaning as previously described.

Methods named *mthName1* through *mthNameN* can be included as shown. Each of these may have an optional modifier shown above as *mthModifier1* through *mthModifierN*. However, every interface method is implicitly **public** and **abstract**. Therefore method modifiers are generally not used. The return types of the methods are *rtype1* through *rtypeN* and their optional parameter lists are *params1* through *paramsN*.

A class can implement one or more interfaces. To do so, it first includes an **implements** clause in its class definition that specifies the interface(s) being implemented. Second, it provides implementations for all of the methods specified by the interface(s). Here is the syntax for the **implements** clause:

clsModifiers class *clsName* extends *superName* implements *intfList* {
  // provide implementations for interfaces

  ...

}

Here, *clsModifiers* are the class modifiers described in the previous chapter. The name of the class is *clsName*. Of course, the **extends** clause is optional. If used, the name of the superclass is *superName*. The keyword **implements** indicates that this class implements one or more interfaces. The names of these interfaces are included in *intfList* and are separated by commas.

If a class implements an interface, it must implement all of the methods declared by that interface. Otherwise, the compiler issues an error message.

EXAMPLES

1. The following application illustrates how to declare interfaces and implement these in various classes. Interface **Shape2D** declares a **getArea( )** method that calculates and returns the area of an enclosed 2D shape. Interface **Shape3D** declares a **getVolume( )** method that calculates and returns the volume of an enclosed 3D shape. **Point3D** contains the coordinates of a point. The abstract class **Shape** declares an abstract **display( )** method and is extended by the **Circle** and **Sphere** classes. The former implements the **Shape2D** interface, and the latter implements the **Shape3D** interface. The **Shapes** class instantiates each of these classes and exercises its methods.

```
interface Shape2D {
  double getArea();
}

interface Shape3D {
  double getVolume();
}

class Point3D {
  double x, y, z;

  Point3D(double x, double y, double z) {
    this.x = x;
    this.y = y;
    this.z = z;
  }
}

abstract class Shape {
  abstract void display();
}

class Circle extends Shape
implements Shape2D {
```

```java
    Point3D center, p; // p is any point on the circumference

    Circle(Point3D center, Point3D p) {
      this.center = center;
      this.p = p;
    }

    public void display() {
      System.out.println("Circle");
    }

    public double getArea() {
      double dx = center.x - p.x;
      double dy = center.y - p.y;
      double d = dx * dx + dy * dy;
      double radius = Math.sqrt(d);
      return Math.PI * radius * radius;
    }
}

class Sphere extends Shape
implements Shape3D {
  Point3D center;
  double radius;

  Sphere(Point3D center, double radius) {
    this.center = center;
    this.radius = radius;
  }

  public void display() {
    System.out.println("Sphere");
  }

  public double getVolume() {
    return 4 * Math.PI * radius * radius * radius / 3;
  }
}

class Shapes {

  public static void main(String args[]) {

    Circle c = new Circle(new Point3D(0, 0, 0), new Point3D(1, 0, 0));
    c.display();
    System.out.println(c.getArea());
```

```
    Sphere s = new Sphere(new Point3D(0, 0, 0), 1);
    s.display();
    System.out.println(s.getVolume());
  }
}
```

Output from this application is shown here:

```
Circle
3.141592653589793
Sphere
4.1887902047863905
```

2. The following example shows an interface that defines a set of constants. Interface **Material** defines a set of string constants for various materials. Abstract class **MaterialObject** has one instance variable named **material** of type **String**. This records the material used to construct that object. Classes **Ball**, **Coin**, and **Ring** extend **MaterialObject**. The constructors initialize the **material** variable. Class **MaterialObjects** instantiates these three classes. A different material is passed to each constructor. The material of each object is displayed.

```
interface Material {
  String bronze = "bronze";
  String gold = "gold";
  String marble = "marble";
  String silver = "silver";
  String wood = "wood";
}

abstract class MaterialObject {
  String material;
}

class Ball extends MaterialObject
  Ball(String material) {
    this.material = material;
  }
}

class Coin extends MaterialObject
  Coin(String material) {
    this.material = material;
```

```
      }
    }

    class Ring extends MaterialObject {
      Ring(String material) {
        this.material = material;
      }
    }

    class MaterialObjects {
      public static void main(String args[]) {
        Ball ball = new Ball(Material.wood);
        Coin coin = new Coin(Material.silver);
        Ring ring = new Ring(Material.gold);
        System.out.println(ball.material);
        System.out.println(coin.material);
        System.out.println(ring.material);
      }
    }
```

Output from this application is shown here:

```
wood
silver
gold
```

EXERCISES

1. What is an interface?

2. What is the default modifier for an interface?

3. What does the **public** modifier for an interface designate?

4. What are the default modifiers for interface variables?

5. What are the default modifiers for interface methods?

6. Write an application that illustrates how to declare interfaces and implement them in various classes. Interfaces **AntiLockBrakes**, **CruiseControl**, and **PowerSteering** declare optional functionality for an automobile. In this simple example, each interface declares one method that has the same name as its

interface. The abstract **Auto** class is extended by the **Model1**, **Model2**, and **Model3** classes. Power steering is available for **Model1** objects. Antilock brakes and cruise control are available for **Model2** objects. Cruise control is available for **Model3** objects. Instantiate each of these classes and exercise its methods.

7.2 *INTERFACE REFERENCES*

You can specify an interface name as the type of a variable. The variable can then reference any object that implements that interface. The compiler issues an error message if you assign an object to the variable that does not implement that interface.

You can access interface variables and methods relative to the interface reference. This is done according to the following syntax:

intfRef.varName
intfRef.mthName(args)

Here, *intfRef* is the variable that is typed as an interface reference. The variable and method names are *varName* and *mthName*, respectively. The optional argument list is *args*. However, only variables and methods defined by the interface can be accessed relative to *intfRef*. The compiler issues an error message if this rule is violated.

Interface references support run-time polymorphism. If you invoke an interface method relative to that reference, the correct implementation is automatically invoked.

EXAMPLE

1. This example illustrates how to declare and use an interface reference variable. Interface **A** declares a **display( )** method. Classes **C1**, **C2**, and **C3** implement that method. The **main( )** method declares variable **a** of type **A**. Therefore, it can hold a reference to any object that implements interface **A**. This is demonstrated by creating objects of class **C1**, **C2**, and **C3** and invoking the **display( )** method relative to the interface reference.

```
interface A {
  void display(String s);
}

class C1 implements A {
  public void display(String s) {
    System.out.println("C1: " + s);
  }
}

class C2 implements A {
  public void display(String s) {
    System.out.println("C2: " + s);
  }
}

class C3 implements A {
  public void display(String s) {
    System.out.println("C3: " + s);
  }
}

class InterfaceReferenceVariable {
  public static void main(String args[]) {
    A a;
    a = new C1();
    a.display("String 1");
    a = new C2();
    a.display("String 2");
    a = new C3();
    a.display("String 3");
  }
}
```

Output from this application is shown here:

```
C1: String 1
C2: String 2
C3: String 3
```

EXERCISES

1. What compile-time error is generated for the following program?

```
interface B {
  void display();
}

class D1 {
}

class D2 implements B {
  public void display() {
    System.out.println("D2");
  }
}

class D3 implements B {
  public void display() {
    System.out.println("D3");
  }
}

class InterfaceReferenceVariable2 {
  public static void main(String args[]) {
    B b;
    b = new D1();
    b.display();
    b = new D2();
    b.display();
    b = new D3();
    b.display();
  }
}
```

2. Write a program that illustrates the use of interface references. Interface **LuminousObject** declares **lightOff( )** and **lightOn( )** methods. Class **SolidObject** is extended by **Cone** and **Cube**. Class **LuminousCone** extends **Cone** and implements **LuminousObject**. Class **LuminousCube** extends **Cube** and implements **LuminousObject**. Instantiate the **LuminousCone** and **LuminousCube** classes. Use interface references to refer to those objects. Invoke the methods of the **LuminousObject** interface via the interface reference.

| 7.3 | *I*NTERFACE INHERITANCE |

You previously saw how the **extends** keyword declares a subclass of an existing class. This same keyword can also be used to define an inheritance relationship between interfaces. Although a subclass may directly extend only one superclass, this same restriction does not apply with interfaces. An interface may directly extend multiple interfaces.

You may indicate that an interface extends one or more interfaces via the following syntax:

```
intfModifier interface intfName extends intfList {
  // interface body
}
```

Here, *intfModifier* is the optional interface modifier described in Section 7.1. The name of the interface is *intfName*.

The **extends** clause declares that this interface extends one or more interfaces. These are known as superinterfaces and are listed by name in *intfList*. Commas separate the interface names.

If a variable with the same name is declared in more than one superinterface, this represents an ambiguity. The compiler generates an error message if that variable is used. Methods with the same signature may be declared by more than one superinterface. However, those methods must have the same return type. Otherwise, the compiler issues an error message.

EXAMPLES

1. The following application illustrates how to use interface inheritance. Interface **L** extends interfaces **J** and **K**. Class **I** implements interface **L**. Therefore, it must provide implementations of all methods defined by interfaces **J**, **K**, and **L**.

```
interface J {
  int j = 200;
  int j1();
}

interface K {
  double k1();
}
```

```
interface L extends J, K {
  boolean l1();
}

class I implements L {

  public int j1() {
    return 4;
  }

  public double k1() {
    return 6.8;
  }

  public boolean l1() {
    return true;
  }
}

class InterfaceInheritance {

  public static void main(String args[]) {
    I i = new I();
    System.out.println(i.j);
    System.out.println(i.j1());
    System.out.println(i.k1());
    System.out.println(i.l1());
  }
}
```

Output from this application is shown here:

```
200
4
6.8
true
```

2. The following program generates a compile-time error. Interface **Base** declares variables **base** and **ambiguous**. Interface **Set1** extends **Base** and declares variables **ambiguous** and **set1**. Interface **Set2** extends **Base** and declares variable **set2**. Interface **Total** extends both **Set1** and **Set2**. It also declares variable **total**. The error occurs at the last statement in the **main( )** method where **ambiguous** is used. This is because that variable is declared in more than one of the interfaces implemented by class **Z**.

```
interface Base {
  int base = 0;
  int ambiguous = 1000;
}

interface Set1 extends Base {
  int set1 = 1;
  int ambiguous = 1000;
}

interface Set2 extends Base {
  int set2 = 2;
}

interface Total extends Set1, Set2 {
  int total = 3;
}

class Z implements Total {
}

class AmbiguousVariable {
  public static void main(String args[]) {
    Z z = new Z();
    System.out.println(z.base);
    System.out.println(z.set1);
    System.out.println(z.set2);
    System.out.println(z.total);
    System.out.println(z.ambiguous); // Error!
  }
}
```

3. The following program generates a compile-time error. Interface
   L1 declares methods **f( )** and **g( )**. Interface **L2** extends **L1** and
   also declares methods **f( )** and **g( )**. However, the return type of
   g( ) in **L1** differs from the return type of **g( )** in **L2**. The
   compiler identifies this as an error.

```
interface L1 {
  void f();
  void g();
}
```

```
interface L2 extends L1 {
  void f();
  int g();
}

class CompileError {
  public static void main(String args[]) {
    System.out.println("Compile-time error");
  }
}
```

EXERCISES

1. Write a program that illustrates interface inheritance. Interface **P** is extended by **P1** and **P2**. Interface **P12** inherits from both **P1** and **P2**. Each interface declares one constant and one method. Class **Q** implements **P12**. Instantiate **Q** and invoke each of its methods. Each method displays one of the constants.

2. Write another program that illustrates interface inheritance. Interface **K1** declares method **methodK( )** and a variable **intK** that is initialized to one. Interface **K2** extends **K1** and declares **methodK( )**. Interface **K3** extends **K2** and declares **methodK( )**. The return type of **methodK( )** is **void** in all interfaces. Class **U** implements **K3**. Its version of **methodK( )** displays the value of **intK**. Instantiate **U** and invoke its method.

7.4 *T HE instanceof OPERATOR*

It is sometimes useful to determine if an object is of a particular class or implements a specific interface. The **instanceof** operator can be used for this purpose, using the following syntax:

varName instanceof *type*

Here, *varName* is an object reference variable and *type* is the name of either a class or an interface. The expression evaluates to **true** if *varName* is a *type*. Otherwise, it evaluates to **false**.

1. This example uses the **instanceof** operator to test if an object is of a particular class. The **abstract** class **Fish** declares one **abstract** method named **display( )**. It also has two **abstract** subclasses named **FreshWaterFish** and **SaltWaterFish**. Some concrete subclasses are defined.

   The **main( )** method creates an array of type **Fish**. Different types of fish are instantiated and assigned to the elements of this array. A loop then iterates through these elements. Notice that the **instanceof** operator is used to identify if a fish is of type **SaltWaterFish**. The net effect is that the **display( )** method is called only for saltwater fish.

```
abstract class Fish {
  abstract void display();
}

abstract class FreshWaterFish extends Fish {
}

abstract class SaltWaterFish extends Fish {
}

class Trout extends FreshWaterFish {
  void display() {
    System.out.println("Trout");
  }
}

class Flounder extends SaltWaterFish {
  void display() {
    System.out.println("Flounder");
  }
}

class Tuna extends SaltWaterFish {
  void display() {
    System.out.println("Tuna");
  }
}

class InstanceofClass {
  public final static int NUMFISH = 4;
```

```
public static void main(String args[]) {

    // Create an array of fish
    Fish fishes[] = new Fish[NUMFISH];

    // Create objects
    fishes[0] = new Trout();
    fishes[1] = new Flounder();
    fishes[2] = new Tuna();
    fishes[3] = new Trout();

    // Demonstrate instanceof operator
    for(int i = 0; i < NUMFISH; i++) {
      Fish fish = fishes[i];
      if(fish instanceof SaltWaterFish) {
        fish.display();
      }
    }
  }
}
```

Output from this application is shown here:

```
Flounder
Tuna
```

2. This example uses the **instanceof** operator to test if an object implements a particular interface. The **Vehicle** interface declares a **drive( )** method. The abstract **Mammal** class is the superclass of the **Bear**, **Elephant**, **Horse**, and **Lion** classes. The **Vehicle** interface is implemented by the **Elephant** and **Horse** classes. However, the **Bear** and **Lion** classes do not implement this interface. The **main( )** method creates and initializes an array of four **Mammal** objects. A loop then iterates through the elements in that array. If the object implements the **Vehicle** interface, the **drive( )** method is invoked.

```
interface Vehicle {
  void drive();
}

abstract class Mammal {
}

class Bear extends Mammal {
}
```

```
class Elephant extends Mammal
implements Vehicle {
  public void drive() {
    System.out.println("Elephant: drive");
  }
}

class Horse extends Mammal
implements Vehicle {
  public void drive() {
    System.out.println("Horse: drive");
  }
}

class Lion extends Mammal {
}

class InstanceofInterface {
  public final static int NUMMAMMALS = 4;

  public static void main(String args[]) {

    // Create an array of mammals
    Mammal mammals[] = new Mammal[NUMMAMMALS];

    // Create objects
    mammals[0] = new Bear();
    mammals[1] = new Elephant();
    mammals[2] = new Horse();
    mammals[3] = new Lion();

    // Demonstrate instanceof operator
    for(int i = 0; i < NUMMAMMALS; i++) {
      if(mammals[i] instanceof Vehicle) {
        Vehicle v = (Vehicle)mammals[i];
        v.drive();
      }
    }
  }
}
```

Output from this application is shown here:

```
Elephant: drive
Horse: drive
```

1. Write a program that demonstrates the **instanceof** operator. Declare interfaces **I1** and **I2**. Interface **I3** extends both of these interfaces. Also declare interface **I4**. Class **X** implements **I3**. Class **W** extends **X** and implements **I4**. Create an object of class **W**. Use the **instanceof** operator to test if that object implements each of the interfaces and is of type **X**.

7.5 *P*ACKAGES

A *package* is a group of classes and interfaces. You can assign the classes and interfaces in a source file to a particular package by using a **package** statement with the following syntax:

package *packageName*;

Here, *packageName* is the name of the package.

If a source file does not contain a **package** statement, its classes and interfaces are placed in a default package. This approach has been used for all examples seen so far in this book. If a **package** statement is used, it must appear as the first statement in that source file. Also, a maximum of one **package** statement may appear in a file. If these rules are violated, a compiler error results.

A package name can be a simple identifier that follows the Java naming conventions. An example is shown here:

```
package engineering;
```

It is also possible to organize packages in a hierarchical manner. In this case, *packageName* would be a sequence of package names each separated by a period. An example is shown here:

```
package engineering.electrical.signals;
```

In this case, the engineering package contains a package named electrical. The electrical package contains a package named signals.

You must establish a directory hierarchy that corresponds to the package hierarchy. The reason for this is that each package must reside in a directory that reflects its full package name. For example, if you define a package named **engineering.electrical.signals** on a Windows platform, the source files for that package must be in a directory named **engineering\electrical\signals**.

The Java class libraries are organized into packages. Some of these are listed in the following table.

Package	Description
java.applet	Allows you to build applets
java.awt	Provides an Abstract Window Toolkit (AWT) so graphical user interfaces can be constructed
java.awt.event	Handles events from AWT components
java.io	Supports input and output
java.lang	Provides core Java functionality
java.net	Enables networking
java.util	Offers utility functionality

EXAMPLE

1. This example illustrates how the classes defined in four separate source files can be grouped into one package named **p**. The source code for **p\PackageDemo.java** is shown in the following listing. An object of class **A** is created and method **a1( )** is called. Similarly, objects of classes **B** and **C** are created and methods are invoked on those objects.

```
package p;

class PackageDemo {

  public static void main(String args[]) {
    A a = new A();
    a.a1();
    B b = new B();
    b.b1();
    C c = new C();
    c.c1();
  }
}
```

The source code for **p\A.java** is shown in the following listing.

```
package p;

class A {
  void a1() {
    System.out.println("a1");
  }
}
```

The source code for **p\B.java** is shown in the following listing.

```
package p;

class B {
  void b1() {
    System.out.println("b1");
  }
}
```

The source code for **p\C.java** is shown in the following listing.

```
package p;

class C {
  void c1() {
    System.out.println("c1");
  }
}
```

Note   *These four files are all in the same directory.*

To build this package, you must change to the parent directory of **p** and issue the following command:

javac p*.java

The **.class** files created by this command are placed in the sub-directory **p**.

To execute this application, remain in the parent directory of **p** and issue the following command:

java p.PackageDemo

Notice that the argument to the Java interpreter is a fully qualified class name. This includes both the package and class names.

Output from this application is shown here:

```
a1
b1
c1
```

1. What is a package?

2. If a source file does not contain a package statement, where are its classes and interfaces placed?

3. If a source file named **X.java** contains the statement "package a.b.c.d," in what directory (relative to the current directory) must it be located? What commands would you give to compile and run this program?

7.6 CLASSPATH

CLASSPATH is an environment variable that determines where the JDK tools such as the Java compiler and interpreter search for a **.class** file. It contains an ordered sequence of directories as well as **.jar** and **.zip** files. (Files with **.jar** and **.zip** suffixes are archives that can contain multiple files.) It is important to have the CLASSPATH variable set correctly when working with packages.

On a Windows platform you may set the value of an environment variable by typing a command such as the following:

```
set classpath=c:\project1;c:\project2
```

You may confirm that CLASSPATH is set correctly by entering the command shown here:

```
echo %classpath%
```

This command displays the current setting of that environment variable.

By default, the JDK tools first attempt to locate a **.class** file relative to the current directory. If this is not successful, the locations specified by CLASSPATH are then searched in sequence. Finally, the Java class libraries are automatically searched. (The Java class libraries are located in a file named **classes.zip** under the **lib** subdirectory where the JDK was installed.)

You only need to change the value of CLASSPATH if you store **.class**, **.jar**, or **.zip** files anywhere other than the current directory.

EXAMPLE

1. Assume that you set the CLASSPATH environment variable on a Windows platform by typing the following command:

   ```
   set classpath=c:\chemistry;c:\physics;c:\calculus;c:\graph
   ```

   To find a class named **logarithmic.Plot**, the tools supplied with the JDK search for the following files in sequence:

   1. logarithmic\Plot.class under the current directory
   2. c:\chemistry\logarithmic\Plot.class
   3. c:\physics\logarithmic\Plot.class
   4. c:\calculus\logarithmic\Plot.class
   5. c:\graph\logarithmic\Plot.class
   6. the Java class libraries

   The first match is used. If none of the files exist, the compiler issues a **NoClassDefFoundError** message. (Errors and exceptions are discussed in the next chapter.)

EXERCISE

1. Assume that you created three packages named **a.b.c.d**, **j.k.l.m**, and **r.s.t**. The **.class** files for these packages are stored in directories c:\lab8\a\b\c, c:\freshman\chem101\j\k\l\m, and c:\seminar\r\s\t, respectively. How should CLASSPATH be set so the classes and interfaces in those three packages can be located by the JDK tools?

| 7.7 | *T*HE *import* STATEMENT |

It is easy to access classes and interfaces in the same package. Their simple names may be used directly. However, to access types in a different package, you cannot use only those simple names. They do not provide sufficient information for the Java compiler to locate the **.class** file.

One solution to this problem is to specify a fully qualified name for a type. For example, one of Java's built-in packages is **java.awt.event**. This package defines the class **MouseEvent**. Thus, to access the class **MouseEvent** in the package **java.awt.event**, you can refer to that type as **java.awt.event.MouseEvent**.

However, frequent use of fully qualified type names can be laborious. Therefore, the **import** statement is provided for your convenience. It has the two forms provided below:

```
import fullyQualifiedTypeName;
import packageName.*;
```

The first form allows you to use a simple name for the class or interface given as *fullyQualifiedTypeName*. The second form allows you to use simple names for the types in the package named *packageName*.

For example, the following statement allows you to use the simple name **MouseEvent** instead of the fully qualified name **java.awt.event.MouseEvent**:

```
import java.awt.event.MouseEvent;
```

You may use simple names for all the types in **java.awt.event** if you use the statement shown here:

```
import java.awt.event.*;
```

You might be wondering why the preceding programs in this book have not used an **import** statement. The answer is that a core set of Java's classes are contained in the package **java.lang** and this package is automatically imported by the Java compiler into every source file. Therefore, you always have the convenience of using simple names for the types in that package.

Importing one package does not import any of its subpackages. Consider the following statement:

```
import java.awt.*;
```

This does not cause the public types in **java.awt.event** to be imported. You must provide another import statement to accomplish this, as shown here:

```
import java.awt.event.*;
```

EXAMPLE

1. The source code for **q\ImportDemo.java** is shown in the following listing. It begins with a **package** statement that places the types defined in this file into a package named **q**. The next two **import** statements allow us to use abbreviated names for the available types defined in packages **r** and **s**. The rest of the listing is straightforward.

```
package q;
import r.*;
import s.*;

class ImportDemo {

  public static void main(String args[]) {
    R r = new R();
    r.r1();
    S s = new S();
    s.s1();
  }
}
```

The source code for **r\R.java** is shown in the following listing. It begins with a package statement that places the class defined in this file into a package named **r**.

```
package r;

public class R {
  public void r1() {
    System.out.println("r1");
  }
}
```

The source code for **s\S.java** is shown in the following listing. It begins with a package statement that places the class defined in this file into a package named **s**.

```
package s;

public class S {
  public void s1() {
    System.out.println("s1");
  }
}
```

To build these three packages, you must change to their parent directories and issue the following commands:

javac q*.java
javac r*.java
javac s*.java

The **.class** files created by these commands are placed in the appropriate subdirectories.

To execute the application, you must remain in the parent directory of **q** and issue the following command:

```
java q.ImportDemo
```

Notice that the argument to the Java interpreter is a fully qualified class name.

Output from this application is shown here:

```
r1
s1
```

EXERCISES

1. Explain the two forms of the **import** statement.

2. Make two alterations to the **q\ImportDemo.java** source file from the preceding example. Specifically, comment out the package statement and the first import statement. Then attempt to rebuild the code. Make certain you understand the compiler errors that occur.

3. Comment out the import statements in **q\ImportDemo.java** and use fully qualified names for types so the file compiles.

7.8 ■ *A*CCESS CONTROL AND PACKAGES

As you learned earlier in this book, the **public**, **protected**, and **private** keywords can be used in variable, constructor, and method modifiers. Now that packages have been covered, it is a good idea to review their meanings:

Keyword	Description
public	Access is allowed from any class.
protected	Access is allowed only from code in the same package or subclasses in different packages.
private	Access is allowed only from code in the same class.

These modifiers are mutually exclusive. Only one may be used. If none is specified, the default is that access is provided only from code in the same package.

EXAMPLE

1. This example illustrates the distinction among **public**, **protected**, and **private** variables. The source code for **e\E.java** is shown in the following listing. This class contains three **int** variables with different modifiers.

```
package e;

public class E {
  public int e1 = 11;
  protected int e2 = 22;
  private int e3 = 33;
}
```

The source code for **f\F.java** is shown in the following listing. This illustrates how a subclass in a different package can access **public** and **protected** members of its superclass.

```
package f;
import e.*;

public class F extends E {

  public void display() {
```

```
    // OK to access public member
    System.out.println(e1);

    // OK to access protected member
    // in our superclass
    System.out.println(e2);

    // Not OK to access private member
    // System.out.println(e3);
  }
}
```

The source code for **g\G.java** is shown in the following listing. This illustrates how a non-subclass in a different package *cannot* access **protected** members of a class.

```
package g;
import e.*;

public class G {

  public void display() {

    // Create an instance of E
    E e = new E();

    // OK to access public member
    System.out.println(e.e1);

    // Not OK to access protected member
    // System.out.println(e.e2);

    // Not OK to access private member
    // System.out.println(e.e3);
  }
}
```

The source code for **h\ProtectedDemo11.java** is shown in the following listing. This is the application that uses classes **f.F** and **g.G**.

```
package h;
import f.F;
import g.G;

class ProtectedDemo {
```

```
   public static void main(String args[]) {

      // Test subclass in a different package
      F f = new F();
      f.display();

      // Test non-subclass in a different package
      G g = new G();
      g.display();
   }
}
```

To build these three packages, you must change to the parent
directory and issue the following commands:

javac e*.java
javac f*.java
javac g*.java
javac h*.java

The **.class** files created by these commands are placed in the
appropriate subdirectories.

To execute the application, you must remain in the parent
directory and issue the following command:

java h.ProtectedDemo

Notice that the argument to the Java interpreter is a fully
qualified class name.

Output from this application is shown here:

```
11
22
11
```

EXERCISES

1. What access is granted by the **public** modifier?

2. What access is granted by the **protected** modifier?

3. What access is granted by the **private** modifier?

4. Experiment with the files **f\F.java** and **g\G.java** by temporarily
   removing the comment characters. What compiler errors
   are generated?

Mastery
Skills Check

Before continuing, you should be able to answer these questions and complete these exercises:

1. What syntax is used to declare an interface?

2. Explain the **instanceof** operator.

3. Explain the **package** statement.

4. Explain how CLASSPATH is used.

5. Explain the **import** statement.

6. What package is automatically imported into every source file?

7. Interfaces are sometimes used to indicate which classes have a certain capability or characteristic. Consider the following classes and interfaces. The abstract class **Animal** has abstract subclasses named **Bird** and **Reptile**. Classes **Dove**, **Eagle**, **Hawk**, **Penguin**, and **Seagull** extend **Bird**. Classes **Rattlesnake** and **Turtle** extend **Reptile**. The **ColdBlooded** interface defines no constants and declares no methods. It is implemented by **Reptile**. The **OceanDwelling** interface also defines no constants and declares no methods. It is implemented by the **Penguin**, **Seagull**, and **Turtle** classes. Define all of these classes and implement the interfaces as specified. Create one instance of each class. Then display all cold-blooded animals and all ocean-dwelling animals.

Cumulative
Skills Check

This section checks how well you have integrated the material in this chapter with that from earlier chapters.

1. Write an application that combines several classes and interfaces. The abstract class **Robot** has concrete subclasses named **RobotA**, **RobotB**, and **RobotC**. Class **RobotA1** extends

RobotA. Classes **RobotB1** and **RobotB2** extend **RobotB**. Class **RobotC1** extends **RobotC**. The **Locomotion** interface declares three methods named **forward( )**, **reverse( )**, **and stop( )**. It is implemented by classes **RobotB** and **RobotC**. The **Sound** interface declares one method named **beep( )**. It is implemented by classes **RobotA1**, **RobotB1**, and **RobotC**. Define all of these classes and implement the interfaces as specified. Create one instance of each class. Then invoke the **beep( )** method of all objects that are of type **Sound**. Also invoke the **stop( )** method of all objects that are of type **Locomotion**.

2. The abstract class **Tent** has concrete subclasses named **TentA**, **TentB**, **TentC**, and **TentD**. The **Waterproof** interface defines no constants and declares no methods. It is implemented by **TentB** and **TentD**. Define all of these classes, and implement the interfaces as specified. Create one instance of each class. Then display all waterproof tents. Place this code in a package named **tents**.

8

Exceptions

AN *exception* is an object that is generated at run-time to describe a problem encountered during the execution of a program. Some causes for an exception are integer division-by-zero, array index negative or out-of-bounds, illegal cast, interrupted I/O operation, unexpected end-of-file condition, missing file, incorrect number format, and malformed Uniform Resource Locator (URL). There are many other examples of exceptions. The causes of these will become clear in subsequent chapters of this book.

The ability to handle these types of problems is an important feature of the Java language. It allows you to write more robust programs. This chapter illustrates how to write code that handles these run-time problems. You will also see how to define and use your own custom exceptions.

Review

Skills Check

Before proceeding, you should be able to answer these questions and perform these exercises.

1. How do interfaces support polymorphism?

2. What happens if the same variable is declared in more than one superinterface?

3. What happens if the same method is declared in more than one superinterface?

4. Declare an interface that contains some constants commonly used in chemistry and physics. The values that should be included are the acceleration of gravity (9.8m/sec/sec), the speed of light (3E8m/sec), and Avogadro's constant (6.02E23). Display the values of these constants.

8.1 EXCEPTION HANDLING

Let us begin our discussion of exceptions by looking at a program that deliberately generates an arithmetic exception when an integer division-by-zero is attempted. It is shown in the following listing:

```
class DivideByZero {

  public static void main(String args[]) {
    a();
  }

  static void a() {
    b();
  }

  static void b() {
    c();
  }

  static void c() {
    d();
  }

  static void d() {
    int i = 1;
    int j = 0;
    System.out.println(i/j);
  }
}
```

Output from this program is shown here:

```
java.lang.ArithmeticException: / by zero
        at DivideByZero.d(DivideByZero.java: 22)
        at DivideByZero.c(DivideByZero.java: 16)
        at DivideByZero.b(DivideByZero.java: 12)
        at DivideByZero.a(DivideByZero.java: 8)
        at DivideByZero.main(DivideByZero.java: 4)
```

You can see that an arithmetic exception object was generated at line 22 in this program. It was handled by the default exception handling mechanism. Information about the exception is displayed, and execution of the application is stopped.

Closely examine the output generated by this program. You can see that **main( )** invoked **a( )**. Method **a( )** invoked **b( )**. Method **b( )** invoked **c( )**. Method **c( )** invoked **d( )**. Each time one method invokes another method, an *activation frame* is placed on the stack. This is necessary so that the processor can correctly return from a method to its caller. Here, the default exception handling mechanisms examine the stack and determine how a method that generates an exception was invoked. We will talk more about activation frames later in this chapter.

The Java language allows you to handle exceptions that occur during execution of a program. This is done by using the following syntax:

```
try {
  // try block
}
catch(ExceptionType1 param1) {
  // exception-handling block
}
catch(ExceptionType2 param2) {
  // exception handling block
}

  ...
catch(ExceptionTypeN param3) {
  // exception handling
}
finally {
  // finally block
}
```

Let us first consider the structure of this code. The **try** statement contains a block of statements enclosed by braces. This is the code you want to monitor for exceptions. If a problem occurs during its execution, an exception is *thrown*. (You will see shortly how this is done with a **throw** statement.)

Immediately following the **try** block is a sequence of **catch** blocks. Each of these begins with the **catch** keyword. An argument is passed to each **catch** block. That argument is the exception object that contains information about the problem.

If a problem occurs during execution of the **try** block, the Java Virtual Machine (JVM) immediately stops executing the **try** block and looks for a **catch** block that can process that type of exception. Any remaining statements in the **try** block are not executed. The search begins at the first **catch** block. If the type of the exception object matches the type of the **catch** block parameter, those statements are executed. Otherwise, the remaining **catch** clauses are examined in sequence for a type match.

One of the biggest advantages of the Java exception handling mechanism is that it allows you to write software that is better organized and easier to understand. You no longer need to distribute code to check and handle errors throughout your program. Instead, a **try** block can be written and, if problems occur during its execution, control proceeds in a well-defined manner to the appropriate **catch** block.

When a **catch** block completes execution, control passes to the statements in the **finally** block. The Java compiler ensures that the **finally** block is executed in all circumstances. When a **try** block completes without problems, the **finally** block executes. Even if a **return** statement is included in a **try** block, the compiler ensures that the **finally** block is executed before the current method returns.

The **finally** block is optional. However, in some applications it can provide a useful way to relinquish resources. For example, you may wish to close files or databases at this point.

Each **try** block must have at least one **catch** or **finally** block. Otherwise, a compiler error occurs. The compiler also checks the type of each **catch** block parameter. If this is not a **java.lang.Throwable** object, an error message is generated.

EXAMPLE

1. This example illustrates the flow of control in a program with exception handling. The application accepts two strings in integer format as its command-line arguments. The first number is divided by the second number and the result is displayed. There are **catch** blocks to handle the different types of exceptions that can occur. If a division-by-zero is attempted, an **ArithmeticException** occurs. An **ArrayIndexOutOfBounds-Exception** occurs if one or both of the command-line arguments is missing. If an argument is not formatted as an integer, a **NumberFormatException** occurs. Try executing this program with these different conditions and observe the results. Notice that the **finally** block always executes. Also observe that the call to **println( )** after the division never executes if an exception occurs.

```
class Divider {

  public static void main(String args[]) {

    try {

      System.out.println("Before Division");
      int i = Integer.parseInt(args[0]);
      int j = Integer.parseInt(args[1]);
      System.out.println(i/j);
      System.out.println("After Division");
    }
    catch(ArithmeticException e) {
      System.out.println("ArithmeticException");
    }
    catch(ArrayIndexOutOfBoundsException e) {
    System.out.println("ArrayIndex"
      "OutOfBoundsException");
    }
    catch(NumberFormatException e) {
      System.out.println("NumberFormatException");
    }
    finally {
      System.out.println("Finally block");
    }
  }
}
```

EXERCISE

1. What is the output from the following program?

```
class ClassCast {

  public static void main(String args[]) {

    try {

      Object obj = new Integer("85");
      System.out.println("Before cast");
```

```
        Double dobj = (Double)obj;
        System.out.println("After cast");
      }
    catch(Exception e) {
        System.out.println(e);
      }
    }
  }
```

8.2 *C*ATCH BLOCK SEARCHES

As previously described, the search for an exception handler begins at the first **catch** block immediately following the **try** block in which the exception occurred. The search continues until the type of the exception object matches the type of the **catch** block parameter.

What happens if none of these **catch** blocks are a type match with the exception object? In that case, the search continues by examining the **catch** blocks of any enclosing **try** block. If a match is not found in the current method, the search continues in the calling method. The search continues up the stack in this manner. If the call stack is followed up to the **main( )** method and a matching **catch** block has still not been located, the default exception handler is then invoked to display the exception and terminate the program.

It is important to remember that any **finally** block is always executed before this search continues beyond the current method.

As previously described, the **catch** blocks associated with a **try** statement are examined in sequence. Once a matching **catch** block is located, any remaining **catch** blocks are not examined.

You will see shortly that exception classes exist in a class hierarchy. For example, **ArithmeticException**, **ArrayIndexOutOfBoundsException**, and **NumberFormatException** are subclasses of **Exception**. Therefore, it would be illogical to define a first **catch** block with a parameter type of **Exception** followed by a second **catch** block with a parameter type of **ArithmeticException**. The second **catch** block would never execute. All exceptions would be handled by the first **catch** block. The Java compiler checks the sequence and parameter types of the **catch** blocks. If a **catch** block parameter has a type that is a subclass of a previous **catch** block parameter, an error message is generated.

EXAMPLE

1. The following program illustrates how the search for a **catch** block is done. In this example, the call stack contains the activation frames for methods **main( )**, **a( )**, **b( )**, **c( )**, and **d( )** when an **ArrayIndexOutOfBoundsException** occurs in **d( )**. There is no matching **catch** block in **d( )**, so its **finally** block executes and the search continues in **c( )**. There is no matching **catch** block in **c( )**, so its **finally** block executes and the search continues in **b( )**. A matching **catch** block is located in **b( )** and this executes. Normal processing resumes. The **finally** block of **b( )** executes. Control returns to methods **a( )** and **main( )** as expected.

```java
class CatchSearch {

  public static void main(String args[]) {
    try {
      System.out.println("Before a");
      a();
      System.out.println("After a");
    }
    catch(Exception e) {
      System.out.println("main: " + e);
    }
    finally {
      System.out.println("main: finally");
    }
  }

  public static void a() {
    try {
      System.out.println("Before b");
      b();
      System.out.println("After b");
    }
    catch(ArithmeticException e) {
      System.out.println("a: " + e);
    }
    finally {
      System.out.println("a: finally");
    }
  }

  public static void b() {
```

```java
    try {
      System.out.println("Before c");
      c();
      System.out.println("After c");
    }
    catch(ArrayIndexOutOfBoundsException e) {
      System.out.println("b: " + e);
    }
    finally {
      System.out.println("b: finally");
    }
  }

  public static void c() {
    try {
      System.out.println("Before d");
      d();
      System.out.println("After d");
    }
    catch(NumberFormatException e) {
      System.out.println("c: " + e);
    }
    finally {
      System.out.println("c: finally");
    }
  }

  public static void d() {
    try {
      int array[] = new int[4];
      array[10] = 10;
    }
    catch(ClassCastException e) {
      System.out.println("d: " + e);
    }
    finally {
      System.out.println("d: finally");
    }
  }
}
```

Output from this program is shown here:

```
Before a
Before b
Before c
Before d
```

```
d: finally
c: finally
b: java.lang.ArrayIndexOutOfBoundsException: 10
b: finally
After b
a: finally
After a
main: finally
```

EXERCISES

1. What is the output from the following program?

```java
class CatchSearch2 {

  public static void main(String args[]) {
    try {
      System.out.println("Before a");
      a();
      System.out.println("After a");
    }
    catch(Exception e) {
      System.out.println("main: " + e);
    }
    finally {
      System.out.println("main: finally");
    }
  }

  public static void a() {
    try {
      System.out.println("Before b");
      b();
      System.out.println("After b");
    }
    catch(ArithmeticException e) {
      System.out.println("a: " + e);
    }
    finally {
      System.out.println("a: finally");
    }
  }

  public static void b() {
```

```
    try {
      System.out.println("Before c");
      c();
      System.out.println("After c");
    }
    catch(ArrayIndexOutOfBoundsException e) {
      System.out.println("b: " + e);
    }
    finally {
      System.out.println("b: finally");
    }
  }

  public static void c() {
    try {
      System.out.println("Before d");
      d();
      System.out.println("After d");
    }
    catch(NumberFormatException e) {
      System.out.println("c: " + e);
    }
    finally {
      System.out.println("c: finally");
    }
  }

  public static void d() {
    try {
      Object obj = new Float("85.56");
      System.out.println("Before cast");
      Double dobj = (Double)obj;
      System.out.println("After cast");
    }
    catch(ClassCastException e) {
      System.out.println("d: " + e);
      int i = 1;
      int j = 0;
      System.out.println("Before division");
      int k = i/j;
      System.out.println("After division");
      System.out.println(k);
    }
    finally {
      System.out.println("d: finally");
    }
```

```
      }
    }
```

2. Does the following program compile?

```
class CatchError {

  public static void main(String args[]) {

    try {
      System.out.println("Try Block");
    }
    catch(Exception e) {
      System.out.println("Exception");
    }
    catch(ArithmeticException e) {
      System.out.println("ArithmeticException");
    }
  }
}
```

8.3 *THE throw STATEMENT*

In the previous examples, you saw that an exception was generated by the JVM when certain run-time problems occurred. It is also possible for your program to explicitly generate an exception. This can be done with a **throw** statement. Its form is as follows:

throw *object*;

Here, *object* must be of type **java.lang.Throwable**. Otherwise, a compiler error occurs.

Inside a **catch** block, you may throw the same exception object that was provided as an argument. This can be done with the following syntax:

catch(*ExceptionType param*) {

  ...

  throw *param*;

  ...

}

Alternatively, you may create and throw a new exception object as follows:

throw new *ExceptionType(args)*;

Here, *ExceptionType* is the type of the exception object and *args* is the optional argument list for its constructor.

When a **throw** statement is encountered, a search for a matching **catch** block begins. Any subsequent statements in the same **try** or **catch** block are not executed.

EXAMPLES

1. The following program illustrates how a **catch** block may re-throw an exception. This can be done so **catch** blocks in the calling methods can also process the exception. In this example, the call stack contains the activation frames for methods **main( )**, **a( )**, **b( )**, **c( )**, and **d( )** when an **ArithmeticException** occurs in **d( )**. There is a matching **catch** block in **d( )**. It contains a **throw** statement that throws the same exception object provided as the argument to that **catch** block. Therefore, a search for a matching **catch** block continues in method **c( )**. It also has a **catch** block that matches the type of the exception object. Therefore, that code executes until another **throw** statement is encountered. This stops execution of the **catch** block, and a search for a matching **catch** block continues in method **b( )**. It also has a **catch** block that matches the type of the exception object. Handling of the exception completes with that **catch** block.

```
class ThrowDemo {

  public static void main(String args[]) {
    try {
      System.out.println("Before a");
      a();
      System.out.println("After a");
    }
    catch(ArithmeticException e) {
      System.out.println("main: " + e);
    }
    finally {
      System.out.println("main: finally");
```

```
      }
    }

    public static void a() {
      try {
        System.out.println("Before b");
        b();
        System.out.println("After b");
      }
      catch(ArithmeticException e) {
        System.out.println("a: " + e);
      }
      finally {
        System.out.println("a: finally");
      }
    }

    public static void b() {
      try {
        System.out.println("Before c");
        c();
        System.out.println("After c");
      }
      catch(ArithmeticException e) {
        System.out.println("b: " + e);
      }
      finally {
        System.out.println("b: finally");
      }
    }

    public static void c() {
      try {
        System.out.println("Before d");
        d();
        System.out.println("After d");
      }
      catch(ArithmeticException e) {
        System.out.println("c: " + e);
        throw e;
      }
      finally {
        System.out.println("c: finally");
      }
    }
```

```
      public static void d() {
        try {
          int i = 1;
          int j = 0;
          System.out.println("Before division");
          System.out.println(i/j);
          System.out.println("After division");
        }
        catch(ArithmeticException e) {
          System.out.println("d: " + e);
          throw e;
        }
        finally {
          System.out.println("d: finally");
        }
      }
    }
```

Output from this program is shown here:

```
Before a
Before b
Before c
Before d
Before division
d: java.lang.ArithmeticException: / by zero
d: finally
c: java.lang.ArithmeticException: / by zero
c: finally
b: java.lang.ArithmeticException: / be zero
b: finally
After b
a: finally
After a
main: finally
```

2. This example illustrates how an exception can be created and thrown. The method **a( )** has a **try** block that contains a **throw** statement. You can see that the **new** operator creates an **ArithmeticException** object via its default constructor.

```
class ThrowDemo2 {

  public static void main(String args[]) {
    try {
      System.out.println("Before a");
```

```
      a();
      System.out.println("After a");
    }
    catch(Exception e) {
      System.out.println("main: " + e);
    }
    finally {
      System.out.println("main: finally");
    }
  }

  public static void a() {
    try {
      System.out.println("Before throw statement");
      throw new ArithmeticException();
    }
    catch(Exception e) {
      System.out.println("a: " + e);
    }
    finally {
      System.out.println("a: finally");
    }
  }
}
```

Output from this program is shown here:

```
Before a
Before throw statement
a: java.lang.ArithmeticException
a: finally
After a
main: finally
```

EXERCISES

1. Write a program that illustrates how to use the **throw** statement. Create a class that has static methods **main( )**, **a( )**, **b( )**, **c( )**, and **d( )**. The **main( )** method invokes **a( )**. Method **a( )** invokes **b( )**. Method **b( )** invokes **c( )**. Method **c( )** invokes **d( )**. Method **d( )** declares a local array with ten elements and then attempts to access the element at position 20. Therefore, an **ArrayIndexOutOfBoundsException** is generated. Each

method has a **catch** block for this type of exception and a **finally** block. The **catch** blocks in **c( )** and **d( )** contain a **throw** statement to propagate this exception to their caller. Use the **println( )** method to monitor the flow of control in your program.

2. What is the output of this program?

```
class ThrowExercise2 {

  public static void main(String args[]) {
    try {
      System.out.println("Before a");
      a();
      System.out.println("After a");
    }
    catch(NumberFormatException e) {
      System.out.println("main: " + e);
    }
    finally {
      System.out.println("main: finally");
    }
  }

  public static void a() {
    try {
      System.out.println("Before b");
      b();
      System.out.println("After b");
    }
    catch(NumberFormatException e) {
      System.out.println("a: " + e);
    }
    finally {
      System.out.println("a: finally");
    }
  }

  public static void b() {
    try {
      System.out.println("Before c");
      c();
      System.out.println("After c");
    }
    catch(NumberFormatException e) {
      System.out.println("b: " + e);
```

```
      }
      finally {
        System.out.println("b: finally");
      }
   }

   public static void c() {
      try {
        System.out.println("Before d");
        d();
        System.out.println("After d");
      }
      catch(ArithmeticException e) {
        System.out.println("c: " + e);
      }
      finally {
        System.out.println("c: finally");
      }
   }

   public static void d() {
      try {
        Integer iobj = new Integer("45.67");
      }
      catch(NumberFormatException e) {
        throw e;
      }
      finally {
        System.out.println("d: finally");
      }
   }
}
```

8.4 | EXCEPTION AND ERROR CLASSES

Each **catch** clause must have exactly one parameter whose type is
Throwable. The Java compiler generates an error message if this is
not done. The **Throwable** class is the superclass of all exception and
error classes. It provides the following constructors:

Throwable()
Throwable(String *message*)

Here, *message* is a string that describes the problem.

This class provides two methods that we will use in this book. The **getMessage( )** method returns the string that was provided to the constructor. Its signature is shown here:

String getMessage()

The **printStackTrace( )** method displays information about the program stack at the time this problem occurred. The form used in this chapter is shown here:

void printStackTrace()

This method displays the stack trace on the standard output stream.

The **Error** class extends **Throwable**. It has more than a dozen subclasses that represent serious problems that can be encountered by the Java Virtual Machine. These include class format errors, stack overflow, memory exhaustion, internal errors, or illegal access. These conditions occur rarely and are not considered further in this book.

The **Exception** class extends **Throwable**. It has subclasses that represent various problems that can occur at run-time and provides the following constructors:

Exception()
Exception(String *message*)

Here, *message* is a string that describes the problem.

Table 8-1 summarizes some subclasses of **Exception**.

Class	Description
ClassNotFoundException	A class cannot be found.
IllegalAccessException	An illegal access to a class was attempted.
InstantiationException	An attempt was made to instantiate an interface or abstract class.
InterruptedException	A thread has been interrupted.
NoSuchFieldException	A field could not be found.
NoSuchMethodException	A method could not be found.
RuntimeException	A run-time exception occurred.

TABLE 8-1 *Some Subclasses of* ***Exception*** ▼

The classes listed in Table 8-1 are defined by the **java.lang** package. There are additional subclasses of **Exception** defined in other packages. For example, the **java.io** package defines **IOException** and a set of subclasses to describe various problems that can occur during input and output operations.

The **RuntimeException** class is one of the most important subclasses of **Exception**. It describes run-time problems that can commonly occur in programs and provides the following constructors:

```
RuntimeException()
RuntimeException(String message)
```

Here, _message_ is a string that describes the problem.

Table 8-2 summarizes some subclasses of **RuntimeException**.

Class	Description
ArrayIndexOutOfBoundsException	An array index is out-of-bounds.
ArithmeticException	An arithmetic exception occurred (e.g., integer division-by-zero).
ClassCastException	An invalid cast attempt was attempted.
NegativeArraySizeException	A negative number was used for an array size.
NullPointerException	A field or method access for a **null** object was attempted.
NumberFormatException	A number is in an illegal format.
SecurityException	An operation is denied for security reasons.
StringIndexOutOfBoundsException	A string index is out-of-bounds.

TABLE 8-2 _Some Subclasses of **RuntimeException**_ ▼

EXAMPLE

1. The following example illustrates the operation of the
printStackTrace( ) method. The call stack for this program
contains activation frames for methods **main( )**, **a( )**, **b( )**,
c( ), and **d( )** when an **ArithmeticException** occurs. The
exception is caught and processed by the exception handler in
main( ), which calls **printStackTrace( )** to display the state of
the stack trace at the time the exception occurred.

```
class PrintStackTraceDemo {

  public static void main(String args[]) {
    try {
      a();
    }
    catch(ArithmeticException e) {
      e.printStackTrace();
    }
  }

  public static void a() {
    try {
      b();
    }
    catch(NullPointerException e) {
      e.printStackTrace();
    }
  }

  public static void b() {
    try {
      c();
    }
    catch(NullPointerException e) {
      e.printStackTrace();
    }
```

```
    }

    public static void c() {
      try {
        d();
      }
      catch(NullPointerException e) {
        e.printStackTrace();
      }
    }

    public static void d() {
      try {
        int i = 1;
        int j = 0;
        System.out.println(i/j);
      }
      catch(NullPointerException e) {
        e.printStackTrace();
      }
    }
  }
```

Output from this program is shown here:

```
java.lang.ArithmeticException: / by zero
   at PrintStackTraceDemo.d(PrintStackTraceDemo.java:43)
   at PrintStackTraceDemo.c(PrintStackTraceDemo.java:32)
   at PrintStackTraceDemo.b(PrintStackTraceDemo.java:23)
   at PrintStackTraceDemo.a(PrintStackTraceDemo.java:14)
   at PrintStackTraceDemo.main(PrintStackTraceDemo.java:5)
```

EXERCISES

1. What are the two subclasses of **Throwable**? Explain the distinction between these.

2. Name an **Exception** subclass that is not a **RuntimeException**.

3. Name six subclasses of **RuntimeException**.

*T*HE *throws* CLAUSE

When you write a method that can throw exceptions to its caller, it is useful to document that fact for other programmers who use your code. This provides them with the opportunity to deal with those exceptions. Similarly, you want to know which exceptions can be thrown from code written by others. This is one aspect of the Java language that helps programmers build more robust software.

A **throws** clause can be used in a constructor declaration for this purpose. It has the following syntax:

```
consModifiers clsName(cparams) throws exceptions {

    // body of constructor

}
```

Here, *consModifiers* are an optional set of modifiers. The name of the class is *clsName*. The optional constructor parameters are shown as *cparams*. A list of some exceptions that can be generated by the constructor is specified by *exceptions*, a comma-delimited set of exception classes.

A **throws** clause can be used in a method declaration as shown here:

```
mthModifiers rtype mthName(mparams) throws exceptions {

    // body of method

}
```

Here, *mthModifiers* are an optional set of modifiers and *rtype* is the return type of the method named *mthName*. Its optional parameters are shown as *mparams*. A list of some exceptions that can be generated by the method is specified by *exceptions*, a comma-delimited set of exception classes.

The Java compiler checks each constructor and method to determine the types of exceptions it can generate. You are required to catch or declare all subclasses of **Exception** other than the **RuntimeException** subclasses. If this is not done, a compiler error message is generated. This feature of Java reminds you to include handlers for these exceptions.

Because run-time exceptions are problems that can occur in almost any method, the Java designers believed it would be inconvenient to require that you include a **throws** clause for these types of problems. However, you may do so.

Also, the Java compiler issues an error message if you have a **catch** block for an exception type that cannot be generated by a **try** block.

1. This example illustrates how a **throws** clause is used. In this example, **main( )** calls **a( )**, which invokes **b( )**. Method **b( )** then calls **c( )**. Finally, method **c( )** invokes a static method named **forName( )** of **Class**. This method can throw a **ClassNotFoundException**. This is not a **RuntimeException**, therefore, you are required to catch or declare this exception in every method in which it can occur. The compiler issues an error message if this is not done. You can see that **c( )** has a **throws** clause indicating this type of exception can be generated. Method **b( )** also has such a **throws** clause. However, method **a( )** does catch this type of exception. Therefore, it does not require a **throws** clause. Experiment with this code by commenting out the **throws** clauses, and observe the compiler error that results.

```
class ThrowsDemo {

  public static void main(String args[]) {
    a();
  }

  public static void a() {
    try {
      b();
    }
    catch(ClassNotFoundException e) {
      e.printStackTrace();
    }
  }

  public static void b() throws ClassNotFoundException {
    c();
  }

  public static void c() throws ClassNotFoundException {
```

```
        Class cls = Class.forName("java.lang.Integer");
        System.out.println(cls.getName());
        System.out.println(cls.isInterface());
    }
}
```

Output from this program is shown here:

```
java.lang.Integer
false
```

EXERCISE

1. Are you required to catch or declare exceptions of class **ArithmeticException**?

2. Are you required to catch or declare exceptions of class **IOException**?

3. Are you required to catch or declare subclasses of **RuntimeException**?

4. A method named **average( )** has one argument that is an array of strings. It converts these to **double** values and returns their average. The method generates a **NullPointerException** if an array element is **null** or a **NumberFormatException** if an element is incorrectly formatted. Write a program that illustrates how to declare and use this method. Include a **throws** clause in the method declaration to indicate that these problems can occur.

8.6 CUSTOM EXCEPTIONS

Java allows you to create your own exception classes so application-specific problems can be handled. This can be done by creating a subclass of **Exception**. You then use the **throws** statement to throw an instance of your exception. You must catch or declare this exception in all methods in which it can occur if it is not a subclass of **RuntimeException**.

EXAMPLE

1. This example illustrates how to create and use your own exceptions. Classes **ExceptionA** and **ExceptionB** extend **Exception**. You are required to catch or declare these exceptions for each method in which they can occur. This is because they are not a subclass of **RuntimeException**. Method **c( )** creates a random number and uses it to determine which type of exception to throw. Notice that the **throws** clause indicates it can generate both of these exception types. Method **b( )** has a **throws** clause that includes only **ExceptionA**. This is because **ExceptionB** is handled by a **catch** block in that method. Finally, method **a( )** has a **catch** block that handles any exception. Therefore, a **throws** clause is not required.

```java
import java.util.*;

class ExceptionSubclass {

  public static void main(String args[]) {
    a();
  }

  static void a() {
    try {
      b();
    }
    catch(Exception e) {
      e.printStackTrace();
    }
  }

  static void b() throws ExceptionA {
    try {
      c();
    }
    catch(ExceptionB e) {
      e.printStackTrace();
    }
  }

  static void c() throws ExceptionA, ExceptionB {
    Random random = new Random();
    int i = random.nextInt();
    if(i % 2 == 0) {
```

```
      throw new ExceptionA("We have a problem");
    }
    else {
      throw new ExceptionB("We have a big problem");
    }
  }
}

class ExceptionA extends Exception {
  public ExceptionA(String message) {
    super(message);
  }
}


class ExceptionB extends Exception {
  public ExceptionB(String message) {
    super(message);
  }
}
```

Sample output from this application is shown here:

```
ExceptionB: We have a big problem
        at ExceptionSubclass.c(ExceptionSubclass.java: 34)
        at ExceptionSubclass.b(ExceptionSubclass.java: 20)
        at ExceptionSubclass.a(ExceptionSubclass.java: 11)
        at ExceptionSubclass.main(ExceptionSubclass.java: 6)
```

EXERCISES

1. Write a program that generates a custom exception if any of its command-line arguments are negative.

2. Does this program compile?

```
class ExceptionSubclassQuestion {

  public static void main(String args[]) {
    a();
  }

  static void a() {

    try {
```

```
        try {
          new ExceptionM("M");
        }
        catch(ExceptionN e) {
          System.out.println("Inner catch");
          e.printStackTrace();
        }
      }
      catch(ExceptionM e) {
        System.out.println("Outer catch");
        e.printStackTrace();
      }
    }
  }

class ExceptionM extends Exception {
  public ExceptionM(String message) {
    super(message);
  }
}


class ExceptionN extends Exception {
  public ExceptionN(String message) {
    super(message);
  }
}
```

Mastery
Skills Check

At this point you should be able to answer these questions and perform these exercises:

1. What is an exception?

2. Name six conditions that generate an exception.

3. What is the superclass of all error and exception classes?

4. What types of exceptions must be caught or declared?

5. A method named **add( )** accepts an array of strings as its argument. It converts these to **double** values and returns their sum. The method generates a **NumberFormatException** if an element is incorrectly formatted. It can also create and throw a custom exception, **RangeException**, if an element is less than 0 or greater than 1. Write a program that illustrates how to declare and use this method. Invoke the method from **main( )**. Catch any exceptions that are thrown and display an informative message for the user. Also, provide a **finally** clause to thank the user for using the program.

Cumulative Skills Check

This section checks how well you have integrated the material in this chapter with that of the earlier chapters.

1. What happens on floating-point division-by-zero? On integer division-by-zero?

2. Write a program that accepts the fully qualified name of a class as its argument. Compute and display how many superclasses exist for that class. (Hint: Use the **forName( )** and **getSuperclass( )** methods of **Class**.) If a **ClassNotFoundException** occurs, catch it and provide an error message for the user.

9

Multithreaded Programming

chapter objectives

THIS chapter demonstrates how to perform multithreaded programming in Java. It begins with an overview and shows two ways you can create a thread.

Java provides mechanisms so you can coordinate the activities of several threads in a process. This is important because data shared by several threads can be corrupted if they are not properly synchronized.

Multithreaded programming requires careful attention to details. One of the problems that can occur is deadlock. This happens when several threads wait forever for access to objects. An example illustrates this kind of design flaw.

Finally, you will see how several threads can communicate with each other.

Review

Skills Check

Before proceeding, you should be able to answer these questions and perform these exercises.

1. What five keywords are used to generate and handle exceptions in Java?

2. Explain how Java searches for a **catch** block to handle an exception.

3. Does the code in a **finally** block always execute?

4. Write a simple program that generates a **StringIndexOutOfBoundsException**, catches the exception, and displays an error message.

5. What output is generated by the following program?

```
class NestedTryBlocks {

  public static void main(String args[]) {
    a();
  }

  static void a() {
    try {
      try {
```

```
      System.out.println("Before"
         "integer division-by-zero");
      int i = 1;
      int j = 0;
      System.out.println(i/j);
      System.out.println("After"
         "integer division-by-zero");
    }
    catch(Exception e) {
      System.out.println("Inner catch block");
      throw e;
    }
    finally {
      System.out.println("Inner finally block");
    }
  }
  catch(Exception e) {
    System.out.println("Outer catch block");
  }
  finally {
    System.out.println("Outer finally block");
  }
}
}
```

9.1 *A N   O V E R V I E W   O F   T H R E A D S*

Modern operating systems manage multiple processes on a computer. Each of these runs in its own address space and can be independently scheduled for execution. A *thread* is a sequence of execution within a process. You may think of a thread as a "lightweight" process. It does not have its own address space but uses the memory and other resources of the process in which it executes. Therefore, the resources required for a thread are substantially less than those required for a process. There may be several threads in one process. The Java Virtual Machine (JVM) manages these and schedules them for execution. The time needed to perform a *context switch* from one thread to another is substantially less than that required for performing such a change between processes. This is another advantage of threads.

Let us consider the life cycle of a thread. A thread moves through several states from its creation to its ultimate death. These possible states are: (1) new, (2) ready, (3) running, (4) waiting, and (5) dead. Figure 9-1 shows the transitions among these states.

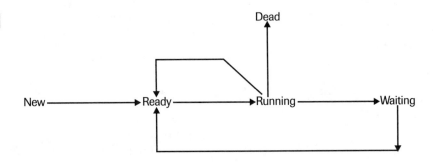

A thread is in the *new* state immediately after it is created and transitions to the *ready* state after it is started. It moves to the *running* state when the JVM selects it for execution. If the thread completes, it transitions to the *dead* state. If it chooses to sleep, wait, or perform an I/O operation, it changes to the *waiting* state. When this sleep, wait, or I/O operation completes, the thread again changes to the *ready* state. The JVM may move a thread from the running to ready state so that another thread has an opportunity to execute. This is discussed later.

One of the functions of the JVM is to schedule threads for execution. When several threads are ready, it selects one of these to execute.

Each thread has a priority. The JVM selects the highest-priority thread in the ready state for execution. A thread does not execute if there are higher-priority threads in the ready state.

If several runnable threads have the same priority, the JVM may *timeslice* the processor among them. After some period of time, the JVM preempts the thread that is currently executing and gives another thread an opportunity to execute. This behavior ensures that the processor time is equitably shared among these threads.

However, not all JVMs provide timeslicing. On those platforms, when a thread begins execution, it is not preempted unless a higher-priority thread becomes ready.

9.2 *C*REATING THREADS

Let's begin with an overview of how to create and manage threads. The **Thread** class in the **java.lang** package allows you to create and manage threads. Each thread is a separate instance of this class.

You may directly extend the **Thread** class as outlined in the following code:

```
class ThreadX extends Thread {
  public void run( ) {
    // logic for the thread
  }
}
```

Here, the class **ThreadX** extends **Thread**. The logic for the thread is contained in the **run( )** method. That method may be very simple or complex. It can create other objects or even initiate other threads.

The program can start an instance of the thread by using the form shown here:

```
ThreadX tx = new ThreadX( );
tx.start( );
```

The first line instantiates the **ThreadX** class. The second line invokes the **start( )** method of that object to start the thread executing. One of the actions of the **start( )** method is to invoke the **run( )** method. It is possible to create and start several instances of **ThreadX** that execute concurrently.

There is another way to create a thread. Declare a class that implements the **Runnable** interface. This interface declares only one method as shown here:

```
public void run( );
```

An example of such a class is shown here:

```
class RunnableY implements Runnable {
  public void run( ) {
    // logic for thread
}
```

The application can start an instance of the thread by using the following code:

```
RunnableY ry = new RunnableY( );
ThreadY ty = new Thread(ry);
ty.start( );
```

The first line instantiates the **RunnableY** class. The second line instantiates the **Thread** class. A reference to the **RunnableY** object is provided as the argument to the constructor. The last line starts the thread.

Now let us look at some of the specific variables and methods of the **Thread** class and then demonstrate their use.

The **Thread** class in the **java.lang** package defines three **int** constants that are used to specify the priority of a thread. These are **MAX_PRIORITY**, **MIN_PRIORITY**, and **NORM_PRIORITY**. They represent the maximum, minimum, and normal thread priorities.

Some of the constructors for **Thread** are as follows:

```
Thread()
Thread(Runnable r)
Thread(Runnable r, String s)
Thread(String s)
```

Here, *r* is a reference to an object that implements the **Runnable** interface and *s* is a string used to identify the thread.

The following table shows some static methods provided by this class.

Method	Description
Thread currentThread()	Returns a reference to the current thread
void sleep(long *msec*) throws InterruptedException	Causes the current thread to wait for *msec* milliseconds
void sleep(long *msec*, int *nsec*) throws InterruptedException	Causes the current thread to wait for *msec* milliseconds plus *nsec* nanoseconds
void yield()	Causes the current thread to yield control of the processor to other threads

Table 9-1 shows some instance methods provided by this class.

Method	Description
String getName()	Returns the name of the thread.
int getPriority()	Returns the priority of the thread.
boolean isAlive()	Returns **true** if this thread has been started and has not yet died. Otherwise, returns **false**.
void join() throws InterruptedException	Causes the caller to wait until this thread dies.
void join(long *msec*) throws InterruptedException	Causes the caller to wait a maximum of *msec* milliseconds until this thread dies. If *msec* is zero, there is no limit for the wait time.

TABLE 9-1   *Some Instance Methods Defined by **Thread*** ▼

Method	Description
void join(long *msec*, int *nsec*) throws InterruptedException	Causes the caller to wait a maximum of *msec* milliseconds plus *nsec* nanoseconds until this thread dies. If *msec* plus *nsec* is zero, there is no limit for the wait time.
void run( )	Comprises the body of the thread. This method is overridden by subclasses.
void setName(String *s*)	Sets the name of this thread to *s*.
void setPriority(int *p*)	Sets the priority of this thread to *p*.
void start( )	Starts the thread.
String toString( )	Returns the string equivalent of this thread.

TABLE 9-1 *Some Instance Methods Defined by* **Thread** *(continued)* ▼

EXAMPLES

1. This example illustrates how to create a thread by subclassing the **Thread** class. Class **ThreadX** extends **Thread** and overrides the **run( )** method. An infinite loop inside that method causes the thread to repetitively sleep for 2000 milliseconds and display the string "Hello". It is necessary to catch the **InterruptedException** that can be thrown by the **sleep( )** method.

   The **main( )** method of **ThreadDemo1** instantiates a **ThreadX** object and calls its **start( )** method. The **start( )** method invokes the **run( )** method.

```
class ThreadX extends Thread {

  public void run() {
    try {
      while(true) {
        Thread.sleep(2000);
        System.out.println("Hello");
      }
    }
    catch(InterruptedException ex) {
      ex.printStackTrace();
    }
  }
}

class ThreadDemo1 {
```

```
    public static void main(String args[]) {

      ThreadX tx = new ThreadX();
      tx.start();
    }
}
```

2. This example illustrates how to create a thread by implementing the **Runnable** interface. Class **RunnableY** implements this interface. The logic of the **run( )** method is identical to that of the preceding example.

   The **main( )** method of **ThreadDemo2** instantiates a **RunnableY** object. It then instantiates a **Thread** object. Notice that a reference to the **RunnableY** object is passed as the argument to **Thread** constructor. The **start( )** method of the **Thread** class is invoked to start the thread.

```
class RunnableY implements Runnable {

  public void run() {
    try {
      while(true) {
        Thread.sleep(2000);
        System.out.println("Hello");
      }
    }
    catch(InterruptedException ex) {
      ex.printStackTrace();
    }
  }
}

class ThreadDemo2 {

  public static void main(String args[]) {

    RunnableY ry = new RunnableY();
    Thread t = new Thread(ry);
    t.start();
  }
}
```

3. This example illustrates how a program can wait for threads to complete. The **ThreadM** class extends **Thread** and displays a string every second for 10 iterations. The **ThreadN** class extends **Thread** and displays a string every two seconds for 20 iterations.

The **main( )** method of **JoinDemo1** creates and starts these two threads and displays a message after they have both completed.

```
class ThreadM extends Thread {

  public void run() {
    try {
      for(int i = 0; i < 10; i++) {
        Thread.sleep(1000);
        System.out.println("ThreadM");
      }
    }
    catch(InterruptedException ex) {
      ex.printStackTrace();
    }
  }
}

class ThreadN extends Thread {

  public void run() {
    try {
      for(int i = 0; i < 20; i++) {
        Thread.sleep(2000);
        System.out.println("ThreadN");
      }
    }
    catch(InterruptedException ex) {
      ex.printStackTrace();
    }
  }
}

class JoinDemo1 {

  public static void main(String args[]) {

    ThreadM tm = new ThreadM();
    tm.start();
    ThreadN tn = new ThreadN();
    tn.start();
    try {
      tm.join();
      tn.join();
      System.out.println("Both threads have finished");
    }
```

```
        catch(Exception e) {
          e.printStackTrace();
        }
      }
    }
```

EXERCISES

1. Write an application that executes two threads. One thread displays "A" every 1,000 milliseconds, and the other displays "B" every 3,000 milliseconds. Create the threads by extending the **Thread** class.

2. Write an application that executes two threads. One thread displays "A" every 1,000 milliseconds, and the other displays "B" every 3,000 milliseconds. Create the threads by implementing the **Runnable** interface.

3. Write an application that creates and starts five threads. Each thread is instantiated from the same class. It executes a loop with ten iterations. Each iteration displays the character 'x' and sleeps between 300 and 800 milliseconds. The application waits for all threads to complete and then displays a message.

Note

*You may see methods named **resume( )**, **stop( )**, and **suspend( )**, in existing Java code. Be advised that these methods are now deprecated.*

9.3 **S**YNCHRONIZATION

This section describes some problems that can occur when multiple threads access shared data. You will see why it is necessary to carefully coordinate their actions. This is important material. Data corruption can occur if a multithreaded program is not designed correctly. This can lead to system failure. Unfortunately, such problems can occur at unpredictable times and be very difficult to reproduce.

The Java language provides some mechanisms to assist you in building robust multithreaded programs. However, you must understand when and how to apply these techniques. This information is also provided here.

As an example, consider a bank account that is shared by multiple customers. Each of these customers can make deposits to or withdrawals from this account. Your application might have a separate thread to process the actions of each user.

Figure 9-2 depicts one possible scheduling of these threads. At time t0, the account balance is initially zero. Thread A is executing and wants to deposit $10 to the account. The current value of the account is read at time t1. However, a context switch from Thread A to Thread B then occurs at time t2. Thread B then reads the value of the account at time t3. It increments this value by $10 at time t4. Another context switch occurs at time t5. This returns control to Thread A. At time t6, it sets the account balance to $10.

The net effect of this sequencing is that the final account balance is only $10. It should be $20. Data corruption has resulted.

The solution to this problem is to *synchronize* the access to this common data. This can be done in two ways. First, a method can be synchronized by using the **synchronized** keyword as a modifier in the method declaration.

When a thread begins executing a **synchronized** instance method, it automatically acquires a *lock* on that object. The lock is automatically relinquished when the method completes. Only one thread may have

FIGURE 9-2

Thread Scheduling ▼

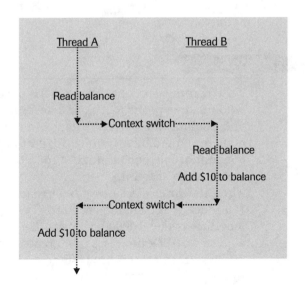

Time	Thread A	Thread B	Balance
t0			$0
t1	Read balance		$0
t2	Context switch		$0
t3		Read balance	$0
t4		Add $10 to balance	$10
t5	Context switch		$10
t6	Add $10 to balance		$10

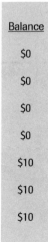

this lock at any time. Therefore, only one thread may execute any of the **synchronized** instance methods of an object at a particular time. If a second thread attempts to execute a **synchronized** instance method for that same object, the JVM automatically causes the second thread to wait until the first thread relinquishes the lock.

When a thread begins executing a **synchronized** static method, it automatically acquires a lock on the associated **Class** object. The lock is automatically relinquished when the method completes. Only one thread may have this lock at any time. Therefore, only one thread may execute any of the **synchronized** static methods of a class at a particular time. If another thread attempts to execute a **synchronized** static method for that same class, the JVM automatically causes that thread to wait until the first thread relinquishes the lock.

Another way to synchronize access to common data is via a **synchronized** statement block. This has the following syntax:

```
synchronized(obj) {
  // statement block
}
```

Here, *obj* is the object to be locked. If you wish to protect instance data, you should lock against that object. If you wish to protect class data, you should lock the appropriate **Class** object.

One important benefit of the Java class libraries is that they are designed to be *thread-safe*. In other words, multiple threads may access their methods.

EXAMPLE

1. This example simulates the actions of several bank customers who make deposits to a shared account. The **Account** class encapsulates the current balance in the account. This value is incremented by a **synchronized** method so it is not corrupted. The **getBalance( )** method returns the current value of the account.

   The **Customer** class extends **Thread**. Its constructor saves a reference to the shared account. The **run( )** method executes a loop that makes 100000 deposits. Each deposit equals $10.

   The **BankDemo** class first creates one **Account** object. Then 10 **Customer** objects are instantiated and started. The **join( )** method is called to wait for each of these threads to complete. Finally, the balance in the account is displayed.

```
class Account {
  private int balance = 0;

  synchronized void deposit(int amount) {
    balance += amount;
  }

  int getBalance() {
    return balance;
  }
}

class Customer extends Thread {
  Account account;

  Customer(Account account) {
    this.account = account;
  }

  public void run() {
    try {
      for(int i = 0; i < 100000; i++) {
        account.deposit(10);
      }
    }
    catch(Exception e) {
      e.printStackTrace();
    }
  }
}

class BankDemo {
  private final static int NUMCUSTOMERS = 10;

  public static void main(String args[]) {

    // Create account
    Account account = new Account();

    // Create and start customer threads
    Customer customers[] = new Customer[NUMCUSTOMERS];
    for(int i = 0; i < NUMCUSTOMERS; i++) {
      customers[i] = new Customer(account);
      customers[i].start();
    }
```

```
// Wait for customer threads to complete
for(int i = 0; i < NUMCUSTOMERS; i++) {
  try {
    customers[i].join();
  }
  catch(InterruptedException e) {
    e.printStackTrace();
  }
}

// Display account balance
System.out.println(account.getBalance());
  }
}
```

This application takes several seconds to execute. Its output is shown here:

```
10000000
```

Note

*It is important to realize that a statement such as "balance += amount;" is not an atomic operation. Although it appears as only one line in the Java source code, the Java compiler generates several bytecode instructions for it. A context switch may occur between any of these instructions and cause problems. Therefore, it is necessary to prevent this by designating the enclosing method as **synchronized**.*

EXERCISES

1. Remove the **synchronized** modifier from the **deposit( )** method in the preceding example. Rebuild the application and execute it several times. What observations can you make about the results?

2. Rewrite the preceding example to use a **synchronized** statement block instead of a **synchronized** method.

9.4 ## **D**EADLOCK

Deadlock is an error that can be encountered in multithreaded programs. It occurs when two or more threads wait indefinitely for each other to relinquish locks. Assume that thread 1 holds a lock on object 1 and waits for a lock on object 2. Thread 2 holds a lock on object 2 and waits for a lock on object 1. Neither of these threads may proceed. Each waits forever for the other to relinquish the lock it needs.

Deadlock situations can also arise that involve more than two threads. Assume that thread 1 waits for a lock held by thread 2. Thread 2 waits for a lock held by thread 3. Thread 3 waits for a lock held by thread 1.

A complete discussion of deadlock is beyond the scope of this book. However, you must be careful to avoid these types of design flaws. Unfortunately, many deadlock errors occur only when threads are scheduled in a certain sequence.

One strategy that is sometimes used for deadlock prevention is to assign a precedence to all lockable objects and never acquire locks out of sequence.

EXAMPLE

1. This example illustrates how a deadlock error can occur. Class **A** has two **synchronized** methods named **a1( )** and **a2( )**. It also has an instance variable **b** that holds a reference to an object of class **B**. The **a1( )** method calls the **b2( )** method of that object.

   Similarly, class **B** has two **synchronized** methods named **b1( )** and **b2( )**. It also has an instance variable **a** that holds a reference to an object of class **A**. The **b1( )** method calls the **a2( )** method of that object.

   Class **Thread1** extends **Thread** and executes a loop that invokes the **a1( )** method of an **A** object. Class **Thread2** extends **Thread** and executes a loop that invokes the **b1( )** method of a **B** object.

   The **DeadlockDemo** class creates instances of the **A** and **B** classes. It then instantiates the **Thread1** and **Thread2** classes and starts these threads. The **join( )** method is used to wait for these threads to complete. A message is displayed if this occurs.

```
class A {
  B b;

  synchronized void a1() {
    System.out.println("Starting a1");
    b.b2();
  }

  synchronized void a2() {
    System.out.println("Starting a2");
  }
}

class B {
  A a;

  synchronized void b1() {
    System.out.println("Starting b1");
    a.a2();
  }

  synchronized void b2() {
    System.out.println("Starting b2");
  }
}

class Thread1 extends Thread {
  A a;

  Thread1(A a) {
    this.a = a;
  }

  public void run() {
    for(int i = 0; i < 100000; i++)
      a.a1();
  }
}

class Thread2 extends Thread {
  B b;

  Thread2(B b) {
    this.b = b;
  }
```

```
  public void run() {
    for(int i = 0; i < 100000; i++)
      b.b1();
  }
}

class DeadlockDemo {

  public static void main(String args[]) {

    // Create objects
    A a = new A();
    B b = new B();
    a.b = b;
    b.a = a;

    // Create threads
    Thread1 t1 = new Thread1(a);
    Thread2 t2 = new Thread2(b);
    t1.start();
    t2.start();

    // Wait for threads to complete
    try {
      t1.join();
      t2.join();
    }
    catch(Exception e) {
      e.printStackTrace();
    }

    // Display message
    System.out.println("Done!");
  }
}
```

The following is sample output from this application:

```
Starting a1
Starting b2
Starting a1
Starting b2
Starting a1
Starting b2
Starting a1
Starting b2
Starting a1
Starting b1
```

Here, the first thread successfully executes four loops. Each time the **a1( )** method calls the **b2( )** method and returns. The first thread calls **a1( )** again. Then a context switch occurs and the second thread calls **b1( )**. Deadlock occurs because the second thread waits for a lock on the **A** object and the first thread waits for a lock on the **B** object.

You may encounter a different sequence of output messages on your machine. However, the potential for deadlock is always present. This is why these problems can be so difficult to identify.

EXERCISE

1. Examine the following program and comment on whether deadlock can occur.

```java
class X {

  synchronized void x1() {
    x2();
  }

  synchronized void x2() {
  }
}

class ThreadX extends Thread {
  X x;

  ThreadX(X x) {
    this.x = x;
  }

  public void run() {
    for(int i = 0; i < 100000; i++)
      x.x1();
  }
}

class DeadlockQuestion {
  private final static int NUMTHREADS = 10;

  public static void main(String args[]) {
```

```
    // Create object
    X x = new X();

    // Create and start threads
    ThreadX threads[] = new ThreadX[NUMTHREADS];
    for(int i = 0; i < NUMTHREADS; i++) {
      threads[i] = new ThreadX(x);
      threads[i].start();
    }

    // Wait for threads to complete
    for(int i = 0; i < NUMTHREADS; i++)
      try {
        threads[i].join();
      }
      catch(Exception e) {
        e.printStackTrace();
      }

    // Display message
    System.out.println("Done!");
  }
}
```

9.5   *T*HREAD COMMUNICATION

The preceding section described how deadlock can occur if a thread acquires a lock and does not relinquish it. This section demonstrates how threads can cooperate with each other. You will see that a thread can temporarily release a lock so other threads can have an opportunity to execute a **synchronized** method or statement block. That lock can be acquired again at a later time.

The class **Object** defines three methods that allow threads to communicate with each other. The **wait( )** method allows a thread that is executing a **synchronized** method or statement block on that object to release the lock and wait for a notification from another thread. It has these three forms:

void wait( ) throws InterruptedException
void wait(long *msec*) throws InterruptedException
void wait(long *msec*, int *nsec*) throws InterruptedException

The first form causes the current thread to wait indefinitely. The second form causes the current thread to wait for *msec* milliseconds. The last form causes the current thread to wait for *msec* milliseconds plus *nsec* nanoseconds.

The **notify( )** method allows a thread that is executing a **synchronized** method or statement block to notify another thread that is waiting for a lock on this object. If several threads are waiting, only one of these is selected. The selection criteria are determined by the implementer of the JVM. The signature of this method is shown here:

```
void notify()
```

The **notifyAll( )** method allows a thread that is executing a **synchronized** method or statement block to notify all threads that are waiting for a lock on this object. The signature of this method is shown here:

```
void notifyAll()
```

It is important to understand that when a thread executes the **notify( )** or **notifyAll( )** method, it does not relinquish its lock at that moment. This occurs only when it leaves the **synchronized** method or statement block.

The net effect of the **notify( )** and **notifyAll( )** methods is that one thread resumes its execution of the **synchronized** method or statement block. It returns from the **wait( )** method and continues executing the next statement.

Because these three methods are implemented by **Object**, they are inherited by all classes. This is an extremely powerful design. Any class has the potential to take advantage of Java's multi-threading capabilities.

EXAMPLE

1. This example shows how multiple threads may communicate with each other. The application has one thread that produces a sequence of integers. These are written to a queue. Several consumer threads read the numbers from the queue and display them.

   The **Producer** class extends **Thread**. Its constructor receives and saves a reference to a **Queue** object. The **run( )** method executes an infinite loop that calls **add( )** to add new entries to the queue.

The **Consumer** class extends **Thread**. Its constructor receives and saves a string and a reference to a **Queue** object. The string is used to uniquely identify that object. Its **run( )** method executes an infinite loop that calls **remove( )** to remove entries from the queue. Each entry is displayed.

The **Queue** class provides temporary storage for the integers generated by the **Producer** object. An array is used to save this data. Variables **r** and **w** indicate the locations at which data should be read and written, respectively. The total number of unread entries in the array is saved in **count**.

The **add( )** method first checks if the array is full. If so, it calls **wait( )**. Otherwise, the integer is written to the array and the **w** and **count** variables are updated. Finally, all waiting threads are notified.

The **remove( )** method first checks if the array is empty. If so, it calls **wait( )**. Otherwise, an integer is read from the array and the **r** and **count** variables are updated. Finally, all waiting threads are notified.

The **main( )** method of **ProducerConsumers** creates and starts one queue, one producer, and three consumers.

```
class Producer extends Thread {
  Queue queue;

  Producer(Queue queue) {
    this.queue = queue;
  }

  public void run() {
    int i = 0;
    while(true) {
      queue.add(i++);
    }
  }
}

class Consumer extends Thread {
  String str;
  Queue queue;

  Consumer(String str, Queue queue) {
```

```java
      this.str = str;
      this.queue = queue;
   }

   public void run() {
     while(true) {
       System.out.println(str + ": " + queue.remove());
     }
   }
}

class Queue {
  private final static int SIZE = 10;
  int array[] = new int[SIZE];
  int r = 0;
  int w = 0;
  int count = 0;

  synchronized void add(int i) {

    // Wait while the queue is full
    while(count == SIZE) {
      try {
        wait();
      }
      catch(InterruptedException ie) {
        ie.printStackTrace();
        System.exit(0);
      }
    }

    // Add data to array and adjust write pointer
    array[w++] = i;
    if(w >= SIZE)
      w = 0;

    // Increment count
    ++count;

    // Notify waiting threads
    notifyAll();
  }

  synchronized int remove() {

    // Wait while the queue is empty
```

```
      while(count == 0) {
        try {
          wait();
        }
        catch(InterruptedException ie) {
          ie.printStackTrace();
          System.exit(0);
        }
      }

      // Read data from array and adjust read pointer
      int element = array[r++];
      if(r >= SIZE)
        r = 0;

      // Decrement count
      --count;

      // Notify waiting threads
      notifyAll();

      // Return element from array
      return element;
    }
}

class ProducerConsumers {

  public static void main(String args[]) {
    Queue queue = new Queue();
    new Producer(queue).start();
    new Consumer("ConsumerA", queue).start();
    new Consumer("ConsumerB", queue).start();
    new Consumer("ConsumerC", queue).start();
  }
}
```

EXERCISE

1. What is the output from this application?

```
class K {
  boolean flag;
```

```java
    synchronized void k1() {
      if(flag == false) {
        flag = true;
        try {
          System.out.println("Calling wait");
          wait();
        }
        catch(Exception e) {
          e.printStackTrace();
        }
      }
      else {
        flag = false;
        System.out.println("Calling notifyAll");
        notifyAll();
      }
    }
}

class ThreadK extends Thread {
  K k;

  ThreadK(K k) {
    this.k = k;
  }

  public void run() {
    k.k1();
    System.out.println("Done");
  }
}

class WaitNotifyDemo {

  public static void main(String args[]) {

    K k = new K();
    new ThreadK(k).start();
    new ThreadK(k).start();
  }
}
```

Mastery
Skills Check

At this point you should be able to perform the following exercises and answer the questions.

1. What is a thread?

2. Name two ways to create a thread.

3. What is deadlock and how can it occur?

4. How can threads communicate with each other?

5. What is the expected behavior of the following program?

```java
class NormPriorityThread extends Thread {

  public void run() {
    for(int i = 0; i < 100000000; i++) {
    }
  }
}


class LowPriorityThread extends Thread {

  public void run() {
    setPriority(MIN_PRIORITY);
    try {
      for(int i = 0; i < Integer.MAX_VALUE; i++)
        System.out.println("Low priority thread: " + i);
    }
    catch(Exception e) {
      e.printStackTrace();
    }
  }
}


class PriorityDemo {

  public static void main(String args[]) {

    // Create and start low priority thread
    LowPriorityThread lpt = new LowPriorityThread();
    lpt.start();
```

```
          // Wait for 2000 milliseconds
          try {
            Thread.sleep(2000);
          }
          catch(Exception e) {
            e.printStackTrace();
          }

          // Create and start normal priority thread
          NormPriorityThread npt = new NormPriorityThread();
          npt.start();
        }
      }
```

6. Write a multithreaded program that simulates how several users may share a limited pool of resources. Each user is represented by a separate thread. A coordinator manages access to these resources. Each user executes an infinite loop that contains the following steps: (a) request a resource from the coordinator, (b) use the resource for five to ten seconds, (c) release the resource to the coordinator, and (d) sleep for three seconds. Display a message each time a user uses a resource. That message should identify the user and the resource.

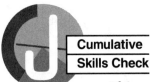

**Cumulative
Skills Check**

This section checks how well you have integrated material in this chapter with that from the preceding chapters.

1. What happens if an exception is generated in a **synchronized** method or statement block? Why is the language defined in this manner?

2. Write a program to display a random integer between 5 and 10 every three seconds.

3. Write a multithreaded program that simulates a set of grasshoppers jumping around in a box. Each grasshopper jumps to a different location every 2 to 12 seconds. Display the new location of a grasshopper after each of these jumps.

10

Introducing the Java Class Libraries

I N order to become a proficient Java programmer, you must understand both the language and the class libraries. The preceding chapters described the primary features of the Java language. The remainder of this book describes the most commonly used functionality in the Java class libraries. Keep in mind that the class libraries are quite extensive. The core functionality alone is organized into more than two dozen classes.

This chapter begins our look at the class libraries by examining the **java.util** package. The utility classes provide functionality that can be used in a wide variety of programming contexts. For example, you have the ability to generate random numbers, work with date and time information, and use calendars. Data structures such as vectors, hash tables, and stacks are available. A class is provided so you can process input strings.

The classes and interfaces demonstrated in this chapter are only a small subset of the **java.util** package. However, they are representative of that package and are very frequently used in the remaining chapters.

Review
Skills Check

Before proceeding, you should be able to answer these questions and perform these exercises.

1. What is the difference between the **notify( )** and **notifyAll( )** methods of **Object**?

2. A set of ten mice continually enter and exit a box. Each mouse spends between 10 and 20 seconds out of the box, enters, spends between 5 and 8 seconds in the box, and exits. A maximum of four mice may be in the box at any time. If the box is full when another mouse wishes to enter, that animal must wait. Write a multithreaded program to simulate the behavior of this system. Establish a separate thread to manage the behavior of each mouse. Display the number of mice inside the box each time a mouse enters or exits.

3. Write a multithreaded program to illustrate the functionality of the **join( )** method of **Thread**. Start three threads named "A1," "A2," and "A3." Each of these threads sleeps for an interval between 10 and 30 seconds and then terminates. Use the **join( )** method to wait for all of these threads to terminate. Then start two threads named "B1" and "B2." Each of these threads sleeps for an interval between 10 and 30 seconds and then terminates. Use the **join( )** method to wait for all of these threads to terminate.

10.1 THE RANDOM CLASS

The **Random** class allows you to generate random **double, float, int,** or **long** numbers. You may also generate numbers that have a Gaussian distribution. This can be very valuable if you are building a simulation of a real-world system. Input data frequently follows such a distribution.

This class provides the following constructors:

```
Random()
Random(long seed)
```

Here, *seed* is a value to initialize the random number generator. The first form uses the current time as the seed.

Table 10-1 summarizes some instance methods provided by this class.

Method	Description
void nextBytes(byte *buffer*[ ])	Fills *buffer* with random numbers.
double nextDouble( )	Returns a random **double** value.
float nextFloat( )	Returns a random **float** value.
double nextGaussian( )	Returns a random **double** value. Numbers obtained from repeated calls to this method have a Gaussian distribution with a mean of 0 and a standard deviation of 1.
int nextInt( )	Returns a random **int** value.
long getLong( )	Returns a random **long** value.
void setSeed(long *seed*)	Seeds the random number generator with *seed.*

TABLE 10-1 *Some Methods Defined by* ***Random*** ▼

EXAMPLE

1. The example generates and displays ten random integers. The default constructor for the **Random** class creates a random number generator. The numbers are obtained by calling the **nextInt( )** method of the generator.

```java
import java.util.*;

class RandomInts {

  public static void main(String args[]) {

    // Create random number generator
    Random generator = new Random();

    // Generate and display 10 random integers
    for(int i = 0; i < 10; i++)
      System.out.println(generator.nextInt());
  }
}
```

EXERCISES

1. Write an application that generates a set of random numbers with a Gaussian distribution. Compute and display the mean value of those numbers. Your program should accept one command-line argument. This is an integer value that determines the number of random numbers to generate. If a command-line argument is missing, generate 100 such numbers. It is not necessary to display the individual numbers.

2. Write an application that uses a seed value to create a random number generator. Display ten numbers obtained from that source. Then use the same seed value to create a second random number generator. Display ten numbers obtained from that source. How do the numbers compare?

10.2 *T*HE DATE CLASS

The **Date** class encapsulates information about a specific date and time. It provides the following constructors:

Date( )
Date(long *msec*)

The first form returns an object that represents the current date and time. The second form returns an object that represents the date and time *msec* milliseconds after the epoch. The epoch is defined as midnight on January 1, 1970 GMT (Greenwich Mean Time).

Table 10-2 summarizes some instance methods provided by this class.

EXAMPLE

1. The following application instantiates a **Date** object with its default constructor. That object encapsulates the current date and time information. Its string equivalent is displayed. Another **Date** object is then instantiated by using a different constructor. Its argument is the number of milliseconds since January 1, 1970 GMT. The string equivalent of this value is displayed.

```
import java.util.*;

class DateDemo {

  public static void main(String args[]) {

    // Get date object initialized
    // to current date and time
    Date currentDate = new Date();

    // Display current date
    System.out.println(currentDate);

    // Get date object initialized to
    // the epoch (Jan 1 1970)
    Date epoch = new Date(0);

    // Display epoch date
    System.out.println(epoch);
  }
}
```

Output from this application is shown here:

```
Sun Feb 08 10:15:23 EST 1998
Wed Dec 31 19:00:00 EST 1969
```

Method	Description
boolean after(Date *d*)	Returns **true** if *d* is after the current date. Otherwise, returns **false**.
boolean before(Date *d*)	Returns **true** if *d* is before the current date. Otherwise, returns **false**.
boolean equals(Date *d*)	Returns **true** if *d* has the same value as the current date. Otherwise, returns **false**.
long getTime( )	Returns the number of milliseconds since the epoch.
void setTime(long *msec*)	Sets the date and time of the current object to represent *msec* milliseconds since the epoch.
String toString( )	Returns the string equivalent of the date.

TABLE 10-2   *Some Instance Methods Defined by* **Date** ▼

EXERCISES

1. Write a program that obtains the number of milliseconds since the epoch and uses this value to calculate the number of days since January 1, 1970.

2. Write a program that adds 100 days to the current date. Display the new date and time.

10.3 *T*HE CALENDAR AND GREGORIAN CALENDAR CLASSES

The abstract **Calendar** class allows you to interpret date and time information. This class defines several **int** constants that are used when you get or set components of the calendar. These are listed here:

AM	AM_PM	APRIL
AUGUST	DATE	DAY_OF_MONTH
DAY_OF_WEEK	DAY_OF_WEEK_IN_MONTH	DAY_OF_YEAR
DECEMBER	DST_OFFSET	ERA
FEBRUARY	FIELD_COUNT	FRIDAY

HOUR	HOUR_OF_DAY	JANUARY
JULY	JUNE	MARCH
MAY	MILLISECOND	MINUTE
MONDAY	MONTH	NOVEMBER
OCTOBER	PM	SATURDAY
SECOND	SEPTEMBER	SUNDAY
THURSDAY	TUESDAY	UNDECIMBER
WEDNESDAY	WEEK_OF_MONTH	WEEK_OF_YEAR
YEAR	ZONE_OFFSET	

Note *The UNDECIMBER constant is used in lunar calendars to represent the thirteenth month of the year.*

The **Calendar** class does not have public constructors. Instead, you may use the static **getInstance( )** method to obtain a calendar initialized to the current date and time. One of its forms is shown here:

Calendar getInstance( )

Table 10-3 summarizes some instance methods provided by this class.

The **GregorianCalendar** class is a concrete subclass of **Calendar**. It provides the logic to manage date and time information according to the rules of the Gregorian calendar. This is the calendar that numbers years starting at the birth of Christ.

It provides several constructors. Some of these are shown here:

GregorianCalendar( )
GregorianCalendar(int *year*, int *month*, int *date*)
GregorianCalendar(int *year*, int *month*, int *date*, int *hour*, int *minute*, int *sec*)
GregorianCalendar(int *year*, int *month*, int *date*, int *hour*, int *minute*)

The first form creates an object initialized with the current date and time. The other forms allow you to specify how various date and time components are initialized.

Method	Description
abstract boolean after(Object *calendarObj*)	Returns **true** if the invoking **Calendar** object contains a date later than the one specified by *calendarObj*. Otherwise, it returns **false**.
abstract boolean before(Object *calendarObj*)	Returns **true** if the invoking **Calendar** object contains a date earlier than the one specified by *calendarObj*. Otherwise, it returns **false**.
abstract boolean equals(Object *calendarObj*)	Returns **true** if the invoking **Calendar** object contains a date equal to the one specified by *calendarObj*. Otherwise, it returns **false**.
final int get(int *calendarField*)	Returns the value of one component of the invoking object. The component is indicated by *calendarField*. Some examples of the components that can be requested are **Calendar.YEAR**, **Calendar.MONTH**, **Calendar.MINUTE**, and so forth.
static Calendar getInstance( )	Returns a **Calendar** object for the default locale and time zone.
final Date getTime( )	Returns a **Date** object equivalent to the time of the invoking object.
final void set(int *year*, int *month*, int *date*, int *hour*, int *minute*, int *second*)	Sets various date and time components of the invoking object.
final void setTime(Date *d*)	Sets various date and time components of the invoking object. This information is obtained from the **Date** object *d*.

TABLE 10-3 *Some Methods Defined by **Calendar*** ▼

The class provides all of the methods defined by **Calendar** and also adds the **isLeapYear( )** method shown here:

boolean isLeapYear( )

This method returns **true** if the current year is a leap year. Otherwise, it returns **false**.

EXAMPLE

1. This example illustrates how to use some methods provided by the **Calendar** class. The static **getInstance( )** method returns a **Calendar** object initialized with the current date and time. The **get( )** method returns information about the field specified by its argument.

```
import java.util.*;

class CalendarDemo {

  public static void main(String args[]) {

    Calendar calendar = Calendar.getInstance();
    System.out.println(calendar.get(Calendar.YEAR));
    System.out.println(calendar.get(Calendar.HOUR));
    System.out.println(calendar.get(
      Calendar.HOUR_OF_DAY));
    System.out.println(calendar.get(Calendar.MINUTE));
  }
}
```

Sample output from this application is shown here:

```
1998
7
19
41
```

EXERCISE

1. Write an application that demonstrates how to use some methods provided by the **GregorianCalendar** class. Instantiate an object of this class. Display the current year and also test if it is a leap year. Also present the current month, week of year, week of month, day of year, and day of week.

| 10.4 | # THE VECTOR CLASS AND ENUMERATION INTERFACE |

The **Vector** class is one of the most important in all of the Java class libraries. Recall that you cannot expand the size of a static array. You may think of a vector as a dynamic array that automatically expands as more elements are added to it. All vectors are created with some initial capacity. When space is needed to accommodate more elements, the capacity is automatically increased. It is for this reason that vectors are commonly used in Java programming.

The class supports the following constructors:

```
Vector( )
Vector(int n)
Vector(int n, int delta)
```

The first form creates a vector with an initial capacity of ten elements. The second form creates a vector with an initial capacity of *n* elements. The final form creates a vector with an initial capacity of *n* elements that increases by *delta* elements each time it needs to expand.

Table 10-4 summarizes the instance methods provided by this class.

Method	**Description**
void addElement(Object *obj*)	Adds *obj* to the vector.
int capacity( )	Returns the capacity.
Object clone( )	Returns a duplicate of the current object.
boolean contains(Object *obj*)	Returns **true** if *obj* is contained by the vector. Otherwise, returns **false**.
void copyInto(Object *array*[ ])	Copies the elements of the current object to *array*.
Object elementAt(int *index*)	Returns the element at *index*.
Enumeration elements( )	Returns an enumeration of the elements.
void ensureCapacity(int *minimum*)	Sets the minimum capacity to *minimum*.
Object firstElement( )	Returns the first element.
int indexOf(Object *obj*)	Searches for the first occurrence of *obj*. Returns its index or –1 if *obj* is not in the vector.

TABLE 10-4   *Methods Defined by* **Vector** ▼

Method	Description
int indexOf(Object *obj*, int *start*)	Searches for the first occurrence of *obj* beginning at index *start*. Returns its index or -1 if *obj* is not in the vector.
void insertElementAt(Object *obj*, int *index*)	Adds *obj* to the vector at *index*.
boolean isEmpty( )	Returns **true** if the vector is empty. Otherwise, returns **false**.
Object lastElement( )	Returns the last element.
int lastIndexOf(Object *obj*)	Searches for the last occurrence of *obj*. Returns its index or -1 if *obj* is not in the vector.
int lastIndexOf(Object *obj*, int *start*)	Searches for the last occurrence of *obj* before index *start*. Returns its index or -1 if *obj* is not in the vector.
void removeAllElements( )	Removes all elements.
boolean removeElement(Object *obj*)	Removes the first instance of *obj* from the vector. Returns **true** if successful. Otherwise, returns **false**.
void removeElementAt(int *index*)	Removes the element at *index*.
void setElementAt(Object *obj*, int *index*)	Assigns *obj* to the element at *index*.
void setSize(int *size*)	Sets the number of elements to *size*. Elements beyond *size* are discarded.
int size( )	Returns the number of elements currently in the vector.
String toString( )	Returns the string equivalent of the vector.
void trimToSize( )	Sets the capacity to the number of elements currently in the vector.

TABLE 10-4 *Methods Defined by **Vector** (continued)* ▼

The **Enumeration** interface allows you to iterate through a set of objects. It defines the two methods shown here:

```
boolean hasMoreElements( )
Object nextElement( )
```

The first method returns **true** if more elements are available. Otherwise, it returns **false**. The second method returns the next available element.

This interface is implemented by the **Vector** class.

EXAMPLES

1. This example illustrates the basics of working with vectors. The default constructor is used to create a vector, and objects are added to it. Note that since **addElement( )** accepts one argument of class **Object**, many different types of objects can be added to the same vector. The **println( )** method is invoked to display the vector. The **insertElementAt( )** and **removeElementAt( )** methods are then demonstrated.

```java
import java.util.*;

class VectorDemo {

  public static void main(String args[]) {

    // Create a vector and its elements
    Vector vector = new Vector();
    vector.addElement(new Integer(5));
    vector.addElement(new Float(-14.14f));
    vector.addElement(new String("Hello"));
    vector.addElement(new Long(120000000));
    vector.addElement(new Double(-23.45e-11));

    // Display the vector elements
    System.out.println(vector);

    // Insert an element into the vector
    String s = new String("String to be inserted");
    vector.insertElementAt(s, 1);
    System.out.println(vector);

    // Remove an element from the vector
    vector.removeElementAt(3);
    System.out.println(vector);
  }
}
```

Output from this application is shown here:

```
[5, -14.14, Hello, 120000000, -2.345E-10]
[5, String to be inserted, -14.14, Hello, 120000000, -2.345E-10]
[5, String to be inserted, -14.14, 120000000, -2.345E-10]
```

The output appears as shown because the **Vector** class overrides the **toString( )** method to return a string equivalent of the vector.

2. This example illustrates the basics of working with the **Enumeration** interface. The application creates a vector and adds several elements to it. Then an **Enumeration** object is obtained from the **elements( )** method of the vector. A loop is then used to iterate through the vector elements. Notice that **hasMoreElements( )** tests if the enumeration has unread elements. If this method returns **true**, the **nextElement( )** method is called to obtain the next element.

```java
import java.util.*;

class EnumerationDemo {

  public static void main(String args[]) {

    // Create a vector and its elements
    Vector vector = new Vector();
    vector.addElement(new Integer(5));
    vector.addElement(new Float(-14.14f));
    vector.addElement(new String("Hello"));
    vector.addElement(new Long(120000000));
    vector.addElement(new Double(-23.45e-11));

    // Display the elements of the vector
    Enumeration e = vector.elements();
    while(e.hasMoreElements()) {
      Object obj = e.nextElement();
      System.out.println(obj);
    }
  }
}
```

Output from this application is shown here:

```
5
-14.14
Hello
120000000
-2.345E-10
```

1. Write an application that generates between 10 and 25 random **double** values that have a Gaussian distribution. Convert these to **Double** objects, save them in a vector, and display the elements of the vector. Use an **Enumeration** to iterate through the elements.

2. Write a program that converts each of its command-line arguments to a **Double** object and stores it in a vector. Then display the elements in the reverse order of how they were entered.

10.5 ▮ *T* HE STACK CLASS

The **Stack** class extends **Vector** and provides a LIFO (last-in, first-out) stack. Here is an excellent example of the power of object-oriented programming. The **Vector** class provides the functionality of a dynamic array. This capability is also needed to implement the **Stack** class. The **Stack** class reuses this implementation and also provides methods to push, pop, and otherwise manipulate the stack. You will see that class inheritance is commonly used throughout the Java class libraries to achieve maximum code reuse.

Table 10-5 summarizes the methods provided by this class.

Method	Description
boolean empty()	Returns **true** if the stack is empty. Otherwise, returns **false**.
Object peek() throws EmptyStackException	Returns the object at the top of the stack but does not remove it from the stack.
Object pop() throws EmptyStackException	Returns the object at the top of the stack and removes it from the stack.
Object push(Object *obj*)	Pushes *obj* onto the stack and also returns *obj*.
int search(Object *obj*)	Searches the stack for *obj*. If not found, returns –1. Otherwise, returns the index at which *obj* is located. The top of the stack is index 1.

TABLE 10-5 *Methods Defined by* **Stack** ▼

EXAMPLE

1. The following application converts each of its command-line arguments to an **Integer** object and pushes it onto a stack. When all command-line arguments have been processed, the elements of the stack are popped and displayed.

```
import java.util.*;

class PushPop {

  public static void main(String args[]) {

    // Create stack
    Stack stack = new Stack();

    // Push elements onto stack
    for(int i = 0; i < args.length; i++)
      stack.push(new Integer(args[i]));

    // Pop elements from stack and display
    while(!stack.empty()) {
      Object obj = stack.pop();
      System.out.println(obj);
    }
  }
}
```

Assume that the user enters the following command:

```
java PushPop 1 2 3 4 5
```

Output from this application would be as shown here:

```
5
4
3
2
1
```

EXERCISE

1. Modify the example so that duplicate values are not stored on the stack.

| 10.6 | ## THE HASHTABLE CLASS |

Hash tables are commonly used in Java programming. They allow you to easily store and retrieve objects. Each entry in a hash table contains a key and a value. Both the key and the value are objects. The keys must be unique; the values need not be. You do not retrieve elements from a hash table by index. Instead, a key is used to obtain the corresponding value. Another name for this type of data structure is *associative array*.

The **Hashtable** class allows you to create and use hash tables. The following are some of its constructors:

```
Hashtable( )
Hashtable(int n)
Hashtable(int n, float lf)
```

Here, *n* is the initial capacity of the hash table and *lf* is its load factor. The latter is a number between 0 and 1. The size of the hash table is automatically increased when the number of entries in the hash table exceeds the product of the capacity and load factor.

Table 10-6 summarizes some of the methods provided by this class.

Method	Description
boolean contains(Object *v*) throws NullPointerException	Returns **true** if the hash table contains *v* as one of its values. Otherwise, returns **false**. The method throws a **NullPointerException** if *v* is null.
boolean containsKey(Object *k*)	Returns **true** if the hash table contains *k* as one of its keys. Otherwise, returns **false**.
boolean containsValue(Object *v*)	Returns **true** if the hash table contains *v* as one of its values. Otherwise, returns **false**.
Enumeration elements( )	Returns an enumeration of the values.
Object get(Object *k*)	Returns the value associated with the key *k*.
boolean isEmpty( )	Returns **true** if the hash table is empty. Otherwise, returns **false**.
Enumeration keys( )	Returns an enumeration of the keys.
Object put(Object *k*, Object *v*) throws NullPointerException	Puts a key/value pair into the hash table. The key is *k* and the value is *v*. The method throws a **NullPointerException** if *k* or *v* is **null**.
Object remove(Object *k*)	Removes the key/value pair whose key is *k*.
int size( )	Returns the number of keys.
String toString( )	Returns the string equivalent of this hash table.

TABLE 10-6   *Some Methods Defined by **Hashtable** ▼*

EXAMPLE

1. This example illustrates the basics of working with a hash table.

```java
import java.util.*;

class HashtableDemo {

  public static void main(String args[]) {

    // Create a hash table and populate it
    Hashtable hashtable = new Hashtable();
    hashtable.put("apple", "red");
    hashtable.put("strawberry", "red");
    hashtable.put("lime", "green");
    hashtable.put("banana", "yellow");
    hashtable.put("orange", "orange");

    // Display the elements of the hash table
    Enumeration e = hashtable.keys();
    while(e.hasMoreElements()) {
      Object k = e.nextElement();
      Object v = hashtable.get(k);
      System.out.println("key = " + k + "; value = " + v);
    }

    // Display the value for 'apple'
    System.out.print("\nThe color of an apple is: ");
    Object v = hashtable.get("apple");
    System.out.println(v);
  }
}
```

Output from this application is shown here:

```
key = strawberry; value = red
key = orange; value = orange
key = apple; value = red
key = lime; value = green
key = banana; value = yellow

The color of an apple is: red
```

1. Write an application that uses a hash table to store information about people. Use the social security number as a key and a **Person** object as a value. A **Person** object should store the following information: name, telephone number, fax number, and e-mail address. Display all of the key/value pairs in the hash table.

10.7 *T*HE STRINGTOKENIZER CLASS

The **StringTokenizer** class allows you to parse a string into tokens. The characters that act as delimiters between tokens can be specified. This functionality can be very useful in some types of applications. For example, you may need to build a program that processes formatted data from a file. Compilers and interpreters also require the ability to examine a string and segment it into tokens according to a set of rules.

This class provides the following constructors:

StringTokenizer(String *str*)
StringTokenizer(String *str*, String *delimiters*)
StringTokenizer(String *str*, String *delimiters*, boolean *delimitersAreTokens*)

Here, *str* is the string to be parsed and *delimiters* contains the characters that separate tokens. If *delimitersAreTokens* is **true**, the tokenizer returns the delimiters as tokens. Otherwise, the delimiters are not returned from the tokenizer.

This class implements the **Enumeration** interface that was discussed early in this chapter. Table 10-7 summarizes some of the methods provided by this class.

Method	Descriptor
int countTokens( )	Returns the number of tokens in the string.
boolean hasMoreTokens( )	Returns **true** if there are more tokens. Otherwise, returns **false**.
String nextToken( )	Returns the next token.
String nextToken(String *delimiters*)	Returns the next token and defines *delimiters* as the set of the delimiter characters.

TABLE 10-7 *Some Methods Defined by StringTokenizer* ▼

EXAMPLE

1. The following application illustrates how to use a string tokenizer. The arguments to the constructor are the string to be parsed and the delimiter characters. The forward slash is the only delimiter used in this example. If **hasMoreTokens( )** returns **true**, there is at least one unread token. The **nextToken( )** method is called to obtain its value.

```java
import java.util.*;

class StringTokenizerDemo {

  public static void main(String args[]) {

    String str =
      "123/45.6/-11.2/41/-90.1/100/99.99/-50/-20";
    StringTokenizer st = new StringTokenizer(str, "/");
    while(st.hasMoreTokens()) {
      String s = st.nextToken();
      System.out.println(s);
    }
  }
}
```

Output from this application is shown here:

```
123
45.6
-11.2
41
-90.1
100
99.99
-50
-20
```

EXERCISE

1. Rewrite the example to use the methods defined by the **Enumeration** interface.

Mastery
Skills Check

At this point you should be able to answer these questions and perform these exercises:

1. What is a vector?

2. What is an enumeration?

3. What is a hash table?

4. Write a program that computes and displays the number of days until Christmas.

5. Write a program that accepts the name of a city as its command-line argument. Display the name of the country in which that city is located. Store the city and country strings in a hash table. Provide appropriate feedback if the user does not include a command-line argument or specifies a city that is not in the hash table.

Cumulative
Skills Check

This section checks how well you have integrated the material in this chapter with that of the earlier chapters.

1. Write an application that displays the calendar for the current month.

2. An application consists of ten tasks. There is a pool of four resources. Each task executes an infinite loop in which it acquires a resource for its exclusive use, uses that resource for one to two seconds, releases the resource, and sleeps for eight seconds. Design and build a multithreaded application that provides this functionality. Use a stack to store the available resources.

11

Input and Output

THIS chapter presents an overview of the most commonly used classes in the **java.io** package. It begins by describing how to work with files and directories. You will then see how to create and use a *stream*. This is an abstraction for either a source or destination of data. Streams are used here to read and write files. You will learn in the next chapter that they can also be used to exchange data over a network connection.

The classes and interfaces used for both character and byte streams are also discussed. These provide sequential access to data. Buffered streams reduce the number of accesses to a physical device, which improves performance. Random access files allow nonsequential access to their data.

A class is provided so you may process a character input stream and generate a sequence of tokens. This is useful for building parsers, compilers, and other tools.

Review
Skills Check

Before proceeding, you should be able to answer these questions and perform these exercises.

1. Construct an application that calculates the number of days remaining in the current year.

2. Design and build a multithreaded application. There is one thread that produces a sequence of integers. These are written to a queue. Several consumer threads read the numbers from the queue and display them. Use a vector for the queue. Enforce a limit on the maximum number of entries that may be in the queue at any time. Provide **synchronized** methods so the threads may safely add and remove queue elements.

3. A factory has ten workers. There is a set of four tools. Each worker executes an infinite loop to acquire two tools, use those tools for 10 to 20 seconds, release the tools, and take a 20-second rest. Design and build a multithreaded application that provides this functionality. Use a stack to hold the available tools. Provide **synchronized** methods so the threads may safely get and release tools.

11.1 FILES AND DIRECTORIES

The **File** class encapsulates information about the properties of a file or directory. These include its read and write permissions, time of last modification, and length. It is also possible to determine the files that are contained in a directory. This is valuable because you can build an application that navigates a directory hierarchy. New directories can be created, and existing files and directories may be deleted or renamed.

The **File** class provides the following constructors:

```
File(String path)
File(String directoryPath, String filename)
File(File directory, String filename)
```

The first form has one parameter that is the *path* to a file or directory. The second form has two parameters. These are the path to a directory and the name of a file in that directory. The last form also has two parameters. These are a **File** object for a directory and the name of a file in that directory. All of these constructors throw a **NullPointerException** if *path* or *filename* is **null**.

File defines two **char** constants. These are **separatorChar** and **pathSeparatorChar**. The former is the character that separates the directory and file portions of a filename. The latter is the character that separates components in a "path-list." Obviously, both of these values are platform dependent. For example, a different value is obtained on a Windows machine than on a UNIX platform.

Table 11-1 summarizes some instance methods provided by this class.

Method	Description
boolean canRead( )	Returns **true** if the file exists and can be read. Otherwise, returns **false**.
boolean canWrite( )	Returns **true** if the file exists and can be written. Otherwise, returns **false**.
boolean delete( )	Deletes the file. Returns **true** if the file is successfully deleted. Otherwise, returns **false**. Note that a directory must be empty before it can be deleted.
boolean equals(Object *obj*)	Returns **true** if the current object and *obj* refer to the same file. Otherwise, returns **false**.
boolean exists( )	Returns **true** if the file exists. Otherwise, returns **false**.
String getAbsolutePath( )	Returns the absolute path to the file.
String getCanonicalPath( )	Returns the canonical path to the file.
String getName( )	Returns the name of the file.
String getParent( )	Returns the parent of the file.
String getPath( )	Returns the path to the file.
boolean isAbsolute( )	Returns **true** if the file path name is absolute. Otherwise, returns **false**.
boolean isDirectory( )	Returns **true** if the file is a directory. Otherwise, returns **false**.
boolean isFile( )	Returns **true** if the file is not a directory. Otherwise, returns **false**.
long lastModified( )	Returns the number of milliseconds between 00:00:00 Greenwich Mean Time, January 1, 1970, and the time of last modification for this file.
long length( )	Returns the number of bytes in the file.
String[ ] list( )	Returns the names of files in the directory.
boolean mkdir( )	Creates a directory with the name of this file. All parent directories must already exist. Returns **true** if the directory was created. Otherwise, returns **false**.
boolean mkdirs( )	Creates a directory with the name of this file. Any missing parent directories are also created. Returns **true** if the directory was created. Otherwise, returns **false**.
boolean renameTo(File *newName*)	Renames the file or directory to *newName*. Returns **true** if the current object has been renamed to *newName*. Otherwise, returns **false**.

TABLE 11-1   *Some Methods Defined by **File***   ▼

EXAMPLE

1. The following application illustrates some of the methods of **File**.

```java
import java.io.*;

class FileDemo {

  public static void main(String args[]) {

    try {

      // Display constants
      System.out.println("pathSeparatorChar = " +
        File.pathSeparatorChar);
      System.out.println("separatorChar = " +
        File.separatorChar);

      // Test some methods
      File file = new File(args[0]);
      System.out.println("getName() = " +
        file.getName());
      System.out.println("getParent() = " +
        file.getParent());
      System.out.println("getAbsolutePath() = " +
        file.getAbsolutePath());
      System.out.println("getCanonicalPath() = " +
        file.getCanonicalPath());
      System.out.println("getPath() = " +
        file.getPath());
      System.out.println("canRead() = " +
        file.canRead());
      System.out.println("canWrite() = " +
        file.canWrite());
    }
    catch(Exception e) {
      e.printStackTrace();
    }
  }
}
```

Assume that the following command is issued on a Windows platform:

```
java FileDemo c:\tyj\examples\io\FileDemo.java
```

In this case, output is as follows:

```
pathSeparatorChar = ;
separatorChar = \
getName() = FileDemo.java
getParent() = c:\tyj\examples\io
getAbsolutePath() = c:\tyj\examples\io\FileDemo.java
getCanonicalPath() = c:\tyj\examples\io\FileDemo.java
getPath() = c:\tyj\examples\io\FileDemo.java
canRead() = true
canWrite() = true
```

EXERCISE

1. Write an application to rename a file. Use the **renameTo( )** method of **File** to accomplish this task. The first command-line argument is the old filename; the second is the new filename.

11.2 *C*HARACTER STREAMS

A *stream* is an abstraction for a source or destination of data. It enables you to use the same techniques to interface with different types of physical devices. For example, an input stream may read its data from a keyboard, file, or memory buffer. An output stream may write its data to a monitor, file, or memory buffer. Other types of devices may also be used as the source or destination for a stream.

There are two types of streams: byte and character. Byte streams allow you to read and write binary data. For example, an application that simulates the behavior of an electric circuit can write a sequence of **float** values to a file. These would represent the value of a signal over a time interval. This binary data could later be retrieved for analysis. You will learn about byte streams later in this chapter.

Character streams allow you to read and write characters and strings. An input character stream converts bytes to characters. An output character stream converts characters to bytes.

You previously learned that Java internally represents characters according to the 16-bit Unicode encoding. However, this may not be the encoding used on a specific machine. Character streams translate between these two formats. A complete discussion of this topic is beyond our scope. It is sufficient to know that the ability to translate between Unicode and other encodings is an important feature because it enables you to write programs that operate correctly for an international marketplace.

Figure 11-1 shows a few of the character streams provided by the **java.io** package. This section discusses the **Writer**, **OutputStreamWriter**, **FileWriter, Reader**, **InputStreamReader**, and **FileReader** classes. The buffered character streams, **BufferedReader** and **BufferedWriter**, are considered in the next section. The important **PrintWriter** class is explained in Section 11-4.

FIGURE 11-1

Some of the Character Stream Classes

▼

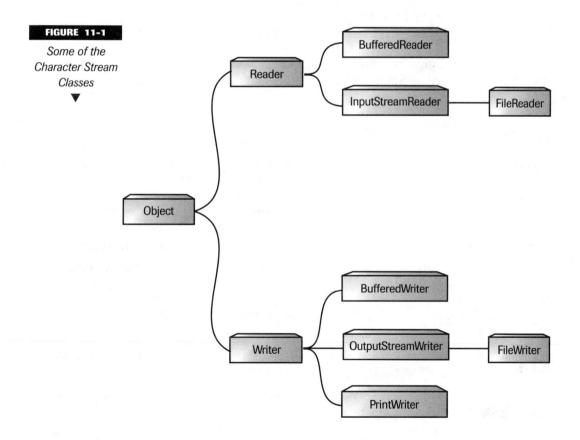

The abstract **Writer** class defines the functionality that is available for all character output streams. It provides the following constructors:

Writer( )
Writer(Object *obj*)

The first form synchronizes on the **Writer** object, and the second form synchronizes on *obj*.

Table 11-2 summarizes the methods provided by this class. All of these can throw an **IOException**. The specific methods that must be implemented by a subclass are indicated in the table. **Writer** provides default implementations of the other methods.

The **OutputStreamWriter** class extends **Writer**. It converts a stream of characters to a stream of bytes. This is done according to the rules of a specific character encoding.

The constructors provided by this class are as follows:

OutputStreamWriter(OutputStream *os*)
OutputStreamWriter(OutputStream *os*, String *encoding*)

Method	Description
void close( )	Closes the output stream. Note: Must be implemented by a subclass.
void flush( )	Writes any buffered data to the physical device represented by that stream. Note: Must be implemented by a subclass.
void write(int *c*)	Writes the lower 16 bits of *c* to the stream.
void write(char *buffer*[ ])	Writes the characters in *buffer* to the stream.
void write(char *buffer*[ ], int *index*, int *size*)	Writes *size* characters from *buffer* starting at position *index* to the stream. Note: Must be implemented by a subclass.
void write(String *s*)	Writes *s* to the stream.
void write(String *s*, int *index*, int *size*)	Writes *size* characters from *s* starting at position *index* to the stream.

TABLE 11-2   *Methods Defined by* **Writer** ▼

Here, *os* is the output stream and *encoding* is the name of a character encoding. The first form of the constructor uses the default character encoding of the user's machine.

The **getEncoding( )** method returns the name of the character encoding. It has this syntax:

String getEncoding( )

The **FileWriter** class extends **OutputStreamWriter** and outputs characters to a file. Some of its constructors are as follows:

FileWriter(String *filepath*) throws IOException
FileWriter(String *filepath*, boolean *append*) throws IOException
FileWriter(File *fileObj*) throws IOException

Here, *filepath* is the full path name of a file and *fileObj* is a **File** object that describes the file. If *append* is **true**, characters are appended to the end of the file. Otherwise, the existing contents of the file are overwritten.

The abstract **Reader** class defines the functionality that is available for all character input streams. Table 11-3 summarizes the methods provided by this class. The specific methods that must be implemented by a subclass are indicated in the table. **Reader** provides default implementations of the other methods.

The **InputStreamReader** class extends **Reader**. It converts a stream of bytes to a stream of characters. This is done according to the rules of a specific character encoding.

The constructors provided by this class are as follows:

InputStreamReader(InputStream *is*)
InputStreamReader(InputStream *is*, String *encoding*)

Here, *is* is the input stream and *encoding* is the name of a character encoding. The first form of the constructor uses the default character encoding of the user's machine.

The **getEncoding( )** method returns the name of the character encoding. It has the following syntax:

String getEncoding( )

Method	Description
void close( )	Closes the input stream. Further read attempts generate an **IOException**. Note: Must be implemented by a subclass.
void mark(int *numChars*)	Places a mark at the current point in the input stream that will remain valid until *numChars* characters are read.
boolean markSupported( )	Returns **true** if **mark( )/reset( )** are supported on this stream.
int read( )	Reads a character from the stream. Waits until data is available.
int read(char *buffer*[ ])	Attempts to read up to *buffer.length* characters into *buffer* and returns the actual number of characters that were successfully read. Waits until data is available.
int read(char *buffer*[ ], int *offset*, int *numChars*)	Attempts to read up to *numChars* characters into *buffer* starting at *buffer*[*offset*] and returns the actual number of characters that were successfully read. Waits until data is available. Note: Must be implemented by a subclass.
boolean ready( )	Returns **true** if the next **read( )** will not wait.
void reset( )	Resets the input pointer to the previously set mark.
int skip(long *numChars*)	Skips over *numChars* bytes of input returning the number of characters actually skipped.

TABLE 11-3   *Methods Defined by **Reader*** ▼

The **FileReader** class extends **InputStreamReader** and inputs characters from a file. Its two most common constructors are shown here:

FileReader(String *filepath*)
FileReader(File *fileObj*)

Either can throw a **FileNotFoundException**. Here, *filepath* is the full path name of a file and *fileObj* is a **File** object that describes the file.

EXAMPLE

1. This example illustrates how to write and read files by using character streams. One application writes to a file. Another reads from a file.

   The program that writes a file is shown in the following listing. It accepts one command-line argument that is the name of the file to create. Twelve strings are written to the file by using the **write( )** method of **FileWriter**.

```java
import java.io.*;

class FileWriterDemo {

  public static void main(String args[]) {

    try {

      // Create a file writer
      FileWriter fw = new FileWriter(args[0]);

      // Write strings to the file
      for(int i = 0; i < 12; i++) {
        fw.write("Line " + i + "\n");
      }

      // Close file writer
      fw.close();
    }
    catch(Exception e) {
      System.out.println("Exception: " + e);
    }
  }
}
```

The program that reads a file is shown in the following listing. It accepts one command-line argument that is the name of the file to read. A **FileReader** object is created. Individual characters are obtained via **read( )** and displayed via **System.out.print( )**. The stream is closed when all characters have been read.

```java
import java.io.*;

class FileReaderDemo {

  public static void main(String args[]) {

    try {

      // Create a file reader
      FileReader fr = new FileReader(args[0]);

      // Read and display characters
```

```
        int i;
        while((i = fr.read()) != -1) {
          System.out.print((char)i);
        }

        // Close file reader
        fr.close();
      }
      catch(Exception e) {
        System.out.println("Exception: " + e);
      }
    }
  }
}
```

To test this example, execute the writer application by entering the following command:

```
java FileWriterDemo output.txt
```

Then execute the reader application by entering this command:

```
java FileReaderDemo output.txt
```

Output should appear as shown here:

```
Line 0
Line 1
Line 2
Line 3
Line 4
Line 5
Line 6
Line 7
Line 8
Line 9
Line 10
Line 11
```

EXERCISES

1. Write an application that reads a file and counts the number of occurrences of each digit between '0' and '9'. Supply the filename as a command-line argument.

2. Write an application that copies one character file to a second character file. The source file is the first command-line argument, and the destination file is the second command-line argument.

11.3 ▐ BUFFERED CHARACTER STREAMS

This section describes how you can buffer input and output for character streams. The following classes are outlined: **BufferedWriter** and **BufferedReader**. The advantage of buffering is that the number of reads and writes to a physical device is reduced. This improves performance.

The **BufferedWriter** class extends **Writer** and buffers output to a character stream. Its constructors are as follows:

BufferedWriter(Writer *w*)
BufferedWriter(Writer *w*, int *bufSize*)

The first form creates a buffered stream using a buffer with a default size. In the second, the size of the buffer is specified by *bufSize*.

This class implements all of the methods defined by **Writer**. In addition, it provides the **newLine( )** method to output a line separator. Its signature is shown below:

void newLine( ) throws IOException

The **BufferedReader** class extends **Reader** and buffers input from a character stream. Its constructors are as follows:

BufferedReader(Reader *r*)
BufferedReader(Reader *r*, int *bufSize*)

The first form creates a buffered stream using a buffer with a default size. In the second, the size of the buffer is specified by *bufSize*.

This class implements all of the functionality defined by **Reader**. In addition, the **readLine( )** method reads newline-terminated strings from a character stream. Its signature is

String readLine( ) throws IOException

This method is frequently used in the examples and exercises of this book. It discards the newline character.

EXAMPLES

1. This example illustrates how to write and read files by using buffered character streams. One application writes to a file and another application reads from a file.

   The program that writes a file is shown in the following listing. It accepts one command-line argument that is the name of the file to create. A **FileWriter** object is created and passed as the argument to the **BufferedWriter** constructor. Twelve strings are written to the file by using the **write( )** method of **BufferedWriter**. Compare this program to **FileWriterDemo** in Section 11-2.

```java
import java.io.*;

class BufferedWriterDemo {

  public static void main(String args[]) {

    try {

      // Create a file writer
      FileWriter fw = new FileWriter(args[0]);

      // Create a buffered writer
      BufferedWriter bw = new BufferedWriter(fw);

      // Write strings to the file
      for(int i = 0; i < 12; i++) {
        bw.write("Line " + i + "\n");
      }

      // Close buffered writer
      bw.close();
    }
    catch(Exception e) {
      System.out.println("Exception: " + e);
    }
  }
}
```

The program that reads a file is shown in the following listing. It accepts one command-line argument that is the name of the file to read. A **FileReader** object is created and passed as the argument to the **BufferedReader** constructor. The **readLine( )** method is used to obtain the individual lines in the file. Note that **readLine( )** discards the newline character it reads. The file reader is closed after all lines have been displayed. Compare this program to **FileReaderDemo** in Section 11-2.

```java
import java.io.*;

class BufferedReaderDemo {

  public static void main(String args[]) {

    try {

      // Create a file reader
      FileReader fr = new FileReader(args[0]);

      // Create a buffered reader
      BufferedReader br = new BufferedReader(fr);

      // Read and display lines from file
      String s;
      while((s = br.readLine()) != null)
        System.out.println(s);

      // Close file reader
      fr.close();
    }
    catch(Exception e) {
      System.out.println("Exception: " + e);
    }
  }
}
```

To test this example, execute the writer application by entering the following command:

```
java BufferedWriterDemo output.txt
```

Then execute the reader application by entering this command:

```
java BufferedReaderDemo output.txt
```

Output should be identical to that of the Section 11-2 example.

2. This example shows how to use a buffered character stream to read input from the keyboard. The program executes an infinite loop that reads a string and displays the number of characters it contains. Each string must be terminated by a newline character.

Notice that **System.in** is passed as the argument to the **InputStreamReader** constructor. This is done because **System.in** is an **InputStream**. The **InputStreamReader** object is then passed as the argument to the **BufferedReader** constructor.

```java
import java.io.*;

class ReadConsole {

  public static void main(String args[]) {

    try {

      // Create an input stream reader
      InputStreamReader isr =
        new InputStreamReader(System.in);

      // Create a buffered reader
      BufferedReader br = new BufferedReader(isr);

      // Read and process lines from console
      String s;
      while((s = br.readLine()) != null) {
        System.out.println(s.length());
      }

      // Close input stream reader
      isr.close();
    }
    catch(Exception e) {
      System.out.println("Exception: " + e);
    }
  }
}
```

EXERCISES

1. Write an application that reads a file, converts each tab character to a space character, and writes its output to another file. The input file is the first command-line argument; the output file is the second command-line argument.

2. Write an application that reads and processes strings from the console. Reverse the sequence of characters in each string and then display it.

11.4 *THE PRINTWRITER CLASS*

The **PrintWriter** class extends **Writer** and displays string equivalents of simple types such as **int**, **float**, **char**, and objects. Its functionality is valuable because it provides a common interface by which many different data types can be output.

This class has these four constructors:

```
PrintWriter(OutputStream outputStream)
PrintWriter(OutputStream outputStream, boolean flushOnNewline)
PrintWriter(Writer writer)
PrintWriter(Writer writer, boolean flushOnNewline)
```

Here, *flushOnNewline* controls whether Java flushes the output stream every time a newline ('\n') character is output. If *flushOnNewline* is **true**, flushing automatically takes place. If **false**, flushing is not automatic. The first and third constructors do not automatically flush. (When a stream is flushed, any data that is internally buffered by the stream is written to the physical device.)

Java's **PrintWriter** objects support the **print( )** and **println( )** methods for all types including **Object**. If an argument is not a simple type, the **PrintWriter** methods will call the object's **toString( )** method and then display the string that is returned from this method.

EXAMPLE

1. This example illustrates how to use some of the **PrintWriter** methods to output characters to the console. Notice that **System.out** is passed as the argument to the **PrintWriter** constructor. You will see later in this chapter that **System.out** is an **OutputStream**.

```java
import java.io.*;

class PrintWriterDemo {

  public static void main(String args[]) {

    try {

      // Create a print writer
      PrintWriter pw = new PrintWriter(System.out);

      // Experiment with some methods
      pw.println(true);
      pw.println('A');
      pw.println(500);
      pw.println(40000L);
      pw.println(45.67f);
      pw.println(45.67);
      pw.println("Hello");
      pw.println(new Integer("99"));

      // Close print writer
      pw.close();
    }
    catch(Exception e) {
      System.out.println("Exception: " + e);
    }
  }
}
```

Output from this application is

```
true
A
500
40000
45.67
45.67
Hello
99
```

1. Modify the example to illustrate how **PrintWriter** can be used to send output to a file. The name of the file is supplied as the command-line argument. Do not automatically flush the output stream when a newline is output.

11.5 **B**YTE STREAMS

This section describes how to write and read files by using byte streams. Recall that byte streams allow a programmer to work with the binary data in a file.

Figure 11-2 shows a few of the byte streams provided by the **java.io** package. Other types of byte streams are also available but they are beyond the scope of this book. This section discusses the **OutputStream**, **FileOutputStream**, **FilterOutputStream**, **BufferedOutputStream**, **DataOutputStream,** and **PrintStream** classes that are used for output, while the **InputStream**, **FileInputStream**, **FilterInputStream**, **BufferedInputStream**, and **DataInputStream** classes are used for input.

The **OutputStream** class defines the functionality that is available for all byte output streams. The following table summarizes the methods provided by this class.

Method	Description
void close( ) throws IOException	Closes the output stream.
void flush( ) throws IOException	Flushes the output stream.
void write(int *i*) throws IOException	Writes lowest-order 8 bits of *i* to the stream.
void write(byte *buffer*[ ]) throws IOException	Writes *buffer* to the stream.

void write(byte *buffer*[ ],
  int *index*, int *size*)
  throws IOException
	Writes *size* bytes from *buffer* starting at position *index* to the stream.

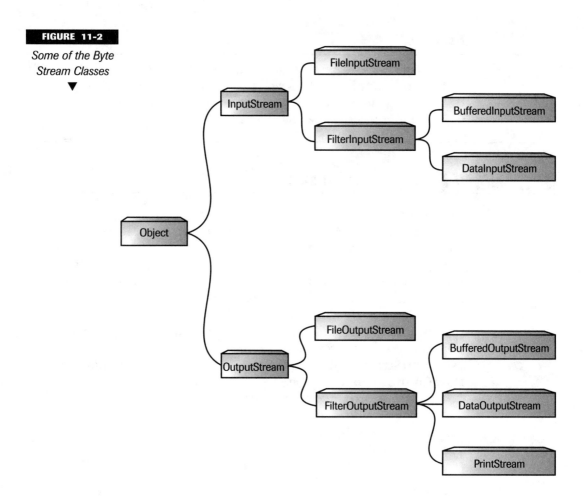

FIGURE 11-2

Some of the Byte Stream Classes
▼

The **FileOutputStream** class extends **OutputStream** and allows you to write binary data to a file. Its most commonly used constructors are as follows:

FileOutputStream(String *filepath*) throws IOException
FileOutputStream(String *filepath*, boolean *append*) throws IOException
FileOutputStream(File *fileObj*) throws IOException

Here, *filepath* is the full path name of a file and *fileObj* is a **File** object that describes the file. If *append* is **true**, characters are appended to the end of the file. Otherwise, the existing contents of the file are overwritten.

The **FilterOutputStream** class extends **OutputStream**. It is used to filter output and provides this constructor:

FilterOutputStream(OutputStream *os*)

Here, *os* is the output stream to be filtered.

You do not directly instantiate **FilterOutputStream**. Instead, you must create a subclass to implement the desired functionality.

The **BufferedOutputStream** class extends **FilterOutputStream** and buffers output to a byte stream. Its constructors are as follows:

BufferedOutputStream(OutputStream *os*)
BufferedOutputStream(OutputStream *os*, int *bufSize*)

The first argument to both constructors is a reference to the output stream. The first form creates a buffered stream by using a buffer with a default size. In the second, the size of the buffer is specified by *bufSize*.

The **DataOutputStream** class extends **FilterOutputStream** and implements **DataOutput**. It allows you to write the simple Java types to a byte output stream. The class provides this constructor:

DataOutputStream(OutputStream *os*)

Here, *os* is the output stream.

The **DataOutput** interface defines methods that can be used to write the simple Java types to a byte output stream. Table 11-4 summarizes the methods declared by this interface. All of these can throw an **IOException**.

UTF-8 encodes a character as one, two, or three bytes. Its advantage is that an ASCII character can be represented as only one byte. This is more compact than the Unicode equivalent.

The **PrintStream** class extends **FilterOutputStream** and provides all of the formatting capabilities we have been using from **System.out** since the beginning of the book. The static **System.out** variable is a **PrintStream**.

Method	Description
void write(int *i*)	Writes *i* to the stream.
void write(byte *buffer*[ ])	Writes *buffer* to the stream.
void write(byte *buffer*[ ], int *index*, int *size*)	Writes *size* bytes from *buffer* starting at position *index* to the stream.
void writeBoolean(boolean *b*)	Writes *b* to the stream.
void writeByte(int *i*)	Writes lowest-order 8 bits of *i* to the stream.
void writeBytes(String *s*)	Writes *s* to the stream.
void writeChar(int *i*)	Writes lowest-order 16 bits of *i* to the stream.
void writeChars(String *s*)	Writes *s* to the stream.
void writeDouble(double *d*)	Writes *d* to the stream.
void writeFloat(float *f*)	Writes *f* to the stream.
void writeInt(int *i*)	Writes *i* to the stream.
void writeLong(long *l*)	Writes *l* to the stream.
void writeShort(short *s*)	Writes *s* to the stream.
void writeUTF(String *s*)	Writes *s* to the stream. Characters are converted from Unicode to UTF-8 encoding.

TABLE 11-4 *Methods Defined by **DataOutput*** ▼

PrintStream has these two constructors:

PrintStream(OutputStream *outputStream*)
PrintStream(OutputStream *outputStream*, boolean *flushOnNewline*)

Here, *flushOnNewline* controls whether Java flushes the output stream every time a newline ('**n**') character is output. If *flushOnNewline* is **true**, flushing automatically takes place. If **false**, flushing is not automatic. The first constructor does not automatically flush.

Java's **PrintStream** objects support the **print( )** and **println( )** methods for all types including **Object**. If an argument is not a simple

type, the **PrintStream** methods will call the object's **toString( )**
method and then print out the result.

*The **PrintStream** class does not correctly handle Unicode characters.*
*Therefore, it is highly recommended that you use the **PrintWriter** class to*
produce console output. The latter class does correctly translate Unicode
*characters to bytes. If you attempt to instantiate **PrintStream**, the JDK*
compiler issues a warning message that the constructors are deprecated. The
deprecation applies for JDK version 1.1 or later. However, the methods of this
class were not deprecated so that you may continue to use them in simple
examples, such as those shown in this book. It is acceptable to use
***PrintStream** for simple test programs. However, use **PrintWriter** for*
production software.

The abstract **InputStream** class defines the functionality that is
available for all byte output streams. Table 11-5 summarizes the
methods provided by this class.

Method	Description
int available( )	Returns the number of bytes currently available for reading.
void close( )	Closes the input stream.
void mark(int *numBytes*)	Places a mark at the current point in the input stream. It remains valid until *numBytes* are read.
boolean markSupported( )	Returns **true** if **mark( )/reset( )** are supported. Otherwise, returns **false**.
int read( )	Reads one byte from the input stream.
int read(byte *buffer*[ ])	Attempts to read up to *buffer.length* bytes into buffer and returns the actual number of bytes that were successfully read.
int read(byte *buffer*[ ], int *offset*, int *numBytes*)	Attempts to read up to *numBytes* bytes into buffer starting at *buffer*[*offset*]. Returns the number of bytes successfully read.
void reset( )	Resets the input pointer to the previously set mark.
int skip(long *numBytes*)	Skips *numBytes* bytes of input. Returns the number of bytes actually skipped.

TABLE 11-5 *Methods Defined by **InputStream*** ▼

The **FileInputStream** class extends **InputStream** and allows you to read binary data from a file. Its most commonly used constructors are as follows:

FileInputStream(String *filepath*) throws FileNotFoundException
FileInputStream(File *fileObj*) throws FileNotFoundException

Here, *filepath* is the full path name of a file and *fileObj* is a **File** object that describes the file.

The **FilterInputStream** class extends **InputStream** and filters an input stream. It provides this constructor:

FilterInputStream(InputStream *is*)

Here, *is* is the input stream to be filtered.

You do not directly instantiate **FilterInputStream**. Instead, you must create a subclass to implement the desired functionality.

The **BufferedInputStream** class extends **FilterInputStream** and buffers input from a byte stream. Its constructors are as follows:

BufferedInputStream(InputStream *is*)
BufferedInputStream(InputStream *is*, int *bufSize*)

The first argument to both constructors is a reference to the input stream. The first form creates a buffered stream by using a buffer with a default size. In the second, the size of the buffer is specified by *bufSize*.

The **DataInputStream** class extends **FilterInputStream** and implements **DataInput**. It allows you to read the simple Java types from a byte input stream. This class provides this constructor:

DataInputStream(InputStream *is*)

Here, *is* is the input stream.

The **DataInput** interface defines methods that can be used to read the simple Java types from a byte input stream. Table 11-6 summarizes the methods defined by this interface. All of these can throw an **IOException**.

Method	Description
boolean readBoolean( )	Reads and returns a **boolean** from the stream.
byte readByte( )	Reads and returns a **byte** from the stream.
char readChar( )	Reads and returns a **char** from the stream.
double readDouble( )	Reads and returns a **double** from the stream.
float readFloat( )	Reads and returns a **float** from the stream.
void readFully(byte *buffer*[ ])	Reads bytes and fills *buffer*.
void readFully(byte *buffer*[ ], int *index*, int *size*)	Reads *size* bytes and fills *buffer* starting at position *index*.
int readInt( )	Reads and returns an **int** from the stream.
long readLong( )	Reads and returns a **long** from the stream.
short readShort( )	Reads and returns a **short** from the stream.
String readUTF( )	Reads a string from the input. Characters are converted from UTF-8 format to Unicode. The string is returned from the method.
int readUnsignedByte( )	Reads and returns an unsigned byte from the stream.
int readUnsignedShort( )	Reads and returns an unsigned short from the stream.
int skipBytes(int *n*)	Skips ahead *n* bytes in the stream.

TABLE 11-6 *Methods Defined by DataInput* ▼

EXAMPLES

1. This example illustrates how to use the **FileOutputStream** and **FileInputStream** classes to write and read files. One application writes to a file and another application reads from a file.

   The program that writes to a file is shown in the following listing. It accepts one command-line argument that is the name of the file to create. Twelve bytes are written to the file by using the **write( )** method of **FileOutputStream**.

```
import java.io.*;

class FileOutputStreamDemo {
```

```
public static void main(String args[]) {

  try {

    // Create a file output stream
    FileOutputStream fos =
      new FileOutputStream(args[0]);

    // Write 12 bytes to the file
    for(int i = 0; i < 12; i++) {
      fos.write(i);
    }

    // Close file output stream
    fos.close();
  }
  catch(Exception e) {
    System.out.println("Exception: " + e);
  }
 }
}
```

The program that reads a file is shown in the following listing. It accepts one command-line argument that is the name of the file to read. A **FileInputStream** object is created. Bytes are obtained via **read( )** and displayed via **System.out.println( )**. The stream is closed when all bytes have been read.

```
import java.io.*;

class FileInputStreamDemo {

  public static void main(String args[]) {

    try {

      // Create a file input stream
      FileInputStream fis =
        new FileInputStream(args[0]);

      // Read and display data
      int i;
      while((i = fis.read()) != -1) {
        System.out.println(i);
      }
```

```
      // Close file input stream
      fis.close();
    }
    catch(Exception e) {
      System.out.println("Exception: " + e);
    }
  }
}
```

To test this example, execute the file output stream application by entering the following command:

```
java FileOutputStreamDemo output.txt
```

Then execute the file input stream application by entering this command:

```
java FileInputStreamDemo output.txt
```

Output from this application is shown here:

```
0
1
2
3
4
5
6
7
8
9
10
11
```

2. This example illustrates how to use the **BufferedOutputStream** and **BufferedInputStream** classes to write and read files. One application writes to a file and another application reads from a file.

 The program that writes to a file is shown in the following listing. It accepts one command-line argument that is the name of the file to create. Twelve bytes are written to the file by using the **write( )** method of **BufferedOutputStream**. Compare this program with **FileOutputStreamDemo**, seen earlier in this section.

```
import java.io.*;
```

```
class BufferedOutputStreamDemo {

  public static void main(String args[]) {

    try {

      // Create a file output stream
      FileOutputStream fos =
        new FileOutputStream(args[0]);

      // Create a buffered output stream
      BufferedOutputStream bos =
        new BufferedOutputStream(fos);

      // Write 12 bytes to the file
      for(int i = 0; i < 12; i++) {
        bos.write(i);
      }

      // Close buffered output stream
      bos.close();
    }
    catch(Exception e) {
      System.out.println("Exception: " + e);
    }
  }
}
```

The program that reads a file is shown in the following listing. It accepts one command-line argument that is the name of the file to read. A **BufferedInputStream** object is created. Bytes are obtained via **read( )** and displayed via **System.out.println( )**. The stream is closed when all bytes have been read. Compare this program with **FileInputStreamDemo**, seen earlier in this section.

```
import java.io.*;

class BufferedInputStreamDemo {

  public static void main(String args[]) {

    try {

      // Create a file input stream
      FileInputStream fis =
```

```
        new FileInputStream(args[0]);

      // Create a buffered input stream
      BufferedInputStream bis =
        new BufferedInputStream(fis);

      // Read and display data
      int i;
      while((i = bis.read()) != -1) {
        System.out.println(i);
      }

      // Close file input stream
      fis.close();
    }
    catch(Exception e) {
      System.out.println("Exception: " + e);
    }
  }
}
```

To test this example, execute the buffered output stream application by entering the following command:

```
java BufferedOutputStreamDemo output.txt
```

Then execute the buffered input stream application by entering this command:

```
java BufferedInputStreamDemo output.txt
```

The output from this example is identical to that of the previous example.

3. This example illustrates how to use the **DataOutputStream** and **DataInputStream** classes to write and read files. One application writes to a file and another reads from a file.

   The program that writes to a file is shown in the following listing. It accepts one command-line argument that is the name of the file to create. Various types of data are written to the file by using the methods of **DataOutputStream**.

```
import java.io.*;

class DataOutputStreamDemo {

  public static void main(String args[]) {
```

```java
        try {

            // Create a file output stream
            FileOutputStream fos =
                new FileOutputStream(args[0]);

            // Create a data output stream
            DataOutputStream dos =
                new DataOutputStream(fos);

            // Write various types of data
            dos.writeBoolean(false);
            dos.writeByte(Byte.MAX_VALUE);
            dos.writeChar('A');
            dos.writeDouble(Double.MAX_VALUE);
            dos.writeFloat(Float.MAX_VALUE);
            dos.writeInt(Integer.MAX_VALUE);
            dos.writeLong(Long.MAX_VALUE);
            dos.writeShort(Short.MAX_VALUE);

            // Close file output stream
            fos.close();
        }
        catch(Exception e) {
            System.out.println("Exception: " + e);
        }
    }
}
```

The program that reads a file is shown in the following listing. It accepts one command-line argument that is the name of the file to read. A **DataInputStream** object is created. The various data types are obtained by calling some of its methods. The stream is closed when all data has been read.

```java
import java.io.*;

class DataInputStreamDemo {

    public static void main(String args[]) {

        try {

            // Create a file input stream
            FileInputStream fis =
```

```
          new FileInputStream(args[0]);

          // Create a data input stream
          DataInputStream dis =
            new DataInputStream(fis);

          // Read and display data
          System.out.println(dis.readBoolean());
          System.out.println(dis.readByte());
          System.out.println(dis.readChar());
          System.out.println(dis.readDouble());
          System.out.println(dis.readFloat());
          System.out.println(dis.readInt());
          System.out.println(dis.readLong());
          System.out.println(dis.readShort());

          // Close file input stream
          fis.close();
        }
        catch(Exception e) {
          System.out.println("Exception: " + e);
        }
      }
    }
```

To test this example, execute the data output stream application by entering the following command:

```
java DataOutputStreamDemo output.txt
```

Then execute the data input stream application by entering this command:

```
java DataInputStreamDemo output.txt
```

The output should be as follows:

```
false
127
A
1.7976931348623157E308
3.4028235E38
2147483647
9223372936854775807
32767
```

1. Write one application that splits a large file into smaller files and a second application that merges these smaller files to re-create the large file. These tools would be useful if you needed to save a large file (e.g., the JDK) onto multiple floppy disks and restore it at a later time.

2. Write one application that writes the first 15 numbers of the Fibonacci series to a file. Use the **writeShort( )** method of **DataOutputStream** to output the numbers. Write a second application that reads this data from a file and displays it. Use the **readShort( )** method of **DataInputStream** to input the numbers. For both applications, specify the name of the file as a command-line argument.

11.6   *R*ANDOM ACCESS FILES

The stream classes examined in the previous sections can only use sequential access to read and write data in a file. The **RandomAccessFile** class allows you to write programs that can seek to any location in a file and read or write data at that point. This type of functionality is very valuable in some programs. For example, it can be used to manage a set of data records that are stored in a file.

This class implements the **DataInput** and **DataOutput** interfaces. It also provides the methods summarized in the following table.

Method	Description
void close( )	Close the file.
long getFilePointer( )	Returns the current position of the file pointer. This identifies the point at which the next byte is read or written.
long length( )	Returns the number of bytes in the file.
int read( )	Reads and returns a byte from the file. Waits until data is available.

Method	Description
int read(byte *buffer*[ ], int *index*, int *size*)	Attempts to read *size* bytes from the file and places these in *buffer* starting at position *index*. Returns the number of bytes actually read. Waits until data is available.
int read(byte *buffer*[ ])	Reads bytes from the file and places these in *buffer*. Returns the number of bytes read. Waits until data is available.
void seek(long *n*)	Positions the file pointer at *n* bytes from the beginning of the file. The next read or write occurs at this position.
int skipBytes(int *n*)	Adds *n* to the file pointer. Returns the actual number of bytes skipped. If *n* is negative, no bytes are skipped.

The most significant of these methods is **seek( )** because it allows random access to any position in the file.

EXAMPLE

1. This example displays the last N bytes of a file. (This is sometimes referred to as the "tail" of the file.) The first command-line argument is the filename; the second is the number of bytes. A **RandomAccessFile** object is created for the file. The **seek( )** method positions the file pointer. The program then enters a loop in which **readByte( )** is used to obtain bytes from the file. These are displayed via **print( )**.

```java
import java.io.*;

class Tail {

  public static void main(String args[]) {

    try {
```

```
    // Create random access file
    RandomAccessFile raf =
      new RandomAccessFile(args[0], "r");

    // Determine number of bytes
    // to display at end of file
    long count = Long.valueOf(args[1]).longValue();

    // Determine file length
    long position = raf.length();

    // Seek to the correct position
    position -= count;
    if(position < 0)
      position = 0;
    raf.seek(position);

    // Read and display the bytes
    while(true) {

      // Read byte
      try {
        byte b = raf.readByte();

        // Display as character
        System.out.print((char)b);
      }
      catch(EOFException eofe) {
        break;
      }
    }
  }
  catch(Exception e) {
    e.printStackTrace();
  }
  }
}
```

To test this application, enter a command as follows. This command displays the last 40 bytes from the file **Tail.java**.

```
java Tail Tail.java 40
```

Output is shown here:

```
e.printStackTrace();
      }
    }
  }
```

---

1. Write a program to display the bytes of a file in reverse sequence. Provide the name of the file as a command-line argument.

11.7 *T*HE STREAMTOKENIZER CLASS

The **StreamTokenizer** class parses the data from a character input stream and generates a sequence of tokens. A *token* is a group of characters that represent a number or word. This functionality can be very valuable if you need to build parsers, compilers, or any program that processes character input.

A constructor for this class is as follows:

StreamTokenizer(Reader *r*)

Here, *r* is a reader.

The class defines four constants. **TT_EOF** and **TT_EOL** indicate end-of-file and end-of-line conditions, respectively. **TT_NUMBER** and **TT_WORD** indicate that a number or word has been read.

Three instance variables provide valuable information. If the current token is a number, **nval** contains its value and **ttype** equals **TT_NUMBER**. If the current token is a string, **sval** contains its value and **ttype** equals **TT_WORD**. Otherwise, **ttype** contains the character that has been read.

The methods provided by this class are summarized in Table 11-7.

Method	Description
void commentChar(int *ch*)	Indicates that *ch* starts a single-line comment.
void eolIsSignificant(boolean *flag*)	If *flag* is **true**, the end-of-line is treated as a token. Otherwise, it is treated as white space.
int lineno( )	Returns the current line number.
void lowerCaseMode(boolean *flag*)	If *flag* is **true**, the token is automatically converted to lowercase. Otherwise, it is not.
int nextToken( )	Returns **TT_NUMBER** if the next token is a number. Returns **TT_WORD** if the next token is a word. Otherwise, returns the character that equals the next token.
void ordinaryChar(int *ch*)	Specifies that *ch* should be treated as an ordinary character. Note: Each ordinary character is returned as a separate token from **nextToken( )**.
void parseNumbers( )	Specifies that numbers should be parsed.
void pushBack( )	Pushes the current token back to the input stream.
void quoteChar(int *ch*)	Defines *ch* as the quote character for string literals.
void resetSyntax( )	Specifies that all characters should be treated as ordinary characters.
void slashSlashComments(boolean *flag*)	If *flag* is **true**, // comments are ignored. Otherwise, they are not.
void slashStarComments(boolean *flag*)	If *flag* is **true**, /* ...*/ comments are ignored. Otherwise, they are not.
String toString( )	Returns the string equivalent of the current token.
void whitespaceChars(int *c1*, int *c2*)	Specifies that all characters in the range *c1–c2* (inclusive) should be treated as white space.
void wordChars(int *c1*, int *c2*)	Specifies that all characters in the range *c1–c2* (inclusive) should be treated as word characters.

TABLE 11-7 *Methods Defined by **StreamTokenizer*** ▼

*The **StreamTokenizer** constructor sets the initial state of the object so that: (a) All byte values from '\u0000' to '\u0020' are treated as white space. (b) All byte values from 'A' to 'Z', 'a' to 'z', and '\u00A0' to '\u00FF' are treated as alphabetic characters. (c) The forward slash is a comment character. (d) Single and double quote characters are the string quote characters. (e) Numbers are parsed. (f) End-of-line conditions are white space. (g) The // and /* ... */ comment styles are not recognized.*

The general procedure to use a stream tokenizer is as follows.

1. Create a **StreamTokenizer** object for a **Reader**.
2. Define how characters are to be processed.
3. Call **nextToken( )** to obtain the next token.
4. Read the **ttype** instance variable to determine the token type.
5. Read the value of the token from the **sval**, **nval**, or **ttype** instance variable.
6. Process the token.
7. Repeat steps 3–6 until **nextToken( )** returns **StreamTokenizer.TT_EOF**.

EXAMPLES

1. This example illustrates how to read a text file and parse its contents. The application accepts one command-line argument that specifies the file to be read. **FileReader**, **BufferedReader**, and **StreamTokenizer** objects are then created.

   The period character is defined as an ordinary character. This must be done so that the period at the end of each sentence is treated as a token.

   The apostrophe character is defined as a word character. This must be done so words that contain an apostrophe are processed as one token.

   A loop then reads and processes each token from the file. The type of the token is indicated by the variable **ttype**. This determines if the variable **sval**, **nval**, or **ttype** is displayed. The line number is also displayed.

When an end-of-file condition is detected, the file reader is closed.

```java
import java.io.*;

class StreamTokenizerDemo {

  public static void main(String args[]) {

    try {

      // Create a file reader
      FileReader fr = new FileReader(args[0]);

      // Create a buffered reader
      BufferedReader br = new BufferedReader(fr);

      // Create a stream tokenizer
      StreamTokenizer st = new StreamTokenizer(br);

      // Define period as ordinary character
      st.ordinaryChar('.');

      // Define apostrophe as word character
      st.wordChars('\'', '\'');

      // Process tokens
      while(st.nextToken() != StreamTokenizer.TT_EOF) {
        switch(st.ttype) {
          case st.TT_WORD:
            System.out.println(st.lineno() + ") " +
              st.sval);
            break;
          case st.TT_NUMBER:
            System.out.println(st.lineno() + ") " +
              st.nval);
            break;
          default:
            System.out.println(st.lineno() + ") " +
              (char)st.ttype);
        }
      }

      // Close file reader
      fr.close();
    }
```

```
        catch(Exception e) {
          System.out.println("Exception: " + e);
        }
      }
    }
```

Assume that the file **tokens.txt** contains the following lines:

```
The price is $23.45.
Is that too expensive?
(I don't think so.)
```

Enter the following command on a Windows platform:

```
java StreamTokenizerDemo tokens.txt
```

Output is as follows:

```
1) The
1) price
1) is
1) $
1) 23.45
1) .
2) Is
2) that
2) too
2) expensive
2) ?
3) (
3) I
3) don't
3) think
3) so
3) .
3) )
```

2. The previous example illustrated how to parse a file that contained words, numbers, and some punctuation marks. This example shows how to process a text file that contains numbers delimited by spaces and commas. Notice that the comma is defined as a whitespace character via a call to **whitespaceChars( )**.

```
import java.io.*;

class StreamTokenizerDemo2 {
```

```
public static void main(String args[]) {

  try {

    // Create a file reader
    FileReader fr = new FileReader(args[0]);

    // Create a buffered reader
    BufferedReader br = new BufferedReader(fr);

    // Create a stream tokenizer
    StreamTokenizer st = new StreamTokenizer(br);

    // Consider commas as white space
    st.whitespaceChars(',', ',');

    // Process tokens
    while(st.nextToken() != StreamTokenizer.TT_EOF) {
      switch(st.ttype) {
        case st.TT_WORD:
          System.out.println(st.lineno() + ") " +
            st.sval);
          break;
        case st.TT_NUMBER:
          System.out.println(st.lineno() + ") " +
            st.nval);
          break;
        default:
          System.out.println(st.lineno() + ") " +
            (char)st.ttype);
      }
    }

    // Close file reader
    fr.close();
  }
  catch(Exception e) {
    System.out.println("Exception: " + e);
  }
  }
}
```

Assume that the file **numbers.txt** contains these lines:

```
34.567, 23, -9.3
21, -23, 90, 7.6
```

Enter the following command on a Windows platform:

```
java StreamTokenizerDemo2 numbers.txt
```

Output is as follows:

```
1) 34.567
1) 23.0
1) -9.3
2) 21.0
2) -23.0
2) 90.0
2) 7.6
```

EXERCISES

1. Use a stream tokenizer to count the number of lines in a text file. (Hint: Use the **eolIsSignificant( )** method.)

2. Write a program that demonstrates the default behavior of the **StreamTokenizer** class. Display numbers, words, and ordinary characters that are returned from the **nextToken( )** method. Test your program by tokenizing a .java file.

Mastery
Skills Check

At this point you should be able to perform the following exercises and answer these questions.

1. What is a stream?

2. What are the similarities and differences between character and byte streams?

3. What are the superclasses of input and output character streams?

4. What are the superclasses of input and output byte streams?

5. Write an application that displays a directory tree. The program should accept one command-line argument. If this represents a file, its name should be displayed. If this represents a directory, the program should recursively determine and display all files and directories that it contains.

6. Modify the directory tree program so that it accepts two command-line arguments. The first must be the name of a file or directory. The second optional argument is a file suffix (e.g., .gif or .html or .wav). Display only those files whose names end with the specified suffix.

7. Modify the filtered directory tree program so it displays the sizes (in bytes) of the individual files.

Cumulative Skills Check

This section checks how well you have integrated material in this chapter with that from the preceding chapters.

1. Build a program that computes the area of a circle. Prompt the user for the radius and display the area. If the user entry is incorrectly formatted or represents a negative number, present the prompt again.

2. Write a program that scans through a file and displays any Java documentation comments. These begin with the three-character sequence /** and terminate with the two-character sequence */. Note that a documentation comment may span several lines. There may also be several documentation comments on the same line.

3. A text file contains data about employees. Each line contains the name, location, and phone number of an employee. Semicolons are used to delimit these data items. Write a program that reads this file and displays each line as shown in the following listing. Use a **StringTokenizer** to parse each line.

```
Name: Joe O'Neil
Location: 1J338
Phone: 3678
```

12

Networking

T HE **java.net** package contains classes that allow you to build distributed applications. This chapter examines some of their functionality.

Internet addresses identify machines on the Internet. A class is provided so you may work with this information.

A socket is one end of a bidirectional communication path that connects applications on two separate machines. It uses the Transmission Control Protocol (TCP) to obtain reliable, sequenced data exchange. In this chapter, you will see how to build client/server applications with sockets.

Alternatively, datagrams may be exchanged between machines. These employ the User Datagram Protocol (UDP) to obtain a more efficient, best-effort delivery. This technique is also demonstrated here.

Finally, you will learn how to retrieve Web resources that are named via Uniform Resource Locators (URLs).

Review
Skills Check

Before proceeding, you should be able to perform these exercises.

1. Read a text file and count the number of times each letter of the alphabet is used. Consider upper- and lowercase letters to be the same. Display these counts for each of the 26 letters of the alphabet.

2. Write a program that quizzes a user on basic arithmetic. The application should prompt a user with a simple addition or subtraction question. The user should be told if his or her answer is correct.

3. A file contains multiple lines of data. Each line contains several tokens separated by whitespace. Write a program that can read and filter a file of this format. The application should display a subset of the tokens that are on each line. The first command-line argument is the name of the file. The second and third command-line arguments specify the index of the first and last token to be displayed.

▰ 12.1 ▰ *INTERNET ADDRESSES*

An Internet address is a 32-bit quantity that identifies a machine connected to the Internet. It is commonly expressed as a sequence of four numbers separated from each other by periods. For example, a machine might have the address "128.34.29.56." You may wish to consult other texts to learn how these 32 bits are formatted. As a point of interest, there is an effort known as IP Version 6 that includes features for the next generation of the Internet Protocol (IP). In that release, an Internet address is increased to 128 bits. However, this chapter uses 32-bit addresses.

An Internet address may also be expressed as a sequence of tokens separated from each other by periods. For example, a machine may have the address "www. mycompany.com." This format is significantly easier for people to remember and communicate. The Domain Name System (DNS) translates an Internet address in dotted string format to a dotted decimal format. Thus, DNS is essentially a clearinghouse for Internet addresses.

Note

The preceding brief discussion of Internet addresses and the DNS is sufficient for the purposes of this book and for most day-to-day uses of Java. However, if the handling of addresses is going to be an important part of your programming future, you will want to learn more about them and the operation of DNS. It is a vital part of the Internet.

The class **InetAddress** in the **java.net** package encapsulates an Internet address. We will be using this class in the examples that follow. Therefore, let us become familiar with its most commonly used methods.

Various instance methods are available to obtain information about the address represented by an **InetAddress** object. They are summarized here:

Method	Description
byte[ ] getAddress( )	Returns an array of bytes containing the address information. The data is in network byte order (highest-order byte in first element).
String getHostAddress( )	Returns a string containing the address information.
String getHostName( )	Returns a string containing the host name.

A commonly used method of **InetAddress** is **getByName( )**. It performs a name-to-address translation by using information provided by DNS and has the following signature:

```
static InetAddress getByName(String hostName)
throws UnknownHostException
```

A host may have several addresses. In that case, the **getAllByName( )** method can be used to obtain an array of **InetAddress** objects. It has this form:

```
static InetAddress[ ] getAllByName(String hostName)
throws UnknownHostException
```

For both of these methods, *hostName* is the name of an Internet host. This may be expressed in either dotted string format (e.g., "www.osborne.com") or a dotted decimal format (e.g. "200.200.200.200"). You will see later in this chapter that it is necessary to create an **InetAddress** object to identify the destination for a datagram.

It is also possible to determine the address of the local host. This is done by the **getLocalHost( )** method:

```
static InetAddress getLocalHost() throws UnknownHostException
```

Here, an **InetAddress** object is returned that encapsulates the information.

EXAMPLE

1. The following example illustrates how to apply some of the methods of **InetAddress**. The application accepts one command-line argument that is an Internet address. This may be in either dotted decimal or string format. It uses the static method **getAllByName( )** to obtain an array of **InetAddress** objects that correspond to that address. For each address, the **getHostName( )** and **getHostAddress( )** methods are called. The **getAddress( )** method is called to obtain an array of bytes that contain the address.

```
import java.net.*;

class InetAddressDemo {
```

```
public static void main(String args[]) {
  try {

    // Get an address
    InetAddress ias[] =
      InetAddress.getAllByName(args[0]);
    for(int i = 0; i < ias.length; i++) {
      System.out.println(ias[i].getHostName());
      System.out.println(ias[i].getHostAddress());
      byte bytes[] = ias[i].getAddress();
      for(int j = 0; j < bytes.length; j++) {
        if(j > 0)
          System.out.print(".");
        if(bytes[j] >= 0)
          System.out.print(bytes[j]);
        else
          System.out.print(bytes[j] + 256);
      }
      System.out.println("");
    }

  }
  catch(Exception e) {
    e.printStackTrace();
  }
 }
}
```

Experiment with this application by using the command line argument "127.0.0.1." By convention, this represents your local machine. The output is shown here:

```
localhost
127.0.0.1
127.0.0.1
```

Also, give an incorrect address such as "abc.def." In that case, an **UnknownHostException** is thrown by **getAllByName( )**.

EXERCISE

---

1. Write an application that illustrates how to use the **getLocalHost( )** method of **InetAddress**. Display the name and address of the local machine.

12.2 **S**ERVER SOCKETS AND SOCKETS

A *socket* is one end of a bidirectional communication path between two machines. It provides a mechanism for two applications to obtain reliable, sequenced data exchange. These features are available because sockets use the Transmission Control Protocol (TCP) in addition to the Internet Protocol (IP).

The **ServerSocket** and **Socket** classes can be used to build client/server applications. Let's look at the functionality they provide.

The **ServerSocket** class is used to build a server application. It listens for incoming requests from clients. The following is one of its constructors:

ServerSocket(int *port*) throws IOException

Here, *port* is the software port on which to listen for incoming client requests. Other forms of the constructor allow you to limit the queue of incoming requests or bind to a specific address.

The **accept( )** method listens for an incoming request from a client. It waits until a request arrives. The signature of this method is shown here:

Socket accept( ) throws IOException

The **accept( )** method returns a **Socket** object. That object may then be used to communicate with the client.

You may close a server socket via the **close( )** method shown here:

void close( ) throws IOException

The **Socket** class is used to exchange data between a client and a server. The following is one of its constructors:

Socket(String *hostName*, int *port*)
throws UnknownHostException, IOException

Here, *hostName* is the name of the server host. This may be either a dotted string or a dotted decimal address. The parameter *port* indicates the software port on that server to which this socket should connect.

After a socket is created, a program must then obtain input and output streams to communicate. The **getInputStream( )** and **getOutputStream( )** methods are used for this purpose. Their signatures are shown here:

InputStream getInputStream( ) throws IOException

OutputStream getOutputStream( ) throws IOException

The **InputStream** and **OutputStream** objects are then typically used to create **DataInputStream** and **DataOutputStream** objects, respectively. Recall from Chapter 11 that these streams can be used to read and write various types of data.

You may close a socket via the **close( )** method shown here:

void close( ) throws IOException

EXAMPLE

1. This example illustrates how to write a simple client/server application. A client contacts the server to obtain a random integer. This value is then displayed.

   The following listing shows the server software. It requires one command-line argument to specify the software port on which this server listens for incoming client requests. The **main( )** method begins by converting this string to an **int** and saving its value in **port**. A random number generator is created. A **ServerSocket** object is created for the specified port. The server then enters an infinite loop. The **accept( )** method is called to wait for incoming client requests. When a request arrives, a **Socket** object is returned from that method. That socket is used for communication with the client. A data output stream is obtained from the socket, and a random integer is written to the client. The socket is closed, and the **accept( )** method is called again.

```java
import java.io.*;
import java.net.*;
import java.util.*;

class ServerSocketDemo {

  public static void main(String args[]) {
    try {

      // Get port
      int port = Integer.parseInt(args[0]);
```

```
        // Create random number generator
        Random random = new Random();

        // Create server socket
        ServerSocket ss = new ServerSocket(port);

        // Create infinite loop
        while(true) {

            // Accept incoming requests
            Socket s = ss.accept();

            // Write result to client
            OutputStream os = s.getOutputStream();
            DataOutputStream dos = new DataOutputStream(os);
            dos.writeInt(random.nextInt());

            // Close socket
            s.close();
        }
    }
    catch(Exception e) {
        System.out.println("Exception: " + e);
    }
  }
}
```

The following listing shows the client software. The application requires two command-line arguments that are the name and port of the server. A **Socket** object is created to communicate with the server application. A data input stream is obtained for that socket, and the random integer generated by the server is read. The result is displayed and the socket is closed.

```
import java.io.*;
import java.net.*;

class SocketDemo {

  public static void main(String args[]) {

    try {

        // Get server and port
        String server = args[0];
```

```
        int port = Integer.parseInt(args[1]);

        // Create socket
        Socket s = new Socket(server, port);

        // Read random number from server
        InputStream is = s.getInputStream();
        DataInputStream dis = new DataInputStream(is);
        int i = dis.readInt();

        // Display result
        System.out.println(i);

        // Close socket
        s.close();
      }
    catch(Exception e) {
      System.out.println("Exception: " + e);
      }
    }
  }
}
```

If you are using a Windows PC, it is easy to observe these applications communicating with each other. Create one DOS window and start the server software by entering the following command:

```
java ServerSocketDemo 4231
```

Here, 4231 is the software port to which incoming requests are directed. The use of 4231 is arbitrary; you may experiment with other values. However, avoid values below 1000.

Create another DOS window and start the client software by entering the following command:

```
java SocketDemo 127.0.0.1 4231
```

Here, the IP address 127.0.0.1 represents your local machine. The second argument to the client application must be the same number that was supplied as the argument to the server application.

The **SocketDemo** application displays one random integer and terminates. However, you may run the application again to generate another random number.

1. Write a server that executes an infinite loop to read a **double** value from a client, square the value, and write the result to the client. Also, write a client application that sends a **double** value to the server application. Specify the value as one of the command line arguments to the client.

12.3 *D*ATAGRAM SOCKETS AND PACKETS

The previous section described how to work with sockets. They use the Transmission Control Protocol (TCP) to provide reliable, sequenced data exchange. In most cases, this functionality is required for your applications.

However, TCP may incur substantial overhead to achieve these reliability characteristics. In some cases, you may not require this functionality. For example, if you are sending a stream of video packets from one machine to another, it does not matter if a few frames are lost or arrive out of sequence. This will probably not be perceptible to the user. Also, if you are building an application that periodically samples data from a large set of clients, it may not be a problem if some information is lost. That missing data can be collected on a subsequent polling cycle.

The User Datagram Protocol (UDP) provides a sensible alternative to TCP for applications such as these. UDP does not guarantee a reliable, sequenced data exchange, and therefore requires much less overhead.

The **java.net** library provides two classes that can be used to build client/server applications with datagrams. These are the **DatagramPacket** and **DatagramSocket** classes. Let us look at the functionality they provide.

The **DatagramPacket** class encapsulates a datagram packet. Its two constructors are shown here:

DatagramPacket(byte[ ] *buffer*, int *size*)
DatagramPacket(byte[ ] *buffer*, int *size*, InetAddress *ia*, int *port*)

The first form of the constructor creates a **DatagramPacket** object that can be used to receive an incoming datagram. In that form, *buffer* is a **byte** array to which incoming data is written. The number of bytes in *buffer* is *size*.

The second form of the constructor creates a **DatagramPacket** object that can be used to transmit an outgoing datagram. In that form, *buffer* is a **byte** array from which outgoing data is read. The number of bytes to read from *buffer* is *size*. The Internet address and port of the recipient are available in *ia* and *port*.

The methods defined by **DatagramPacket** are summarized in Table 12-1.

The DatagramSocket class is used to send or receive datagrams. Two of its constructors are shown here:

```
DatagramSocket( ) throws SocketException
DatagramSocket(int port) throws SocketException
```

The first form of the constructor binds the datagram socket to any available port. The second form binds the socket to *port*.

The **receive( )** method listens for an incoming datagram. It waits until a datagram arrives. The signature of this method is as follows:

```
void receive(DatagramPacket dp) throws IOException
```

Here, *dp* is a **DatagramPacket** object in which incoming data is stored.

Method	Description
InetAddress getAddress( )	For received datagrams, returns the address of the sending machine. For datagrams to be transmitted, returns the address of the destination machine.
byte[ ] getData( )	Returns a byte array containing the data.
int getLength( )	Returns the number of bytes in the packet.
int getPort( )	Returns the port.
void setAddress(InetAddress ia)	Sets the address to *ia*.
void setData(byte buffer[ ])	Sets the data to that contained in *buffer*.
void setLength(int size)	Sets the size of the packet to *size*.
void setPort(int port)	Sets the port to *port*.

TABLE 12-1 *Methods Defined by **DatagramPacket*** ▼

The **send( )** method transmits a datagram. The signature of this method is as follows:

void send(DatagramPacket *dp*) throws IOException

Here, *dp* is a **DatagramPacket** object that contains the data to be sent and the destination host and port.

You may close a datagram socket via the **close( )** method shown here:

void close() throws IOException

EXAMPLE

1. This example illustrates how to use the **DatagramSocket** and **DatagramPacket** classes. It includes one application that transmits a datagram and another application that executes an infinite loop to receive and display datagrams.

   The sender application is invoked with three command-line arguments. These are the address and port of the server and a word. The word is sent to the server in a datagram packet.

   The receiver application is invoked with one command-line argument. This is the software port to which it listens for incoming packets. When it receives a packet, it displays the enclosed word.

   Source code for the receiver is shown in the following listing. Its one command-line argument is converted to an **int** and saved in **port**. A **DatagramSocket** object is created for that port. After creating a buffer to hold incoming packets, the application begins an infinite loop. Inside that loop, it creates a **DatagramPacket** object to hold incoming packets. The **receive( )** method of the socket waits for incoming requests. After a packet is received, the **getData( )** method of **DatagramPacket** is called to obtain its data. This is displayed, and control passes to the top of the loop.

```
import java.net.*;

class DatagramReceiver {
  private final static int BUFSIZE = 20;

  public static void main(String args[]) {
```

```
try {

    // Obtain port
    int port = Integer.parseInt(args[0]);

    // Create a DatagramSocket object for the port
    DatagramSocket ds = new DatagramSocket(port);

    // Create a buffer to hold incoming data
    byte buffer[] = new byte[BUFSIZE];

    // Create infinite loop
    while(true) {

        // Create a datagram packet
        DatagramPacket dp =
            new DatagramPacket(buffer, buffer.length);

        // Receive data
        ds.receive(dp);

        // Get data from the datagram packet
        String str = new String(dp.getData());

        // Display the data
        System.out.println(str);
    }
}
catch(Exception e) {
    e.printStackTrace();
}
}
}
```

Source code for the sender is shown in the following listing. This application accepts three command-line arguments: the name of the destination machine, the destination port, and a word to send to the receiver. An **InetAddress** object is created for the destination address. A **DatagramSocket** object is created to send a datagram packet. Note that the constructor binds the socket to any available port. A **DatagramPacket** object is created. This packet contains not only the data to be sent but also the destination address and port. Finally, the **send( )** method of the socket is called to transmit the packet.

```java
import java.net.*;

class DatagramSender {

  public static void main(String args[]) {
    try {

      // Create destination Internet address
      InetAddress ia =
        InetAddress.getByName(args[0]);

      // Obtain destination port
      int port = Integer.parseInt(args[1]);

      // Create a datagram socket
      DatagramSocket ds = new DatagramSocket();

      // Create a datagram packet
      byte buffer[] = args[2].getBytes();
      DatagramPacket dp =
        new DatagramPacket(buffer, buffer.length,
          ia, port);

      // Send the datagram packet
      ds.send(dp);
    }
    catch(Exception e) {
      e.printStackTrace();
    }
  }
}
```

EXERCISE

1. Write an application that can receive datagram packets. Display the Internet address and port of the sending machine. You can use the **DatagramSender** developed in the example to generate these packets.

12.4 ■ *UNIFORM RESOURCE LOCATORS*

A Uniform Resource Locator (URL) identifies a Web resource. The format of a URL is as follows:

protocol://host:port/file

Here, *protocol* is the protocol to be used when retrieving this resource. Commonly used protocols include ftp and http. The *host* parameter identifies the machine from which the resource may be retrieved. The *port* parameter is optional and identifies the software port on the server. Default port values are used for various protocols if this parameter is omitted. The *file* parameter identifies a specific file on the server.

The **URL** class encapsulates information about a URL. The following are some of its constructors:

```
URL(String protocol, String host, int port, String file)
    throws MalformedURLException
URL(String protocol, String host, String file)
    throws MalformedURLException
URL(String urlString)
    throws MalformedURLException
```

Here, the *protocol, host, port,* and *file* parameters have the meanings previously described. The *urlString* parameter combines all of these items into one string.

The **openStream( )** method opens and returns an input stream for the URL. Its signature is shown here:

```
InputStream openStream( ) throws IOException
```

The contents of the resource can then be read from that input stream.

The class also provides the methods shown here:

```
String getFile( )
String getHost( )
String getPort( )
String getProtocol( )
```

These can be used to obtain the individual components of a URL.

Other constructors and methods are available, but they are beyond the scope of this book.

EXAMPLE

1. The following application creates a "mini-browser" that illustrates how to read the contents of a resource identified by a URL. The URL is supplied as a command-line argument and is passed as the argument to the **URL** constructor. The **openStream( )** method returns an input stream that can be used to retrieve the contents of that resource. A loop then reads blocks of data from the resource and displays this information as characters on the standard output. Note that this simple application works for resources that contain ordinary text. However, other types of resources that have binary data cannot be presented by this program.

```java
import java.io.*;
import java.net.*;

class URLDemo {

  public static void main(String args[]) {
    try {

      // Obtain url
      URL url = new URL(args[0]);

      // Obtain input stream
      InputStream is = url.openStream();

      // Read and display data from url
      byte buffer[] = new byte[1024];
      int i;
      while((i = is.read(buffer)) != -1) {
        System.out.write(buffer, 0, i);
      }
    }
    catch(Exception e) {
      e.printStackTrace();
    }
  }
}
```

You can easily test this file by using a local file on your PC. Create a file named **c:\test.txt** that has the contents shown here:

```
This is a text file
that can be used to
test my Java application.
```

To test this application, open a DOS window and enter the following command:

```
java URLDemo file:/test.txt
```

The application outputs the contents of the file.

If you are connected to the Internet, you may test the program by supplying a URL that uses HTTP. For example:

```
java URLDemo http://www.osborne.com
```

The application outputs the HTML source for the default page at the site.

EXERCISE

---

1. Write a program to display the protocol, host, port, and file components of a URL.

**Mastery
Skills Check**

Before continuing, you should be able to answer these questions:

1. What are the two formats commonly used to express Internet addresscs?

2. What class encapsulates an Internet address?

3. Explain the distinction between server sockets and sockets.

4. What two classes are used to build applications that use the User Datagram Protocol (UDP) for communication?

5. What is the format of a URL?

**Cumulative
Skills Check**

This section checks how well you have integrated material in this chapter with that from the preceding chapters.

1. Most client/server applications use a multithreaded server so independent sessions can be managed for each client. Design and build an application by using this technique. Each server thread receives messages from a client. Each message contains a number. Add this number to a running total and return the current total to the client. The client executes an infinite loop that does the following: (a) prompts the user for a number, (b) sends that value to the server, (c) receives the current total, and (d) displays the total.

2. Write one application that executes an infinite loop to receive datagrams and display the data they contain. Write a second application that executes an infinite loop to generate a random number, transmit this value to the first application via a datagram, and sleep for 20 seconds. Test with several instances of the second application.

13

Applets

A LL of the programs presented so far in this book have been applications. This chapter describes how to build and use applets—the small programs that are executed by using a Web browser or a tool such as the applet viewer. The applet viewer is included in the Java Development Kit (JDK). Applets are the most common type of Java program in use today.

You will also be introduced to some of the classes in the **java.awt** package. These are used here to build simple applets that display strings, shapes, and images. Classes are also available so you can work with different colors and fonts.

Applets are typically referenced in a Web page. The complete HTML (Hypertext Markup Language) syntax for doing this is explained. You will see that when a browser requests a page, it also retrieves any referenced applets and executes them.

The superclass of all applets is **java.applet.Applet**. This class and its superclasses are discussed. They provide substantial functionality that is available to any applet.

You will see how to use images in applets.

Finally, multithreading and double buffering are described. This is important material for creating applets that display animations.

Review
Skills Check

Before proceeding, you should be able to answer these questions and perform these exercises.

1. What protocol is used to transmit information via sockets?

2. What protocol is used to transmit datagrams?

3. Write a server that generates a random number every two seconds and sends it to a set of clients. Use sockets to transmit this information to the clients. Write a client that receives and displays each value.

13.1 **A N OVERVIEW OF APPLETS**

An applet is a program that can be referenced by the HTML source code of a Web page. It is dynamically downloaded from a Web server to a browser. The applet then executes within the environment provided by the browser. Alternatively, you may use a tool such as the applet viewer to run it. All of the applets in this book may be tested in this manner.

It is important to recognize that downloading code from the Internet and executing it on your computer is inherently dangerous. Therefore, applets do not have the same capabilities as Java applications. They are restricted to operating within the confines of a "sandbox." In other words, code that is "untrusted" is not allowed to operate outside certain boundaries.

For example, applets are normally not allowed to read or write to your local disk. This would obviously be risky because they could accidentally or maliciously destroy any data stored on that device. They cannot execute any native code. (Native code is written in languages other than Java, such as C or C + + .) If this were permitted, the applet could completely circumvent the "sandbox" constraints. Similarly, starting other applications on the user's machine is prohibited.

An applet may open a socket connection back to the host from which it was downloaded, but not to any other host. The reason for this restriction can be understood if you imagine a configuration in which a firewall protects a corporate Intranet from computer hackers. Assume that an employee has downloaded an applet from the Internet to a PC or workstation. If that applet is allowed to open sockets to any machine, it would then have the potential to steal proprietary information and send it back to the hacker's machine. This must be prevented. Therefore, an applet is not allowed to contact any of those private machines.

These restrictions are the defaults needed to safeguard a user's machine from damage by untrusted code. However, the Java security architecture continues to evolve. There are now mechanisms that allow a user to relax the limitations of the "sandbox" for applets that come from trusted sources. The mechanism that allows a user to distinguish a trusted from an untrusted applet is the digital signature. You can think of a digital signature as analogous to a handwritten signature. A digital signature can be associated with an applet. This identifies the organization or individual that produced the applet. If the user trusts the integrity and quality of that source, he or she may choose to relax the limitations of the "sandbox" for that applet. Additional details of the Java security mechanisms are beyond the scope of this book. However, it is recommended that you check the Sun Microsystems Web site for more information.

Your First Java Applet

Let's develop and test a simple Java applet. Its purpose is to display a string within the applet display area. The following illustration shows how this applet appears.

The source code for this applet is shown in the following listing. Let's consider each of these lines.

The first and second lines import the **java.applet.Applet** and **java.awt.Graphics** classes. You will see that the **Applet** class is the superclass of all applets. The **Graphics** class is provided by the Abstract Window Toolkit (AWT). A more complete description of its functionality is provided later in this chapter. For the moment, it is sufficient to know that this class allows you to draw strings, lines, and other shapes in the applet area.

The next four lines define a Java comment. Within that comment is Hypertext Markup Language (HTML) source code. The applet tag specifies which class contains the code for this applet. It also defines the width and height in pixels of the display area. We will examine the applet tag and all of its possible attributes later in this chapter. You will see that the applet viewer reads the HTML and interprets the information that is contained between the applet tags. Don't get confused: The HTML is not part of the applet and is not used by a Web browser. It is used only by the applet viewer.

The next line declares that **FirstApplet** extends **Applet**. Each applet that you create must extend this class.

Next, a method named **paint( )** is defined. This method is responsible for generating the output of the applet. It accepts a **Graphics** object as its one argument. You will learn later that the **paint( )** method is automatically invoked whenever the applet needs to be displayed.

The actual output of the string is done by calling the **drawString( )** method of the **Graphics** object. The first argument to this method is the string to be displayed. The second and third arguments are the x and y coordinates at which to begin the string.

To understand the meaning of these arguments, you must understand the coordinate system that is used to position output via the **Graphics** object. The upper-left corner of the applet is always the origin at 0,0. The x coordinates increase as you move to the right. The y coordinates increase as you move down.

```
import java.applet.Applet;
import java.awt.Graphics;
/*
  <applet code="FirstApplet" width=200 height=200>
  </applet>
*/

public class FirstApplet extends Applet {

  public void paint(Graphics g) {

    g.drawString("This is my first applet!", 20, 100);
  }
}
```

Compile this code and then enter the following command:

```
appletviewer FirstApplet.java
```

The applet viewer tool is one of the tools included in the Java Developer Kit (JDK). It executes an applet by using the HTML source code included in the comment at the top of the Java source file. Recall that the width and height attributes of the applet tag define the dimensions of the applet display area.

As mentioned in the previous section, applets may also be executed by a Web browser. The details of doing this are described later in this chapter.

EXAMPLE

1. The following applet draws a line between two points in the applet display area. It is similar in structure to **FirstApplet**. However, it uses another method provided by the **Graphics** object called **drawLine( )**. This method displays a line connecting two points in the applet display area. It accepts four **int** arguments. These are the x and y coordinates of the first point and the x and y coordinates of the second point.

```java
import java.applet.Applet;
import java.awt.Graphics;
/*
  <applet code="DrawLine" width=200 height=200>
  </applet>
*/

public class DrawLine extends Applet {

  public void paint(Graphics g) {
    g.drawLine(10, 10, 180, 110);
  }
}
```

The following illustration shows how this applet appears.

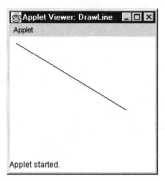

1. Experiment with **FirstApplet** by changing the coordinates at which the string is displayed.

2. Experiment with **DrawLine** by modifying the coordinates used for the end points. Also display several lines in the applet area.

13.3 *THE LIFE CYCLE OF AN APPLET*

You already know that a Java application begins execution at the **main( )** method of a class. However, an applet executes within an environment provided by a Web browser or a tool such as the applet viewer. Therefore, it does not have a **main( )** method. Instead, there are four methods that are called during the life cycle of an applet: **init( )**, **start( )**, **stop( )**, and **destroy( )**. They are defined by the **java.applet.Applet** class and, therefore, are inherited by every applet. Let's discuss each of them.

The **init( )** method is called only when the applet begins execution. It is common to place code here that needs to be executed only once, such as reading parameters that are defined in the HTML file. You will see later in this chapter how to pass parameters to an applet.

The **start( )** method is executed after the **init( )** method completes execution. In addition, this method is called by the applet viewer or Web browser to resume execution of the applet. The **stop( )** method is called by the applet viewer or Web browser to suspend execution of an applet. Therefore, the **start( )** and **stop( )** methods may be called multiple times during the life cycle of the applet.

You will see that **stop( )** is invoked when the applet viewer is minimized and **start( )** is called when the applet viewer is later maximized.

Also, the **stop( )** method is called if the user is viewing a Web page that contains the applet and then goes to another page. The **start( )** method is called if the user returns to the page that contains the applet. Finally, the **destroy( )** method is called by the applet viewer or Web browser before the applet is terminated. The **stop( )** method is invoked before **destroy( )**.

EXAMPLE

1. This example illustrates when the **init( )**, **start( )**, **stop( )**, and **destroy( )** methods are called during the life cycle of an applet. The variable named **str** holds a reference to a string. Each time the **init( )**, **start( )**, and **stop( )** methods are called, the name of that method is appended to **str**. The **destroy( )** method is overridden to display a string on the console. When this applet first begins, you can see it displays **init; start**. If you minimize and maximize the applet window, you can observe that the applet then displays **init; start; stop; start**. This is because the **stop( )** method was called when the applet was minimized and the **start( )** method was called when it was maximized.

```java
import java.applet.Applet;
import java.awt.Graphics;
/*
  <applet code="AppletLifecycle" width=300 height=50>
  </applet>
*/

public class AppletLifecycle extends Applet {
  String str = "";

  public void init() {
    str += "init; ";
  }

  public void start() {
    str += "start; ";
  }

  public void stop() {
    str += "stop; ";
  }

  public void destroy() {
    System.out.println("destroy");
  }

  public void paint(Graphics g) {
    g.drawString(str, 10, 25);
  }
}
```

Output from this applet is shown here:

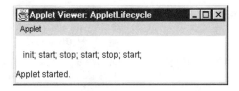

EXERCISE

1. What are the four methods that are called by an applet viewer or browser during the lifetime of an applet? When are they invoked?

13.4 *T*HE GRAPHICS CLASS

In the previous section, you saw how to create simple applets that displayed strings and lines. This was done by using functionality provided by the **java.awt.Graphics** class. This section examines this class in more detail.

A **Graphics** object encapsulates a set of methods that can perform graphics output. Specifically, it allows you to draw lines, ovals, rectangles, strings, images, characters, and arcs.

Some of the commonly used methods of the **Graphics** class are summarized in Table 13-1.

Method	Description
void drawArc(int *x*, int *y*, int *w*, int *h*, int *degrees0*, int *degrees1*)	Draws an arc between *degrees0* and *degrees1*. The center of the arc is the center of a rectangle with upper-left corner at coordinates *x* and *y*, width *w*, and height *h*. Zero degrees is at position 3pm on a watch. The angle increases in a counterclockwise direction.
void drawImage(Image *img*, int *x*, int *y*, ImageObserver *io*)	Draws the image *img* so its upper-left corner is at *x,y*. Updates about the progress of this activity are sent to *io*.
void drawLine(int *x0*, int *y0*, int *x1*, int *y1*)	Draws a line between the points at *x0,y0* and *x1,y1*.

TABLE 13-1   *Some Methods of the* **Graphics** *Class* ▼

Method	Description
void drawOval(int *x*, int *y*, int *w*, int *h*)	Draws an oval. The center of the shape is the center of a rectangle with upper-left corner at coordinates *x* and *y*, width *w*, and height *h*.
void drawPolygon(int *x*[ ], int *y*[ ], int *n*)	Draws a polygon with *n* corners. The coordinates are given by the elements of *x* and *y*. The first and last points are automatically connected.
void drawPolyline(int *x*[ ], int *y*[ ], int *n*)	Draws a polyline with *n* points. The coordinates are given by the elements of *x* and *y*. The first and last points are not automatically connected.
void drawRect(int *x*, int *y*, int *w*, int *h*)	Draws a rectangle with upper-left corner at coordinates *x* and *y*, width *w*, and height *h*.
void drawString(String *str*, int *x*, int *y*)	Draws *str* at location *x,y*.
void fillArc(int *x*, int *y*, int *w*, int *h*, int *degrees0*, int *degrees1*)	Fills an arc between *degrees0* and *degrees1*. The center of the arc is the center of a rectangle with upper-left corner at coordinates *x* and *y*, width *w*, and height *h*. Zero degrees is at position 3pm on a watch.
void fillOval(int *x*, int *y*, int *w*, int *h*)	Fills an oval. The center of the shape is the center of a rectangle with upper-left corner at coordinates *x* and *y*, width *w*, and height *h*.
void fillPolygon(int *x*[ ], int *y*[ ], int *n*)	Fills a polygon with *n* corners. The coordinates are given by the elements of *x* and *y*.
void fillRect(int *x*, int *y*, int *w*, int *h*)	Fills a rectangle with upper-left corner at coordinates *x* and *y*, width *w*, and height *h*.
Color getColor( )	Gets the color of the current object.
Font getFont( )	Gets the font of the current object.
FontMetrics getFontMetrics( )	Gets the font metrics of the current object.

TABLE 13-1　*Some Methods of the **Graphics** Class (continued)* ▼

Some of these methods are now demonstrated in the examples and exercises. The remaining methods are covered in the rest of the chapter. More detail about the classes used as parameter and return types is also provided later.

1. The following applet draws an arc from 0 to 135 degrees. It uses the **drawArc( )** method of the **Graphics** object to draw the arc.

```
import java.applet.Applet;
import java.awt.Graphics;
/*
  <applet code="DrawArc" width=200 height=200>
  </applet>
*/

public class DrawArc extends Applet {

  public void paint(Graphics g) {
    g.drawArc(20, 20, 160, 160, 0, 135);
  }
}
```

Output from this applet is shown here:

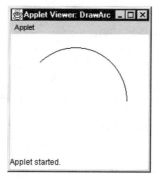

2. The following applet draws a polygon. It uses the **drawPolygon( )** method of the **Graphics** object to draw the shape.

```
import java.applet.Applet;
import java.awt.Graphics;
/*
  <applet code="DrawPolygon" width=200 height=200>
  </applet>
*/
```

```
public class DrawPolygon extends Applet {

  public void paint(Graphics g) {
    int n = 5;
    int xdata[] = new int[n];
    int ydata[] = new int[n];
    xdata[0] = 10;
    ydata[0] = 100;
    xdata[1] = 60;
    ydata[1] = 10;
    xdata[2] = 70;
    ydata[2] = 140;
    xdata[3] = 140;
    ydata[3] = 90;
    xdata[4] = 190;
    ydata[4] = 10;
    g.drawPolygon(xdata, ydata, n);
  }
}
```

Output from this applet is shown here:

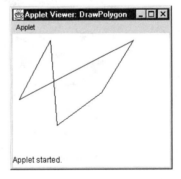

EXERCISE

1. Write an applet that draws a rectangle. The dimensions of the applet should be 500 × 300 pixels. The rectangle should be centered in the applet and have a width and height of 300 and 200 pixels, respectively.

2. Write an applet that draws a circle. The dimensions of the applet should be 500 × 300 pixels. The circle should be centered in the

applet and have a radius of 100 pixels. (Hint: Use the
drawOval( ) method of **Graphics**.)

13.5   *U*SING COLORS

The **java.awt.Color** class is used to work with color. Each instance of
this class represents a particular color. This section demonstrates how
to draw colored strings, lines, and shapes in an applet. It is possible to
fill a shape such as an oval or rectangle with a color. You will see later
in this chapter how to set the background and foreground colors of an
applet.

This class has the following three constructors:

Color(int *red*, int *green*, int *blue*)
Color(int *rgb*)
Color(float *r*, float *g*, float *b*)

Here, *red*, *green*, and *blue* are **int** values that range between 0 and 255,
inclusive. The argument *rgb* contains an encoding of a color in which
the red, green, and blue components are specified in bits 23 to 16, 15 to
8, and 7 to 0, respectively. Finally, *r*, *g*, and *b* are **float** values that
range between 0.0 and 1.0f, inclusive.

The **Color** class also defines several constants that represent specific
colors. These are **black**, **blue**, **cyan**, **darkGray**, **gray**, **green**,
lightGray, **magenta**, **orange**, **pink**, **red**, **white**, and **yellow**.

Table 13-2 summarizes some of the methods defined by this class.

Method	Description
static int HSBtoRGB(float *h*, float *s*, float *b*)	Returns an **int** encoding of a color whose hue, saturation, and brightness are specified by *h*, *s*, and *b*. These values range between 0.0f and 1.0f. Hue is the color. Its values represent red, orange, yellow, green, blue, indigo, and violet as the hue varies from 0.0f to 1.0f. Saturation represents the purity of the color. Brightness indicates the strength of the color. A brightness value of zero is black.

TABLE 13-2   *Some Methods Defined by **Color** ▼*

Method	Description
static float[ ] RGBtoHSB(int *r*, int *g*, int *b*, float *hsb*[ ])	Returns an array of float elements with the hue, saturation, and brightness values for the color whose red, green, and blue components are specified by *r*, *g*, and *b*. The argument *hsb* is the array in which these values are stored. A new array is allocated if *hsb* is **null**.
Color brighter( )	Returns a brighter version of the current object.
Color darker( )	Returns a darker version of the current object.
static Color decode(String *str*) throws NumberFormatException	Returns a **Color** object corresponding to *str*. This argument must contain the decimal, octal, or hex encoding of a color.
boolean equals(Object *obj*)	Returns **true** if the current object and *obj* represent the same color value.
int getBlue( )	Returns the blue component of the current object.
int getGreen( )	Returns the green component of the current object.
int getRGB( )	Returns an **int** encoding of the current object.
int getRed( )	Returns the red component of the current object.

TABLE 13-2   *Some Methods Defined by **Color** (continued)* ▼

EXAMPLES

1. The following applet demonstrates how to display a blue string in an applet. The code is similar to what has been seen previously. Here, the **setColor( )** method of the **Graphics** class is invoked to set the current color of the graphics context.

```
import java.applet.Applet;
import java.awt.Color;
import java.awt.Graphics;
/*
  <applet code="BlueString" width=300 height=100>
  </applet>
*/

public class BlueString extends Applet {

  public void paint(Graphics g) {
    g.setColor(Color.blue);
```

```
    g.drawString("Blue String", 100, 50);
  }
}
```

Output from this applet is shown here:

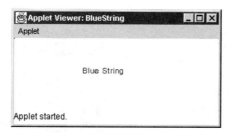

2. The following applet displays 13 vertical color bars that
    correspond to the constants defined by the **Color** class. The
    ColorBars class extends **Applet**. It creates an array of **Color**
    objects named **colors** that is initialized to contain the 13 colors
    specified by the constants of the **Color** class. The **paint( )**
    method is overridden to create the 13 color bars. The width of
    each bar is calculated. A loop then displays each bar. This is
    done by calling **setColor( )** to set the color of the graphics
    context and then calling **fillRect( )** to draw a rectangle filled
    with that color.

```java
import java.applet.Applet;

import java.awt.*;

/*
  <applet code="ColorBars" width=260 height=260>
  </applet>
*/

public class ColorBars extends Applet {
  Color colors[] = { Color.black, Color.blue, Color.cyan,
    Color.darkGray, Color.gray, Color.green,
      Color.lightGray,
    Color.magenta, Color.orange, Color.pink, Color.red,
    Color.white, Color.yellow };

  public void paint(Graphics g) {
    int deltax = 260/colors.length;
    for(int i = 0; i < colors.length; i++) {
```

```
         g.setColor(colors[i]);
         g.fillRect(i * deltax, 0, (i + 1) * deltax, 260);
      }
   }
}
```

Output from this applet is shown here:

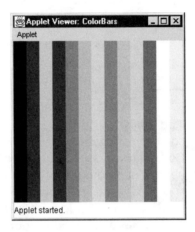

3. A color may be specified by its red, green, and blue components. Alternatively, it may be specified by its hue, saturation, and brightness (HSB) values. This applet illustrates how to fill a triangle with a color identified by the HSB model. The static **HSBtoRGB( )** method is used to convert HSB parameters to an **int** that contains encoded RGB components. This value is then passed as the argument to the **Color** constructor.

```
import java.applet.Applet;
import java.awt.*;
/*
   <applet code="ColoredTriangle" width=400 height=200>
   </applet>
*/

public class ColoredTriangle extends Applet {

   public void paint(Graphics g) {
      int n = 3;
      int xdata[] = new int[n];
      int ydata[] = new int[n];
      xdata[0] = 50;
      ydata[0] = 150;
```

```
        xdata[1] = 200;
        ydata[1] = 50;
        xdata[2] = 350;
        ydata[2] = 150;
        int rgb = Color.HSBtoRGB(1.0f, 1.0f, 1.0f);
        g.setColor(new Color(rgb));
        g.fillPolygon(xdata, ydata, n);
    }
}
```

Output from this applet is shown here:

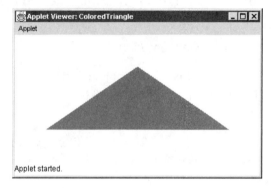

EXERCISES

1. Modify the **ColorBars** example to draw horizontal color bars.
2. Experiment with the **ColoredTriangle** by using different values for hue, saturation, and brightness.

13.6 *D*ISPLAYING TEXT

You have previously seen how the **drawString( )** method of the **Graphics** class is used. This section describes additional capabilities for controlling the appearance and placement of a string in an applet. For example, you will learn how to display strings by using different fonts. This is necessary in many applets. For example, tables and graphs use various fonts for titles, axes, data, and other information. You will also learn how to center text in an applet and how to display multiple lines of text.

A font determines the size and appearance of characters in a string. Information about a font is encapsulated by the **java.awt.Font** class.

The following is one of its constructors:

Font(String *name*, int *style*, int *ps*)

Here, *name* identifies the font. Some commonly used font names are Serif, SansSerif, and Monospaced. The *style* may be **BOLD**, **ITALIC**, or **PLAIN**. The point size of the font is *ps*.

After a font has been created, you may then use it in a graphics context. This is done by calling the **setFont( )** method of the **Graphics** class. This method has the following format:

void setFont(Font *font*)

Here, *font* is a **Font** object. After this method is called, any strings that are output via the **drawString( )** method are displayed with that font.

The **java.awt.FontMetrics** class allows you to get several metrics about the size of a font. In addition, you may also determine the size of a string that is displayed in that font. These quantities are provided in pixels. You will see that they are necessary to calculate the position at which to draw a string in an applet.

The specific metrics that are available are the ascent, descent, leading, and height. Let's describe their meaning. When a string is displayed, all of its characters are aligned to a horizontal *baseline*. Characters extend above and below that line. The number of pixels above the baseline is the *ascent*. The number of pixels below the baseline is the *descent*. The number of pixels between the descent of one line and the ascent of the next line is the *leading*. The sum of the ascent, descent, and leading is the *height*.

The one constructor for this class is

FontMetrics(Font *font*)

Here, *font* indicates the font for which metrics are wanted.

Some of the commonly used methods in this class are summarized in the following table. All of these methods return a value in pixels.

Method	Description
int charWidth(char *c*)	Returns the width of *c*.
int charWidth(int *i*)	Returns the width of the character in the lowest 16 bits of *i*.

Method	Description
int getAscent( )	Returns the ascent.
int getDescent( )	Returns the descent.
int getHeight( )	Returns the height.
int getLeading( )	Returns the leading.
int stringWidth(String *str*)	Returns width of *str.*

EXAMPLES

1. The following applet illustrates use of the **Font** class. A horizontal baseline is drawn in light gray across the middle of the applet display area. This is done by calling the **setColor( )** and **drawLine( )** methods of the **Graphics** object. A **Font** object is created for "Serif" font, bold style, and point size 36. This is passed as the argument to the **setFont( )** method of the **Graphics** object. A string is drawn in black at the baseline. This is done by calling the **setColor( )** and **drawString( )** methods of the **Graphics** object.

```
import java.applet.Applet;
import java.awt.*;
/*
   <applet code="FontDemo" width=200 height=200>
   </applet>
*/

public class FontDemo extends Applet {

  public void paint(Graphics g) {

    // Draw baseline
    int baseline = 100;
    g.setColor(Color.lightGray);
    g.drawLine(0, baseline, 200, baseline);

    // Draw string
    g.setFont(new Font("Serif", Font.BOLD, 36));
    g.setColor(Color.black);
    g.drawString("Wxyz", 5, baseline);
  }
}
```

Output from this applet is shown here:

2. The following applet illustrates use of the **FontMetrics** class. Two strings of characters are displayed on two consecutive lines. Horizontal lines are displayed in light gray. These mark the baseline minus the ascent and the baseline plus the descent. The **paint( )** method begins by initializing the variable named **baseline**. A light gray horizontal line is drawn at the baseline. A **Font** object is created and is provided as the argument to the **setFont( )** method. The **drawString( )** method is used to display a string positioned at the baseline. A **FontMetrics** object is obtained via the **getFontMetrics( )** method of the **Graphics** object. The ascent, descent, leading, and height are obtained and used to position all subsequent display operations.

```java
import java.applet.*;
import java.awt.*;
/*
   <applet code="FontMetricsDemo" width=300 height=200>
   </applet>
*/

public class FontMetricsDemo extends Applet {

  public void paint(Graphics g) {

    // Draw baseline
    int baseline = 100;
```

```java
        g.setColor(Color.lightGray);
        g.drawLine(0, baseline, 300, baseline);

        // Draw string
        Font font = new Font("Serif", Font.BOLD, 36);
        g.setFont(font);
        g.setColor(Color.black);
        g.drawString("Wxyz", 5, baseline);
        g.setColor(Color.lightGray);

        // Get FontMetrics
        FontMetrics fm = g.getFontMetrics(font);

        // Draw line at baseline - ascent
        int ascent = fm.getAscent();
        int y = baseline - ascent;
        g.drawLine(0, y, 300, y);

        // Draw line at baseline + descent
        int descent = fm.getDescent();
        y = baseline + descent;
        g.drawLine(0, y, 300, y);

        // Draw line at baseline + descent + leading
        int leading = fm.getLeading();
        y = baseline + descent + leading;
        g.drawLine(0, y, 300, y);

        // Draw line at baseline + height
        int height = fm.getHeight();
        y = baseline + height;
        g.drawLine(0, y, 300, y);

        // Draw string
        g.setColor(Color.black);
        g.drawString("\"'?/^{9}|[0]*@#", 5, y);
        g.setColor(Color.lightGray);

        // Draw line at baseline + height + descent
        y = baseline + height + descent;
        g.drawLine(0, y, 300, y);
    }
}
```

Output from this applet is shown here:

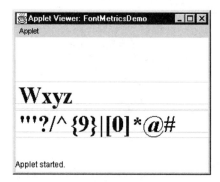

---

1. Experiment with **FontDemo** to show how its output changes when a different font, style, and point size are used.

2. Experiment with **FontMetricsDemo** to show how its output changes when a different font, style, and point size are used.

13.7 **U**SING APPLET DIMENSIONS

The previous sections illustrated how to display strings, lines, and shapes in an applet by using the drawing methods of the **Graphics** class. Each of these methods required arguments to indicate where the output should be positioned.

This section describes how to dynamically determine the dimensions of an applet. The data can then be used to calculate the arguments that should be passed to the drawing methods of the **Graphics** class. For example, you can display a circle at the center of an applet. If the applet is resized, the circle remains positioned at its center.

The **getSize( )** method is used to determine the size of an applet. It has the form shown here:

Dimension getSize( )

A **Dimension** object encapsulates a width and height. The following are some of its constructors:

Dimension(Dimension *d*)
Dimension(int *w*, int *h*)

Here, *d* is a **Dimension** object. The arguments *w* and *h* represent the width and height in pixels. The class has two instance variables **width** and **height** of type **int**.

EXAMPLES

1. The following applet shows how the **getSize( )** method can be used to draw a circle that remains centered in the applet display area even as the applet is resized. Notice that the width and height of the area are compared. The smaller dimension is used to calculate the radius of the circle. This design ensures that the circle always remains completely visible in the display area no matter how the applet is resized. The radius of the circle is 0.4 times either the width or height of the applet. (The smaller of the two quantities is used.)

```
import java.applet.*;
import java.awt.*;
/*
  <applet code="Circle" width=200 height=200>
  </applet>
*/

public class Circle extends Applet {

  public void paint(Graphics g) {
    Dimension d = getSize();
    int xc = d.width/2;
    int yc = d.height/2;
    int radius = (int)((d.width < d.height) ?
      0.4 * d.width : 0.4 * d.height);
    g.drawOval(xc - radius, yc - radius, 2 * radius, 2 *
      radius);
  }
}
```

Output from this applet is shown here:

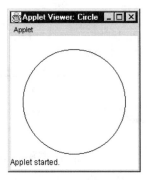

2. The following applet demonstrates how to position a string in the center of an applet. The **paint( )** method creates and sets the font for the graphics context. It then gets a **FontMetrics** object that contains information about that font. The dimensions of the applet are obtained via the **getSize( )** method. The width of the string in pixels is obtained via the **stringWidth( )** method. These values are used to compute the x coordinate at which the string should begin. The y coordinate is computed by adding the descent to the vertical center of the applet.

```
import java.applet.*;
import java.awt.*;
/*
  <applet code="CenterString" width=300 height=200>
  </applet>
*/

public class CenterString extends Applet {

  public void paint(Graphics g) {

    // Set string
    String s = "Teach Yourself Java";
```

```
        // Create and set font
        Font f = new Font("SansSerif", Font.BOLD, 20);
        g.setFont(f);

        // Get font metrics
        FontMetrics fm = g.getFontMetrics();

        // Calculate starting position of string
        Dimension d = getSize();
        int x = d.width/2 - fm.stringWidth(s)/2;
        int y = d.height/2 + fm.getDescent();

        // Draw string
        g.drawString(s, x, y);
    }
}
```

Output from this applet is shown here:

EXERCISES

1. Write an applet that draws two lines in its display area. The first line begins at the upper-left corner and extends to the lower-right corner. The second line begins at the upper-right corner and extends to the lower-left corner. Use the **getSize( )** method so that the applet operates correctly even if it is resized.

2. Write an applet that plots f(x) = sin(x) + (1/2) * sin(2x) + (1/3) * sin(3x) + (1/4) * sin(4x). Let x range from −Math.PI to Math.PI. Scale the plot so it fits within the available area as the applet is resized. Your plot should appear as shown here:

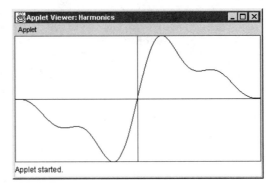

![13.8] ***U*SING APPLETS IN A WEB PAGE**

You have previously seen how the applet viewer uses the HTML source code at the beginning of a **.java** file to display an applet. It is also possible to embed an applet in a Web page. You can then supply the URL for that Web page to a browser and it presents the applet. The complete syntax for an applet tag in HTML is shown in the following listing. Optional lines are enclosed in brackets.

```
<applet

[codebase=url]

code=clsName

[alt=text]

[name=appName]

width=wpixels
```

```
height=hpixels

[align=alignment]

[vspace=vspixels]

[hspace=hspixels

>

[<param name=pname1 value=value1>]

[<param name=pname2 value=value2>]

    . . .

[<param name=pnameN value=valueN>]

</applet>
```

The second line in this listing defines an optional parameter known as *code base*. This is the location from which the **.class** files for the applet are retrieved. You can assign a URL to code base. However, if code base is not specified in the < applet > tag, the **.class** files for the applet are retrieved from the same location where the HTML document was obtained. That location is known as *document base.*

The code parameter of the < applet > tag is required. It is assigned the name of the applet class, *clsName*. Browsers that cannot support applets use *text* as an alternate representation of this applet. Each instance of an applet on a Web page may be assigned a unique name shown above as *appName*.

The width and height of the applet must be specified in *wpixels* and *hpixels*.

The *alignment* of the applet may have a value of LEFT, RIGHT, TOP, BOTTOM, MIDDLE, BASELINE, TEXTTOP, ABSMIDDLE, or ABSBOTTOM. These constants have the same meanings as they do in HTML when used to align images. The vertical and horizontal spacing around the applet may be specified as *vspixels* and *hspixels*.

Parameters may be passed to an applet via a series of param tags. In the syntax shown above, the names of the parameters are *pname1* through *pnameN*. The values of these parameters are *value1* through *valueN*.

1. The following Web page is retrieved by specifying the URL "http://host1/page.html." The HTML file and **photo1.jpg** are retrieved from host1. However, the file **Example1.class** and any other **.class** files are retrieved from host2. The code base is the machine from which the **.class** files for the applet are retrieved. The document base is the machine from which all other files are retrieved.

```
<img src="photo1.jpg" width=200 height=200>
<br>
<applet code="Example1" codebase="host2" width=300
  height=300>
</applet>
```

1. The following Web page is retrieved by specifying the URL "http://host3/page.html." From which machines are the different components of this Web page retrieved? What is code base? What is document base?

```
<img src="photo2.jpg" width=200 height=200>
<br>
<applet code="Example2" codebase="host4" width=300
  height=300>
</applet>
```

13.9   *THE APPLET CLASS*

All applets extend the **java.applet.Applet** class. This section takes a brief look at the functionality of this class and its superclasses.

Figure 13-1 shows the inheritance relationships among the superclasses of **Applet**. State and behavior are inherited from **java.lang.Object**, **java.awt.Component**, **java.awt.Container**, and

FIGURE 13-1

Applet and its superclasses

▼

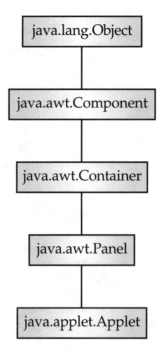

java.awt.Panel. A complete discussion of all these classes must wait until Chapter 15 when the Abstract Window Toolkit (AWT) is studied. However, we will take a brief look at them here.

The abstract **Component** class represents many of the different types of elements you can include in a graphical user interface. Some examples of the components that can be presented are buttons, choices, lists, and scroll bars. These and other types of elements are described in Chapter 15. Because an applet is also a component, you can receive and process events from it by using the same techniques that apply to other user interface elements. This is a considerable advantage and provides another example of the power of object-oriented programming.

There are more than 100 methods provided by this class. Only a small subset of these are summarized in Table 13-3. They are the methods used in this chapter.

The abstract **Container** class is a component that may contain other components. You will see in Chapter 15 that this design allows us to easily build sophisticated user interfaces. A concrete subclass of **Component** is **Panel**.

Method	Description
Image createImage(int *width*, int *height*)	Returns an **Image** object of dimensions *width* and *height*.
Font getFont( )	Returns the current font.
FontMetrics getFontMetrics(Font *font*)	Returns the font metrics for *font*.
Color getForeground( )	Returns the foreground color.
Dimension getSize( )	Returns the size of this component.
public void paint(Graphics *g*)	Paints the component on *g*.
void repaint( )	Requests that the JVM schedule a call to **update( )**.
void setBackground(Color *c*)	Sets the background color to *c*.
void setFont(Font *f*)	Sets the font to *f*.
void setForeground(Color *c*)	Sets the foreground color to *c*.
public void update(Graphics *g*)	Fills the component with its background color and calls **paint( )**.

TABLE 13-3   *Some Methods Defined by* **Component** ▼

The **Applet** class extends **Panel**. It defines the **init( )**, **start( )**, **stop( )**, and **destroy( )** methods that are used to manage the applet life cycle. These were discussed earlier in this chapter. Methods are also provided so that an applet can interact with its environment. Table 13-4 summarizes some of the methods defined by this class.

Method	Description
void destroy( )	Destroys this applet.
AppletContext getAppletContext( )	Returns the applet context.
URL getCodeBase( )	Returns the code base.
URL getDocumentBase( )	Returns the document base.
Image getImage(URL *url*)	Returns an **Image** object for the image at *url*.

TABLE 13-4   *Some Methods Defined by* **Applet** ▼

Method	Description
Image getImage(URL *url*, String *imgName*)	Returns an **Image** object for the image named *imgName* relative to *url*.
String getParameter(String *pName*)	Returns the value of parameter *pName*.
void init( )	Initializes this applet.
void showStatus(String *str*)	Displays *str* on the status line.
void start( )	Starts this applet.
void stop( )	Stops this applet.

TABLE 13-4   *Some Methods Defined by **Applet*** (continued) ▼

The examples in this section demonstrate some of this functionality. The remaining methods are discussed in the rest of this chapter.

EXAMPLES

1. The **setBackground( )** and **setForeground( )** methods are illustrated in the following applet. These set the background color to yellow and the foreground color to blue. A square and a line are then drawn. They appear in blue.

```java
import java.applet.*;
import java.awt.*;
/*
  <applet code="BackgroundForeground" width=200
    height=200>
  </applet>
*/

public class BackgroundForeground extends Applet {

  public void paint(Graphics g) {
    setBackground(Color.yellow);
    setForeground(Color.blue);
    g.drawLine(0, 0, 200, 200);
    g.fillRect(100, 40, 50, 50);
  }
}
```

Output from this applet is shown here:

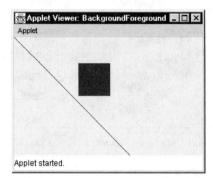

2. This example illustrates how to use the **getParameter( )** method to work with parameters provided in the associated HTML source. The background and foreground colors are the first two parameters. The string values for these parameters are the hexadecimal formats for white and black. The third parameter is a string that is displayed in the center of the applet.

The **paint( )** method obtains the values of these parameters and saves them in variables named **background**, **foreground**, and **message**. The static **decode( )** method of **Color** is called to obtain objects representing the background and foreground colors. The background and foreground colors of the applet are then set. The message is then displayed in the center of the applet. Notice how this is done. The current font and its associated font metrics are obtained. The **stringWidth( )** method of **FontMetrics** returns the width of its argument in pixels. This information plus the width of the applet are used to compute the position of the string. The string is displayed via the **drawString( )** method.

```java
import java.applet.*;
import java.awt.*;
/*
  <applet code="AppletParameters" width=300 height=300>
  <param name="background" value="0xffffff">
  <param name="foreground" value="0x000000">
  <param name="message" value="Testing Applet
    Parameters">
  </applet>
*/
```

```
public class AppletParameters extends Applet {

  public void paint(Graphics g) {
    String background = getParameter("background");
    String foreground = getParameter("foreground");
    String message = getParameter("message");
    setBackground(Color.decode(background));
    setForeground(Color.decode(foreground));
    Font font = getFont();
    FontMetrics fm = getFontMetrics(font);
    Dimension d = getSize();
    int x = (d.width - fm.stringWidth(message))/2;
    int y = d.height/2;
    g.drawString(message, x, y);
  }
}
```

Output from this applet is shown here:

EXERCISE

1. Write an applet that draws an ellipse. Accept two parameters that are the sizes of the two axes in pixels. Center the ellipse in the applet. (Hint: Use the **drawOval( )** method of **Graphics**.)

2. Write an applet that sets the background color to cyan and draws a circle of radius 50 pixels centered in the middle of the applet. The dimensions of the applet should be 120 × 120 pixels. Fill the circle with a magenta color.

![13.10]   **T***HE APPLETCONTEXT CLASS*

The **java.applet.AppletContext** interface defines methods that allow an applet to interact with the context (or environment) in which it is executing. This context is provided by either a tool such as the applet viewer or a Web browser.

Table 13-5 summarizes the methods declared by this interface.

Method	Description
Applet getApplet(String *appName*)	Returns the applet named *appName*. (Note: A name is assigned to an applet instance via the HTML syntax described in the previous section.)
Enumeration getApplets( )	Returns an enumeration of the applets in the current context.
AudioClip getAudioClip(URL *url*)	Returns an **AudioClip** object for the audio clip at *url*.
Image getImage(URL *url*)	Returns an **Image** object for the image at *url*.
void showDocument(URL *url*)	Retrieves and shows the document at *url*.
void showDocument(URL *url*, String *target*)	Retrieves the document at *url* and displays it in *target*.
void showStatus(String *str*)	Displays *str* in the status line.

TABLE 13-5   *Methods Declared by* **AppletContext** ▼

The first form of **showDocument( )** causes the Web browser to retrieve and display the Web page identified by *url*. The second form of **showDocument( )** allows you to specify where this Web page is displayed. The argument target may be "_self" (show in current frame), "_parent" (show in parent frame), "_top" (show in top frame), and "_blank" (show in a new browser window). It may also equal the name of a frame.

Many browsers allow you to divide their display area into frames. These are rectangular regions that can independently display different URLs. A Web page can use the < frameset > tag to define how its display areas are to be divided into frames. A simple example of this technique is shown in the following listing. The display is divided into two columns. The left and right columns are 25 percent and 75 percent of the browser window, respectively.

```
<frameset cols="25%,75%">
<frame name="left" src="left.html">
<frame name="right" src="right.html">
</frameset>
```

Framesets provide additional functionality. For example, you can specify a fixed width in pixels for a frameset or define nested framesets. Consult other texts for more information.

The **AppletContext** interface is implemented by the applet viewer. However, these methods do not have the same functionality as you would find in a Web browser environment. For example, if you use the **showDocument( )** method in an applet and then execute that applet with the applet viewer, you will find that this method has no effect.

EXAMPLES

1. The following example illustrates the operation of the **showDocument( )** method. It divides the browser area into two frames. The applet appears in the top frame and uses the **showDocument( )** method to retrieve a URL and display it in the bottom frame. The example has been tested successfully with Internet Explorer 4.0.

   There are four files for this example. The contents of **ShowDocument.html** are shown in the following listing. This is the file that the user requests via the Web browser. It defines a frameset with two frames named "frame1" and "frame2". These two frames are always equal in height.

   ```
   <frameset rows="50%,50%">
   <frame name="frame1" src="frame1.html">
   <frame name="frame2" src="frame2.html">
   </frameset>
   ```

   The contents of **frame1.html** are shown in the following listing. This file contains the applet tag.

   ```
   <applet code="ShowDocument" width=200 height=50>
   </applet>
   ```

The contents of **frame2.html** are shown in the following listing. This file is initially presented in the bottom frame during the time the Web page is being retrieved. The bottom frame is then overwritten with that page.

```
<B>This is frame2.html</B>
```

The contents of **ShowDocument.java** are shown in the following listing. Its **init( )** method gets the applet context and invokes the **showDocument( )** method to retrieve the Web page at **www.osborne.com** and display it in the frame named "frame2". If a problem occurs, the **showStatus( )** method is called to report the exception. The **paint( )** method uses the **drawString( )** method of the **Graphics** object to display a name for this applet.

```
import java.applet.*;
import java.awt.*;
import java.net.*;
/*
  <applet code="ShowDocument" width=200 height=50>
  </applet>
*/

public class ShowDocument extends Applet {

  public void init() {
    AppletContext ac = getAppletContext();
    try {
      URL url = new URL("http://www.osborne.com");
      ac.showDocument(url, "frame2");
    }
    catch(Exception e) {
      showStatus("Exception: " + e);
    }
  }

  public void paint(Graphics g) {
    g.drawString("ShowDocument Applet", 10, 25);
  }
}
```

2. The following applet displays its dimensions on the status line. The **paint( )** method gets the size of the applet and then displays its width and height.

```
import java.applet.*;
import java.awt.*;
/*
  <applet code="ShowDimension" width=200 height=200>
  </applet>
*/

public class ShowDimension extends Applet {

  public void paint(Graphics g) {

    // Obtain dimension
    Dimension d = getSize();

    // Display on status line
    showStatus("width = " + d.width + "; height = " +
      d.height);
  }
}
```

EXERCISE

1. Write an applet that uses **showStatus( )** to display the name of the current month, day, and year. Also display this information in the applet.

13.11   *U SING IMAGES*

This section describes how to write applets that display images. Only a brief overview of this topic is provided here. The Java class libraries provide additional capabilities for image processing that are beyond the scope of this book.

The **getImage( )** method of the **Applet** class returns a **java.awt.Image** object. That method has the two forms shown here:

Image getImage(URL *url*)
Image getImage(URL *base*, String *fileName*)

The first form accepts one argument that is an absolute URL to identify the image resource. The second form accepts two arguments. Its first argument is an URL to identify the base location from where the image file can be downloaded, and its second argument is the name of a specific file.

The **drawImage( )** method of the **Graphics** class initiates the downloading of an image and displays subsets of the image data as it is downloaded to a user's machine. The method has several forms. The one used in this book is:

boolean drawImage(Image *img*, int *x*, int *y*, ImageObserver *io*)

Here, *img* is a reference to the **Image** object that was returned from **getImage( )**. The coordinates where the upper-left corner of the image should be positioned are given as *x* and *y*. The last parameter is a reference to an object that implements the **ImageObserver** interface. This interface is implemented by all components. In this book, the applet itself is provided as an image observer.

EXAMPLE

---

1. This example illustrates how to write an applet that displays an image. The name of the file (relative to the document base for this applet) is provided as a parameter in the HTML code. The **init( )** method calls **getImage( )** to obtain an **Image** object. Its first argument is an URL that provides the location from where the image should be retrieved. Its second argument is a string that contains the name of the file relative to the location specified by the first argument. It is important to understand that the **getImage( )** method returns immediately. It does not even initiate download of image data.

   The **paint( )** method invokes the **drawImage( )** method of the **Graphics** object. The first argument to this method is a reference to the **Image** object. The second and third arguments specify the x, y coordinates of the upper-left corner where the image should appear on the display. The final argument is a reference to the applet itself. The **drawImage( )** method initiates the download of the image. As the data arrives at the user's machine, the **paint( )** method is called periodically to display this information.

```
import java.applet.*;
import java.awt.*;
/*
  <applet code="DrawImage" width=280 height=280>
  <param name="file" value="kids2.jpg">
  </applet>
*/

public class DrawImage extends Applet {
  Image image;

  public void init() {
    image = getImage(getDocumentBase(),
      getParameter("file"));
  }

  public void paint(Graphics g) {
    g.drawImage(image, 0, 0, this);
  }
}
```

Output from this applet is shown here:

EXERCISE

1. Write an applet that accepts multiple parameters that identify
   a set of images. Select one of these images at random and
   display it.

13.12 USING THREADS

Chapter 9 explained how to build multithreaded applications. This section demonstrates how to build applets that use threads. The information you previously learned is applicable here.

The examples presented so far have used the **paint( )** method to draw strings, lines, shapes, or images. Recall that this method is inherited from the **Component** class. However, applets that use threads commonly need to update the display. For example, an applet that provides an animation or simulation will need to do this.

You cannot invoke the **paint( )** method directly to update the display. The reason is that the Java Virtual Machine (JVM) schedules a number of important tasks. Updating the display is only one of these. Garbage collection, I/O, and thread management are others. The JVM decides when the screen can be updated.

Therefore, your applet must invoke the **repaint( )** method to request an update of the applet display. When the JVM determines that it is appropriate to perform this work, it calls the **update( )** method.

The default implementation of the **update( )** method clears the applet display with the background color and then invokes the **paint( )** method.

Your program may override both the **update( )** and **paint( )** methods. Let's now look at two examples that illustrate how this is done.

EXAMPLE

1. This applet displays a counter in its center. The counter begins at zero and is incremented every second. The **init( )** method initializes the counter and starts a thread. The **run( )** method contains the body of the thread. It executes an infinite loop that calls the **repaint( )** method, sleeps for one second, and increments the counter. The **paint( )** method displays the current value of the counter as a string in the center of the applet.

Note *The **update( )** method has not been overridden. Therefore, the applet is cleared with the background color before the **paint( )** method is invoked.*

```
import java.applet.*;
import java.awt.*;
/*
  <applet code="Counter" width=250 height=100>
  </applet>
*/

public class Counter extends Applet
implements Runnable {
  int counter;
  Thread t;

  public void init() {

    // Initialize counter
    counter = 0;

    // Start thread
    t = new Thread(this);
    t.start();
  }

  public void run() {
    try {
      while(true) {

        // Request a repaint
        repaint();

        // Sleep before displaying next count
        Thread.sleep(1000);

        // Increment counter
        ++counter;
      }
    }
    catch(Exception e) {
    }
  }

  public void paint(Graphics g) {

    // Set font
    g.setFont(new Font("Serif", Font.BOLD, 36));
```

```
        // Get font metrics
        FontMetrics fm = g.getFontMetrics();

        // Display counter
        String str = "" + counter;
        Dimension d = getSize();
        int x = d.width/2 - fm.stringWidth(str)/2;
        g.drawString(str, x, d.height/2);
    }
}
```

Sample output from this applet is shown here:

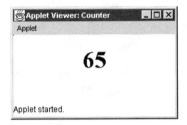

2. This applet draws a dot at a random location in its display area every 200 milliseconds. Any dots that already exist are not erased. Therefore, dots accumulate as the applet executes.

   The **init( )** method starts a thread. The **run( )** method contains the body of the thread. It executes an infinite loop that calls the **repaint( )** method and then sleeps for 200 milliseconds. The **paint( )** method selects a random location in the applet and displays a 2 × 2 solid rectangle at that position.

Note   *The **update( )** method has been overridden. Therefore, the applet display area is not cleared with the background color before the **paint( )** method is invoked. This causes the dots to accumulate as the applet executes.*

```
import java.applet.*;
import java.awt.*;
/*
  <applet code="Dots" width=250 height=100>
  </applet>
```

```
*/

public class Dots extends Applet
implements Runnable {
  Thread t;

  public void init() {

    // Start thread
    t = new Thread(this);
    t.start();
  }

  public void run() {
    try {
      while(true) {

        // Request a repaint
        repaint();

        // Sleep before displaying next dot
        Thread.sleep(200);
      }
    }
    catch(Exception e) {
    }
  }

  public void update(Graphics g) {
    paint(g);
  }

  public void paint(Graphics g) {

    // Pick a random point in the applet
    Dimension d = getSize();
    int x = (int)(Math.random() * d.width);
    int y = (int)(Math.random() * d.height);

    // Draw a dot at that location
    g.fillRect(x, y, 2, 2);
  }
}
```

Sample output from this applet is shown here:

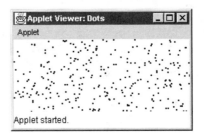

1. Write an applet that moves a 5 × 5 pixel-filled rectangle along a circular trajectory that is 100 pixels in radius and is located at the center of the applet.

2. Modify the **Dots** example so that the points are connected by lines. When a new dot is added to the applet, draw a line between it and the last dot.

13.13 *D*OUBLE BUFFERING

The previous section demonstrated how to build applets that use threads to update their display area. Recall that the default implementation of the **update( )** method clears the entire display area with the background color. The **paint( )** method is then called to generate the output of the applet. This can sometimes cause an annoying "flicker" in the display. It occurs because the screen is frequently being cleared with one color and drawn with a different color.

This section demonstrates how a technique known as *double buffering* can be used to avoid display "flicker" in applets. The **update( )** method is overridden so that the display is not cleared. Instead, it simply invokes the **paint( )** method.

Inside the **paint( )** method, all drawing operations are done to a buffer. The buffer is then copied to the screen.

A background buffer can be created via the **createImage( )** method of **Component**. It has this form:

Image createImage(int *width*, int *height*)

Here, *width* and *height* specify the size of the buffer. We will create a buffer that has the same dimensions as the applet.

A graphics context for this buffer can be obtained via the **getGraphics( )** method of **Image**. It has the form shown here:

Graphics getGraphics()

Drawing operations are then done by using this graphics context.

The buffer can be copied to the screen by using the **drawImage( )** method of **Graphics**. The form for this method was seen in Section 4 of this chapter.

EXAMPLES

1. This example shows a solid circle that moves from left to right across the applet display area. The flicker effect should be noticeable.

```java
import java.applet.*;
import java.awt.*;
/*
  <applet code="NoDoubleBuffer" width=300 height=100>
  </applet>
*/

public class NoDoubleBuffer extends Applet
implements Runnable {
    int x = 0;
    Thread t;

    public void init() {

      // Start thread
      t = new Thread(this);
      t.start();
    }

    public void run() {
      try {
        while(true) {
```

```
        // Request a repaint
        repaint();

        // Sleep before update
        Thread.sleep(100);
      }
    }
    catch(Exception e) {
    }
  }

  public void paint(Graphics g) {

    // Draw filled circle
    Dimension d = getSize();
    g.fillOval(x, d.height/4, 50, 50);

    // Increment x
    x += 5;
    if(x + 50 > d.width)
      x = 0;
  }
}
```

Output from this applet is shown here:

2. This example illustrates how to provide double buffering for the animation seen in the previous example. The **init( )** method now creates a buffer that has the same dimensions as the applet. The **update( )** method is overridden so that the applet display area is not cleared. Instead, the **paint( )** method is called.

A graphics context is created for the buffer when the **paint( )** method is first called. A reference to this object is saved in the instance variable **bufferg**. It can then be used in subsequent calls to **paint( )**. Drawing operations are then done to the buffer. The screen is updated via **drawImage( )**.

Execute this applet and observe that it does not exhibit the same
flicker problem as the previous example.

```java
import java.applet.*;
import java.awt.*;
/*
  <applet code="DoubleBuffer" width=300 height=100>
  </applet>
*/

public class DoubleBuffer extends Applet
implements Runnable {
  int x = 0;
  Thread t;
  Image buffer;
  Graphics bufferg;

  public void init() {

    // Start thread
    t = new Thread(this);
    t.start();

    // Create buffer
    Dimension d = getSize();
    buffer = createImage(d.width, d.height);
  }

  public void run() {
    try {
      while(true) {

        // Request a repaint
        repaint();

        // Sleep before update
        Thread.sleep(100);
      }
    }
    catch(Exception e) {
    }
  }

  public void update(Graphics g) {
    paint(g);
  }
```

```
public void paint(Graphics g) {

    // Get graphics object for buffer
    if(bufferg == null)
      bufferg = buffer.getGraphics();

    // Draw to buffer
    Dimension d = getSize();
    bufferg.setColor(Color.white);
    bufferg.fillRect(0, 0, d.width, d.height);
    bufferg.setColor(Color.black);
    bufferg.fillOval(x, d.height/4, 50, 50);

    // Update screen
    g.drawImage(buffer, 0, 0, this);

    // Increment x
    x += 5;
    if(x + 50 > d.width)
      x = 0;
  }
}
```

EXERCISE

1. Write an applet that simulates an analog meter as shown in the following illustration. The parameters to the applet define the amplitude and frequency (in cycles/second) of a sine wave and the maximum and minimum values that can be displayed by the meter. Use double buffering techniques to avoid display flicker.

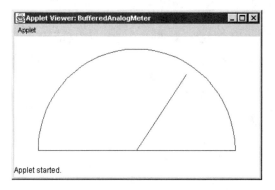

Mastery
Skills Check

At this point you should be able to answer these questions and perform these exercises:

1. Name four restrictions that are placed on an applet by the "sandbox" model.

2. What class provides methods to draw lines and shapes in an applet?

3. What are the ascent, descent, leading, and height of a font?

4. Name ten methods provided by **Component**.

5. What HTML tag is used to embed an applet in a Web page?

6. What is the distinction between code base and document base? When do they have different values?

7. Name two methods provided by **AppletContext** and state what function they provide.

8. What are the primary methods executed during the life cycle of an applet?

9. Write an applet that contains a 10 × 10 solid blue square. The square moves at a constant speed. It bounces off the borders of the applet display area. Each time the square collides with a border, its speed remains unchanged but its velocity changes. Use double buffering to avoid display flicker.

10. Write an applet that presents a message in its display area. The applet begins by displaying the first character of the message, waiting for t1 milliseconds, adding the second character, waiting for t1 milliseconds, adding the third character, and so forth. This operation continues until all of the characters of the message are visible. When all characters have been presented, the entire message remains visible for t2 milliseconds. Then the display area is cleared and the cycle repeats. The applet should accept three parameters. The first parameter is named "message". This is the string to be displayed. The second parameter is named "t1" and is the number of milliseconds between characters. The third

parameter is named "t2" and is the number of milliseconds for which the entire message remains visible. Use double buffering to avoid display flicker.

Cumulative Skills Check

This section checks how well you have integrated the material in this chapter with that of the earlier chapters.

1. Write an applet that displays a sequence of images in an infinite loop. The applet should accept a parameter named "count" that equals the total number of images. Another parameter named "msec" determines the number of milliseconds between images. There are also parameters named "file0", "file1", "file2", and so forth to specify the files from which each image can be read.

2. Write an applet that displays a different image based on the day of the week. The applet should accept seven parameters that identify the image files.

3. Write a multithreaded applet that simulates an analog clock. Show minute and hour hands.

14

An Introduction to Event Handling

T
HE graphical user interface of an applet can include a variety of components. Some examples are buttons, check boxes, choices, lists, scroll bars, text areas, text fields, and menus. A user may interact with an applet via these elements. In addition, the mouse and keyboard can also provide input.

An event is generated each time a user interacts with an applet in this manner—for example, when a button is pressed, the mouse is dragged, a scroll bar is manipulated, or a menu item is selected.

This chapter begins our discussion of event handling. It describes how an applet can receive and process input from the mouse. The next chapter teaches you how to process input from the other types of user interface elements.

The delegation event model specifies how an event can be generated by one object and sent to other objects for processing. You will learn about the classes and interfaces that are defined in the **java.awt.event** package for handling events. These are the foundation on which event handling is built in Java.

Adapter, inner, and anonymous inner classes are also described in this chapter. They provide mechanisms that make it easier to construct event handling code.

Review

Skills Check

Before proceeding, you should be able to answer these questions and perform these exercises.

1. Write an applet that displays the waveform $y(x) = \sin(x) * \sin(10x)$. Let values on the x-axis range from $-2 * \text{Math.PI}$ to $2 * \text{Math.PI}$. Your applet should appear as shown in the following illustration.

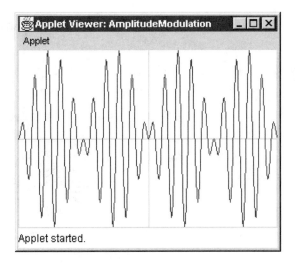

2. Build an applet that displays a horizontal rectangle in its center. Let the rectangle fill with color from left to right. Provide applet parameters to specify the width, height, and color of the rectangle and the number of milliseconds required to fill it. Use double buffering to avoid display flicker. Your applet should appear as shown in the following illustration.

3. Write an applet that generates and displays a set of points. Each point is 1×1 pixel in size. The x and y coordinates of each point are randomly selected and have a Gaussian distribution. A point whose x and y coordinates are zero is positioned at the center of the applet display area. The applet generates and displays these points in an infinite loop. Your applet should appear as shown in the following illustration. Notice that the points are clustered in the center of the applet and are not uniformly distributed.

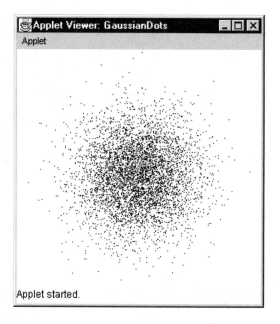

The programs shown in the beginning of this book are text-based console applications. Applets provide a graphical user interface (GUI). Aside from the obvious visual differences, the major distinction between the two is that a GUI-based program is event-driven and a console application is not. If you are familiar with Windows programming, you already understand the difference. If not, the following explanation will help.

A person interacts with an applet via a set of user interface elements that are displayed on the screen. The keyboard and mouse are also sources of input. You will see in the next chapter that the Abstract Window Toolkit (AWT) provides a set of standard components, such as buttons, check boxes, and scroll bars, with which a user interface can be constructed. It is important to realize that your applet does not poll these components for events. Such a design would be very wasteful of processor resources. Instead, an applet is *event-driven*. That is, the code to handle a particular type of event is invoked only when such an event occurs.

The Java run-time system notifies the applet about an event by calling an event handler that has been supplied by the applet. Upon receipt of the event, the applet handles the event and then returns control to the run-time system. This process of receiving and responding to events continues until the applet terminates. It is important to understand that the user interacts with the applet when he or she wants. The applet does not enter a "mode," such as inputting a string using **readLine( )**, in which it waits for the user to type characters. Instead, each user-input interaction generates its own event.

There are various ways in which an event-driven interface can be defined, and the specific mechanism is determined by the *event model*. Java Development Kit (JDK) version 1.1 introduced the *delegation event model*. This provides an efficient means for an event to be sent from a source to one or more listeners. JDK version 1.0 used a different event model that is not described in this book. It is still supported for backward compatibility. However, the JDK compiler issues warning messages if you attempt to use those older methods. The messages state that the methods are deprecated. All new code should be designed by using the delegation event model. You may also wish to convert older code so that it uses this technique.

The delegation event model provides a standard mechanism for a source to generate an event and send it to a set of listeners. Let us look first at events and then examine the specific responsibilities of sources and listeners.

An *event* is an object that describes some state change in a source. It can be generated when a person interacts with an element in a graphical user interface—for example, pressing a button, clicking the mouse, double-clicking on a list box entry, or closing a window.

A *source* generates events. It has three main responsibilities. First, it must provide methods that allow listeners to register and unregister for notifications about a specific type of event. Second, it must generate the event. Finally, it must send the event to all registered listeners. The event may be unicast to a single listener or multicast to several listeners. It is possible for a source to generate several types of events. In that case, multiple registration/unregistration methods would be provided.

The methods implemented by a source that allow listeners to register and unregister for events are as follows:

```
public void addTypeListener(TypeListener el)
public void addTypeListener(TypeListener el) throws
   TooManyListenersException
public void removeTypeListener(TypeListener el)
```

Here, *Type* is the type of the event and *el* is the event listener. The first form allows several listeners to register for the same type of event. The second form is provided if only one listener may register to receive that type of event. The last form allows a listener to unregister for notifications about a specific type of event.

A *listener* receives event notifications. It has three main responsibilities. First, it must register to receive notifications about specific events. It does so by calling the appropriate registration method of the source. Second, it must implement an interface to receive events of that type. Finally, it must unregister if it no longer wants to receive those notifications. It does so by calling the appropriate unregistration method of the source.

The delegation event model can be depicted as shown in Figure 14-1. Here, a source multicasts an event to a set of listeners. The listeners implement an interface to receive notifications about that type of event. In effect, the source *delegates* the processing of the event to one or more listeners.

Let us consider how the delegation event model applies to a button in a graphical user interface. This component generates an event when

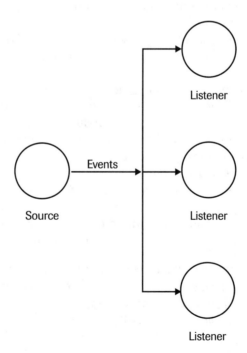

FIGURE 14-1

The Delegation Event Model

▼

it is pressed. An object of class **java.awt.event.ActionEvent** is created to encapsulate information about the event.

The **java.awt.Button** class provides the following methods so listeners may register and unregister to receive action events:

```
void addActionListener(ActionListener al)
void removeActionListener(ActionListener al)
```

Here, *al* is a reference to the listener object.

Finally, the **java.awt.eventActionListener** interface must be implemented by a listener. This defines one method to receive action events as follows:

```
void actionPerformed(ActionEvent ae)
```

Here, *ae* is a reference to the action event.

(Action events may also be generated by other types of user interface components. The next chapter discusses this topic in more detail and shows how to build code that handles these types of events.)

EXERCISES

1. What are the three responsibilities of event sources?

2. What are the three responsibilities of event listeners?

3. What are the forms of the registration and unregistration methods implemented by event sources?

14.2 *E VENT CLASSES*

A set of classes are provided to represent the various types of AWT events. The relationships among them are shown in Figure 14-2. Let us briefly consider some of these classes.

The **EventObject** class extends **Object** and is part of the **java.util** package. Its constructor has this form:

```
EventObject(Object src)
```

Here, *src* is the object that generates the event.

FIGURE 14-2

*The Java Event
Class Hierarchy*
▼

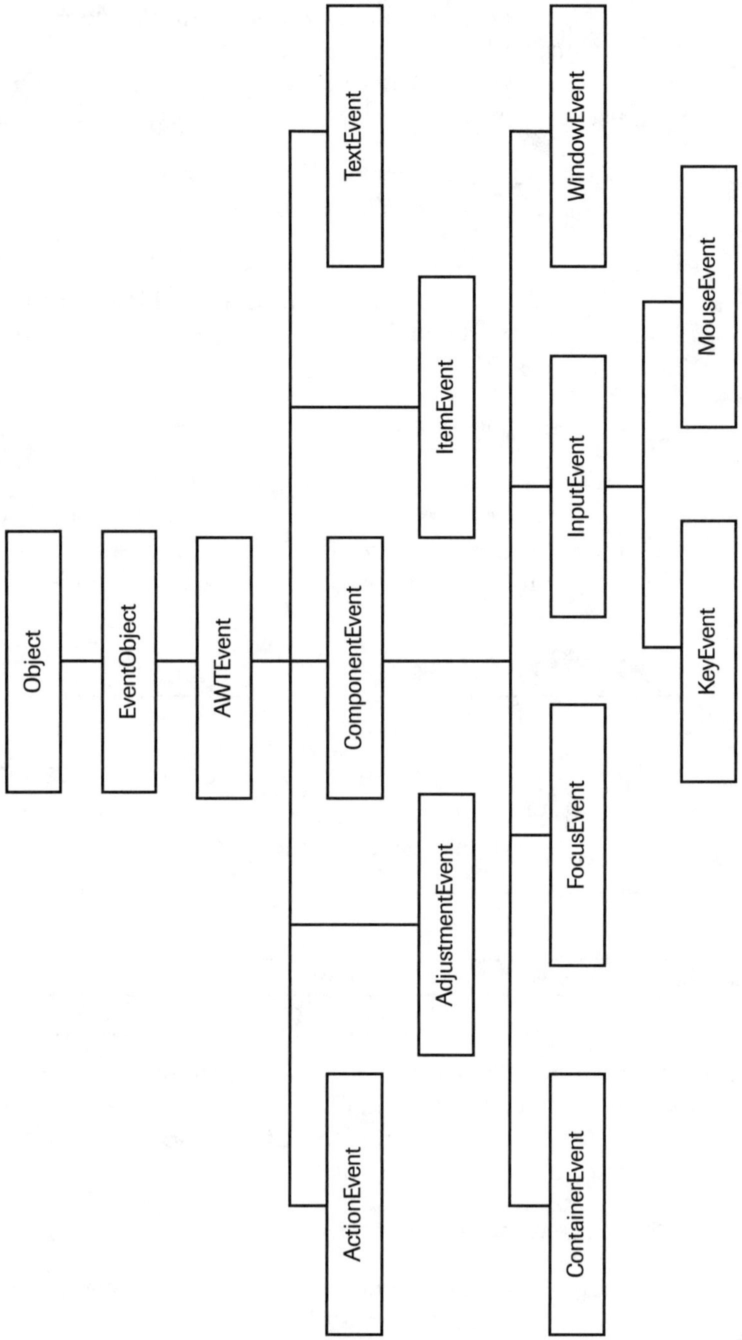

This class has the two methods shown here:

Object getSource( )
String toString( )

The **getSource( )** method returns the object that generated the event, and the **toString( )** method returns a string equivalent of the event.

The abstract **AWTEvent** class extends **EventObject** and is part of the **java.awt** package. All of the AWT event types are subclasses of **AWTEvent**. These events are discussed throughout the rest of this chapter.

One of its constructors has this form:

AWTEvent(Object *source*, int *id*)

Here, *source* is the object that generates the event and *id* identifies the type of the event. The possible values of *id* are described in the remainder of this section.

Two of its methods are shown here:

int getId( )
String toString( )

The **getId( )** method returns the type of the event, and the **toString( )** method returns the string equivalent of the event.

Table 14-1 lists the main event classes in **java.awt.event** and summarizes some of the conditions that cause them to be generated.

Let us examine the constants and methods defined by the **ComponentEvent**, **InputEvent**, and **MouseEvent** classes.

The **ComponentEvent** class extends **AWTEvent**. It defines **int** constants that are used to identify four types of component events. The constants and their meanings are given in the following table:

Constant	**Description**
COMPONENT_HIDDEN	The component was hidden.
COMPONENT_MOVED	The component was moved.
COMPONENT_RESIZED	The component was resized.
COMPONENT_SHOWN	The component became visible.

Event	Generated When
ActionEvent	A button is pressed, a list item is double-clicked, or a menu item is selected.
AdjustmentEvent	A scroll bar is manipulated.
ComponentEvent	A component is hidden, moved, resized, or becomes visible.
ContainerEvent	A component is added to or removed from a container.
FocusEvent	A component gains or loses keyboard focus.
InputEvent	A mouse or key event occurs.
ItemEvent	A check box or list item is clicked, a choice selection is made, or a checkable menu item is selected or deselected.
KeyEvent	Input is received from the keyboard.
MouseEvent	The mouse is dragged or moved, clicked, pressed, or released. Also generated when the mouse enters or exits a component.
TextEvent	The value of a text area or text field is changed.
WindowEvent	A window is activated, closed, deactivated, deiconified, iconified, opened, or quit.

TABLE 14-1   *The Primary Event Classes* ▼

ComponentEvent has this constructor:

ComponentEvent(Component *src*, int *type*)

Here, *src* is a reference to the object that generated this event. The type of the event is *type*.

ComponentEvent is the superclass of **ContainerEvent**, **FocusEvent**, **InputEvent**, and **WindowEvent**.

The **getComponent( )** method returns the component that generated this event. It is shown here:

Component getComponent()

InputEvent is a subclass of **ComponentEvent** and is the superclass for component input events. Its subclasses are **KeyEvent** and **MouseEvent**. The **InputEvent** class defines seven **int** constants that can be used to obtain information about any modifiers associated with this event. These are **ALT_MASK**, **BUTTON1_MASK**,

BUTTON2_MASK, **BUTTON3_MASK**, **CTRL_MASK**, **META_MASK**, and **SHIFT_MASK**.

The **isAltDown( )**, **isControlDown( )**, **isMetaDown( )**, and **isShiftDown( )** methods test if these modifiers were pressed at the time the event was generated. The forms of these methods are shown here:

```
boolean isAltDown()
boolean isControlDown()
boolean isMetaDown()
boolean isShiftDown()
```

The **getModifiers( )** method returns an **int** that contains all of the modifier flags for the event. Its signature is shown here:

```
int getModifiers()
```

The **MouseEvent** class extends **InputEvent**. It defines **int** constants that can be used to identify types of mouse events. The constants and their meanings are given in the following table:

Constant	Description
MOUSE_CLICKED	The mouse was clicked.
MOUSE_DRAGGED	The mouse was dragged.
MOUSE_ENTERED	The mouse entered a component.
MOUSE_EXITED	The mouse exited from a component.
MOUSE_MOVED	The mouse was moved.
MOUSE_PRESSED	The mouse was pressed.
MOUE_RELEASED	The mouse was released.

MouseEvent is a subclass of **InputEvent** and has this constructor:

MouseEvent(Component *src*, int *type*, long *when*, int *modifiers*, int *x*, int *y*, int *clicks*, boolean *triggersPopup*)

Here, *src* is a reference to the component that generated this event. The type of the event is *type*. The *modifiers* argument indicates which modifiers were pressed when this mouse event occurred. The coordinates of the mouse are in *x* and *y*. The click count is in *clicks*. The *triggersPopup* flag indicates if this event causes a pop-up menu to appear on this platform. (Pop-up menus are beyond the scope of this book.)

The most commonly used methods in this class are **getX( )** and **getY( )**. These return the coordinates of the mouse when the event occurred. Their forms are shown here:

```
int getX()
int getY()
```

The **getPoint( )** method returns a **Point** object that has the location of the mouse event relative to the source component. It is shown here:

```
Point getPoint()
```

The **Point** class is defined in the **java.awt** package. Objects of this class encapsulate the coordinates of a point. The class has two public instance variables named **x** and **y**. These can be used to obtain the location of that point.

The **translatePoint( )** method changes the location of the event. Its form is

```
void translatePoint(int x, int y)
```

Here, the arguments x and y are added to the coordinates of the event.

The **getClickCount( )** method obtains the number of mouse clicks for this event. Its signature is:

```
int getClickCount()
```

EXERCISES

1. What class must be extended by all event classes?

2. When are mouse events generated?

3. What are the superclasses of **MouseEvent**?

14.3 EVENT LISTENERS

The **java.util.EventListener** interface does not define any constants or methods but exists only to identify those interfaces that process events. All event listener interfaces must extend this interface. Table 14-2 shows the relationship between the AWT event types and the listener interfaces that define methods to process those events. All of these interfaces are declared in the **java.awt.event** package.

Let us consider the methods provided by the **Component** class that allow a listener to register and unregister for mouse events, as follows:

> void addMouseListener(MouseListener *ml*)
> void addMouseMotionListener(MouseMotionListener *mml*)
> void removeMouseListener(MouseListener *ml*)
> void removeMouseMotionListener(MouseMotionListener *mml*)

Here, *ml* is the mouse listener and *mml* is the mouse motion listener.

The **MouseListener** interface defines several methods to receive mouse events. Their forms are shown below:

> void mouseClicked(MouseEvent *me*)
> void mouseEntered(MouseEvent *me*)
> void mouseExited(MouseEvent *me*)
> void mousePressed(MouseEvent *me*)
> void mouseReleased(MouseEvent *me*)

Event Class	Listener Interface
ActionEvent	ActionListener
AdjustmentEvent	AdjustmentListener
ComponentEvent	ComponentListener
ContainerEvent	ContainerListener
FocusEvent	FocusListener
ItemEvent	ItemListener
KeyEvent	KeyListener
MouseEvent	MouseListener, MouseMotionListener
TextEvent	TextListener
WindowEvent	WindowListener

TABLE 14-2 *AWT Event Classes and Listener Interfaces* ▼

The **MouseMotionListener** interface defines two methods to receive mouse events, as follows:

void mouseDragged(MouseEvent *me*)
void mouseMoved(MouseEvent *me*)

Here, *me* is the **MouseEvent** object generated by the source. Components generate mouse events. The appropriate method of all registered listeners is invoked and the event is passed as an argument to that method.

EXAMPLES

1. The following applet illustrates how to process mouse click, enter, exit, press, and release events. These are received via the **MouseListener** interface. The **init( )** method registers the applet itself as a listener for these events. The **mouseClicked( )** method is called when the mouse is clicked. It sets the background color to blue. The **mouseEntered( )** and **mouseExited( )** methods are called when the mouse enters or exits the applet. These set the background color to green and red, respectively. The **mousePressed( )** and **mouseReleased( )** methods are called when the mouse is pressed and released. These set the background color to white and yellow, respectively. Notice that it is necessary to call **repaint( )** to refresh the display so the color change becomes visible.

```
import java.applet.*;
import java.awt.*;
import java.awt.event.*;
/*
  <applet code="MouseEvents" width=300 height=300>
  </applet>
*/

public class MouseEvents extends Applet
implements MouseListener {

  public void init() {
    addMouseListener(this);
  }

  public void mouseClicked(MouseEvent me) {
```

```
        setBackground(Color.blue);
        repaint();
    }

    public void mouseEntered(MouseEvent me) {
      setBackground(Color.green);
      repaint();
    }

    public void mouseExited(MouseEvent me) {
      setBackground(Color.red);
      repaint();
    }

    public void mousePressed(MouseEvent me) {
      setBackground(Color.white);
      repaint();
    }

    public void mouseReleased(MouseEvent me) {
      setBackground(Color.yellow);
      repaint();
    }
}
```

2. The following applet illustrates how to process mouse drag events. When the user presses the mouse, a line is drawn from the center of the applet to the current mouse position. As the mouse is dragged, the line moves. One end of the line always remains fixed at the center of the applet. The other end of the line moves to track the mouse position. When the mouse is released, the line disappears.

   The **MouseMotionEvents** class extends **Applet** and implements both the **MouseListener** and **MouseMotionListener** interfaces. An instance variable **p** of type **Point** holds a reference to the current position of the mouse when it is pressed. The **init( )** method invokes both the **addMouseListener( )** and **addMouseMotionListener( )** so the applet may receive notifications about all mouse events that it generates. Notice that a reference to the applet itself is passed as the argument to these methods.

   The **mousePressed( )** method obtains the current position of the mouse via the **getPoint( )** method of **MouseEvent**. The return value from this method is assigned to **p**. An update of the display is requested via the call to **repaint( )**. This makes the line appear as soon as the user presses the mouse.

The **mouseReleased( )** method sets **p** to **null** and calls **repaint( )**. This makes the line disappear as soon as the user releases the mouse.

The **mouseDragged( )** method updates **p** and calls **repaint( )**. This causes one end of the line to track the cursor position when the mouse is being dragged.

The **paint( )** method draws a line from the center of the applet to **p**.

```java
import java.applet.*;
import java.awt.*;
import java.awt.event.*;
/*
  <applet code="MouseMotionEvents" width=300 height=300>
  </applet>
*/

public class MouseMotionEvents extends Applet
implements MouseListener, MouseMotionListener {
  Point p;

  public void init() {
    addMouseListener(this);
    addMouseMotionListener(this);
  }

  public void mouseClicked(MouseEvent me) {
  }

  public void mouseEntered(MouseEvent me) {
  }

  public void mouseExited(MouseEvent me) {
  }

  public void mousePressed(MouseEvent me) {
    p = me.getPoint();
    repaint();
  }

  public void mouseReleased(MouseEvent me) {
    p = null;
    repaint();
  }
```

```java
public void mouseDragged(MouseEvent me) {
  p = me.getPoint();
  repaint();
}

public void mouseMoved(MouseEvent me) {
}

public void paint(Graphics g) {
  if(p != null) {
    Dimension d = getSize();
    int xc = d.width/2;
    int yc = d.height/2;
    g.drawLine(xc, yc, p.x, p.y);
  }
}
}
```

Output from this applet is shown in the following illustration:

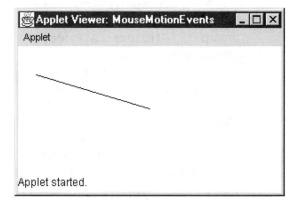

EXERCISES

1. What interface must be extended by all listener interfaces?

2. What are the two listener interfaces that can receive mouse events?

3. Write an applet that tracks the position of the mouse when it is dragged or moved. Draw a 10 × 10-pixel rectangle filled with black at the current mouse position.

| 14.4 | A *DAPTER CLASSES* |

You saw in the previous section that the **MouseListener** interface declares five methods. These are called when the mouse is clicked, pressed, or released. Mouse events also occur when the mouse enters or exits a component. An applet can implement this interface and register itself to receive mouse events. However, it must implement all of the five methods declared by that interface. This can be inconvenient. Adapter classes make it easy to deal with this situation.

An adapter class provides empty implementations of all methods in a particular listener interface. It can be useful if you want to override only some of the methods defined by that interface.

Table 14-3 summarizes the adapter classes in the **java.awt.event** package and the listener interfaces that are implemented by each.

EXAMPLE

1. This example illustrates how to use the **MouseAdapter** class. The **MouseAdapterDemo** class extends **Applet**. Its **init( )** method sets the background color of the applet to green. An instance of **MyMouseAdapter** is created and registered to receive mouse events.

   The **MyMouseAdapter** class extends **MouseAdapter** and overrides the **mousePressed( )** and **mouseReleased( )** methods. When the mouse is pressed, the color of the applet changes to red. It changes to green when the mouse is released.

   It is important to notice that a reference to the applet is provided to the **MyMouseAdapter** constructor. This is necessary so that the adapter can invoke methods of the applet.

```
import java.applet.*;
import java.awt.*;
import java.awt.event.*;
/*
  <applet code="MouseAdapterDemo" width=100 height=100>
  </applet>
*/

public class MouseAdapterDemo extends Applet {

  public void init() {
    setBackground(Color.green);
    addMouseListener(new MyMouseAdapter(this));
```

```
      }
    }

class MyMouseAdapter extends MouseAdapter {
  MouseAdapterDemo mad;

  public MyMouseAdapter(MouseAdapterDemo mad) {
    this.mad = mad;
  }

  public void mousePressed(MouseEvent me) {
    mad.setBackground(Color.red);
    mad.repaint();
  }

  public void mouseReleased(MouseEvent me) {
    mad.setBackground(Color.green);
    mad.repaint();
  }
}
```

EXERCISES

1. Explain why an adapter class is useful.

2. Use adapter classes to write an applet that changes to cyan while the mouse is being dragged. At all other times, the applet should be white.

Adapter Class	Listener Interface
ComponentAdapter	ComponentListener
ContainerAdapter	ContainerListener
FocusAdapter	FocusListener
KeyAdapter	KeyListener
MouseAdapter	MouseListener
MouseMotionAdapter	MouseMotionListener
WindowAdapter	WindowListener

TABLE 14-3 *Adapter Classes* ▼

14.5 INNER CLASSES

An *inner class* is defined within the scope of an expression or another class. Therefore, it has access to the variables and methods in that scope. This section demonstrates how to create and use such classes. You will see that they make it easier to build adapter classes.

The following listing outlines the general form of an applet that uses an inner class as an adapter for mouse events. Observe that **MyMouseAdapter** is defined within the scope of **MouseInnerDemo**. Therefore, it may directly access the variables and methods of **MouseInnerDemo**. It is not necessary for the adapter class to receive a reference to the applet.

The **init( )** method of the applet instantiates the adapter class and registers that object to receive mouse listener events.

```
public class MouseInnerDemo extends Applet {

  public void init( ) {
    ...
    addMouseListener(new MyMouseAdapter());
  }

  class MyMouseAdapter extends MouseAdapter {

    public void mousePressed(MouseEvent me) {
      ...
    }
  }
}
```

EXAMPLE

1. This example illustrates how an inner class can be used to simplify the handling of a mouse event. The **MouseInnerDemo** class extends **Applet**. Its **init( )** method sets the background color to green. An instance of **MyMouseAdapter** is created and registered to receive mouse events.

    The **MyMouseAdapter** class extends **MouseAdapter** and overrides the **mousePressed( )** and **mouseReleased( )** methods. When the mouse is pressed, the color of the applet changes to red. It changes to green when the mouse is released.

Compare this code carefully with the **MouseAdapterDemo** in the previous section. Here, the **MyMouseAdapter** class is defined within the scope of **MouseInnerDemo**. Therefore, it has access to the variables and methods of the latter class. It can invoke the **setBackground( )** and **repaint( )** methods of the applet directly. It is no longer necessary to provide a constructor for **MyMouseAdapter** that accepts and saves a reference to the applet.

```java
import java.applet.*;
import java.awt.*;
import java.awt.event.*;
/*
  <applet code="MouseInnerDemo" width=100 height=100>
  </applet>
*/

public class MouseInnerDemo extends Applet {

  public void init() {
    setBackground(Color.green);
    addMouseListener(new MyMouseAdapter());
  }

  class MyMouseAdapter extends MouseAdapter {

    public void mousePressed(MouseEvent me) {
      setBackground(Color.red);
      repaint();
    }

    public void mouseReleased(MouseEvent me) {
      setBackground(Color.green);
      repaint();
    }
  }
}
```

Note

*When you compile this file with the JDK compiler, two **.class** files are created. These are **MouseInnerDemo.class** and **MouseInnerDemo$MyMouseAdapter.class**. The name of the latter file shows that **MyMouseAdapter** is defined within the scope of **MouseInnerDemo**.*

1. Explain the scope of an inner class.

2. Use inner classes to write an applet that changes to cyan while the mouse is being dragged. At all other times, the applet should be white.

14.6 *A* NONYMOUS INNER CLASSES

An *anonymous inner class* is an inner class that does not have a name. This section demonstrates how to create and use such classes. You will see that they make it easier to build adapter classes.

The syntax to define an anonymous inner class is:

new *clsName*( ) { ... }

Here, *clsName* is the name of the superclass for our anonymous inner class. Its body is defined between the opening and closing braces.

The following listing outlines the general form of an applet that uses an anonymous inner class as an adapter for mouse events.

The **init( )** method of the applet instantiates an anonymous adapter class and registers that object to receive mouse listener events. The anonymous inner class extends **MouseAdapter** and provides an implementation of the **mousePressed( )** method.

```
public class MouseAnonymousDemo extends Applet {

    public void init( ) {
        ...
        addMouseListener(new MouseAdapter() {

            public void mousePressed(MouseEvent me) {
                ...
            }
        });
    }
}
```

If you compare this outline with the previous discussion of inner classes, you can see that anonymous inner classes allow us to build very compact code to handle events.

EXAMPLE

1. This example illustrates the use of anonymous inner classes.
   The **MouseAnonymousDemo** class extends **Applet**. Its **init( )**
   method sets the background color to green. An anonymous inner
   class is then instantiated and registered to receive mouse events.

   The syntax "new MouseAdapter( ) { ... }" indicates to the Java
   compiler that an anonymous inner class that extends
   MouseAdapter is being defined. That class overrides the
   mousePressed( ) and **mouseReleased( )** methods. When the
   mouse is pressed, the color of the applet changes to red. It
   changes to green when the mouse is released.

   Compare this code carefully with the **MouseInnerDemo** in
   the previous section.

```java
import java.applet.*;
import java.awt.*;
import java.awt.event.*;
/*
  <applet code="MouseAnonymousDemo" width=100 height=100>
  </applet>
*/

public class MouseAnonymousDemo extends Applet {

  public void init() {
    setBackground(Color.green);
    addMouseListener(new MouseAdapter() {

      public void mousePressed(MouseEvent me) {
        setBackground(Color.red);
        repaint();
      }

      public void mouseReleased(MouseEvent me) {
        setBackground(Color.green);
        repaint();
      }
    });
  }
}
```

1. Use anonymous inner classes to write an applet that changes to cyan while the mouse is being dragged. At all other times, the applet should be white.

Mastery
Skills Check

At this point you should be able to answer these questions:

1. Explain the delegation event model.

2. What is the superclass of all event classes?

3. What interface must all listener interfaces extend?

4. Which two listener interfaces receive mouse events?

5. What is an adapter class?

6. What is an inner class? Why is it useful when handling events?

7. What is an anonymous inner class? Why is it useful when handling events?

Cumulative
Skills Check

This section checks how well you have integrated the material in this chapter with that of the earlier chapters.

1. Write an applet that initially appears with its background color equal to black. Each time the mouse is clicked, the background color becomes a little brighter. In other words, successive mouse clicks smoothly change the background color from black to dark gray to light gray to white. (Hint: Use the **setBackground( )** method of **Component**.)

2. Write an applet that allows you to interactively draw a circle in its display area. The point at which you press the mouse defines its center. Then drag the mouse from this point to define its radius. As you drag the mouse, the radius of the circle dynamically changes. When you release the mouse, the radius is fixed. You can erase the display area and draw another circle by pressing and dragging the mouse again. Use anonymous inner classes to handle specific mouse and mouse motion events.

3. Write an applet whose display area smoothly changes color from one random value to another. If the mouse is pressed, the color changes should suspend. When the mouse is released, the color changes should resume. (Hint: One way to generate colors that change smoothly in this manner is to independently vary their red, green, and blue components. Use a different sine wave for each color component to smoothly change its value.)

15

The Abstract Window Toolkit

THE Abstract Window Toolkit (AWT) allows you to build graphical user interfaces for applets and applications. Its classes and interfaces are located in the **java.awt** package and other subpackages. This chapter begins by considering some of the classes that allow you to create different elements on a screen such as buttons, check boxes, lists, and others. Three types of layout managers are considered. These determine where elements are positioned in a user interface. Panels are also discussed because they provide another way to organize the screen. Windows, frames, menus, and menu bars are described. Finally, dialogs and file dialogs, which can be used to collect information from a user, are covered.

This chapter also continues our discussion of event handling. More information is provided about the classes and interfaces in the **java.awt.event** package. You will learn about the different events that are generated by the AWT components. These events are sent to your program via the delegation event model that was described in the previous chapter. The associated listener interfaces are also studied.

The **java.awt** package is very large. There is not sufficient space to cover all of its capabilities. However, the most commonly used features are described. You will be able to build very attractive and powerful applets and applications after you master this material.

Review
Skills Check

Before proceeding, you should be able to answer these questions and perform these exercises.

1. Write an applet that displays a sequence of images. Suspend the animation when the user clicks the mouse on an image. Resume the animation when the user clicks again.

2. Write an applet that animates a stick figure of a windmill. The arms of the windmill should initially be stationary. Start the arms moving when the mouse is dragged. Stop the arms when the mouse is clicked. Your applet should appear as shown in the following illustration:

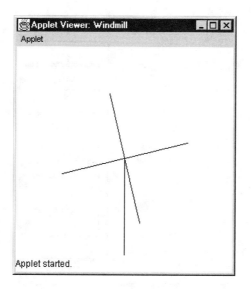

15.1 ■ *O*VERVIEW

The abstract **Component** class was introduced in Chapter 13. You saw that applets inherit considerable functionality from this class. Because user interface elements are also components, the knowledge you learned in the last two chapters is still applicable.

Figure 15-1 shows some of the classes that extend **Component**. Each of them is described in this chapter.

Recall from Chapter 13 that the **Container** class extends **Component**. You may think of a container as a component that can hold references to a number of other components. This capability is enormously powerful. It allows us to build graphical user interfaces that nest containers within containers. Each container has an associated **LayoutManager** object that determines where to position its components. The **java.awt** package includes several types of layout managers. Some of these are described later in this chapter.

The abstract **Container** class provides only a default constructor. Some of its commonly used methods are shown in Table 15-1.

The **add( )** method provided by the **Container** class is used frequently in the first half of this chapter. You will see that we can

FIGURE 15-1

Some subclasses
*of **Component***
▼

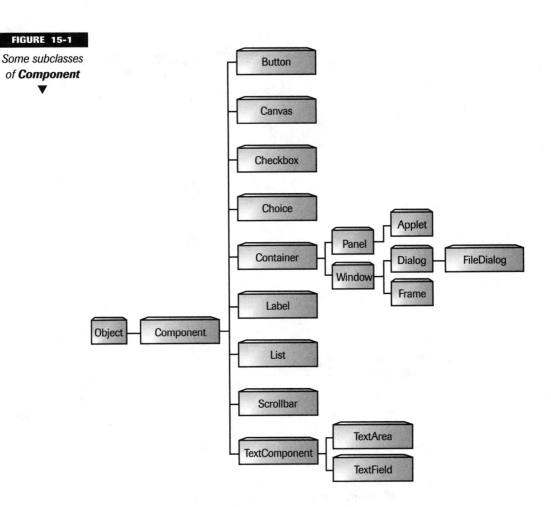

instantiate labels, buttons, check boxes, and other types of user interface elements and add them to an applet.

The **Panel** class is a concrete subclass of **Container**. You will see later how it can hold various types of user interface components. It provides these constructors:

```
Panel( )
Panel(LayoutManager lm)
```

Here, *lm* is the layout manager to be used for that panel.

Method	Description
Component add(Component *c*)	Adds *c* to the container and returns *c*.
Component add(Component *c*, Object *obj*)	Adds *c* to the container as specified by *obj* and returns *c*.
void addContainerListener (ContainerListener *cl*)	Registers *cl* to receive container events.
Insets getInsets( )	Returns the **Insets** object for this container.
void remove(Component *c*)	Removes *c* from the container.
void removeContainerListener (ContainerListener *cl*)	Unregisters *cl* to receive container events.
void setLayout(LayoutManager *lm*)	Sets *lm* as the layout manager for this container.

TABLE 15-1   *Some Methods Defined by **Container*** ▼

Finally, the **Applet** class extends **Panel**. This means that an applet inherits all of the functionality of its **Component**, **Container**, and **Panel** superclasses. In the next few sections, you will see how the **add( )** method inherited from **Component** is used to include components in the applet display area.

Let us begin by studying each of these components separately and then advance to building applets and applications that integrate them.

15.2 LABELS

A *label* is a string that appears on a graphical user interface. It can be changed by your program but cannot be changed by a user. Labels are very frequently used in programs—often placed, for example, before text fields to inform the user about the input that is expected.

The **Label** class defines these constructors:

```
Label( )
Label(String str)
Label(String str, int align)
```

Here, *str* is the text for the label. The argument *align* is a constant that indicates if the label should be left justified, centered, or right justified. The constants **LEFT**, **CENTER**, or **RIGHT** are used to set the value of *align*.

The methods to read and write the alignment value are as follows:

```
int getAlignment( )
void setAlignment(int align)
```

Here, *align* is defined as described for the constructor.

The methods to read and write the text are as follows:

```
String getText( )
void setText(String str)
```

Here, *str* is the text for the label.

Follow these steps to use a label in an applet:

1. Create a **Label** object.

2. Invoke the **add( )** method to add the **Label** object to the applet.

These steps are illustrated in the example and exercise.

EXAMPLE

1. The following program shows an applet that contains three labels. Each of the alignment styles is illustrated.

```
import java.applet.*;
import java.awt.*;
/*
  <applet code="Labels" width=200 height=120>
  </applet>
*/

public class Labels extends Applet {

  public void init() {
    String s = "This is a very long label";
    Label 11 = new Label(s, Label.LEFT);
    add(11);
    Label 12 = new Label(s, Label.CENTER);
    add(12);
    Label 13 = new Label(s, Label.RIGHT);
    add(13);
  }
}
```

Output from this applet is shown here:

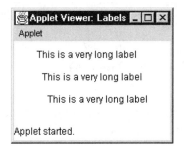

---

1. Write an applet that displays "Good morning" if the current time is between 12 a.m. and 12 p.m., "Good afternoon" if the current time is between 12 p.m. and 6 p.m., and "Good evening" if the current time is between 6 p.m. and 12 a.m.

15.3 *B*UTTONS

A *button* is a component that simulates the appearance of a push button on an electronic instrument. When the user clicks the mouse inside its boundaries, the button changes appearance to provide feedback for the user.

The **Button** class defines these constructors:

```
Button()
Button(String str)
```

Here, *str* is the text for the button.

An action event is generated each time a button is pressed. The methods by which other objects register and unregister to receive action events generated by this component are as follows:

```
void addActionListener(ActionListener al)
void removeActionListener(ActionListener al)
```

Here, *al* is the action listener.

You can read and write the label on a button via the following methods:

```
String getLabel( )
void setLabel(String str)
```

Here, *str* is the string to be used as a label for the button.

An action listener may use the following method to obtain a command string associated with an action event generated by the button:

```
String getActionCommand( )
```

The following method sets the string that is returned by the **getActionCommand( )** method.

```
void setActionCommand(String str)
```

Here, *str* is the string to be returned from the **getAction-Command( )** method.

The **java.awt.event.ActionEvent** class defines four constants to identify the types of modifier keys that can be pressed when an action event is generated. These are **ALT_MASK**, **CTRL_MASK**, **META_MASK**, and **SHIFT_MASK**.

The class provides the constructors shown here:

```
ActionEvent(Object src, int type, String cmd)
ActionEvent(Object src, int type, String cmd, int modifiers)
```

Here, *src* is the object that generated the event. The type of the command is *type,* and the associated command is *cmd.* The argument *modifiers* specifies which modifier keys (ALT, CTRL, META, and/or SHIFT) were pressed when the event occurred.

The command can be obtained via the **getActionCommand( )** method shown here:

```
String getActionCommand( )
```

The return value from this method is the action command.

The modifiers can be obtained via the **getModifiers( )** method shown here:

```
int getModifiers( )
```

The return value can be decoded by using the constants defined by this class.

The **java.awt.event.ActionListener** interface defines one method that must be implemented by an action listener, as follows:

void actionPerformed(ActionEvent *ae*)

Here, *ae* is the action event.

Follow these steps to use a button in an applet:

1. Create a **Button** object.

2. Register the applet to receive action events generated by the button.

3. Invoke the **add( )** method to add the **Button** object to the applet.

4. Implement the **ActionListener** interface in the applet.

These steps are illustrated in the example and exercise.

EXAMPLE

1. The following applet contains three buttons and one label. When a button is pressed, the label displays the string associated with that button. Notice that the **init( )** method creates the buttons and registers the applet itself to receive action events generated by those components. The **actionPerformed( )** method is invoked when an action event is generated by any of the buttons. It receives an **ActionEvent** object as its argument. The **getActionCommand( )** method is called to obtain the string on the button. This value is passed as the argument to the **setText( )** method of the label.

```
import java.applet.*;
import java.awt.*;
import java.awt.event.*;
/*
  <applet code="ButtonEvents" width=400 height=60>
  </applet>
*/

public class ButtonEvents extends Applet
implements ActionListener {
```

```
      Label label;

  public void init() {
    Button b1 = new Button("Apple");
    b1.addActionListener(this);
    add(b1);
    Button b2 = new Button("Banana");
    b2.addActionListener(this);
    add(b2);
    Button b3 = new Button("Orange");
    b3.addActionListener(this);
    add(b3);
    label = new Label("                ");
    add(label);
  }

  public void actionPerformed(ActionEvent ae) {
    label.setText(ae.getActionCommand());
  }
}
```

Output from this applet is shown here:

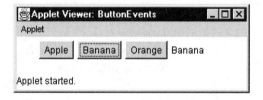

EXERCISE

1. Write an applet that contains one button. Initialize the label on the button to "Start." When the user presses the button, change the label to "Stop." Toggle the button label between these two values each time the button is pressed.

15.4 ANVASES

A *canvas* provides a rectangular area on which you can draw. This is valuable because you can create graphs and other diagrams on the canvas by using methods of the **Graphics** class.

The **Canvas** class extends **Component** and provides this constructor:

Canvas()

You may override the **paint( )** method to draw on the canvas.

EXAMPLE

1. This example shows how to create a canvas and draw on it. Two cycles of a sine wave are displayed. The waveform is centered at the origin. The **MyCanvas** class extends **Canvas** and overrides its **paint( )** method to produce both the axes and plot. The **CanvasDemo** class extends **Applet**. Its **init( )** method instantiates **MyCanvas**, sets its size, and adds that object to the applet.

```
import java.applet.*;
import java.awt.*;
/*
  <applet code="CanvasDemo" width=501 height=200>
  </applet>
*/

class MyCanvas extends Canvas {

  public void paint(Graphics g) {

    // Draw axes
    g.setColor(Color.lightGray);
    Dimension d = getSize();
    g.drawRect(0, 0, d.width - 1, d.height - 1);
    g.drawLine(0, d.height/2, d.width, d.height/2);
    g.drawLine(d.width/2, 0, d.width/2, d.height - 1);

    // Draw waveform
    g.setColor(Color.blue);
    double dx = 4 * Math.PI / d.width;
    double x = -2 * Math.PI;
```

```
      int h = d.height;
      for(int i = 0; i < d.width - 1; i++) {
        int y1 = (int)((h - h * Math.sin(x)) / 2);
        int y2 = (int)((h - h * Math.sin(x + dx)) / 2);
        g.drawLine(i, y1, i + 1, y2);
        x += dx;
      }
    }
}

public class CanvasDemo extends Applet {

  public void init() {
    MyCanvas myCanvas = new MyCanvas();
    myCanvas.setSize(401, 150);
    add(myCanvas);
  }
}
```

Output from this applet is shown here:

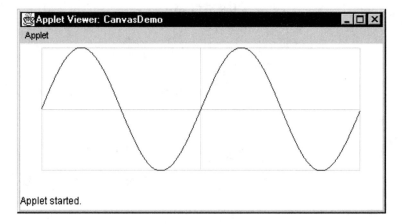

EXERCISE

1. Modify the example so it displays y(x) = Math.sin(10x) * Math.sin(x).

15.5	*C*HECK BOXES

A *check box* is a component that combines a label and small box. Depending on the state of the option represented by that check box, there may or may not be a check mark in the box. The state of that check box is changed by clicking the mouse on the box. You will see that programs frequently present a set of check boxes so a user can efficiently select a set of options.

The **Checkbox** class defines these constructors:

```
Checkbox( )
Checkbox(String str)
Checkbox(String str, boolean state)
Checkbox(String str, boolean state, CheckboxGroup grp)
Checkbox(String str, CheckboxGroup grp, boolean state)
```

Here, *str* is the text for the check box. If *state* is **true**, a check mark appears in the box. Otherwise, the box is cleared. The last two forms of the constructor are used to group several check boxes together. The parameter *grp* is a reference to the check box group. (The use of check box groups is discussed in the next section.)

An item event is generated when the state of a check box changes. The methods by which other objects register and unregister to receive these events are as follows:

```
void addItemListener(ItemListener il)
void removeItemListener(ItemListener il)
```

Here, *il* is the item listener.

You may read and write the state of a check box via the following methods:

```
boolean getState( )
void setState(boolean value)
```

Here, if *value* is **true**, a check mark is placed inside the box. Otherwise, the box is cleared.

You may read and write the label of a check box via the following methods:

```
String getLabel( )
void setLabel(String str)
```

Here, *str* is the string to be used as a label for the check box.

The **Checkbox** class also defines the following two methods by which groups of check boxes may be managed:

```
CheckboxGroup getCheckboxGroup( )
void setCheckboxGroup(CheckboxGroup grp)
```

Here, *grp* is the group to which this check box belongs. (Section 15-6 discusses check box groups.)

The **java.awt.event.ItemEvent** class defines two constants to identify the types of item events. These are **DESELECTED** and **SELECTED**.

It provides this constructor:

```
ItemEvent(ItemSelectable src, int type, Object item, int state)
```

Here, *src* is the object that generated the event. The type of the event is *type*. The entry that generated the event is identified as *item* and its state is provided as *state*.

The item can be obtained via the **getItem( )** method shown here:

```
Object getItem( )
```

The return value from this method is the item that generated the event.

The component that generated this event can be obtained via the **getItemSelectable( )** method shown here:

```
ItemSelectable getItemSelectable( )
```

The return value from this method is the component that generated the event.

The state change (i.e., **DESELECTED** or **SELECTED**) for the item can be obtained via the **getStateChange( )** method shown here:

```
int getStateChange( )
```

The **java.awt.ItemSelectable** interface is implemented by the **Checkbox**, **Choice**, **List**, and **CheckboxMenuItem** classes. It defines the methods shown here:

```
void addItemListener(ItemListener il)
Object[ ] getSelectedObjects( )
void removeItemListener(ItemListener il)
```

The first and third methods are the registration and unregistration methods. The argument *il* is a reference to the listener object.

The second method returns an array of references to the objects that were selected. For a check box, there is only one element in this array. However, you will see later in this chapter that a list box may be configured to allow multiple selections. In that case, the **getSelectedObjects( )** method can return more than one object.

The **java.awt.event.ItemListener** interface defines one method that must be implemented by an item listener, as follows:

void itemStateChanged(ItemEvent *ie*)

Here, *ie* is the item event.

Follow these steps to use a check box in an applet:

1. Create a **Checkbox** object.

2. Register the applet to receive item events generated by the check box.

3. Invoke the **add( )** method to add the **Checkbox** object to the applet.

4. Implement the **ItemListener** interface in the applet.

These steps are illustrated in the example and exercise.

EXAMPLE

1. The following applet contains three check boxes and a label. When a check box is clicked, the label reports its new state. Notice that the **init( )** method creates the check boxes and registers the applet itself to receive item events generated by those components. The **itemStateChanged( )** method is invoked when an item event is generated by any of the check boxes. It receives an **ItemEvent** object as its argument. The **getItemSelectable( )** method is called to obtain a reference to the object that generated the item event. The return value from this method is cast to a **Checkbox**. The **getLabel( )** and **getState( )** methods are then used to obtain the label and state of the check box. These values are passed as the argument to the **setText( )** method of the label.

Note

*The return value from **getItemSelectable( )** is an object that implements the **ItemSelectable** interface. It must be cast to a **Checkbox** so that the **getLabel( )** and **getState( )** methods can be invoked. Recall from Chapter 7 that an interface reference variable may only be used to call the methods declared by that interface.*

```java
import java.applet.*;
import java.awt.*;
import java.awt.event.*;
/*
  <applet code="CheckboxEvents" width=400 height=60>
  </applet>
*/

public class CheckboxEvents extends Applet
implements ItemListener {
  Label label;

  public void init() {
    Checkbox cb1 = new Checkbox("Apple");
    cb1.addItemListener(this);
    add(cb1);
    Checkbox cb2 = new Checkbox("Banana");
    cb2.addItemListener(this);
    add(cb2);
    Checkbox cb3 = new Checkbox("Orange");
    cb3.addItemListener(this);
    add(cb3);
    label = new Label("                    ");
    add(label);
  }

  public void itemStateChanged(ItemEvent ie) {
    Checkbox cb = (Checkbox)ie.getItemSelectable();
    label.setText(cb.getLabel() + " " + cb.getState());
  }
}
```

Output from this applet is shown here:

```
Applet Viewer: CheckboxEvents                    _ □ ×
Applet

        □ Apple   ☑ Banana   □ Orange   Banana true

Applet started.
```

---

1. Write an applet that contains three check boxes and a 30 ×
   30-pixel canvas. The three check boxes should be labeled "Red",
   "Green", and "Blue". The selections of the check boxes determine
   the color of the canvas. For example, if the user selects both
   "Red" and "Blue", the canvas should be purple. (Hint: Use the
   setBackground( ) and **repaint( )** methods to change the color
   of the canvas.)

15.6   *C*HECK BOX GROUPS

A *check box group* is a set of check boxes. Only one of these may be set
at any time. If the user clicks on one element in a check box group,
that check box is set. Other members of the same group are
automatically cleared. An item event is generated when the state of a
check box changes. You will see that programs frequently present a
check box group so that a user can select only one option from a
set of options.

The **CheckboxGroup** class defines only this constructor:

CheckboxGroup( )

You may obtain the group member that is currently set via the
method shown here:

Checkbox getSelectedCheckbox( )

You may set a particular check box in the group via this method:

void setSelectedCheckbox(Checkbox *cb*)

Here, *cb* is the check box to be set.

The check boxes in a check box group are sometimes called *radio buttons.* You will see that they have a different appearance than the check boxes seen in the previous section.

Follow these steps to use a check box group in an applet:

1. Create a **CheckboxGroup** object.

2. Create a **Checkbox** object. Pass a reference to the **CheckboxGroup** object to the **Checkbox** constructor.

3. Register the applet to receive item events generated by the check box.

4. Invoke the **add( )** method to add the **Checkbox** object to the applet.

5. Repeat steps 2–4 for each check box in the group.

6. Implement the **ItemListener** interface in the applet.

These steps are illustrated in the example and exercise.

EXAMPLE

1. The following applet contains three check boxes and a label. When a check box is clicked, the label reports its new state. The **init( )** method creates the check boxes and registers the applet itself to receive item events generated by those components. Notice the form of the **Checkbox** constructors. The second argument identifies the group to which this check box should be added. This is the mechanism used to group check boxes. The third argument specifies the initial state of that check box. The **itemStateChanged( )** method is invoked when an item event is generated by any of the check boxes. It receives an **ItemEvent** object as its argument. The **getItemSelectable( )** method is called to obtain a reference to the object that generated the item event. The return value from this method is cast to a **Checkbox**. The **getLabel( )** and **getState( )** methods are then used to obtain the label and state of the check box. These values are passed as the argument to the **setText( )** method of the label.

```java
import java.applet.*;
import java.awt.*;
import java.awt.event.*;
/*
  <applet code="CheckboxGroupEvents" width=400 height=60>
  </applet>
*/

public class CheckboxGroupEvents extends Applet
implements ItemListener {
  Label label;

  public void init() {
    CheckboxGroup cbg = new CheckboxGroup();
    Checkbox cb1 = new Checkbox("Apple", cbg, true);
    cb1.addItemListener(this);
    add(cb1);
    Checkbox cb2 = new Checkbox("Banana", cbg, false);
    cb2.addItemListener(this);
    add(cb2);
    Checkbox cb3 = new Checkbox("Orange", cbg, false);
    cb3.addItemListener(this);
    add(cb3);
    label = new Label("                ");
    add(label);
  }

  public void itemStateChanged(ItemEvent ie) {
    Checkbox cb = (Checkbox)ie.getItemSelectable();
    label.setText(cb.getLabel() + " " + cb.getState());
  }
}
```

Output from this applet is shown here:

EXERCISE

1. Write an applet that contains a check box group with three check boxes labeled "Red," "Green," and "Blue." There is also a 30 × 30-pixel canvas. The selections of the check boxes determine the color of the canvas. Your applet should appear as shown in the following illustration:

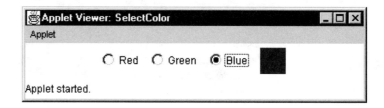

15.7 CHOICES

A *choice* is a component that provides a type of menu. When a user clicks on a choice, it displays all of the allowed selections. When the user selects one of those items, the choice returns to its normal state in which it displays only the current selection. Choices are valuable because they need only a minimum amount of space on the display.

The **Choice** class defines only the constructor shown here:

Choice()

The commonly used methods of **Choice** are summarized in Table 15-2.

An item event is generated when a user selects one of the entries in a choice. Table 15-2 shows that **Choice** provides registration and unregistration methods for **ItemListener** objects.

Follow these steps to use a choice in an applet:

1. Create a **Choice** object.

2. Add items to the choice.

3. Register the applet to receive item events generated by the choice.

4. Invoke the **add( )** method to add the **Choice** object to the applet.

5. Implement the **ItemListener** interface in the applet.

These steps are illustrated in the example and exercise.

Method	Description
void add(String *str*) throws NullPointerException	Adds *str* as an item.
void addItem(String *str*) throws NullPointerException	Adds *str* as an item.
void addItemListener(ItemListener *il*)	Registers *il* to receive item events generated by this choice.
String getIndex(int *i*)	Returns the string at index *i* in this choice.
int getSelectedIndex( )	Returns the index of the selected item.
String getSelectedItem( )	Returns the selected item.
Object[ ] getSelectedObjects( )	Returns an array with one object, which is the selected item.
void insert(String *str*, int *i*) throws IllegalArgumentException	Inserts *str* before the item at index *i*.
void remove(int *i*) throws IllegalArgumentException	Removes the item at index i.
void removeAll( )	Removes all items.
void removeItemListener (ItemListener *il*)	Unregisters *il* to receive item events generated by this choice.
void select(int *i*) throws IllegalArgumentException	Selects the item at index *i*.
void select(String *str*) throws IllegalArgumentException	Selects the item *str*.

TABLE 15-2   *Some Methods Defined by* ***Choice***   ▼

EXAMPLE

1. The following applet contains two choices and a label. When an item in a choice is selected, the label reports its value. The **init( )** method creates the choices, adds items to them, and registers the applet itself to receive item events generated by those components. The **itemStateChanged( )** method is invoked when an item event is generated by either of the choices. It receives an **ItemEvent** object as its argument. The **getItemSelectable( )** method is called to obtain a reference to the object that generated the item event. The return value from this method is cast to a **Choice**. The **getSelectedItem( )** method is then used to obtain the chosen item. This value is passed as the argument to the **setText( )** method of the label.

```
import java.applet.*;
import java.awt.*;
import java.awt.event.*;
/*
  <applet code="ChoiceEvents" width=400 height=60>
  </applet>
*/

public class ChoiceEvents extends Applet
implements ItemListener {
  Label label;

  public void init() {
    Choice c1 = new Choice();
    c1.addItem("Red");
    c1.addItem("Orange");
    c1.addItem("Yellow");
    c1.addItem("Green");
    c1.addItem("Blue");
    c1.addItem("Indigo");
    c1.addItem("Violet");
    c1.addItemListener(this);
    add(c1);
    Choice c2 = new Choice();
    c2.addItem("North");
    c2.addItem("South");
    c2.addItem("East");
    c2.addItem("West");
```

```
        c2.addItemListener(this);
        add(c2);
        label = new Label("                    ");
        add(label);
    }

    public void itemStateChanged(ItemEvent ie) {
        Choice c = (Choice)ie.getItemSelectable();
        label.setText(c.getSelectedItem());
    }
}
```

Output from this applet is shown here:

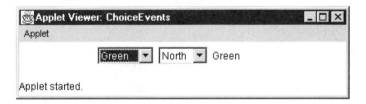

EXERCISE

1. Write an applet that contains one choice element and a 30 × 30-pixel canvas. The items in the choice element should be "Red", "Green", and "Blue". The choice selection should determine the color of the canvas.

15.8 *TEXT FIELDS AND TEXT AREAS*

A *text field* allows a user to enter one line of text. A *text area* allows a user to enter multiple lines of text. Both of these components can also be used to display output.

They generate text events when a character is entered by a user. A text field also generates an action event when a user presses the ENTER key.

Both the **TextField** and **TextArea** classes extend **TextComponent**. The commonly used methods of that class are summarized in Table 15-3.

The **TextField** class defines these constructors:

```
TextField( )
TextField(String str)
TextField(int cols)
TextField(String str, int cols)
```

Here, *str* is the text for the field. The argument *cols* indicates the width of the field in characters.

Method	Description
void addTextListener(TextListener *tl*)	Registers *tl* to receive text events generated by this component.
String getSelectedText( )	Returns a string with any text that has been selected by the user.
int getSelectionEnd( )	Returns the index of the last character of selected text.
int getSelectionStart	Returns the index of the first character of selected text.
String getText( )	Returns a string with the contents of this component.
boolean isEditable( )	Returns **true** if the component is editable. Otherwise, returns **false**.
void removeTextListener(TextListener *tl*)	Unregisters *tl* to receive text events generated by this component.
void select(int *start*, int *end*)	Selects the text from index *start* to index *end*.
void selectAll( )	Selects all of the text in this component.
void setEditable(boolean *flag*)	If *flag* is **true**, the component may be edited. Otherwise, it cannot be edited.
void setSelectionEnd(int *end*)	Ends the selected text at index *end*.
void setSelectionStart(int *start*)	Starts the selected text at index *start*.
void setText(String *str*)	Sets the text of the component to *str*.

TABLE 15-3   *Some Methods Defined by **TextComponent*** ▼

The commonly used methods of **TextField** are summarized in the following table.

Method	Description
void addActionListener(ActionListener *al*)	Registers *al* to receive action events generated by this component.
char getEchoChar( )	Returns the echo character for this component.
void setEchoChar(char *c*)	Sets the echo character for this component.
void removeActionListener (ActionListener *al*)	Unregisters *al* to receive action events generated by this component.

The **TextArea** class defines these constructors:

```
TextArea( )
TextArea(String str)
TextArea(int rows, int cols)
TextArea(String str, int rows, int cols)
TextArea(String str, int rows, int cols, int scrollbars)
```

Here, *str* is the text for the area. The *rows* and *cols* arguments indicate the number of rows and columns in the component. The *scrollbars* argument indicates if horizontal and/or vertical scroll bars should be created. Its possible values are: **SCROLLBARS_BOTH**, **SCROLLBARS_HORIZONTAL_ONLY**, **SCROLLBARS_VERTICAL_ONLY**, and **SCROLLBARS_NONE**.

There is one method to add text to the end of the component, as follows:

```
void append(String str)
```

Here, *str* is the string to be appended to the component.

Another method allows you to insert text in the component, as follows:

```
void insert(String str, int index)
```

Here, *str* is the string to be inserted immediately before the character at position *index*.

You may replace a subset of the characters in this component with this method:

void replaceRange(String *str*, int *start*, int *end*)

Here, *str* is the string to replace the range of characters between positions *start* and *end*.

The **java.awt.event.TextEvent** class provides the constructor shown here:

TextEvent(Object *src*, int *type*)

Here, *src* is the object that generated the event and *type* is the type of the command.

A text event object does not include the character that has been entered. Instead, you must use the methods provided by the text area and text field to read the character.

The **java.awt.TextListener** interface defines one method that must be implemented by a text listener, as follows:

void textValueChanged(TextEvent *te*)

Here, *te* is the text event.

Follow these steps to use a text field in an applet:

1. Create a **TextField** object.

2. Register the applet to receive action and/or text events generated by the text field.

3. Invoke the **add( )** method to add the **TextField** object to the applet.

4. Implement the **ActionListener** and **TextListener** interfaces in the applet.

These steps are illustrated in the example and exercise.

EXAMPLE

1. The following applet contains both a text field and a text area. The **addActionListener( )** and **addTextListener( )** methods register the applet itself to receive action and text events generated by the text field. Notice that the applet is declared to implement the **ActionListener** and **TextListener** interfaces. The text field generates an action event when the user presses the ENTER key. It generates a text event when a new character is

entered. The **actionPerformed( )** method is invoked when an action event occurs. It receives an **ActionEvent** object as an argument and invokes its **getActionCommand( )** method to obtain the contents of the text field. This information is appended to the text area and the text field is cleared. The **textValueChanged( )** method is invoked when a text event occurs. It receives a **TextEvent** object as an argument. This argument is not used in this example. Instead, the **getText( )** method of **TextField** is called to obtain the contents of the text field. This information is appended to the text area.

```java
import java.applet.*;
import java.awt.*;
import java.awt.event.*;
/*
  <applet code="TextFieldEvents" width=400 height=200>
  </applet>
*/

public class TextFieldEvents extends Applet
implements ActionListener, TextListener {
  TextArea ta;
  TextField tf;

  public void init() {
    tf = new TextField(20);
    tf.addActionListener(this);
    tf.addTextListener(this);
    add(tf);
    ta = new TextArea(10, 20);
    add(ta);
  }

  public void actionPerformed(ActionEvent ae) {
    ta.append("ActionEvent: " +
      ae.getActionCommand() + "\n");
    tf.setText("");
  }

  public void textValueChanged(TextEvent te) {
    ta.append("TextEvent: " +
      tf.getText() + "\n");
  }
}
```

Output from this applet is shown here:

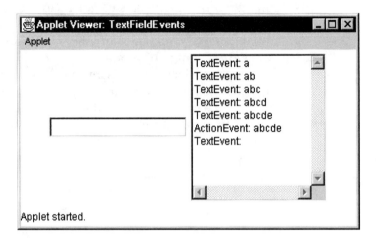

EXERCISE

1. Write an applet that contains a label with the string "Name: ", a 20-character text field initialized to your name, a label with the string "Password: ", and a 20-character text field that is initially empty. Allow the user to change either of these fields. The echo character for the password field should be '*'.

15.9 *L ISTS*

A *list* is a component that allows a user to select one or more items. If the list is not large enough to display all of the allowed selections, scroll bars are automatically provided so a user may scan through the entire list. An action event is generated when a user double-clicks on an item in a list. An item event is generated when a user selects or deselects one of the entries.

The **List** class defines these constructors:

```
List()
List(int rows)
List(int rows, boolean multiple)
```

Here, *rows* is the number of items that are visible to a user. This determines the size of the component. If *multiple* is **true**, a user may select multiple entries in a list. Otherwise, only one item may be selected.

The commonly used methods of **List** are summarized in Table 15-4. Follow these steps to use a list in an applet:

1. Create a **List** object.

2. Add items to the list.

3. Register the applet to receive action and/or item events generated by the list.

4. Invoke the **add( )** method to add the **List** object to the applet.

5. Implement the **ActionListener** and **ItemListener** interfaces in the applet.

These steps are illustrated in the example and exercise.

EXAMPLE

1. The following applet contains a list and a text area. The list does not allow multiple selections. When an item in the list is double-clicked, the text area displays this action event. When an item in the list is selected, the text area displays this item event.

The **init( )** method creates the list, adds items to it, registers the applet itself to receive both action and item events, and adds the list to the applet. The text area is then created and added to the applet.

The **actionPerformed( )** method is invoked when an action event is generated by the list. It receives an **ActionEvent** object as its argument. The **getActionCommand( )** method is called to obtain the list item. This value is passed as the argument to the **append( )** method of the text area.

The **itemStateChanged( )** method is invoked when an item event is generated by the list. It receives an **ItemEvent** object as its argument. The **getItemSelectable( )** method is called to obtain a reference to the object that generated the item event. The return value from this method is cast to a **List**. The **getSelectedItem( )** method is then used to obtain the chosen

Method	Description
void add(String *str*)	Adds *str* as an item.
void add(String *str*, int *i*)	Adds *str* as an item at index *i*.
void addActionListener(ActionListener *al*)	Registers *al* to receive action events generated by this list.
void addItemListener(ItemListener *il*)	Registers *il* to receive item events generated by this list.
void deselect(int *i*)	Deselects the item at index *i*.
String getItem(int *i*)	Returns the item at index *i*.
int getItemCount()	Returns the total number of items.
String[ ] getItems()	Returns an array of strings that contains all items.
int getSelectedIndex()	Returns the index of the selected item.
int[ ] getSelectedIndexes()	Returns an int array containing the indexes of selected items.
String getSelectedItem()	Returns the selected item.
String[ ] getSelectedItems()	Returns an array of strings that contains the selected items.
Object[ ] getSelectedObjects()	Returns an array of objects that contains the selected items.
boolean isMultipleMode()	Returns **true** if multiple items may be selected. Otherwise, returns **false**.
void remove(String *str*)	Removes *str* from the list.
void remove(int *i*)	Removes the item at index *i*.
void removeAll()	Removes all items.
void removeActionlistener(ActionListener *al*)	Unregisters *al* to receive action events generated by this list.
void removeItemListener(ItemListener *il*)	Unregisters *il* to receive item events generated by this list.
void select(int *i*) throws IllegalArgumentException	Selects the item at index *i*.
void setMultipleMode(boolean *flag*)	If *flag* is **true**, a user may select multiple items. Otherwise, only one item may be selected.

TABLE 15-4 *Some Methods Defined by **List*** ▼

item. This value is passed as the argument to the **append( )** method of the text area.

```
import java.applet.*;
import java.awt.*;
import java.awt.event.*;
/*
  <applet code="ListEvents" width=400 height=200>
  </applet>
*/

public class ListEvents extends Applet
implements ActionListener, ItemListener {
  TextArea ta;

  public void init() {
    List list = new List();
    list.add("Hydrogen");
    list.add("Helium");
    list.add("Carbon");
    list.add("Oxygen");
    list.add("Potassium");
    list.add("Phosphorus");
    list.addActionListener(this);
    list.addItemListener(this);
    add(list);
    ta = new TextArea(10, 20);
    add(ta);
  }

  public void actionPerformed(ActionEvent ae) {
    ta.append("ActionEvent: " +
      ae.getActionCommand() + "\n");
  }

  public void itemStateChanged(ItemEvent ie) {
    List list = (List)ie.getItemSelectable();
    ta.append("ItemEvent: " +
      list.getSelectedItem() + "\n");
  }
}
```

Output from this applet is shown here:

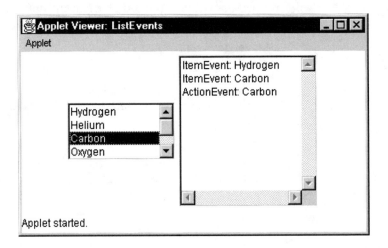

1. Write an applet that contains a single selection list and a 30 x 30-pixel canvas. The items in the list are the 13 colors defined by the constants of the **Color** class. The list selection determines the color of the canvas.

15.10 SCROLL BARS

A scroll bar is a component that allows a user to select any **int** value within a range defined by a minimum and maximum. A scroll bar contains a slider that may be dragged to continuously vary its value. Alternatively, the user may click on one of the buttons at either end of the scroll bar or in the area between the slider and the buttons. These operations also modify its value.

The **Scrollbar** class defines these constructors:

```
Scrollbar()
Scrollbar(int orientation)
Scrollbar(int orientation, int value, int width, int min, int max)
```

Here, *orientation* indicates if the scroll bar is oriented horizontally or vertically. It is assigned the value **HORIZONTAL** or **VERTICAL**. The argument *value* represents the initial value of the scroll bar. The width of the slider is *width*. The range of the scroll bar is determined by the *min* and *max* arguments.

The commonly used methods of **Scrollbar** are summarized in the following table.

Method	Description
void addAdjustmentListener (AdjustmentListener *al*)	Registers *al* to receive adjustment events generated by this scroll bar.
int getValue( )	Returns the value of the scroll bar.
void setValue(int *i*)	Sets the value of the scroll bar to *i*.
void removeAdjustmentListener (AdjustmentListener *al*)	Unregisters *al* to receive adjustment events generated by this scroll bar.

An adjustment event is generated whenever the value represented by a scroll bar changes. The **java.awt.event.AdjustmentEvent** class defines five constants to identify the specific type of this event. These are **BLOCK_DECREMENT**, **BLOCK_INCREMENT**, **TRACK**, **UNIT_DECREMENT**, and **UNIT_INCREMENT**. The first two constants indicate that the user clicked between the slider and one of the buttons. The third constant indicates that the slider was dragged. The last two constants indicate that the user pressed one of the buttons at either end of the scroll bar.

The **AdjustmentEvent** class provides the constructor shown here:

AdjustmentEvent(Adjustable *src*, int *id*, int *type*, int *value*)

Here, *src* is the object that generated the event. The type of the event is *type,* and the value of the scroll bar is *value*.

The source of the event can be obtained via the **getAdjustable( )** method shown here:

Adjustable getAdjustable( )

The type of the event can be obtained via the **getAdjustmentType( )** method shown here:

int getAdjustmentType( )

The return value from this method is one of the five constants previously mentioned.

The value of the scroll bar can be obtained via the **getValue( )** method shown here:

int getValue( )

The **java.awt.event.AdjustmentListener** interface defines one method that must be implemented by an adjustment listener, as follows:

void adjustmentValueChanged(AdjustmentEvent *ae*)

Here, *ae* is the adjustment event.

Follow these steps to use a scroll bar in an applet:

1. Create a **Scrollbar** object.

2. Register the applet to receive adjustment events generated by the scroll bar.

3. Invoke the **add( )** method to add the **Scrollbar** object to the applet.

4. Implement the **AdjustmentListener** interface in the applet.

These steps are illustrated in the example and exercise.

EXAMPLE

1. The following applet contains a scroll bar and a text area. When the value of the scroll bar is changed, the text area displays the current value.

   The **init( )** method creates the scroll bar and registers the applet itself to receive adjustment events. The text area is then created. The **adjustmentValueChanged( )** method is invoked when an adjustment event is generated by the scroll bar. It

receives an **AdjustmentEvent** object as its argument. The
getAdjustable( ) method is called to obtain a reference to the
object that generated the adjustable event. The return value
from this method is cast to a **Scrollbar**. The **getValue( )**
method is then used to obtain the value of the scroll bar. This
value is passed as the argument to the **append( )** method of
the text area.

```java
import java.applet.*;
import java.awt.*;
import java.awt.event.*;
/*
  <applet code="ScrollbarEvents" width=400 height=200>
  </applet>
*/

public class ScrollbarEvents extends Applet
implements AdjustmentListener {
  TextArea ta;

  public void init() {
    Scrollbar sb =
      new Scrollbar(Scrollbar.HORIZONTAL, 50, 5, 0, 100);
    sb.addAdjustmentListener(this);
    add(sb);
    ta = new TextArea(10, 20);
    add(ta);
  }

  public void adjustmentValueChanged(AdjustmentEvent ae)
{
    Scrollbar sb = (Scrollbar)ae.getAdjustable();
    ta.append("AdjustmentEvent: " + sb.getValue() +
      "\n");
  }
}
```

Output from this applet is shown here:

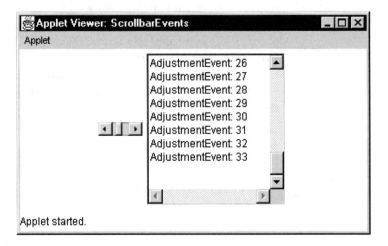

---

1. Write an applet that contains three scroll bars and a 30 × 30-pixel canvas. The scroll bars adjust the red, green, and blue components of the canvas color. Your applet should appear as shown in the following illustration:

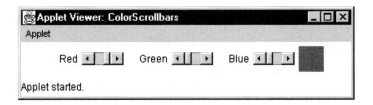

15.11 *L AYOUT MANAGERS*

The previous sections demonstrated some of the components available for building a graphical user interface. Recall that the **add( )** method was used to add a component to an applet. However, it was not necessary for you to specify a precise location for that element. Instead, its placement was determined by a layout manager.

Layout managers provide significant benefits. First, it is not necessary to calculate the coordinates at which an element should be placed. This time-consuming and error-prone work is done for you. Second, if an applet is resized, the layout manager dynamically adjusts the placement of the elements. Third, components typically have different sizes on different platforms. Therefore, it is not possible to specify one set of coordinates that will be suitable in all environments. The layout manager handles this task for you. It is yet another aspect of the Java class libraries that provides platform-independence.

It is possible for you to specify a position and size for each component. However, this is discouraged because your code is no longer platform-independent. Therefore, this technique is not discussed in this book.

A layout manager is associated with each **Container** object. The methods to get and set this association are as follows:

```
LayoutManager getLayout( );
void setLayout(LayoutManager lm)
```

Here, *lm* is a reference to an object that implements the **LayoutManager** interface.

This section begins our look at the most commonly used layout managers. You will see that they employ different strategies to position components.

Let us begin our discussion with **FlowLayout**. This is the default layout manager for an applet. This class places components in a row that is centered in the available space. If the components cannot fit in the current row, another row is started.

The **FlowLayout** class has these constructors:

```
FlowLayout( )
FlowLayout(int align)
FlowLayout(int align, int hgap, int vgap)
```

Here, *align* indicates how the components are aligned in a row. The horizontal and vertical gap in pixels between components may be set to *hgap* and *vgap*.

The **FlowLayout** class also defines three constants that can be used to specify the alignment of components. These are **LEFT**, **CENTER**, and **RIGHT**.

1. The following applet illustrates the operation of the **FlowLayout** manager. The **setLayout( )** method that **Applet** inherits from **Container** is used to explicitly assign a layout manager for this applet. The argument to this method is an instance of **FlowLayout**. The **init( )** method creates **Button** objects and invokes the **add( )** method to add each of these to the applet.

```
import java.applet.*;
import java.awt.*;
/*
  <applet code="FlowLayoutApplet" width=300 height=200>
  </applet>
*/

public class FlowLayoutApplet extends Applet {

  public void init() {
    setLayout(new FlowLayout(FlowLayout.LEFT, 5, 5));
    for(int i = 0; i < 20; i++) {
      add(new Button("Button" + i));
    }
  }
}
```

Output from this applet is shown here:

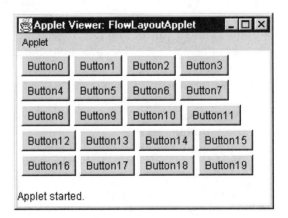

1. Experiment with the **FlowLayoutApplet** by changing the alignment, horizontal gap, and vertical gap values for its constructor.

15.12 *B*ORDER LAYOUT

The **BorderLayout** class allows a programmer to specify the placement of a component. This is done by using the geographic terms "North", "South", "East", "West", or "Center". The components are placed around the periphery with the sizes they require. The component in the center uses the remaining space.

The **BorderLayout** class has these constructors:

```
BorderLayout( )
BorderLayout(int hgap, int vgap)
```

The first form uses no gaps between components. The second form allows you to set the horizontal and vertical gaps between components to *hgap* and *vgap*.

A different form of the **add( )** method must be used in conjunction with a border layout manager, as follows:

```
void add(Component comp, Object obj)
```

Here, *comp* is the component to be added to the applet and *obj* is a string that identifies its position via one of the geographic terms.

EXAMPLE

1. The following applet illustrates the operation of the **BorderLayout** manager. The **setLayout( )** method that **Applet** inherits from **Container** is used to explicitly assign a layout manager for this applet. The argument to this method is an instance of **BorderLayout**. The **init( )** method creates **Button** objects and invokes the **add( )** method to add these to the applet.

```
import java.applet.*;
import java.awt.*;
/*
  <applet code="BorderLayoutApplet" width=300 height=300>
  </applet>
*/

public class BorderLayoutApplet extends Applet {

  public void init() {
    setLayout(new BorderLayout(5, 5));
    Button b1 = new Button("North");
    Button b2 = new Button("South");
    Button b3 = new Button("East");
    Button b4 = new Button("West");
    Button b5 = new Button("Center");
    add(b1, "North");
    add(b2, "South");
    add(b3, "East");
    add(b4, "West");
    add(b5, "Center");
  }
}
```

Output from this applet is shown here:

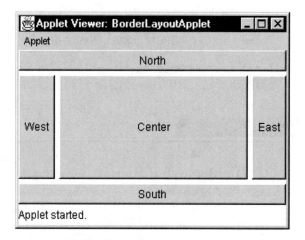

1. Experiment with the **BorderLayoutApplet** by changing the horizontal and vertical gap values for its constructor. Also change the sizes of the labels used for the buttons to observe the behavior of **BorderLayout**.

15.13 — GRID LAYOUT AND INSETS

The **GridLayout** class automatically arranges components in a grid. All components are created with equal size.

The **GridLayout** class has these constructors:

```
GridLayout( )
GridLayout(int rows, int cols)
GridLayout(int rows, int cols, int hgap, int vgap)
```

Here, *rows* and *cols* determine the number of rows and columns in the grid. The horizontal and vertical gap in pixels between components may be set by *hgap* and *vgap*.

The **Insets** class encapsulates information about the top, left, bottom, and right margins around the boundary of a container. It provides this constructor:

```
Insets(int top, int left, int bottom, int right)
```

Here, each of the arguments represents the border in pixels around the periphery of a container. There are also four instance variables—**top**, **left**, **bottom**, and **right**—of type **int**.

In order to specify the insets for a container, you override its **getInsets( )** method. Inside that method, create and return an **Insets** object.

1. The following applet illustrates operation of the **GridLayout** manager. The **setLayout( )** method that **Applet** inherits from **Container** is used to explicitly assign a layout manager for this applet. The argument to this method is an instance of

GridLayout. The arguments to the **GridLayout** constructor indicate that a grid of three rows and two columns should be created. The **init( )** method creates **Button** objects and invokes the **add( )** method to add these to the applet.

The **getInsets( )** method is inherited from the **Container** class. It is overridden to create and return an **Insets** object. A margin of 10 pixels is defined for the top, left, bottom, and right borders of the applet.

```java
import java.applet.*;
import java.awt.*;
/*
  <applet code="GridLayoutApplet" width=200 height=200>
  </applet>
*/

public class GridLayoutApplet extends Applet {

  public void init() {
    setLayout(new GridLayout(3, 2));
    Button b1 = new Button("A");
    Button b2 = new Button("B");
    Button b3 = new Button("C");
    Button b4 = new Button("D");
    Button b5 = new Button("E");
    Button b6 = new Button("F");
    add(b1);
    add(b2);
    add(b3);
    add(b4);
    add(b5);
    add(b6);
  }

  public Insets getInsets() {
    return new Insets(10, 10, 10, 10);
  }
}
```

Output from this applet is shown here:

EXERCISE

1. Experiment with **GridLayoutApplet** by using different horizontal and vertical gap values. Modify the parameters to the **Insets** constructor. Also resize the applet and observe how the buttons are automatically resized.

15.14 *P*ANELS

The **Panel** class extends **Container**. It appears as a rectangular area in which other components are arranged. A layout manager is associated with a panel and determines the placement of those components. You can set the layout manager that is used for a panel.

It is possible to nest panels within other panels. This can be done because a **Panel** object is also a **Component**. In this manner you can have more control over the appearance of your user interface. Different layout managers can be used to arrange different areas of the display.

EXAMPLE

---

1. This applet illustrates how nested panels can be used to create a graphical user interface. The top of the display area contains three check boxes labeled "Red", "Green", and "Blue". The center of the display area contains six buttons labeled "Button 0" through "Button 5" that are arranged in a grid of three rows and two columns. The bottom of the display area contains a label.

```java
import java.applet.*;
import java.awt.*;
/*
  <applet code="PanelDemo" width=200 height=300>
  </applet>
*/

public class PanelDemo extends Applet {

  public void init() {

    // Set layout manager
    setLayout(new BorderLayout());

    // Create panel for "North"
    Panel pn = new Panel();
    Checkbox cb1 = new Checkbox("Red", true);
    pn.add(cb1);
    Checkbox cb2 = new Checkbox("Green", false);
    pn.add(cb2);
    Checkbox cb3 = new Checkbox("Blue", false);
    pn.add(cb3);
    add(pn, "North");

    // Create panel for "Center"
    Panel pc = new Panel();
    pc.setLayout(new GridLayout(3, 2));
    for(int i = 0; i < 6; i++)
      pc.add(new Button("Button " + i));
    add(pc, "Center");

    // Create panel for "South"
    Panel ps = new Panel();
    Label label = new Label("This is the South Panel");
```

```
        ps.add(label);
        add(ps, "South");
    }
}
```

Output from this applet is shown here:

1. Create an applet whose display is organized as one row and two columns. The first column contains three radio buttons labeled "Red", "Green", and "Blue". The second column contains four check boxes labeled "Annuities", "Bonds", "Options", and "Stocks". Your applet should appear as shown in the following illustration:

15.15 **W**INDOWS AND FRAMES

The **Window** class extends **Container** and provides a separate window without a title or menu bar. You typically will not instantiate this class. However, it has two subclasses, **Frame** and **Dialog**, that are commonly used in applets and applications. The former class is demonstrated in this section and the latter class is explained in Section 15-17.

This class has the following constructor:

Window(Frame *parent*)

Here, *parent* is the owner of this window.

Objects may register and unregister to receive window events via these methods:

void addWindowListener(WindowListener *wl*)
void removeWindowListener(Windowlistener *wl*)

Here, *wl* is the window listener.

The **pack( )** method is called to lay out the components in a window and set its initial size. It has the form shown here:

    void pack( )

A new window is initially invisible. To make it appear, invoke the **show( )** method as follows:

    void show( )

Finally, when you finish using a window, you should relinquish its resources by calling the **dispose( )** method shown here:

    void dispose( )

A **Window** object generates events when a window is activated, closed, closing, deactivated, deiconified, iconified, or opened. A **java.awt.event.WindowEvent** object is created to describe this event. It provides a method that allows you to obtain a reference to the window that generated the event. The signature of this method is shown here:

    Window getWindow( )

The **WindowListener** interface is implemented by objects that receive window events. It defines these seven methods:

    void windowActivated(WindowEvent we)
    void windowClosed(WindowEvent we)
    void windowClosing(WindowEvent we)
    void windowDeactivated(WindowEvent we)
    void windowDeiconified(WindowEvent we)
    void windowIconified(WindowEvent we)
    void windowOpened(WindowEvent we)

Here, *we* is the **WindowEvent** object generated by the source. The **windowActivated( )** and **windowDeactivated( )** methods are called when a window is activated or deactivated. The **windowClosing( )** method is called when a user requests that a window be closed. (The application should call **setVisible( )** or **destroy( )** on the associated **Window** object in response to this event.) The **windowClosed( )** method is called after a **Window** object has been closed via **setVisible( )** or **destroy( )**. The **windowDeiconified( )** and

windowIconified( ) methods are called after a window is deiconified or iconified. The **windowOpened( )** method is called when a window is initially opened.

The **Frame** class extends **Window** and provides title and menu bars. This is equivalent to what you have seen as a standard window in a graphical user interface. It has these constructors:

```
Frame()
Frame(String title)
```

Here, *title* is the string displayed in the title bar.

You may get and set the menu bar via these methods:

```
MenuBar getMenuBar()
void setMenuBar(MenuBar mb)
```

Here, *mb* is the **MenuBar** object to be added. We will look at the menu bar in the next section.

You may get and set the title via these methods:

```
String getTitle()
void setTitle(String str)
```

Here, *str* is the string that is used in the title bar of the frame.

The minimum steps to use a frame in an application or applet are:

1. Create a subclass of **Frame**.

2. Handle the window closing event of that subclass.

3. Create an application or applet that instantiates the subclass, invokes the **show( )** method to make the frame visible, and calls the **setSize( )** method to set the dimensions of the frame.

These steps are illustrated in the examples and the exercise.

EXAMPLES

1. This example illustrates how to write an application that creates a **Frame**. The class **Frame1** extends **Frame**. Its constructor uses **super( )** to invoke the superclass constructor and initialize the title bar for this frame. The **addWindowListener( )** method is called so an anonymous inner class can receive and process

window events. The **windowClosing( )** method causes the application to exit when the window is closing. The **main( )** method of **FrameApplication** instantiates **Frame1**, invokes the **show( )** method to make it visible, and invokes **setSize( )** to set the size of the window.

```java
import java.awt.*;
import java.awt.event.*;

class Frame1 extends Frame {

  Frame1(String title) {
    super(title);
    addWindowListener(new WindowAdapter() {
      public void windowClosing(WindowEvent we) {
        System.exit(0);
      }
    });
  }
}

public class FrameApplication {
  public static void main(String args[]) {
    Frame1 f1 = new Frame1("Frame1");
    f1.show();
    f1.setSize(200, 200);
  }
}
```

Output from this application is shown here:

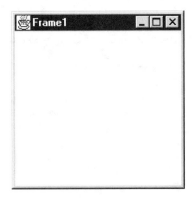

2. This example illustrates how to write an applet that creates a frame. The applet appears with one button labeled "Create Frame." When this button is pressed, a new frame appears.

Web browsers typically warn a user if a frame has been created by an applet. For example, the string "Warning: Applet Window" can automatically appear at the top or bottom of such a frame. This is a security feature of Java. A hacker can write an applet that presents a window prompting the user for sensitive information such as a login and password. Hopefully, the warning message will make a user cautious about supplying such data. The applet viewer does not exhibit this type of behavior.

The code for **Frame2** is similar to that of the previous example. Here, the **windowClosing( )** method invokes **dispose( )** to relinquish any resources that are used by this window. The **FrameApplet** class extends **Applet** and implements **ActionListener**. Its **init( )** method creates a button and registers the applet itself to receive action events from that component. The **actionPerformed( )** method performs the same functions as the **main( )** method seen in the previous example.

```
import java.applet.*;
import java.awt.*;
import java.awt.event.*;
/*
  <applet code="FrameApplet" width=250 height=200>
  </applet>
*/

class Frame2 extends Frame {

  Frame2(String title) {
    super(title);
    addWindowListener(new WindowAdapter() {
      public void windowClosing(WindowEvent we) {
        dispose();
      }
    });
  }
}
```

```
public class FrameApplet extends Applet
implements ActionListener {

  public void init() {
    Button b = new Button("Create Frame");
    b.addActionListener(this);
    add(b);
  }

  public void actionPerformed(ActionEvent ae) {
    Frame2 f2 = new Frame2("Frame2");
    f2.show();
    f2.setSize(200, 200);
  }
}
```

Output from this applet is shown here:

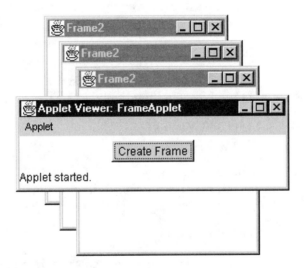

EXERCISE

1. Enhance the **FrameApplet** example so that a count is displayed in
each frame that is created. In other words, the first frame contains a
label of 1, the second frame contains a label of 2, and so forth.

15.16 MENUS AND MENU BARS

A frame may contain a menu bar. This presents a set of options for the user. When the mouse is clicked on an option, a drop-down list of suboptions appears. Each of these suboptions may also have suboptions associated with it. Some suboptions may be checkable. That is, a check mark may appear next to the suboption when it has been selected.

Figure 15-2 shows the relationships among the classes that provide this functionality.

The **MenuComponent** class is the superclass of all other classes shown on this diagram. The font used for a menu-related string may be set via its **setFont( )** method shown here:

void setFont(Font *f*)

Here, *f* is the font to be used.

The **MenuBar** class encapsulates the functionality of a menu bar. It has this constructor:

MenuBar( )

There is an **add( )** method that allows **Menu** objects to be added to the menu bar. That method has this signature:

Menu add(Menu *m*)

Here, *m* is the **Menu** to be added to the **MenuBar**. This object is also returned by the method.

The **Menu** class encapsulates the functionality of a drop-down set of menu items. One of its constructors is

Menu(String *str*)

Here, *str* is the string to be displayed for the menu.

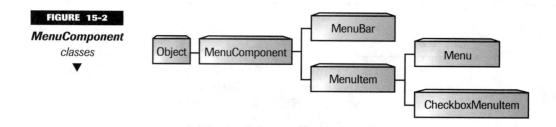

There is an **add( )** method that allows **MenuItem** or **String** objects to be added to the menu, as follows:

MenuItem add(MenuItem *mi*)
void add(String *str*)

Here, *mi* is a **MenuItem** to be added to the menu and *str* is a string to be added to the menu. The first form of this method also returns the menu item.

The **MenuItem** class encapsulates an item in a menu. One of its constructors is

MenuItem(String *str*)

Here, *str* is the string to be displayed for the menu item.

Menu items generate action events when they are selected or deselected. Objects register and unregister to receive these action events via the following methods:

void addActionListener(ActionListener *al*)
void removeActionListener(ActionListener *al*)

Here, *al* is the action listener.

In addition, a menu item may be enabled or disabled via the **setEnabled( )** method, as follows:

void setEnabled(boolean *flag*)

If *flag* is **true**, the menu item is enabled. Otherwise, it is disabled.

The **CheckboxMenuItem** class encapsulates a check box menu item. Some of its constructors are as follows:

CheckboxMenuItem(String *str*)
CheckboxMenuItem(String *str*, boolean *flag*)

Here, *str* is the string to be displayed for the check box menu item. If *flag* is **true**, the item is checked. Otherwise, it is not checked.

Check box menu items generate item events when they are selected or deselected. Objects register and unregister to receive these item events via the following methods:

void addItemListener(ItemListener *il*)
void removeItemListener(ItemListener *il*)

Here, *il* is the item listener.

You may read and write the state of a check box menu item via the **getState( )** and **setState( )** methods shown here:

```
boolean getState()
void setState(boolean flag)
```

If *flag* is **true**, the check box menu item is set. Otherwise, it is cleared.

Follow these steps to create and use a menu bar in a frame:

1. Create a **MenuBar** object.

2. Invoke **setMenuBar( )** to add the **MenuBar** object to the frame.

Follow these steps to create and use a menu in a menu bar:

1. Create a **Menu** object.

2. Invoke **add( )** to add the menu to the menu bar.

Follow these steps to create and use an item in a menu:

1. Create a **CheckboxMenuItem** or **MenuItem** object.

2. Invoke **add( )** to add the item to the menu.

3. Register the frame to receive action or item events generated by the item.

These steps are illustrated in the example and exercise.

EXAMPLE

1. The following applet illustrates how to work with menu bars, menus, menu items, and check box menu items. The applet contains a text area. This is used to report about the action and item events generated by the menu items and check box menu items. A frame that contains a menu bar is created when the applet begins.

   The class **MenuFrame** extends **Frame** and implements **ActionListener**, **ItemListener**, and **WindowListener**. Its constructor accepts both a string to be presented on the title bar and a reference to the applet that invokes this constructor. The frame is registered to process its own window events. A

MenuBar object is created and passed as an argument to the **setMenuBar( )** method. A menu named "A" with menu items named "A1", "A2", and "A3" is created and added to the menu bar. A menu named "B" with menu items named "B1" and "B2" is created and added to the menu bar. A menu named "B3" with menu items named "B31", "B32", and "B33" is created and added to the menu named "B3". A menu named "C" with menu items named "C1" and "C2" is created and added to the menu bar. Finally, a menu named "D" with check box menu items named "D1" and "D2" is created and added to the menu bar. In all cases, the frame is registered to receive action events generated by the menu items and item events generated by the check box menu items.

The **actionPerformed( )** method is called to process the action events. It appends a string to the text area of the applet. Similarly, the **itemStateChanged( )** method is called to process item events. It also appends a string to the text area of the applet.

The **windowClosing( )** method is overridden to relinquish the resources used by this frame.

The **MenuItemEvents** class extends **Applet**. Its **init( )** method instantiates **MenuFrame**, makes it visible, and sets its size. It also creates a text area in which to report about menu-related events.

```
import java.applet.*;
import java.awt.*;
import java.awt.event.*;
/*
  <applet code="MenuItemEvents" width=400 height=200>
  </applet>
*/

class MenuFrame extends Frame
implements ActionListener, ItemListener, WindowListener {
  MenuItemEvents menuItemEvents;

  MenuFrame(String title, MenuItemEvents menuItemEvents) {
    super(title);
    this.menuItemEvents = menuItemEvents;
    addWindowListener(this);
```

```java
// Create and set menu bar
MenuBar mb = new MenuBar();
setMenuBar(mb);

// Create menu A
Menu a = new Menu("A");
mb.add(a);
MenuItem a1 = new MenuItem("A1");
a1.addActionListener(this);
a.add(a1);
MenuItem a2 = new MenuItem("A2");
a2.addActionListener(this);
a.add(a2);
MenuItem a3 = new MenuItem("A3");
a3.addActionListener(this);
a.add(a3);

// Create menu B
Menu b = new Menu("B");
mb.add(b);
MenuItem b1 = new MenuItem("B1");
b1.addActionListener(this);
b.add(b1);
MenuItem b2 = new MenuItem("B2");
b2.addActionListener(this);
b.add(b2);

// Create sub-menu for B3
Menu b3 = new Menu("B3");
b.add(b3);
MenuItem b31 = new MenuItem("B31");
b31.addActionListener(this);
b3.add(b31);
MenuItem b32 = new MenuItem("B32");
b32.addActionListener(this);
b3.add(b32);
MenuItem b33 = new MenuItem("B33");
b33.addActionListener(this);
b3.add(b33);

// Create menu C
Menu c = new Menu("C");
mb.add(c);
MenuItem c1 = new MenuItem("C1");
c1.addActionListener(this);
c.add(c1);
```

```java
      MenuItem c2 = new MenuItem("C2");
      c2.addActionListener(this);
      c.add(c2);

      // Create menu D
      Menu d = new Menu("D");
      mb.add(d);
      CheckboxMenuItem d1 = new CheckboxMenuItem("D1");
      d1.addItemListener(this);
      d.add(d1);
      CheckboxMenuItem d2 = new CheckboxMenuItem("D2");
      d2.addItemListener(this);
      d.add(d2);
   }

   public void actionPerformed(ActionEvent ae) {
      menuItemEvents.ta.append("ActionEvent: " +
         ae.getActionCommand() + "\n");
   }

   public void itemStateChanged(ItemEvent ie) {
      CheckboxMenuItem cbmi =
         (CheckboxMenuItem)ie.getSource();
      menuItemEvents.ta.append("ItemEvent: " +
         cbmi.getLabel() + "\n");
   }

   public void windowActivated(WindowEvent we) {
   }

   public void windowClosed(WindowEvent we) {
   }

   public void windowClosing(WindowEvent we) {
      dispose();
   }

   public void windowDeactivated(WindowEvent we) {
   }

   public void windowDeiconified(WindowEvent we) {
   }

   public void windowIconified(WindowEvent we) {
   }
```

```
      public void windowOpened(WindowEvent we) {
      }
  }

public class MenuItemEvents extends Applet {
  TextArea ta;

  public void init() {
    MenuFrame mf = new MenuFrame("MyFrame", this);
    mf.show();
    mf.setSize(200, 200);
    ta = new TextArea(10, 20);
    add(ta);
  }
}
```

Output from this applet is shown here:

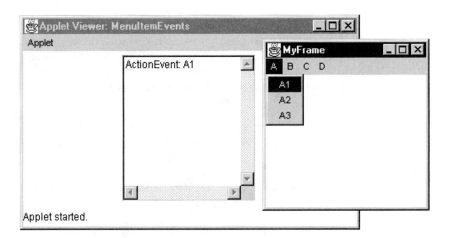

---

1. Create an application that displays a frame with a menu bar. When a user selects any menu or menu item, display that selection on a text area in the center of the frame. Define the menus as done in the previous example.

| 15.17 | # *D*IALOGS AND FILE DIALOGS |

Dialogs are commonly presented in graphic user interfaces to display information or obtain input. A *modal* dialog does not permit a user to make another window in the application active until it has been closed. A *modeless* dialog allows a user to switch to another window in the application before closing the dialog. Let us now demonstrate how to use dialogs.

The **Dialog** class extends **Window**. It provides a window in which all of the user interface components that have been discussed so far may be used.

This class has these constructors:

```
Dialog(Frame parent)
Dialog(Frame parent, boolean flag)
Dialog(Frame parent, String title)
Dialog(Frame parent, String title, boolean flag)
```

Here, *parent* is a reference to the owner of the dialog. The dialog is modal if *flag* is **true**. Otherwise, it is modeless. The title bar is initialized with *title*.

This class has several methods. The **show( )** method is used to make a dialog visible. Its signature is shown here:

```
void show()
```

The **FileDialog** class extends **Dialog** and provides a dialog that allows a user to select a file for reading or writing. This is very useful for applications that need to save data to a file and later retrieve that data. This class defines two **int** constants named **LOAD** and **SAVE**. These determine if the file dialog is being used to select a file for reading or writing.

It has these constructors:

```
FileDialog(Frame parent)
FileDialog(Frame parent, String str)
FileDialog(Frame parent, String str, int rw)
```

Here, *parent* is the frame that creates this dialog. The title bar of the file dialog is initialized from *str*. The final argument indicates if this file dialog identifies a file for loading or saving. If *rw* is **LOAD**, a file is being identified for reading. If *rw* is **SAVE**, a file is being identified for writing. The first two forms create a dialog to load a file.

You may get or set the file selection via the **getFile( )** or **setFile( )** methods, which have these signatures:

```
String getFile()
void setFile(String str)
```

Here, *str* is the name of the file that should be displayed in the file dialog. Follow these steps to create a dialog:

1. Define a subclass of **Dialog**.

2. Inside the constructor: create and arrange user interface elements, invoke **pack( )** to lay out components and set the initial size of this dialog box, and register to receive window events.

3. Call **dispose( )** when you are finished with the dialog.

Follow these steps to use your dialog:

1. Instantiate the **Dialog** subclass.

2. Call **setVisible( )** to make the dialog visible.

3. Call **setSize( )** to set the dimensions of the dialog.

EXAMPLES

1. The following application illustrates how to use the **Dialog** class. It creates a frame that contains a button labeled "Message Dialog". When this button is pressed, a modal dialog appears. The dialog contains a label and a button labeled "OK". It is dismissed when the button is pressed.

   The **MessageDialogDemo** class extends **Frame** and implements **ActionListener**. The **main( )** method creates an instance of this class, makes it visible, and sets its initial size. The constructor sets the layout manager, instantiates the button, registers the applet to listen for action events, and creates an anonymous inner class to handle window events. When the button is pressed, the **actionPerformed( )** method is called. It creates the dialog and invokes **show( )** to make it visible.

   The **MessageDialog** class extends **Dialog** and implements **ActionListener**. The constructor creates a user interface with a label and a button. These components are laid out and the initial size of the dialog is determined by the **pack( )** method. An anonymous inner class is created to handle window events. The **getInsets( )** method returns an **Insets** object that encapsulates the margins of the dialog. Finally, the **dispose( )** method is called when an action event is generated by the button. This is done to remove the dialog from the screen and relinquish any operating system resources that were allocated for it.

```java
import java.awt.*;
import java.awt.event.*;

public class MessageDialogDemo extends Frame
implements ActionListener {
  Button b;

  public static void main(String args[]) {
    MessageDialogDemo mdd = new MessageDialogDemo();
    mdd.setVisible(true);
    mdd.setSize(200, 100);
  }

  MessageDialogDemo() {
    super("Messager Dialog Demo");

    // Set layout manager
    setLayout(new FlowLayout());

    // Create button
    b = new Button("Message Dialog");
    b.addActionListener(this);
    add(b);

    // Anonymous inner class handles window events
    addWindowListener(new WindowAdapter() {
      public void windowClosing(WindowEvent we) {
        System.exit(0);
      }
    });
  }

  public void actionPerformed(ActionEvent ae) {
    String message = "This is the message";
    MessageDialog md =
      new MessageDialog(this, "Message Dialog", true, message);
    md.show();
```

```java
      }
  }

class MessageDialog extends Dialog
implements ActionListener {
  Button ok;

  MessageDialog(Frame parent, String title,
  boolean mode, String message) {
    super(parent, title, mode);

    // Create and add "Center" panel
    Panel pc = new Panel();
    Label label = new Label(message);
    pc.add(label);
   add(pc, "Center");

    // Create and add "South" panel
    Panel ps = new Panel();
    ok = new Button("OK");
    ok.addActionListener(this);
    ps.add(ok);
    add(ps, "South");

    // Lay out components and set the initial size
    // of this dialog box
    pack();

    // Anonymous inner class handles window events
    addWindowListener(new WindowAdapter() {
      public void windowClosing(WindowEvent we) {
        System.exit(0);
      }
    });
  }

  public Insets getInsets() {
    return new Insets(40, 20, 20, 20);
  }


  public void actionPerformed(ActionEvent ae) {
    dispose();
  }
}
```

Output from this application is shown here:

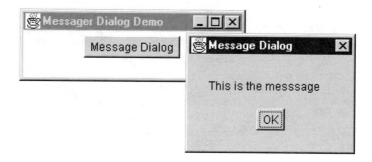

2. The following application illustrates how to use the **FileDialog** class. It creates a frame that contains two buttons and a text field. One of the buttons is labeled "Load." If a user presses this button, a dialog to select a file for reading appears. The other button is labeled "Save." If a user presses this button, a dialog to select a file for writing appears. In either case, once the user specifies a file and presses the Open or Save button on the dialog, the name of the file is displayed in the text field.

The **DialogApplication** class extends **Frame** and implements **ActionListener** and **WindowListener**. The **main( )** method creates an instance of this class, makes it visible, and sets its initial size.

The constructor sets the layout manager, instantiates the buttons and text field, and registers the frame to receive any action or window events.

The **actionPerformed( )** method is called when one of the buttons is pressed. It calls the **getSource( )** method of the **ActionEvent** object to obtain a reference to the object that generated this action event. If this is the load button, the **FileDialog** constructor is invoked with its second argument equal to **FileDialog.LOAD**. Otherwise, the second argument is **FileDialog.SAVE**. The **show( )** method is called to make the file dialog visible. This method does not return until after the user presses the Open, Save, or Cancel button in the file dialog. When control returns to the **actionPerformed( )** method, the **getFile( )** method is invoked to obtain the filename specified by the user. If no file has been selected, this method returns **null**. Otherwise, it returns the name of the file. This string is then written to the text field.

```java
import java.awt.*;
import java.awt.event.*;

public class DialogApplication extends Frame
implements ActionListener, WindowListener {
  Button l, s;
  TextField tf;

  public static void main(String args[]) {
    DialogApplication da = new DialogApplication();
    da.setVisible(true);
    da.setSize(400, 100);
  }

  DialogApplication() {
    super("Dialog Application");
    setLayout(new FlowLayout());
    l = new Button("Load");
    l.addActionListener(this);
    add(l);
    s = new Button("Save");
    s.addActionListener(this);
    add(s);
    tf = new TextField(20);
    add(tf);
    addWindowListener(this);
  }

  public void actionPerformed(ActionEvent ae) {
    FileDialog fd;
    if(ae.getSource() == l) {
      fd = new FileDialog(this, "File Dialog",
        FileDialog.LOAD);
    }
    else {
      fd = new FileDialog(this, "File Dialog",
        FileDialog.SAVE);
    }
    fd.show();
    String filename = fd.getFile();
    if(filename != null) {
      tf.setText(filename);
    }
  }
```

```
public void windowActivated(WindowEvent we) {
}

public void windowClosed(WindowEvent we) {
}

public void windowClosing(WindowEvent we) {
  System.exit(0);
}

public void windowDeactivated(WindowEvent we) {
}

public void windowDeiconified(WindowEvent we) {
}

public void windowIconified(WindowEvent we) {
}

public void windowOpened(WindowEvent we) {
}
}
```

Output from this application is shown here:

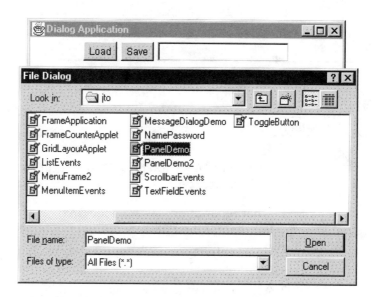

1. Write an application that creates a frame with one button. Each time the button is pressed, a modal dialog box appears that displays a random color in a 100 × 100-pixel canvas in the dialog box. Your application should appear as shown in the following illustration:

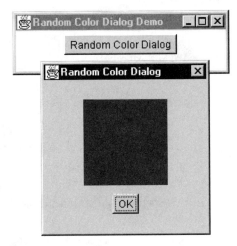

Mastery
Skills Check

At this point you should be able to answer these questions and perform these exercises:

1. What types of events are generated by a button, canvas, check box, choice, text field, text area, list, and scroll bar?

2. Name three types of layout managers and briefly explain their operation.

3. When is a window event generated?

4. What types of events are generated by menu items and check box menu items?

5. Construct an application that displays a button and a 50 × 50-pixel canvas. Label the button "Color Dialog" and fill the canvas with a red color. When a user presses the button, open a modal dialog box that allows the color of the canvas to be changed. The dialog box should have three scroll bars that can adjust the red, green, and blue components of the color. As the scroll bars are manipulated, the color of the canvas should change immediately. There should be a button at the bottom of the dialog box so the user can dismiss it. Your application should appear as shown in the following illustration:

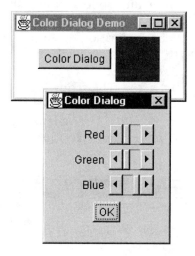

Cumulative
Skills Check

This section checks how well you have integrated the material in this chapter with that of the earlier chapters.

1. Write an application that creates a frame with one button. Each time the button is pressed, a modal dialog box appears that displays the current date. Your application should appear as shown in the following illustration:

2. Design and build a simple chat service. Use a client/server architecture for the software. Allow multiple instances of the client application to communicate with a server application via TCP/IP sockets. Each client application presents a text area and a text field. A user types a message into the text field and hits the ENTER key. The string is sent to the server and is echoed back to all clients. Messages received from the server are appended to the text area. Your client application should appear as shown in the following illustration:

3. Write an applet that displays a calendar for the current month and year. It should appear as shown in the following illustration:

			July 1998			
Sun	Mon	Tue	Wed	Thu	Fri	Sat
			1	2	3	4
5	6	7	8	9	10	11
12	13	14	15	16	17	18
19	20	21	22	23	24	25
26	27	28	29	30	31	

Applet Viewer: CalendarApplet

Applet

Applet started.

16

Topics for Further Investigation

THE previous chapters covered the fundamentals of Java programming. You are now in an excellent position to develop some useful applets and applications.

However, there is other important functionality that has not been covered in this book. This was developed by Sun Microsystems in cooperation with other industry partners. A brief examination of these topics is included in this chapter.

Review

Skills Check

Before proceeding, you should be able to answer these questions and perform these exercises.

1. What functionality is added to the **Window** class by the **Frame** class?

2. What method must be invoked to make windows and dialogs visible?

3. What is the default layout manager for a window?

4. What is the default layout manager for a panel?

5. Write an applet that simulates the operation of a calculator. Provide a text field at the top of the applet to echo button presses and display results. Provide a set of buttons arranged in a 6 × 3 grid. There are ten buttons for the digits 0 to 9, four buttons for the arithmetic operations, a button to change the sign of a number, a button to clear the values of the calculator, and buttons for the period and equals sign.

6. Write an applet that contains two radio buttons and a canvas. The canvas is filled with a color gradient. The canvas is black at one end and white at the opposite end. The radio buttons control whether a horizontal or vertical gradient is displayed. Your applet should appear as shown in the following illustrations.

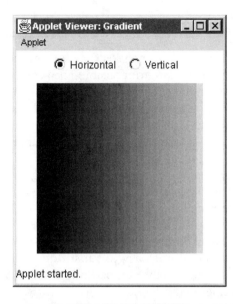

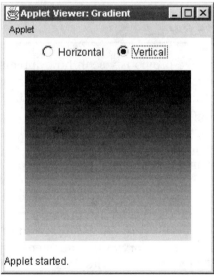

16.1 SWING

Swing is a set of classes that can provide more powerful and flexible interfaces than are possible with the AWT. There are additional types of elements such as tabbed panes, scroll panes, trees, and tables. In addition, familiar components such as buttons have more capabilities in Swing. For example, a button may have both an image and a text string associated with it. Also, the image can be changed as the state of the button changes.

Unlike AWT components, Swing components are not built by using platform-specific code. Instead, they are entirely written in Java and, therefore, are platform-independent. The term *lightweight* is used to describe such elements.

Swing components also provide a pluggable look-and-feel. This means that it is easy to substitute another appearance and behavior for an element. This can be done dynamically. You may even design your own look-and-feel.

16.2 SERVLETS

You have previously seen how applets dynamically extend the functionality of a Web browser. Servlets are Java objects that dynamically extend the functionality of a Web server. The classes for a servlet can be dynamically loaded from local or remote storage. In this respect, it is similar to an applet. However, a servlet does not present a user interface. Instead, it typically provides the business logic for a Web application. This is often done by accessing files and databases.

Each servlet can be addressed via a separate URL. A browser can issue a request for that URL to start the servlet. The Web server may also start servlets when it begins execution. Arguments can be passed to the servlet at initialization. In addition, arguments can be provided each time the servlet is requested. A servlet can read data from an HTTP request and write data to an HTTP response. In this manner, it can interact with the browser.

Applets and servlets can be used to build a Web application. The former provide the user interface and the latter provide the core functionality for that service.

16.3 *JAVA DATABASE CONNECTIVITY (JDBC)*

Relational databases are commonly used to store information. Each database consists of a set of tables and each table contains a set of records. The actual data exists in these records. Applications use a high-level language known as Structured Query Language (SQL) to work with a relational database. SQL provides the ability to manipulate data. For example, you can retrieve, update, insert, or delete one or more records. The structure of the database can also be manipulated via SQL.

Java Database Connectivity (JDBC) allows a Java program to access a relational database. It is included with the JDK and defines classes and interfaces to represent the abstractions that a programmer commonly needs when working with a relational database. These include database connections, SQL statements, result sets, and metadata. Metadata is "data about the data". That is, it describes the database itself.

Java Database Connectivity (JDBC) provides a uniform interface to a variety of relational databases. It operates with database products that provide the Open Database Connectivity (ODBC) interface.

16.4 *OBJECT SERIALIZATION AND REMOTE METHOD INVOCATION (RMI)*

Serialization is the ability to save the state of several objects to a stream. The stream is typically associated with a file. This allows an application to start execution, create a set of objects, save their state, and terminate.

Deserialization is the ability to restore the state of several objects from a stream. This allows an application to start execution, read a file, restore a set of objects from the data in that file, and proceed.

If an object contains references to other objects, these are also saved. The process is recursive, so an attempt to serialize one object can cause many other objects to be serialized. The mechanisms are designed to correctly handle sets of objects that have circular references to each other.

Remote Method Invocation (RMI) allows a Java object that executes on one machine to invoke a method of a Java object that executes another machine. This is an important feature because it allows you to build distributed applications.

Objects can be passed as arguments to remote method calls or returned as values. This is done by using the Object Serialization facilities to transmit the state of an object from one machine to another.

16.5 JAVA BEANS AND JAVA ENTERPRISE JAVA BEANS

Hardware engineers are able to design and construct a system by using components. These building blocks can be simple (such as resistors, capacitors, inductors) or complex (such as digital signal processors, multiplexers, analog/digital converters). Someone knowledgeable about this technology can read the associated specifications and learn how the parts can be connected to provide a solution.

However, software engineers have not been as successful in getting the benefits of reuse and interoperability. A common mechanism for connecting pieces of software has been lacking. The procedures to configure components so they operate as desired in a particular application environment have been non-standard. Because of these incompatibilities, it has not been possible to use a builder tool to visually configure and connect software supplied by multiple vendors.

These shortcomings are overcome by JavaBeans. Java Beans are software components written in Java. They allow you to rapidly create applications by configuring and connecting components called Beans. These components may be supplied by multiple software vendors. Although JavaBeans is a sophisticated and powerful software technology, it is straightforward to use.

The JavaBeans specification defines the mechanisms by which components perform common tasks such as communicating with each other, interacting with tools and saving/restoring their configuration. A Bean has all the benefits of the "write once, run anywhere" paradigm that is the foundation of Java.

A builder tool allows you to visually configure and connect a set of Beans. It uses a mechanism called *introspection* to dynamically determine valuable information about a component. Specifically, the properties, events, and methods of a component can easily be determined if the designer follows some simple naming patterns. This is essential so you can install Beans on your machine and immediately begin working with them.

A Bean developer can provide property editors and customizers. These provide a graphical user interface through which that component can be configured.

The Bean Developer Kit (BDK) is a simple example of a builder tool. It can be downloaded without charge from the JavaSoft Web site (**java.sun.com**). The BDK also includes a set of demonstration components and their source code. Several other vendors also supply tools that allow you to work with Beans.

A set of Beans, supporting classes, and associated resources can be packaged into a Java Archive (JAR) file. This provides a convenient mechanism to deliver software components to users.

JavaBeans is an important software technology. To learn more about it, see "JavaBeans Programming from the Ground Up" by Joseph O'Neil. The book was edited by Herb Schildt and is also available from Osborne/McGraw-Hill.

The Enterprise JavaBeans specification defines a set of services that are available for Java components that execute on a server. For example, a naming service is available so components can be identified. Support for transactions is available. A transaction is a set of changes that typically involve several components. It must be done in an "all-or-nothing" manner. In other words, if a problem is encountered, the transaction must be aborted and any partial changes must be "rolled back." This means that the previous state of those objects must be restored.

16.6 ENTERPRISE SERVICES

There are several APIs that provide functionality for building enterprise applications. Some of these are briefly summarized here:

API	Functionality
Java Naming and Directory Interface (JNDI)	Provides a common interface to heterogeneous naming and directory services
Java Management API (JMAPI)	Allows the development of integrated system, network, and service management applications

API	Functionality
Java Message Service (JMS)	Provides a common interface to enterprise messaging services
Java Interface Definition Language (IDL)	Allows Java programs to connect with CORBA (Common Object Request Broker Architecture) systems
Java Transaction Services (JTS)	Allows heterogeneous software in a transaction processing environment to interoperate
Java Electronic Commerce Framework (JECF)	Allows you to build applications that handle money

16.7 JAVA MEDIA AND COMMUNICATION APIS

Several APIs allow developers to build multimedia applications.

The Java 2-D API allows developers to construct user interfaces with high-quality 2-D graphics, text, and images. It provides a consistent framework for device and resolution-independent graphics.

The Java 3-D API allows developers to build more advanced user interfaces with 3-D virtual worlds. High-level constructs to create, manipulate, and render 3-D geometry are available.

The Java Media Framework API provides capabilities for media capture, playback, and conferencing. You can access a very high quality sound synthesis engine with the Java Sound API. Speech recognition and synthesis is available with the Java Speech API. Telephony functions can be performed via the Java Telephony API.

16.8 SECURITY

Applets downloaded from a network source are normally not trusted. Therefore, they are blocked from accessing your file system or performing other potentially dangerous operations. This is known as the "sandbox" model of security. In other words, untrusted applets are severely limited in terms of the operations they can perform. This default behavior is appropriate when you cannot be certain about the origin of an applet.

However, recent enhancements allow you to provide *signed* applets with selective access to network resources. A complete discussion of cryptography and digital signatures is beyond the scope of this book. However, you may think of a digital signature as analogous to a handwritten signature. An applet that is developed by Sun Microsystems, for example, can be digitally signed by that company. You may wish to relax some of the "sandbox" constraints for any applet which is signed by that company.

16.9 JAVA IN CONSUMER DEVICES

The capabilities of Java are also available for developers building applications for various consumer devices.

JavaCard provides a specialized Java Virtual Machine (JVM) that executes on a smart card. Simple applets can be loaded into the card and executed.

EmbeddedJava is targeted for very simple, high-volume devices. Resources are very limited in this environment. These applications run on real-time operating systems. Examples are pagers, smart cards, controllers, and instruments.

PersonalJava is targeted for devices that support graphical user interfaces and network connectivity. Examples are mobile phones, portable computers, and set-top boxes.

16.10 CONCLUDING COMMENTS

Knowledge of Java technology is a prerequisite for software professionals. This book has given you a foundation on which to build. However, this area of technology continues to evolve rapidly. You should frequently check the Web page at **java.sun.com** to keep informed about the latest developments.

Appendix A

Answers

CHAPTER 1

EXERCISES

1.9

1.
```
class VariableDemo {
    public static void main(String args[]) {
        int num = 1000;
        System.out.println(num + " is the value of num");
    }
}
```

2. The compiler complains that variables **c** and **flag** may not have been initialized.

EXERCISES

1.10

1.
```
class JulietQuote {
    public static void main(String args[]) {
        String s = "Juliet said: " +
            "\"Romeo, where art thou?\"";
        System.out.println(s);
    }
}
```

2.
```
class ConcatenationDemo {
    public static void main(String args[]) {
        String myName = "Joe " + "O'Neil";
        System.out.println(myName);
    }
}
```

EXERCISES

1.11

1. 5 % 3 + 1 = 3, 5 / 3 + 1 = 2, 5 * 3 + 1 = 16

2.
```
class DrivingTime {
    public static void main(String args[]) {
        float h = 3000/75;
        System.out.println(h +
            " hours are required to drive " +
            "from New York to Los Angeles ");
    }
}
```

3. Yes

4. -2.3, 2.3

■ **1.12** *E XERCISES*

1. float
2. long

■ **1.13** *E XERCISES*

1. No. The compiler issues an error message about the assignment "short s2 = s1 + 1;" reporting that an explicit cast is needed to convert an **int** to a **short**. The right side of the assignment statement is automatically converted to an **int**.
2. An incorrect value can be assigned to the variable on the left side of the assignment statement.

■ **1.14** *E XERCISES*

1. Yes
2. Yes

■ **1.15** *E XERCISES*

1. No. All array elements must be the same type.
2.
```
class FourByteArray {
   public static void main(String args[]) {
     byte array[] = new byte[4];
     array[0] = 11;
     array[1] = 26;
     array[2] = 56;
     array[3] = -90;
     System.out.println(array[0]);
     System.out.println(array[1]);
     System.out.println(array[2]);
     System.out.println(array[3]);
   }
}
```

3.
```
class AverageValue {
   public static void main(String args[]) {
     double da[] = new double[4];
     da[0] = 1E307;
     da[1] = 1.1E307;
     da[2] = 1.2E307;
     da[3] = 1.3E307;
     double total = da[0];
     total += da[1];
     total += da[2];
```

```
      total += da[3];
      System.out.println("Average = " + total/4);
   }
}
```

EXERCISES

1.
```
class FloatArray {

   public static void main(String args[]) {

      // Declare, allocate, initialize
      float myarray[][] = {
        { -56.7f },
        { 500.1f, 70.70f },
        { 100.9f, 0.5f, 20.20f }
      };

      // Display length
      System.out.println("myarray.length = " +
        myarray.length);

      // Display elements
      System.out.println(myarray[0][0]);
      System.out.println(myarray[1][0]);
      System.out.println(myarray[1][1]);
      System.out.println(myarray[2][0]);
      System.out.println(myarray[2][1]);
      System.out.println(myarray[2][2]);
   }
}
```

2.
```
class ArrayLengths {
   public static void main(String args[]) {
      int iarray[][] = {
        { 44 },
        { -22, 16 },
        { 11, -12, 99 }
      };
      System.out.println("iarray.length = " + iarray.length);
      System.out.println("iarray[0].length = " + iarray[0].length);
      System.out.println("iarray[1].length = " + iarray[1].length);
      System.out.println("iarray[2].length = " + iarray[2].length);
   }
}
```

3.
```
class Matrix3D {
   public static void main(String args[]) {
      byte array[][][] = {
        { { 4, 5, 6 }, { 1, 2, 3 }, { 5, 7, 8 } },
        { { 2, 0, 5 }, { 9, 8, 7 }, { 4, 4, 3 } },
        { { 0, 0, 0 }, { 1, 1, 1 }, { 2, 2, 2 } }
      };
```

```
      System.out.print(array[0][0][0] + ", ");
      System.out.print(array[0][0][1] + ", ");
      System.out.print(array[0][0][2] + ", ");
      System.out.print(array[0][1][0] + ", ");
      System.out.print(array[0][1][1] + ", ");
      System.out.print(array[0][1][2] + ", ");
      System.out.print(array[0][2][0] + ", ");
      System.out.print(array[0][2][1] + ", ");
      System.out.println(array[0][2][2] + ", ");

      System.out.print(array[1][0][0] + ", ");
      System.out.print(array[1][0][1] + ", ");
      System.out.print(array[1][0][2] + ", ");
      System.out.print(array[1][1][0] + ", ");
      System.out.print(array[1][1][1] + ", ");
      System.out.print(array[1][1][2] + ", ");
      System.out.print(array[1][2][0] + ", ");
      System.out.print(array[1][2][1] + ", ");
      System.out.println(array[1][2][2] + ", ");

      System.out.print(array[2][0][0] + ", ");
      System.out.print(array[2][0][1] + ", ");
      System.out.print(array[2][0][2] + ", ");
      System.out.print(array[2][1][0] + ", ");
      System.out.print(array[2][1][1] + ", ");
      System.out.print(array[2][1][2] + ", ");
      System.out.print(array[2][2][0] + ", ");
      System.out.print(array[2][2][1] + ", ");
      System.out.print(array[2][2][2] + ", ");
   }
}
```

*M*ASTERY SKILLS CHECK: *Chapter 1*

1. Applets require a Web browser or a tool such as the applet viewer to provide an execution environment. Applications are directly interpreted by a Java interpreter.
2. Bytecodes are a platform-independent representation of a program. They are generated by the Java compiler.
3. An object is a region of storage that defines state and behavior.
4. A class is a template for an object.
5. Encapsulation is a mechanism that associates a set of data with the code that manipulates it.
6. Inheritance is a mechanism that allows a class to be defined as a specialization of another class.
7. Polymorphism is a mechanism that allows you to have several different implementations of an interface.
8. **main( )**
9. **boolean**, **char**, **byte**, **short**, **int**, **long**, **double**, **float**

10. A type cast converts from one type to another. It is required when a narrowing conversion is performed.
11. Declare the array name and allocate space for the array elements.
12. Use the syntax *varName*.length where *varName* is the name of the array.
13. Single-line, multiline, and documentation
14. No

CHAPTER 2

REVIEW SKILLS CHECK: Chapter 2

1. Java is platform-independent because the same bytecodes can be interpreted by Java Virtual Machines on different platforms.
2. Here are some packages: (a) **java.applet**: Allows you to build applets. (b) **java.awt**: Allows you to build GUIs. (c) **java.awt.event**: Handles events from AWT components. (d) **java.io**: Handles I/O. (e) **java.lang**: Core functionality.
3. A narrowing conversion occurs when a type is cast to another type with a smaller number of bits.
4. **print( )** and **println( )**
5. When a **char**, **byte**, or **short** is used in an expression, its value is automatically elevated to **int** during the evaluation of that expression.
6. 123count, new-word

2.1 EXERCISES

1. A method is a set of program statements which has been assigned a name. It can return a value and accept arguments.
2. **String**
3. **void**
4. A run-time error
5. A **throws** clause indicates that the method can generate specific types of exceptions.

2.2 EXERCISES

1.
```
class SquareRoot {
    public static void main(String args[]) {
        System.out.println(Math.sqrt(23.45));
```

```
      }
    }

2. class Exponentiation {
     public static void main(String args[]) {
       System.out.println(Math.pow(2, 12));
     }
   }

3. class Triangle {
     public static void main(String args[]) {
       double a = 4.5;
       double b = 8.9;
       double hypotenuse = Math.sqrt(a * a + b * b);
       System.out.println("Sides are " + a + " " + b);
       System.out.println("Hypotenuse is " + hypotenuse);
     }
   }
```

2.3 EXERCISES

```
1. class Last10Chars {
     public static void main(String args[]) {
       String s = "One Two Three Four Five Six Seven";
       int len = s.length();
       String substring = s.substring(len - 10, len);
       System.out.println(substring);
     }
   }

2. class LastNumber {
     public static void main(String args[]) {
       String s1 = "67.89,55.87,-56.45,11.22,78.9";
       int i1 = s1.lastIndexOf(',');
       String s2 = s1.substring(i1 + 1);
       System.out.println(s2);
     }
   }
```

2.4 EXERCISES

```
1. class IntToHexString {
     public static void main(String args[]) {
       System.out.println(Integer.toHexString(100));
     }
   }
```

2.
```
class ParseInt {
    public static void main(String args[]) {
        String s = "125";
        int i = Integer.parseInt(s);
        i = i + 10;
        System.out.println(i);
    }
}
```

2.5 EXERCISES

1.
```
class IntegerEquals {
    public static void main(String args[]) {
        Integer iobj1 = new Integer(5);
        Integer iobj2 = new Integer("5");
        System.out.println(iobj1.equals(iobj2));
    }
}
```

2. An object reference variable has the value **null** when it does not reference any object.

2.6 EXERCISES

1. Garbage collection is the mechanism that reclaims the memory resources of an object when it is no longer referenced by a variable.
2. It prevents programming errors that could otherwise occur by incorrectly deleting or failing to delete objects.
3. An object becomes eligible for garbage collection when it is no longer referenced by any variable. However, the JVM determines exactly when this task is performed.

2.7 EXERCISES

1.
```
class CharacterDemo {
    public static void main(String args[]) {
        System.out.println(Character.isDigit('8'));
        System.out.println(Character.isLetter('A'));
        System.out.println(Character.isLetterOrDigit('A'));
        System.out.println(Character.isLowerCase('a'));
        System.out.println(Character.toLowerCase('A'));
    }
}
```

2.
```
class ShortDemo {
    public static void main(String args[]) {
        String strOctal = "77";
        String strHex = "23";
```

```
              String strDecimal = "156";
              short o = Short.parseShort(strOctal, 8);
              short h = Short.parseShort("23", 16);
              short d = Short.parseShort(strDecimal, 10);
              int sum = o + h + d;
              System.out.println("The sum is " + sum);
          }
      }
```

2.8 EXERCISES

```
1. class StringBufferAppend {
       public static void main(String args[]) {
          StringBuffer sb = new StringBuffer("abcde");
          sb.append("fgh");
          sb.append("ijklmnop");
          System.out.println(sb);
          System.out.println("sb.capacity = " + sb.capacity());
          System.out.println("sb.length = " + sb.length());
       }
   }

2. class StringBufferInsert {
       public static void main(String args[]) {
          StringBuffer sb = new StringBuffer("abcde");
          sb.insert(0, "012345");
          System.out.println(sb);
       }
   }

3. class StringBufferReverse {
       public static void main(String args[]) {
          StringBuffer sb1 = new StringBuffer("abcde");
          sb1.append("abcdefghij");
          StringBuffer sb2 = sb1.reverse();
          System.out.println(sb1);
          System.out.println(sb2);
       }
   }
```

2.9 EXERCISES

```
1. class FloatArray {
       public static void main(String args[]) {
          Float array[] = new Float[5];
          array[0] = new Float(3.4);
          array[1] = new Float(-7);
          array[2] = Float.valueOf("8.5");
          array[3] = Float.valueOf("6.02e23");
          array[4] = new Float(3.4e38);
          System.out.println(array.length);
          System.out.println(array[0]);
```

```
        System.out.println(array[1]);
        System.out.println(array[2]);
        System.out.println(array[3]);
        System.out.println(array[4]);
    }
}
```

2.
```
class ObjectArray {
    public static void main(String args[]) {
        Object array[] = new Object[5];
        array[0] = new Integer(4);
        array[1] = new String("Hello");
        array[2] = new Boolean("true");
        array[3] = new Character('a');
        array[4] = new Double(45.67);
        System.out.println(array[0]);
        System.out.println(array[1]);
        System.out.println(array[2]);
        System.out.println(array[3]);
        System.out.println(array[4]);
    }
}
```

2.10 *E*XERCISES

1.
```
class Multiply2Doubles {
    public static void main(String args[]) {
        // Get first double
        double d1 = Double.valueOf(args[0]).doubleValue();
        // Get second double
        double d2 = Double.valueOf(args[1]).doubleValue();
        // Display their product
        double product = d1 * d2;
        System.out.println("Product is " + product);
    }
}
```

2.
```
class Circle {
    public static void main(String args[]) {
        // Get radius
        double radius = Double.valueOf(args[0]).doubleValue();
        // Display Area
        double area = Math.PI * radius * radius;
        System.out.println("Area is " + area);
    }
}
```

2.11 *E*XERCISES

1.
```
class CurrentTimeMillis {
    public static void main(String args[]) {
        System.out.println(System.currentTimeMillis());
```

```
      }
    }
```

MASTERY SKILLS CHECK: Chapter 2

1. Static variables and methods are associated with a class. They are accessed relative to the name of a class.
2. Instance variables and methods are associated with an object. They are accessed relative to an object reference.
3. *type objRef* = new *clsName(args)*;
4. **Boolean, Character, Byte, Short, Integer, Long, Double, Float**
5. NaN (Not a Number)
6.
```
class MoonWeight {
    public static void main(String args[]) {
        // Get earth weight
        double ew = Double.valueOf(args[0]).doubleValue();
        // Display moon weight
        double mw = ew * .17;
        System.out.println("Moon weight: " + mw);
    }
}
```

7.
```
class Angle {
    public static void main(String args[]) {
        // Get angle in degrees
        double degrees = Double.valueOf(args[0]).doubleValue();
        // Convert to radians
        double radians = degrees * Math.PI/180;
        // Display trig values
        System.out.println("cos = " + Math.cos(radians));
        System.out.println("sin = " + Math.sin(radians));
        System.out.println("tan = " + Math.tan(radians));
    }
}
```

CUMULATIVE SKILLS CHECK: Chapter 2

1.

Keyword	**Meaning**
boolean	Boolean type
byte	Byte type
char	Char type
class	Class definition
double	Double type
float	Float type
int	Int type
long	Long type
new	New operator

Keyword	Meaning
short	Short type
static	Static variable or method

2.
```java
class EightTypes {

    public static void main(String args[]) {

        Boolean bool = Boolean.valueOf(args[0]);
        Character c = new Character(args[1].charAt(0));
        Byte b = Byte.valueOf(args[2]);
        Short s = Short.valueOf(args[3]);
        Integer i = Integer.valueOf(args[4]);
        Long l = Long.valueOf(args[5]);
        Float f = Float.valueOf(args[6]);
        Double d = Double.valueOf(args[7]);

        System.out.println(bool);
        System.out.println(c);
        System.out.println(b);
        System.out.println(s);
        System.out.println(i);
        System.out.println(l);
        System.out.println(f);
        System.out.println(d);
    }
}
```

3.
```java
class CharacterArray {

    public static void main(String args[]) {

        // Create and initialize array
        Character array[] = new Character[5];
        array[0] = new Character('A');
        array[1] = new Character('B');
        array[2] = new Character('C');
        array[3] = new Character('D');
        array[4] = new Character('E');

        // Create string buffer
        StringBuffer sb = new StringBuffer();

        // Append array elements to buffer
        sb.append(array[0]);
        sb.append(array[1]);
        sb.append(array[2]);
        sb.append(array[3]);
        sb.append(array[4]);

        // Display string buffer
        System.out.println(sb);
    }
}
```

*C*HAPTER 3

*R*EVIEW SKILLS CHECK: Chapter 3

1. A static variable exists for the lifetime of a class. An instance variable exists only for the lifetime of an object. A local variable exists only for one invocation of a method.
2. Static method: **Math.max( )**. Static variable: **Math.PI**.
3. **byteValue( )**, **doubleValue( )**, **floatValue( )**, **intValue( )**, **longValue( )**, **shortValue( )**.
4.
```
class Logarithm {
    public static void main(String args[]) {
        double d = Double.valueOf(args[0]).doubleValue();
        System.out.println(Math.log(d));
    }
}
```

3.1 *E*XERCISES

1.
```
class EvenOdd {
    public static void main(String args[]) {
        int i = Integer.valueOf(args[0]).intValue();
        if((i % 2) == 0) System.out.print("Even");
        if((i % 2) == 1) System.out.print("Odd");
        if((i % 2) == -1) System.out.print("Odd");
    }
}
```

2.
```
class LengthConverter {
    public static void main(String args[]) {
        double d = Double.valueOf(args[0]).doubleValue();
        if(args[1].equalsIgnoreCase("Feet"))
            System.out.print(d/3.28 + " Meters");
        if(args[1].equalsIgnoreCase("Meters"))
            System.out.print(d * 3.28 + " Feet");
    }
}
```

3.2 *E*XERCISE

1.
```
class ZeroDivide {
    public static void main(String args[]) {
        double d1 = Double.valueOf(args[0]).doubleValue();
        double d2 = Double.valueOf(args[1]).doubleValue();
        if(d2 == 0) System.out.print("Cannot divide by zero");
```

```
        else System.out.print("Answer is: " + d1/d2);
    }
}
```

3.3 **E**XERCISE

1. No. An opening brace is missing at the end of the first line.

3.4 **E**XERCISES

1.
```
public class CountTo100 {
    public static void main(String args[]) {
        for(int i = 0; i < 101; i = i + 1)
            System.out.print(i + " ");
    }
}
```

2.
```
class Multiple17 {
    public static void main(String args[]) {
        for(int i = 17; i < 101; i = i + 1) {
            if((i % 17) == 0) System.out.print(i + " ");
        }
    }
}
```

3.
```
class Factors {
    public static void main(String args[]) {
        int num = Integer.valueOf(args[0]).intValue();
        for(int i = 2; i < (num/2) + 1; i = i + 1) {
            if((num % i) == 0) System.out.print(i + " ");
        }
    }
}
```

3.5 **E**XERCISES

1.
```
class Count20To30 {
    public static void main(String args[]) {
        for(int i = 20; i <= 30; i++) {
            System.out.print(i + " ");
        }
    }
}
```

2.
```
class AfterIncrementDecrement {
    public static void main(String args[]) {
        int a = 1;
        ++a;
        int b = a;
        --b;
```

```
        System.out.println(a + " " + b);
    }
}
```

3.7 EXERCISES

1. Prints the numbers from 0 to 99, inclusive.
2. Yes
3. If **a** is less than zero

3.8 EXERCISE

```
1. class TernaryOperatorDemo2 {
       public static void main(String args[]) {
           int i = 9;
           System.out.println((i % 2 == 0) ? "Even" : "Odd");
       }
   }
```

MASTERY SKILLS CHECK: Chapter 3

```
1. if(expression) {
       // statement block
   }
   else {
       // statement block
   }
```

```
2. for(initialization; test; increment) {
       // statment block
   }
```

3.

Relational Operator	Meaning
==	Equals
!=	Not equals
>	Greater than
<	Less than
>=	Greater than or equals
<=	Less than or equals
!=	Not equal

4.

Boolean Logical Operator	Meaning
&	AND
|	OR
^	Exclusive OR
!	NOT
&&	AND (short circuit)
||	OR (short circuit)
==	Equal
!=	Not equal

5.
```
class IntArray {
  public static void main(String args[]) {
    int array[] = new int[10];
    int i = -1;
    for(int index = 0; index < 10; index++) {
      array[index] = i--;
    }
    for(int index = 0; index < 10; index++) {
      System.out.println(array[index]);
    }
  }
}
```

*C*UMULATIVE SKILLS CHECK: Chapter 3

1.
```
class SquaresCubes {
  public static void main(String args[]) {
    for(int i2 = 1; i < 11; i++) {
      int square = i * i;
      int cube = square * i;
      System.out.println(i + " " + square + " " + cube);
    }
  }
}
```

2. The increment operator is + +, and it adds one to a variable. The decrement operator is --, and it subtracts one from a variable.

3.
```
class Table {
  public static void main(String args[]) {
    for(int i = 1; i <= 100; i++) {
      System.out.print(i + "\t");
      if((i % 5) == 0) System.out.println("");
    }
  }
}
```

4. The *&* operator always evaluates both of its operands. The *&&* operator does not evaluate its right operand if the left operand is false.

CHAPTER 4

REVIEW SKILLS CHECK: Chapter 4

1. A block of code consists of zero or more statements enclosed by braces.
2. The tab character is represented by the two-character sequence \t.
3. ++count or count++
4. boolean

4.1 EXERCISES

1. An **else** always associates with the nearest **if** within the same block that does not already have an **else** associated with it.
2. To if(count ==5)

4.2 EXERCISES

1.
```
class Countdown {
  public static void main(String args[]) {
    int i = Integer.valueOf(args[0]).intValue();
    for(int j = i; j > 0; j--)
      System.out.print(j + " ");
    System.out.print("\u0007"); // Bell
  }
}
```

2.
```
class Progression {
  public static void main(String args[]) {
    for(int i = 1; i < 1000; i += i)
      System.out.print(i + " ");
  }
}
```

4.3 EXERCISES

1.
```
class SumArguments {
  public static void main(String args[]) {
    int i = args.length;
    double sum = 0;
    while(i > 0) {
      double d = Double.valueOf(args[i - 1]).doubleValue();
      sum = sum + d;
      --i;
```

```
        }
        System.out.print("Sum is " + sum);
    }
}
```

2.
```
class SumRandom {
    public static void main(String args[]) {
        double sum = 0;
        while(true) {
            sum += Math.random();
            System.out.println(sum);
            if(sum > 20)
                break;
        }
    }
}
```

4.4 EXERCISES

1.
```
class Fibonacci {
    public static void main(String args[]) {
        int count = 0;
        int i = 0;
        int j = 1;
        do {
            System.out.print(j + " ");
            int k = i + j;
            i = j;
            j = k;
        } while(++count < 15);
    }
}
```

2.
```
int i = 0;
while(i < 10) {
    // statements
    i = i + 2;
}
```

4.5 EXERCISES

1.
```
class CommandLineArguments {
    public static void main(String args[]) {
        int count = 0;
        for(int i = 0; i < args.length; i++)
            count += args[i].length();
        System.out.println("Total number of characters: " +
            count);
    }
}
```

2.
```
class Primes100To200 {
  public static void main(String args[]) {
    for(int number = 101; number < 200; number++) {
      // Test for factors
      boolean prime = true;
      for(int i = 2; i <= number/2; i++)
        if((number % i) == 0) prime = false;
      // Display if prime
      if(prime == true) {
        System.out.print(number + " ");
      }
    };
  }
}
```

4.6   *EXERCISE*

1.
```
class ArgumentChecker {
  public static void main(String args[]) {
    for(int i = 0; i < args.length; i++) {
      char ch = args[i].charAt(0);
      if(!Character.isLetter(ch) ||
         !Character.isUpperCase(ch)) {
        System.out.print("Arguments must begin " +
          "with an upper case letter");
        break;
      }
    }
  }
}
```

4.7   *EXERCISE*

1.
```
class OddNumbers {
  public static void main(String args[]) {
    for(int i = 1; i < 101; i++) {
      if(i % 2 == 0)
        continue;
      System.out.print(i + " ");
    }
  }
}
```

4.8   *EXERCISE*

---

1. Constant expressions are required for the **case** statements.

| 4.9 | **E**XERCISES |

1.
```
255
15
255
254
-256
63
63
1020
```

2.
```
class CountOnes {
  public static void main(String args[]) {
    byte count = 0;
    int number = Integer.parseInt(args[0]);
    for(int i = 31; i >= 0; i--) {
      if((number & 0x80000000) != 0)
        ++count;
      number <<= 1;
    }
    System.out.println(count + " bits are set");
  }
}
```

MASTERY SKILLS CHECK: Chapter 4

1. **for(;;) { ... }** or **while(true) { ... }** or **do { ... } while(true)**
2. A **break** statement stops execution of the enclosing loop. Execution resumes at the next statement following the loop.
3. A **continue** statement forces the next iteration of the loop to take place, skipping any code in between itself and the test condition.
4. Yes
5.
```
for(int i = 10; i > 0; i--) {
  // ...
}
```

6. The **do** loop always executes its statement block at least once.
7. The **> >** operator means shift right with sign extension. The **> > >** operator means shift right with zero fill.

CUMULATIVE SKILLS CHECK: Chapter 4

1.
```
class MoneyAdder {
  public static void main(String args[]) {
    float sum = 0;
    int i = 0;
    while(i < args.length) {
```

```
          int quantity = Integer.parseInt(args[i]);
          ++i;
          float value = 1;
          if(args[i].equals("pennies"))
            value = 1;
          else if(args[i].equals("nickels"))
            value = 5;
          else if(args[i].equals("dimes"))
            value = 10;
          else if(args[i].equals("quarters"))
            value = 25;
          else {
            System.out.print("Unrecognized coin");
            return;
          }
          sum += quantity * value;
          ++i;
        }
        System.out.println("Sum is $" + sum/100);
      }
    }

2. class SpanishTranslator {
     public static void main(String args[]) {
       if(args[0].equals("One"))
         System.out.println("Uno");
       else if(args[0].equals("Two"))
         System.out.println("Dos");
       else if(args[0].equals("Three"))
         System.out.println("Tres");
       else if(args[0].equals("Four"))
         System.out.println("Quatro");
       else if(args[0].equals("Five"))
         System.out.println("Cinco");
       else
         System.out.println("Unrecognized input");
     }
   }
```

*C*HAPTER 5

*R*EVIEW SKILLS CHECK: Chapter 5

1. initialization, test, and increment
2. A **do** loop will always execute the code in the loop at least once, since the expression controlling the loop is tested at the bottom of the loop. A **while** loop tests its expression at the top of the loop. Therefore, the code in its loop may never execute.

3.
```java
class RandomTotal {
    public static void main(String args[]) {
        double total = 0;
        while(total <= 100) {
            double random = 9 * Math.random() + 1;
            System.out.println(random);
            total += random;
            System.out.println("Total = " + total);
        }
    }
}
```

4.
```java
class SortNumbers {

    public static void main(String args[]) {

        // Declare, allocate, and initialize array
        int size = args.length;
        double data[] = new double[size];
        for(int i = 0; i < size; i++)
            data[i] = Double.valueOf(args[i]).doubleValue();

        // Sort the array
        for(int i = 0; i < size - 1; i++) {
            for(int j = i; j < size; j++) {
                if(data[j] > data[i]) {
                    double temp = data[j];
                    data[j] = data[i];
                    data[i] = temp;
                }
            }
        }

        // Display the array in ascending order
        for(int i = 0; i < size; i++)
            System.out.print(data[i] + " ");
    }
}
```

5. & (AND), | (OR), ^ (Exclusive OR), ~ (Complement), > > (Shift right with sign extension), > > > (Shift right with zero fill), < < (Shift left with zero fill), & = (AND and assignment), | = (OR and assignment), ^ = (Exclusive OR and assignment), > > = (Shift right with sign extension and assignment), > > > = (Shift right with zero fill and assignment), < < = (Shift left with zero fill and assignment)

5.2 ***E*XERCISES**

1.
```java
class Person {
    String name;
    int age;
```

```
        float salary;
    }

    class PersonExample {

      public static void main(String args[]) {

        Person p = new Person();
        p.name = "John Doe";
        p.age = 21;
        p.salary  = 29100f;
        System.out.println("p.name = " + p.name);
        System.out.println("p.age = " + p.age);
        System.out.println("p.salary = " + p.salary);
      }
    }

2. class Sphere {
      double x;
      double y;
      double z;
      double radius;
    }

    class SphereExample {

      public static void main(String args[]) {

        Sphere s = new Sphere();
        s.x = 100;
        s.y = -40;
        s.z = 56.5;
        s.radius = 8;
        System.out.println("s.x = " + s.x);
        System.out.println("s.y = " + s.y);
        System.out.println("s.z = " + s.z);
        System.out.println("s.radius = " + s.radius);
      }
    }
```

3. A class is a template that can be used to create many objects. The class determines the form of each object.

5.3 EXERCISES

```
1. class Person2 {
      String name;
      int age;
      float salary;

      Person2(String aname, int aage, float asalary) {
        name = aname;
        age = aage;
        salary = asalary;
```

```
      }
    }

    class PersonConstructor {

      public static void main(String args[]) {

        Person2 p = new Person2("John Doe", 21, 29100f);
        System.out.println("p.name = " + p.name);
        System.out.println("p.age = " + p.age);
        System.out.println("p.salary = " + p.salary);
      }
    }
```

2.
```
   class Sphere2 {
       double x;
       double y;
       double z;
       double radius;

       Sphere2(double ax, double ay, double az, double aradius) {
         x = ax;
         y = ay;
         z = az;
         radius = aradius;
       }
     }

     class SphereConstructor {

       public static void main(String args[]) {

         Sphere2 s = new Sphere2(100, -40, 56.5, 8);
         System.out.println("s.x = " + s.x);
         System.out.println("s.y = " + s.y);
         System.out.println("s.z = " + s.z);
         System.out.println("s.radius = " + s.radius);
       }
     }
```

<hr>

5.4 **E**XERCISES

1.
```
   class Circle {
       double x;
       double y;
       double radius;

       Circle(double aradius) {
         radius = aradius;
       }
       Circle(double ax, double ay, double aradius) {
         x = ax;
         y = ay;
         radius = aradius;
```

```
      }
    }

    class CircleOverloadConstructors {

      public static void main(String args[]) {

        Circle c1 = new Circle(4);
        System.out.println("c1.x = " + c1.x);
        System.out.println("c1.y = " + c1.y);
        System.out.println("c1.radius = " + c1.radius);
        Circle c2 = new Circle(17.5, 18.4, 6);
        System.out.println("c2.x = " + c2.x);
        System.out.println("c2.y = " + c2.y);
        System.out.println("c2.radius = " + c2.radius);
      }
    }
```

2.
```
   class Sphere {
     double x;
     double y;
     double z;
     double radius;

     Sphere() {
       radius = 1;
     }

     Sphere(double aradius) {
       radius = aradius;
     }

     Sphere(double ax, double ay, double az, double aradius) {
       x = ax;
       y = ay;
       z = az;
       radius = aradius;
     }
   }

   class SphereOverloadConstructors {

     public static void main(String args[]) {

       Sphere s1 = new Sphere();
       System.out.println("s1.x = " + s1.x);
       System.out.println("s1.y = " + s1.y);
       System.out.println("s1.z = " + s1.z);
       System.out.println("s1.radius = " + s1.radius);
       Sphere s2 = new Sphere(2);
       System.out.println("s2.x = " + s2.x);
       System.out.println("s2.y = " + s2.y);
       System.out.println("s2.z = " + s2.z);
       System.out.println("s2.radius = " + s2.radius);
       Sphere s3 = new Sphere(100, -40, 56.5, 8);
       System.out.println("s3.x = " + s3.x);
```

```
            System.out.println("s3.y = " + s3.y);
            System.out.println("s3.z = " + s3.z);
            System.out.println("s3.radius = " + s3.radius);
        }
    }
```

1.
```
class Sphere {
    double x;
    double y;
    double z;
    double radius;

    Sphere() {
      this(0, 0, 0, 1);
    }

    Sphere(double radius) {
      this(0, 0, 0, radius);
    }

    Sphere(double x, double y, double z, double radius) {
      this.x = x;
      this.y = y;
      this.z = z;
      this.radius = radius;
    }
}

class SphereThis {

  public static void main(String args[]) {

    Sphere s = new Sphere(1.1, 3.4, -9.8, 10);
    System.out.println("s.x = " + s.x);
    System.out.println("s.y = " + s.y);
    System.out.println("s.z = " + s.z);
    System.out.println("s.radius = " + s.radius);
  }
}
```

1.
```
class Sphere {
    double x;
    double y;
    double z;
    double radius;

    Sphere() {
      this(0, 0, 0, 1);
```

```
      }

      Sphere(double radius) {
        this(0, 0, 0, radius);
      }

      Sphere(double x, double y, double z, double radius) {
        this.x = x;
        this.y = y;
        this.z = z;
        this.radius = radius;
      }

      void move(double x, double y, double z) {
        this.x = x;
        this.y = y;
        this.z = z;
      }

      void scale(double a) {
        radius *= a;
      }
    }

    class SphereMethods {

      public static void main(String args[]) {

        Sphere s = new Sphere(1.1, 3.4, -9.8, 10);
        s.move(-40, -40, -40);
        s.scale(0.1);
        System.out.println("s.x = " + s.x);
        System.out.println("s.y = " + s.y);
        System.out.println("s.z = " + s.z);
        System.out.println("s.radius = " + s.radius);
      }
    }
```

5.7 EXERCISE

```
1. class SpanishTranslator {

     static String translate(String english) {

       // Perform translation
       String spanish;
       english = english.toLowerCase();
       if(english.equals("one"))
         spanish = "Uno";
       else if(english.equals("two"))
         spanish = "Dos";
       else if(english.equals("three"))
         spanish = "Tres";
       else if(english.equals("four"))
```

```
      spanish = "Quatro";
    else if(english.equals("five"))
      spanish = "Cinco";
    else
      spanish = "Unknown";
    return spanish;
  }
}

class SpanishTranslatorDemo {
  public static void main(String args[]) {
    String s = SpanishTranslator.translate(args[0]);
    System.out.println(s);
  }
}
```

5.8 EXERCISES

1. 100
   1000

2. 1000
   0 1 2 3 4
   1000

5.9 EXERCISE

```
1. class Sphere {
     double x;
     double y;
     double z;
     double radius;

     Sphere() {
       this(0, 0, 0, 1);
     }

     Sphere(double radius) {
       this(0, 0, 0, radius);
     }

     Sphere(double x, double y, double z, double radius) {
       this.x = x;
       this.y = y;
       this.z = z;
       this.radius = radius;
     }

     void move(double x) {
       this.x = x;
     }
```

```
        void move(double x, double y) {
          this.x = x;
          this.y = y;
        }

        void move(double x, double y, double z) {
          this.x = x;
          this.y = y;
          this.z = z;
        }

        void scale(double a) {
          radius *= a;
        }
      }

      class SphereOverloadMethod {

        public static void main(String args[]) {

          Sphere s = new Sphere(1.1, 3.4, -9.8, 10);
          s.move(-40, -40, -40);
          s.scale(0.1);
          System.out.println("s.x = " + s.x);
          System.out.println("s.y = " + s.y);
          System.out.println("s.z = " + s.z);
          System.out.println("s.radius = " + s.radius);
        }
      }
```

5.10 EXERCISES

1. abcde
   abcde

2. sba = aaaaa
   sbb = bbbbb
   sba = aaaaa
   sbb = bbbbbddddd

MASTERY SKILLS CHECK: Chapter 5

```
1. class clsName {
     // instance variable declarations
     type1 varName1 = value1;
     type2 varName2 = value2;
     ...
     typeN varNameN = valueN;

     // constructors
     clsName(cparams1) {
```

```
    // body of constructor
  }
  clsName(cparams2) {
    // body of constructor
  }
  ...
  clsName(cparamsN) {
    // body of constructor
  }

  // methods
  rtype1 mthName1(mparams1) {
    // body of method
  }
  rtype2 mthName2(mparams2) {
    // body of method
  }
  ...
  rtypeN mthNameN(mparamsN) {
    // body of method
  }
}
```

2. A constructor is a special method that creates and initializes an object of a particular class.

3. A type signature is a combination of a method name and the sequence of its parameter types. The Java compiler issues an error message if more than one method has the same type signature.

4. The scope of a variable is the region of a program in which it may be directly accessed.

5. Variable hiding occurs when a local variable has the same name as a static or instance variable.

6. Method overloading occurs when two or more methods have the same name but a different signature.

7. All arguments to a method are passed by value. This includes simple types, array references, and object references. (Remember that a method does not receive a copy of an entire array or object, but rather receives a copy of the reference.)

8. The scope of a local variable is limited to the method in which it is declared. An instance variable is available to all methods in a class. Also, instance variables are initialized to default values when an object is created. However, local variables are not.

9. The scope of the variable **i** is limited to the **for** loop. It is undefined in the last statement.

CUMULATIVE SKILLS CHECK: *Chapter 5*

1.
```
class Rock {
   float mass;

   Rock(float mass) {
     this.mass = mass;
   }
}

class RockArray {
   static int NUMROCKS = 10;

   public static void main(String args[]) {

     // Create the rocks
     Rock rocks[] = new Rock[NUMROCKS];
     for(int i = 0; i < NUMROCKS; i++) {
       float mass = (float)(9 * Math.random() + 1);
       rocks[i] = new Rock(mass);
     }

     // Display the mass of each rock
     float total = 0f;
     for(int i = 0; i < NUMROCKS; i++) {
       float mass = rocks[i].mass;
       System.out.println(mass);
       total += mass;
     }

     // Display the total mass
     System.out.println("Total = " + total);
   }
}
```

2.
```
class Trapezoid {
   double height, base1, base2;

   public Trapezoid(double height, double base1, double base2) {
     this.height = height;
     this.base1 = base1;
     this.base2 = base2;
   }

   public double getArea() {
     return 0.5 * height * (base1 + base2);
   }
}

class TrapezoidDemo {

   public static void main(String args[]) {

     Trapezoid trapezoid = new Trapezoid(6, 5, 8);
```

```
        System.out.println(trapezoid.getArea());
    }
}
```

3. i = 3; s = New string; d = 6.02E23

CHAPTER 6

REVIEW SKILLS CHECK: Chapter 6

1. The **this** keyword can be used to refer to the current object. It also can be used by one constructor to explicitly invoke another constructor of the same class.

2. Arguments are passed by value.

3. The signature of a method is a combination of its name and the sequence of its parameter types.

4.
```
class Planet {
    String name;
    int moons;

    Planet(String name, int moons) {
        this.name = name;
        this.moons = moons;
    }

    void display() {
        System.out.println(name + " has " +
            moons + " moons");
    }
}

class SolarSystem {
    Planet planets[];

    SolarSystem() {

        // Create planets
        planets = new Planet[9];
        planets[0] = new Planet("Mercury", 0);
        planets[1] = new Planet("Venus", 0);
        planets[2] = new Planet("Earth", 1);
        planets[3] = new Planet("Mars", 2);
        planets[4] = new Planet("Jupiter", 16);
        planets[5] = new Planet("Saturn", 18);
        planets[6] = new Planet("Uranus", 15);
        planets[7] = new Planet("Neptune", 8);
        planets[8] = new Planet("Pluto", 1);
    }
```

```
      void display() {
        for(int i = 0; i < planets.length; i++) {
          planets[i].display();
        }
      }
    }

    class SolarSystemDemo {

      public static void main(String args[]) {
        SolarSystem solarSystem = new SolarSystem();
        solarSystem.display();
      }
    }
```

6.1 **E**XERCISE

1. The compilation error occurs at the line "c = new Parent( )" because the types are incompatible for assignment. An object of class **Child** is always of class **Parent**. However, an object of class **Parent** is not always of class **Child**.

6.2 **E**XERCISES

1.
```
class M {
   float f;
   String str;
}

class N extends M {
  Double d1;
}

class Mn {
  public static void main(String args[]) {
    N obj = new N();
    obj.f = 34.5f;
    obj.str = "This is a string";
    obj.d1 = new Double(-23.45e-2);
    System.out.println("obj.f = " + obj.f);
    System.out.println("obj.str = " + obj.str);
    System.out.println("obj.d1 = " + obj.d1);
  }
}
```

2.
```
class S {
   Integer x;
}

class T extends S {
  StringBuffer x;
```

```
      }
      class St {
        public static void main(String args[]) {
          S s = new S();
          s.x = new Integer(5);
          System.out.println("s.x = " + s.x);
          T t = new T();
          t.x = new StringBuffer("Hello");
          System.out.println("t.x = " + t.x);
        }
      }
```

3.
```
   class G {
     static int x = 100;
   }

   class H extends G {
     int x = 50;

     void display() {
       System.out.println("x = " + x);
       System.out.println("super.x = " + super.x);
     }
   }

   class Gh {
     public static void main(String args[]) {
       H h = new H();
       h.display();
     }
   }
```

6.3	***EXERCISES***

1. Hello from B3

2.
```
   class Bond {
     void display() {
       System.out.println("Bond");
     }
   }

   class ConvertibleBond extends Bond {
     void display() {
       System.out.println("Convertible Bond");
     }
   }

   class MethodOverriding4 {
     public static void main(String args[]) {
       Bond bonds[] = new Bond[6];
       bonds[0] = new Bond();
       bonds[1] = new ConvertibleBond();
```

```
        bonds[2] = new ConvertibleBond();
        bonds[3] = new Bond();
        bonds[4] = new Bond();
        bonds[5] = new ConvertibleBond();
        for(int i = 0; i < 6; i++)
          bonds[i].display();
    }
  }
```

6.4 *EXERCISE*

```
1. class I2 {
     String getDescription() {
       return "I2";
     }
   }

   class J2 extends I2 {
     String getDescription() {
       return "J2 " + super.getDescription();
     }
   }

   class K2 extends J2 {
     String getDescription() {
       return "K2 " + super.getDescription();
     }
   }

   class SuperForMethods2 {

     public static void main(String args[]) {

       System.out.println("Instantiating I2");
       I2 obj = new I2();
       System.out.println(obj.getDescription());

       System.out.println("Instantiating J2");
       obj = new J2();
       System.out.println(obj.getDescription());

       System.out.println("Instantiating K2");
       obj = new K2();
       System.out.println(obj.getDescription());
     }
   }
```

6.5 *EXERCISE*

2. Because a superclass constructor must execute before a subclass constructor.

EXERCISES

1. No. The modifiers are mutually exclusive. A **final** class cannot be extended. An **abstract** class cannot be instantiated and is typically extended by other classes.

2. An **abstract** class cannot be instantiated. A concrete class can be instantiated. Abstract classes are usually extended by one or more concrete classes.

3.
```java
abstract class Shape {
  void display() {
  }
}

class Circle extends Shape {
  void display() {
    System.out.println("Circle");
  }
}

class Rectangle extends Shape {
  void display() {
    System.out.println("Rectangle");
  }
}

class Rhombus extends Shape {
  void display() {
    System.out.println("Rhombus");
  }
}

class Trapezoid extends Shape {
  void display() {
    System.out.println("Trapezoid");
  }
}

class Triangle extends Shape {
  void display() {
    System.out.println("Triangle");
  }
}

class AbstractClassDemo2 {
  public static void main(String args[]) {
    Shape s = new Circle();
    s.display();
    s = new Rectangle();
    s.display();
    s = new Rhombus();
    s.display();
    s = new Trapezoid();
    s.display();
    s = new Triangle();
```

```
        s.display();
    }
}
```

EXERCISES

1.
```
class V {
    static final int v = 5;
}

class StaticFinal {

    public static void main(String args[]) {
        System.out.println(V.v);
    }
}
```

2. A compile-time error occurs.

EXERCISES

1. **public**: The method can be invoked by any code that can access this class. **static**: The method is static. **void**: The method does not return a value.

2.
```
abstract class Vehicle {
    abstract int numWheels();
}

class Car extends Vehicle {
    int numWheels() {
        return 4;
    }
}

class Truck extends Vehicle {
    int numWheels() {
        return 8;
    }
}

class VehicleTest {
    public static void main(String args[]) {
        Vehicle v1 = new Car();
        System.out.println("A car has " + v1.numWheels() + " wheels");
        Vehicle v2 = new Truck();
        System.out.println("A truck has " + v2.numWheels() + " wheels");
    }
}
```

6.10 EXERCISES

```
1. class Foo {
     static int i = 7;
     int j;

     Foo(int j) {
       this.j = j;
     }

     public String toString() {
       return "Foo: i = " + i + "; j = " + j;
     }
   }

   class ToString {

     public static void main(String args[]) {
       Foo foo = new Foo(23);
       System.out.println(foo);
     }
   }

2. class ClassDemo2 {

     public static void main(String args[]) {

       Integer obj = new Integer("7");
       Class cls = obj.getClass();
       Class supercls = cls.getSuperclass();
       System.out.println(supercls.getName());
     }
   }
```

MASTERY SKILLS CHECK: Chapter 6

1. The word *polymorphism* literally means "many forms." *Run-time polymorphism* means that the appropriate implementation of a method is selected at run-time.
2. The dynamic method dispatch mechanism selects the appropriate implementation to execute based on the class of the executing object. This forms the basis for run-time polymorphism because it allows a class to have multiple subclasses that implement a method in different ways.

```
3. abstract class Fruit {
     String color;

     public String toString() {
       return getClass().getName() + ": " +
         color;
     }
   }
```

```
   class Apple extends Fruit {

     Apple() {
       color = "Red";
     }
   }

   class Banana extends Fruit {

     Banana() {
       color = "Yellow";
     }
   }

   class Orange extends Fruit {

     Orange() {
       color = "Orange";
     }
   }

   class Strawberry extends Fruit {

     Strawberry() {
       color = "Red";
     }
   }

   class FruitTypes {
     public static void main(String args[]) {
       Fruit fruit = new Apple();
       System.out.println(fruit);
       fruit = new Banana();
       System.out.println(fruit);
       fruit = new Orange();
       System.out.println(fruit);
       fruit = new Strawberry();
       System.out.println(fruit);
     }
   }

4. abstract class Airplane {
     String serial;

     public Airplane(String serial) {
       this.serial = serial;
     }

     abstract int getPassengers();

     public String toString() {
       Class cls = getClass();
       return cls.getName() + ": " +
         serial + " " + getPassengers();
     }
```

```
}

class B747 extends Airplane {
  final static int PASSENGERS = 500;

  public B747(String serial) {
    super(serial);
  }

  public int getPassengers() {
    return PASSENGERS;
  }
}


class B757 extends Airplane {
  final static int PASSENGERS = 300;

  public B757(String serial) {
    super(serial);
  }

  public int getPassengers() {
    return PASSENGERS;
  }
}

class B767 extends Airplane {
  final static int PASSENGERS = 400;

  public B767(String serial) {
    super(serial);
  }

  public int getPassengers() {
    return PASSENGERS;
  }
}

class AirplaneTypes {
  static int NUMAIRPLANES = 6;

  public static void main(String args[]) {

    // Declare and allocate space
    Airplane airplanes[] = new Airplane[NUMAIRPLANES];

    // Create airplanes
    airplanes[0] = new B747("UA1233");
    airplanes[1] = new B767("UA8793");
    airplanes[2] = new B757("UA6733");
    airplanes[3] = new B757("UA4523");
    airplanes[4] = new B747("UA9772");
    airplanes[5] = new B767("UA2331");

    // Display airplanes
```

```
      for(int i = 0; i < NUMAIRPLANES; i++) {
        Airplane a = airplanes[i];
        System.out.println(a);
      }
    }
  }
```

CUMULATIVE SKILLS CHECK: *Chapter 6*

1. Method overloading occurs when several methods in the same class have the same name but different signatures. Method overriding occurs when a subclass defines a method with the same name and signature as one of its superclasses.

2. The keyword **super** can be used to access a variable or invoke a method in the immediate superclass of a class. It can also be used by one constructor to explicitly invoke one of the constructors of its immediate superclass.

3.
```
abstract class Monster {

  public String toString() {
    return getClass().getName();
  }
}

class Vampire extends Monster {
}

class Werewolf extends Monster {
}

class Zombie extends Monster {
}

class MonsterTypes {
  static int NUMMONSTERS = 6;

  public static void main(String args[]) {

    // Declare and allocate space for the monsters
    Monster monsters[] = new Monster[NUMMONSTERS];

    // Create monsters
    monsters[0] = new Zombie();
    monsters[1] = new Vampire();
    monsters[2] = new Werewolf();
    monsters[3] = new Zombie();
    monsters[4] = new Werewolf();
    monsters[5] = new Vampire();

    // Display monsters
    for(int i = 0; i < NUMMONSTERS; i++)
      System.out.println(monsters[i]);
```

```
      }
    }
4. abstract class Widget {
     String color;
     abstract int getMass();
     public String toString() {
       return getClass().getName() + ": " +
         color + ", " + getMass();
     }
   }

   class WidgetA extends Widget {
     final static int MASS = 4;

     WidgetA(String color) {
       this.color = color;
     }

     int getMass() {
       return MASS;
     }
   }


   class WidgetB extends Widget {
     final static int MASS = 1;

     WidgetB(String color) {
       this.color = color;
     }

     int getMass() {
       return MASS;
     }
   }

   class WidgetC extends Widget {
     final static int MASS = 5;

     WidgetC(String color) {
       this.color = color;
     }

     int getMass() {
       return MASS;
     }
   }

   class WidgetD extends Widget {
     final static int MASS = 17;

     WidgetD(String color) {
       this.color = color;
     }
```

```
    int getMass() {
      return MASS;
    }
  }

class WidgetTypes {
  static int NUMWIDGETS = 6;

  public static void main(String args[]) {

    // Declare and allocate space for the widgets
    Widget widgets[] = new Widget[NUMWIDGETS];

    // Create widgets
    widgets[0] = new WidgetC("Red");
    widgets[1] = new WidgetA("Green");
    widgets[2] = new WidgetD("Yellow");
    widgets[3] = new WidgetB("Magenta");
    widgets[4] = new WidgetA("Black");
    widgets[5] = new WidgetC("White");

    // Process widgets
    int totalMass = 0;
    for(int i = 0; i < NUMWIDGETS; i++) {
      Widget w = widgets[i];
      System.out.println(w);
      totalMass += w.getMass();
    }

    // Display total mass
    System.out.println("Total mass = " + totalMass);
  }
}
```

CHAPTER 7

REVIEW SKILLS CHECK: Chapter 7

1. Variable hiding occurs when a variable has the same name as a variable in a superclass.
2. **abstract, final, public**
3. **final**, private, **protected, public**, static, transient, volatile
4. private, **protected, public**
5. **abstract, final**, native, private, **protected, public**, static, **synchronized**
6. A superclass constructor executes before the constructor of a class executes.

7. ```
class Water {
  public final static float BOILING = 100;
```
```

```
    public final static float FREEZING = 0;
    public final static float DENSITY = 1;
}

class WaterDemo {
  public static void main(String args[]) {
    System.out.println(Water.FREEZING);
    System.out.println(Water.BOILING);
    System.out.println(Water.DENSITY);
  }
}
```

7.1 **E**XERCISES

1. An interface is a group of constants and method declarations. It is an abstract description of *what* needs to be done but not *how* it is done.
2. The default modifier for an interface provides access only for code in the same package.
3. The **public** modifier for an interface indicates it can be accessed from code in any other package.
4. **public, static, final**
5. **public** and **abstract**
6. ```
   interface AntiLockBrakes {
       void antiLockBrakes();
   }

   interface CruiseControl {
     void cruiseControl();
   }

   interface PowerSteering {
     void powerSteering();
   }

   abstract class Auto {
   }

   class Model1 extends Auto
   implements PowerSteering {
     public void powerSteering() {
       System.out.println("Model1: powerSteering");
     }
   }

   class Model2 extends Auto
   implements AntiLockBrakes, CruiseControl {
     public void antiLockBrakes() {
       System.out.println("Model2: antiLockBrakes");
     }
     public void cruiseControl() {
       System.out.println("Model2: cruiseControl");
     }
   ```
   ```

```
   }

class Model3 extends Auto
implements CruiseControl {
  public void cruiseControl() {
    System.out.println("Model3: cruiseControl");
  }
}

class Autos {
  public static void main(String args[]) {

    Model1 model1 = new Model1();
    model1.powerSteering();

    Model2 model2 = new Model2();
    model2.antiLockBrakes();
    model2.cruiseControl();

    Model3 model3 = new Model3();
    model3.cruiseControl();
  }
}
```

EXERCISES

1. The line "b = new D1( );" generates an error because the types are incompatible for assignment. Class **D1** does not implement interface **B**.

2.
```
interface LuminousObject {
  void lightOff();
  void lightOn();
}

class SolidObject {
}

class Cone extends SolidObject {
}

class LuminousCone extends Cone
implements LuminousObject {

  public void lightOff() {
    System.out.println("LuminousCone: lightOff");
  }

  public void lightOn() {
    System.out.println("LuminousCone: lightOn");
  }
}

class Cube extends SolidObject {
}
```

```
class LuminousCube extends Cube
implements LuminousObject {

  public void lightOff() {
    System.out.println("LuminousCube: lightOff");
  }

  public void lightOn() {
    System.out.println("LuminousCube: lightOn");
  }
}

class LuminousObjects {
  private final static int NUMOBJECTS = 2;

  public static void main(String args[]) {

    LuminousObject luminousObjects[];
    luminousObjects = new LuminousObject[NUMOBJECTS];

    luminousObjects[0] = new LuminousCone();
    luminousObjects[1] = new LuminousCube();

    for(int i = 0; i < NUMOBJECTS; i++)
      luminousObjects[i].lightOn();

    for(int i = 0; i < NUMOBJECTS; i++)
      luminousObjects[i].lightOff();
  }
}
```

7.3 *E*XERCISES

1.
```
interface P {
  int p = 0;
  void fp();
}

interface P1 extends P {
  int p1 = 1;
  void fp1();
}

interface P2 extends P {
  int p2 = 2;
  void fp2();
}

interface P12 extends P1, P2 {
  int p12 = 12;
  void fp12();
}
```

```
class Q implements P12 {
  public void fp() {
    System.out.println("fp: " + p);
  }
  public void fp1() {
    System.out.println("fp1: " + p1);
  }
  public void fp2() {
    System.out.println("fp2: " + p2);
  }
  public void fp12() {
    System.out.println("fp12: " + p12);
  }
}

class InheritanceExample {
  public static void main(String args[]) {
    Q q = new Q();
    q.fp();
    q.fp1();
    q.fp2();
    q.fp12();
  }
}
```

2.
```
interface K1 {
  int intK = 1;
  void methodK();
}

interface K2 extends K1 {
  void methodK();
}

interface K3 extends K2 {
  void methodK();
}

class U implements K3 {
  public void methodK() {
    System.out.println(intK);
  }
}

class InheritanceExercise {
  public static void main(String args[]) {
    U u = new U();
    u.methodK();
  }
}
```

| 7.4 | **E**XERCISE |

1.
```
interface I1 {
}

interface I2 {
}

interface I3 extends I1, I2 {
}

interface I4 {
}

class X implements I3 {
}

class W extends X implements I4 {
}

class InstanceofTest {
  public static void main(String args[]) {
    W w = new W();
    if(w instanceof I1)
      System.out.println("w implements I1");
    if(w instanceof I2)
      System.out.println("w implements I2");
    if(w instanceof I3)
      System.out.println("w implements I3");
    if(w instanceof I4)
      System.out.println("w implements I4");
    if(w instanceof X)
      System.out.println("w is an instance of X");
  }
}
```

| 7.5 | **E**XERCISES |

1. A package is a group of classes and interfaces.
2. the default package
3. It must be located in the subdirectory a\b\c\d (relative to the current directory. Use the command **javac a\b\c\d\X.java** to compile this file. Issue the command **java a.b.c.d.X** to execute the program.

| 7.6 | **E**XERCISE |

1. Use this command:
   set classpath = c:\lab8;c:\freshman\chem101;c:\seminar.

7.7　EXERCISE

1. One form imports a specific type. It appears as "import *fullyQualifiedTypeName*;". Another form imports all of the available types in a specific package. It appears as "import *packageName.**;".

7.8　EXERCISES

1. The variable, constructor, or method can be accessed by any other class.
2. The variable, constructor, or method can be accessed by code in the same package or subclasses in different packages.
3. The variable, constructor, or method can only be accessed by code in the same class.
4. For **f\F.java**: The compiler complains that variable **e3** in class **e.E** is not accessible from class **f.F**. For **g\G.java**: The compiler complains that variables **e2** and **e3** in class **e.E** is not accessible from class **g.G**.

MASTERY SKILLS CHECK: Chapter 7

1. The general syntax to declare an interface is shown here:

```
intfModifier interface intfName extends intfList {
   // interface variable and method declarations
}
```

2. The **instanceof** operator tests if an object is of a particular class or implements a specific interface.
3. The **package** statement designates the package into which a file's classes and interfaces are placed.
4. CLASSPATH is an environment variable that contains an ordered list of directories and archives. The JDK tools search for a .class file relative to the current directory. If this is not successful, the locations specified by CLASSPATH are then searched in sequence. Finally, the Java class libraries are searched.
5. The **import** statement allows you to use abbreviated names for a specific class or interface or for all of the classes and interfaces in a package.
6. **java.lang**
7.
```
class AnimalTypes {
   private final static int NUMANIMALS = 7;

   public static void main(String args[]) {

      // Declare and allocate space for an array
      Animal animals[] = new Animal[NUMANIMALS];
```

```
     // Initialize array entries
     animals[0] = new Dove();
     animals[1] = new Eagle();
     animals[2] = new Hawk();
     animals[3] = new Penguin();
     animals[4] = new Seagull();
     animals[5] = new Rattlesnake();
     animals[6] = new Turtle();

     // Display all cold blooded animals
     System.out.println("Cold blooded animals:");
     for(int i = 0; i < NUMANIMALS; i++) {
       if(animals[i] instanceof ColdBlooded) {
         System.out.println(animals[i]);
       }
     }

     // Display all ocean dwelling
     System.out.println("Ocean dwelling animals:");
     for(int i = 0; i < NUMANIMALS; i++) {
       if(animals[i] instanceof OceanDwelling) {
         System.out.println(animals[i]);
       }
     }
   }
}

interface ColdBlooded {
}

interface OceanDwelling {
}

abstract class Animal {
}

abstract class Bird extends Animal {
}

class Dove extends Bird {
  public String toString() {
    return "Dove";
  }
}

class Eagle extends Bird {
  public String toString() {
    return "Eagle";
  }
}

class Hawk extends Bird {
  public String toString() {
    return "Hawk";
  }
}
```

```
class Penguin extends Bird
implements OceanDwelling {
  public String toString() {
    return "Penguin";
  }
}

class Seagull extends Bird
implements OceanDwelling {
  public String toString() {
    return "Seagull";
  }
}

abstract class Reptile extends Animal
implements ColdBlooded {
}

class Rattlesnake extends Reptile {
  public String toString() {
    return "Rattlesnake";
  }
}

class Turtle extends Reptile
implements OceanDwelling {
  public String toString() {
    return "Turtle";
  }
}
```

*C*UMULATIVE SKILLS CHECK: *Chapter 7*

```
1. class RobotTypes {
     private final static int NUMROBOTS = 7;

     public static void main(String args[]) {

       // Declare and allocate space for an array
       Robot robots[] = new Robot[NUMROBOTS];

       // Initialize array entries
       robots[0] = new RobotA();
       robots[1] = new RobotA1();
       robots[2] = new RobotB();
       robots[3] = new RobotB1();
       robots[4] = new RobotB2();
       robots[5] = new RobotC();
       robots[6] = new RobotC1();

       // Exercise the 'beep' method on all robots
       // that implement the Sound interface
```

```
      for(int i = 0; i < NUMROBOTS; i++) {
        if(robots[i] instanceof Sound) {
          Sound sound = (Sound)robots[i];
          sound.beep();
        }
      }

      // Exercise the 'stop' method on all robots
      // that implement the Locomotion interface
      for(int i = 0; i < NUMROBOTS; i++) {
        if(robots[i] instanceof Locomotion) {
          Locomotion locomotion = (Locomotion)robots[i];
          locomotion.stop();
        }
      }
    }
}

interface Locomotion {
  void forward();
  void reverse();
  void stop();
}

interface Sound {
  void beep();
}

abstract class Robot {
}

class RobotA extends Robot {
}

class RobotA1 extends RobotA
implements Sound {

  public void beep() {
    System.out.println("RobotA1: beep");
  }
}

class RobotB extends Robot
implements Locomotion {

  public void forward() {
    System.out.println("RobotB: forward");
  }

  public void reverse() {
    System.out.println("RobotB: reverse");
  }

  public void stop() {
    System.out.println("RobotB: stop");
  }
}
```

```
      }

      class RobotB1 extends RobotB
      implements Sound {

        public void beep() {
          System.out.println("RobotB1: beep");
        }
      }

      class RobotB2 extends RobotB {
      }

      class RobotC extends Robot
      implements Locomotion, Sound {

        public void forward() {
          System.out.println("RobotC: forward");
        }

        public void reverse() {
          System.out.println("RobotC: reverse");
        }

        public void stop() {
          System.out.println("RobotC: stop");
        }

        public void beep() {
          System.out.println("RobotC: beep");
        }
      }

      class RobotC1 extends RobotC {
      }
```

2.
```
   package tents;

   abstract class Tent {
   }

   class TentA extends Tent {
   }

   class TentB extends Tent
   implements Waterproof {
   }

   class TentC extends Tent {
   }

   class TentD extends Tent
   implements Waterproof {
   }

   interface Waterproof {
```

```
      }

      class Tents {

        public static void main(String args[]) {

          Tent tents[] = new Tent[4];
          tents[0] = new TentA();
          tents[1] = new TentB();
          tents[2] = new TentC();
          tents[3] = new TentD();

          for(int i = 0; i < 4; i++) {
            if(tents[i] instanceof Waterproof) {
              Class cls = tents[i].getClass();
              System.out.println(cls.getName());
            }
          }
        }
      }
```

CHAPTER 8

REVIEW SKILLS CHECK: Chapter 8

1. Polymorphism means "one interface, many implementations." The declaration of a class may indicate that it implements an interface. That interface may be implemented in different ways by its subclasses. The correct implementation is chosen by the dynamic dispatch mechanism in Java.

2. A compiler error is issued if the variable is used. This is done because the variable is ambiguous.

3. A compiler error is issued only if the methods have the same signature but different return types.

4.
```
public interface PhysicalConstants {
    double G = 9.8;
    double C = 3E8;
    double A = 6.02E23;
}

class PhysicalConstantsDemo {
    public static void main(String args[]) {
        System.out.println(PhysicalConstants.G);
        System.out.println(PhysicalConstants.C);
        System.out.println(PhysicalConstants.A);
    }
}
```

8.1 EXERCISE

1. Before cast
   java.lang.ClassCastException: java.lang.Integer

8.2 EXERCISES

1. Before a
   Before b
   Before c
   Before d
   Before cast
   d: java.lang.ClassCastException: java.lang.Float
   Before division
   d: finally
   c: finally
   b: finally
   a: java.lang.ArithmeticException: / by zero
   a: finally
   After a
   main: finally

2. No. The compiler issues an error because the statement
   "catch(ArithmeticException e)" is never reached.

8.3 EXERCISES

```
1. class ThrowExercise {

    public static void main(String args[]) {
      try {
        System.out.println("Before a");
        a();
        System.out.println("After a");
      }
      catch(ArrayIndexOutOfBoundsException e) {
        System.out.println("main: " + e);
      }
      finally {
        System.out.println("main: finally");
      }
    }

    public static void a() {
      try {
        System.out.println("Before b");
        b();
        System.out.println("After b");
      }
      catch(ArrayIndexOutOfBoundsException e) {
        System.out.println("a: " + e);
```

```
      }
      finally {
        System.out.println("a: finally");
      }
    }

    public static void b() {
      try {
        System.out.println("Before c");
        c();
        System.out.println("After c");
      }
      catch(ArrayIndexOutOfBoundsException e) {
        System.out.println("b: " + e);
      }
      finally {
        System.out.println("b: finally");
      }
    }

    public static void c() {
      try {
        System.out.println("Before d");
        d();
        System.out.println("After d");
      }
      catch(ArrayIndexOutOfBoundsException e) {
        System.out.println("c: " + e);
        throw e;
      }
      finally {
        System.out.println("c: finally");
      }
    }

    public static void d() {
      try {
        int array[] = new int[10];
        System.out.println("Before assignment");
        array[20] = 1;
        System.out.println("After assignment");
      }
      catch(ArrayIndexOutOfBoundsException e) {
        System.out.println("d: " + e);
        throw e;
      }
      finally {
        System.out.println("d: finally");
      }
    }
  }
```

2. Before a
   Before b
   Before c
   Before d

```
d: finally
c: finally
b: java.lang.NumberFormatException: 45.67
b: finally
After b
a: finally
After a
main: finally
```

8.4 | **E**XERCISES

1. **java.lang.Error** and **java.lang.Exception**. The former represent rare conditions that you should not catch (e.g., no available memory). The latter represent conditions that you may catch and handle (e.g., array index out of bounds).
2. **ClassNotFoundException**
3. **ArrayIndexOutOfBounds, ArithmeticException, NegativeArraySizeException, NullPointerException, NumberFormatException, StringIndexOutOfBoundsException**

8.5 | **E**XERCISES

1. No, because it is a subclass of **RuntimeException**.
2. Yes, because it is not a subclass of **RuntimeException**.
3. No.
4.
```
class ThrowsExercise {

    public static void main(String args[]) {

        // Create an array of strings
        String strings[] = new String[6];
        strings[0] = "45";
        strings[1] = "-578";
        strings[2] = "22";
        strings[3] = "100";
        strings[4] = "-1";
        // Omit the following line to get a NullPointerException
        strings[5] = "3000";
        // Include the following line to get a NumberFormatException
        // strings[5] = "300..";

        // Compute average string length
        try {
            System.out.println(average(strings));
        }
        catch(NullPointerException e) {
            System.out.println("Null pointer exception");
        }
        catch(NumberFormatException e) {
```

```
      System.out.println("Number format exception");
    }
  }

  static double average(String array[])
  throws NullPointerException, NumberFormatException {
    double sum = 0;
    for(int i = 0; i < array.length; i++) {
      double d = Double.valueOf(array[i]).doubleValue();
      sum += d;
    }
    return sum/array.length;
  }
}
```

8.6 EXERCISES

1.
```
class NegativeArgumentExceptionDemo {

  public static void main(String args[])
  throws NegativeArgumentException {

    for(int i = 0; i < args.length; i++) {
      double d = Double.valueOf(args[i]).doubleValue();
      if(d < 0) {
        String str = "Negative command line argument: ";
        str += d;
        throw new NegativeArgumentException(str);
      }
    }
  }
}

class NegativeArgumentException extends Exception {
  public NegativeArgumentException(String message) {
    super(message);
  }
}
```

2. No. The compiler issues an error because **ExceptionN** is not thrown in the body of the **try** statement.

MASTERY SKILLS CHECK: Chapter 8

1. An *exception* is an object that is generated to describe a problem encountered during the execution of a problem.
2. integer-division-by-zero, array index negative or out-of-bounds, interrupted I/O operation, unexpected end-of-file condition, missing file, incorrect number format
3. **java.lang.Throwable**

4. You must catch or declare all non-**Runtime** exceptions.

5.
```java
class MasteryExercise {

  public static void main(String args[]) {
    try {
      System.out.println("The sum is " + add(args));
    }
    catch(NumberFormatException e) {
      System.out.println(e);
    }
    catch(RangeException e) {
      System.out.println(e);
    }
    finally {
      System.out.println("Thanks for using this program");
    }
  }

  static double add(String args[])
  throws NumberFormatException, RangeException {
    double sum = 0;
    for(int i = 0; i < args.length; i++) {
      double d = Double.valueOf(args[i]).doubleValue();
      if(d < 0 || d > 1)
        throw new RangeException(d);
      sum += d;
    }
    return sum;
  }
}

class RangeException extends Exception {
  double d;

  public RangeException(double d) {
    this.d = d;
  }

  public String toString() {
    return "Argument " + d + " must be between 0 and 1";
  }
}
```

CUMULATIVE SKILLS CHECK: Chapter 8

1. The result is **NaN** (Not-A-Number). Floating-point division by zero does not generate an exception. Integer division by zero generates an **ArithmeticException**.

2.
```java
class CountSuperclasses {

  public static void main(String args[]) {
    try {
```

```
      int count = countSuperclasses(args[0]);
      System.out.println(count);
    }
    catch(ClassNotFoundException e) {
      System.out.println("Class was not found");
    }
    catch(Exception e) {
      System.out.println("Specify class name as argument");
    }
  }

  static int countSuperclasses(String classname)
  throws ClassNotFoundException {
    Class cls = Class.forName(classname);
    int count = 0;
    while((cls = cls.getSuperclass()) != null) {
      ++count;
    }
    return count;
  }
}
```

CHAPTER 9

REVIEW SKILLS CHECK: Chapter 9

1. try, throw, catch, finally, throws
2. The search for an exception handler begins at the first **catch** block immediately following the **try** block in which the exception occurred. Each **catch** block is examined in sequence to determine if the type of the exception object matches the type of the **catch** block parameter. If a type match is found, the **catch** block is executed. Otherwise, the search continues. The **catch** blocks associated with any enclosing **try** statement are examined. If no **catch** blocks are located in the method, the search continues in the calling method. This process continues as the call stack is followed to the **main( )** method. If a matching **catch** block is not located, the default exception handler is then invoked to display the exception and terminate the program.
3. Yes.
4.
```
class StringIndexOutOfBounds {

  public static void main(String args[]) {

    try {

      String s = "This is a string";
      int length = s.length();
```

```
        System.out.println(s.charAt(length));
      }
      catch(Exception e) {
        e.printStackTrace();
      }
    }
  }
```

5. Before integer division-by-zero
   Inner catch block
   Inner finally block
   Outer catch block
   Outer finally block

9.2 EXERCISES

```
1. class MyThread3 extends Thread {
     String str;
     long msec;

     MyThread3(String str, long msec) {
       this.str = str;
       this.msec = msec;
     }

     public void run() {
       try {
         while(true) {
           Thread.sleep(msec);
           System.out.println(str);
         }
       }
       catch(InterruptedException ex) {
         ex.printStackTrace();
       }
     }
   }

   class ThreadDemo3 {

     public static void main(String args[]) {

       MyThread3 ta = new MyThread3("A", 1000);
       MyThread3 tb = new MyThread3("B", 3000);
       ta.start();
       tb.start();
     }
   }

2. class MyThread4 implements Runnable {
     String str;
     long msec;

     MyThread4(String str, long msec) {
```

```
    this.str = str;
    this.msec = msec;
    new Thread(this).start();
  }

  public void run() {
    try {
      while(true) {
        Thread.sleep(msec);
        System.out.println(str);
      }
    }
    catch(InterruptedException ex) {
      ex.printStackTrace();
    }
  }
}

class ThreadDemo4 {

  public static void main(String args[]) {

    MyThread4 ta = new MyThread4("A", 1000);
    MyThread4 tb = new MyThread4("B", 3000);
  }
}
```

3.
```
class MyThread extends Thread {

  public void run() {
    try {
      for(int i = 0; i < 10; i++) {
        int msec = (int)(300 + 500 * Math.random());
        Thread.sleep(msec);
        System.out.print('x');
      }
    }
    catch(InterruptedException ex) {
      ex.printStackTrace();
    }
  }
}

class FiveThreads {
  private static int NUMTHREADS = 5;

  public static void main(String args[]) {

    // Create threads
    MyThread threads[] = new MyThread[NUMTHREADS];
    for(int i = 0; i < NUMTHREADS; i++) {
      threads[i] = new MyThread();
    }

    // Start threads
    for(int i = 0; i < NUMTHREADS; i++) {
```

```
        threads[i].start();
      }

      // Wait for these threads to complete
      for(int i = 0; i < NUMTHREADS; i++) {
        try {
          threads[i].join();
        }
        catch(Exception e) {
          e.printStackTrace();
        }
      }

      // Display a message
      System.out.println("\nAll threads have completed");
    }
  }
```

9.3 **E*XERCISES***

1. The final account balance is not 10000000. In addition, several executions of the program do not yield the same results.

2.
```
class Account2 {
  private int balance;

  void deposit(int amount) {
    synchronized(this) {
      balance += amount;
    }
  }

  int getBalance() {
    return balance;
  }
}

class Customer2 extends Thread {
  Account2 account;

  Customer2(Account2 account) {
    this.account = account;
  }

  public void run() {
    try {
      for(int i = 0; i < 100000; i++) {
        account.deposit(10);
      }
    }
    catch(Exception e) {
      e.printStackTrace();
    }
  }
```

```
    }

class BankDemo2 {
  private final static int NUMCUSTOMERS = 100;

  public static void main(String args[]) {

    // Create account
    Account2 account = new Account2();

    // Create and start customer threads
    Customer2 customers[] = new Customer2[NUMCUSTOMERS];
    for(int i = 0; i < NUMCUSTOMERS; i++) {
      customers[i] = new Customer2(account);
      customers[i].start();
    }

    // Wait for customer threads to complete
    for(int i = 0; i < NUMCUSTOMERS; i++) {
      try {
        customers[i].join();
      }
      catch(InterruptedException e) {
        e.printStackTrace();
      }
    }

    // Display account balance
    System.out.println(account.getBalance());
  }
}
```

9.4	***E*XERCISE**

1. Deadlock cannot occur in this program. Although there are several threads, they only wait for access to one object. There is no possibility that threads might hold locks that are needed by each other. Also note that **synchronized** method **x1( )** invokes **synchronized** method **x2( )**. This also does not present a possibility of deadlock. When a thread acquires a lock on an object, it may call any number of **synchronized** methods of that same object.

9.5	***E*XERCISE**

1. ```
Calling wait
Calling notifyAll
Done
Done
```
```

▰▰ *M*ASTERY SKILLS CHECK: *Chapter 9*

1. A *thread* is a sequence of execution in a process.
2. Extend the **Thread** class or implement the **Runnable** interface.
3. Deadlock is an error condition that occurs when two or more threads wait indefinitely for each other to relinquish locks.
4. Threads can communicate with each other via the **wait( )**, **notify( )**, and **notifyAll( )** methods.
5. The low-priority thread executes for two seconds. During that time, it outputs strings with an increasing counter value. The normal-priority thread then begins execution. The execution of the low-priority thread is suspended. The normal-priority threads executes for a few seconds. During that time, no visible output is generated. When the normal-priority thread completes, the low-priority thread resumes.
6.
```java
class Resource {
    boolean allocated;
    int rid;

    Resource(int rid) {
        allocated = false;
        this.rid = rid;
    }

    void use(int uid) {
        try {
            System.out.println("User " + uid + " uses resource " + rid);
            Thread.sleep((int)(5000 + 5000 * Math.random()));
        }
        catch(Exception e) {
            e.printStackTrace();
        }
    }
}

class ResourceCoordinator {
    private final static int NUMRESOURCES = 3;
    private int totalAllocated;
    private Resource resources[];

    ResourceCoordinator() {

        // Initialize totalAllocated
        totalAllocated = 0;

        // Create resources
        resources = new Resource[NUMRESOURCES];
        for(int rid = 0; rid < NUMRESOURCES; rid++) {
            resources[rid] = new Resource(rid);
        }
    }
```

```
      synchronized Resource get() {

        // Wait for an available resource
        while(totalAllocated == NUMRESOURCES) {
          try {
            wait();
          }
          catch(InterruptedException ie) {
            ie.printStackTrace();
            System.exit(0);
          }
        }

        // Allocate an available resource
        Resource r = null;
        for(int i = 0; i < NUMRESOURCES; i++) {
          if(resources[i].allocated == false) {
            resources[i].allocated = true;
            r = resources[i];
            break;
          }
        }

        // Increment totalAllocated
        ++totalAllocated;

        // Notify waiting threads
        notifyAll();

        // Return the resource
        return r;
      }

      synchronized void put(Resource r) {

        // Mark resource as available
        r.allocated = false;

        // Decrement totalAllocated
        -totalAllocated;

        // Notify waiting threads
        notifyAll();
      }
    }

class User extends Thread {
  ResourceCoordinator rc;
  int uid;

  User(ResourceCoordinator rc, int uid) {
    this.rc = rc;
    this.uid = uid;
  }

  public void run() {
```

```
    try {
      while(true) {
        Resource r = rc.get();
        r.use(uid);
        rc.put(r);
        sleep(3000);
      }
    }
    catch(Exception e) {
      e.printStackTrace();
    }
  }
}

class ResourcePoolDemo {
  private final static int NUMUSERS = 10;

  public static void main(String args[]) {

    // Create a resource coordinator
    ResourceCoordinator rc = new ResourceCoordinator();

    // Create and start user threads
    for(int uid = 0; uid < NUMUSERS; uid++) {
      new User(rc, uid).start();
    }
  }
}
```

CUMULATIVE SKILLS CHECK: *Chapter 9*

1. If an exception is generated in a **synchronized** method or statement block, the lock on that object is relinquished. This is done so that other threads are not blocked indefinitely.

2.
```
class RandomIntegers {

  public static void main(String args[]) {

    try {

      while(true) {

        int i = (int)(5 * Math.random() + 5);
        System.out.println(i);
        Thread.sleep(3000);
      }
    }
    catch(Exception e) {
      e.printStackTrace();
    }
  }
}
```

3.
```java
class Grasshopper extends Thread {

  public final static int NUMGRASSHOPPERS = 6;
  static Grasshopper grasshoppers[];
  static {
    grasshoppers = new Grasshopper[NUMGRASSHOPPERS];
    for(int i = 0; i < NUMGRASSHOPPERS; i++) {
      grasshoppers[i] = new Grasshopper();
    }
  }

  int x, y;

  public Grasshopper() {
    x = (int)(100 * Math.random());
    y = (int)(100 * Math.random());
  }

  public void run() {
    try {
      while(true) {
        int msec = (int)(10000 * Math.random() + 2000);
        Thread.sleep(msec);
        x = (int)(100 * Math.random());
        y = (int)(100 * Math.random());
        System.out.println("Grasshopper at x = " + x +
          " y = " + y);
      }
    }
    catch(Exception e) {
    }
  }

}

class GrasshopperDemo {

  public static void main(String args[]) {

    for(int i = 0; i < Grasshopper.NUMGRASSHOPPERS; i++)
      new Grasshopper().start();
  }
}
```

CHAPTER 10

REVIEW SKILLS CHECK: Chapter 10

1. The **notify( )** method notifies one of the threads that is waiting to access an object. The **notifyAll( )** method notifies all of the threads that are waiting to access an object.

2.
```java
class Mouse extends Thread {
  Box box;

  Mouse(Box box) {
    this.box = box;
  }

  public void run() {

    try {

      while(true) {

        // Stay out of the box for 10-20 sec
        long out = (long)(10000 * Math.random() + 10000);
        Thread.sleep(out);

        // Enter the box
        box.enter(this);

        // Stay in the box for 5-8 sec
        long in = (long)(5000 * Math.random() + 3000);
        Thread.sleep(in);

        // Exit the box
        box.exit(this);
      }
    }
    catch(Exception e) {
      e.printStackTrace();
    }
  }
}

class Box {
  private static int CAPACITY = 4;
  int count;

  synchronized void enter(Mouse mouse) {

    // Wait while the box is full
    try {
      while(count == CAPACITY) {
        wait();
```

```
        }
      }
      catch(InterruptedException ie) {
        ie.printStackTrace();
        System.exit(0);
      }

      //Increment count
      ++count;

      // Display count
      System.out.println(count);
    }

    synchronized void exit(Mouse mouse) {

      // Decrement count
      --count;

      // Display count
      System.out.println(count);

      // Notify a waiting thread
      notify();
    }
  }

  class BoxAndMice {

    public static void main(String args[]) {

      Box box = new Box();

      for(int i = 0; i < 10; i++)
        new Mouse(box).start();
    }
  }

3. class MyThread extends Thread {
    String name;

    public MyThread(String name) {
      this.name = name;
    }

    public void run() {
      try {
        System.out.println("Thread " + name + " starting");
        int t = (int)(20000 * Math.random() + 10000);
        Thread.sleep(t);
        System.out.println("Thread " + name + " terminating");
      }
      catch(Exception e) {
      }
    }
  }
```

```
class JoinDemo {

  public static void main(String args[]) {

    // Create threads
    MyThread a1 = new MyThread("A1");
    MyThread a2 = new MyThread("A2");
    MyThread a3 = new MyThread("A3");

    // Start the threads
    a1.start();
    a2.start();
    a3.start();

    // Wait for the threads to finish
    try {
      a1.join();
      a2.join();
      a3.join();
    }
    catch(Exception e) {
      e.printStackTrace();
    }

    // Create threads
    MyThread b1 = new MyThread("B1");
    MyThread b2 = new MyThread("B2");

    // Start the threads
    b1.start();
    b2.start();

    // Wait for the threads to finish
    try {
      b1.join();
      b2.join();
    }
    catch(Exception e) {
      e.printStackTrace();
    }
  }
}
```

```
1. import java.util.*;

class GaussianMean {

  public static void main(String args[]) {

    // Determine number of random numbers
    int count = 100;
```

```java
    if(args.length > 0) {
      count = Integer.parseInt(args[0]);
    }

    // Generate random numbers
    Random generator = new Random();
    double total = 0;
    for(int i = 0; i < count; i++) {
      total += generator.nextGaussian();
    }

    // Display the mean of these numbers
    System.out.println("Mean = " + total/count);
  }
}
```

2.
```java
import java.util.*;

class RandomSeed {

  public static void main(String args[]) {

    // Create 1st random number generator
    Random generator = new Random(100);

    // Generate and display 10 random integers
    System.out.println("First generator:");
    for(int i = 0; i < 10; i++)
      System.out.println(generator.nextInt());

    // Create 2nd random number generator
    generator = new Random(100);

    // Generate and display 10 random integers
    System.out.println("Second generator:");
    for(int i = 0; i < 10; i++)
      System.out.println(generator.nextInt());
  }
}
```

The same sequence of numbers is produced by each generation.

10.2 EXERCISES

1.
```java
import java.util.*;

class DaysSinceEpoch {

  public static void main(String args[]) {

    // Get date object initialized
    // to current date and time
    Date currentDate = new Date();

    // Get msec since epoch
    long msec = currentDate.getTime();
```

```
          // Calculate the equivalent number of days
          long days = msec/(24 * 60 * 60 * 1000);

          // Display the equivalent number of days
          System.out.println(days);
      }
   }
```

2.
```
import java.util.*;

class Add100Days {

   public static void main(String args[]) {

      // Get date object initialized
      // to current date and time
      Date date = new Date();

      // Get number of msec since epoch
      long msec = date.getTime();

      // Add 100 days to msec
      msec += 100 * 24 * 60 * 60 * 1000L;

      // Update time
      date.setTime(msec);

      // Display future date information
      System.out.println(date);
   }
}
```

10.3 EXERCISE

1.
```
import java.util.*;

class GregorianCalendarDemo {

   public static void main(String args[]) {
      GregorianCalendar gc = new GregorianCalendar();
      int year = gc.get(Calendar.YEAR);
      System.out.println(year);
      System.out.println(gc.isLeapYear(year));
      System.out.println("Month = " +
         gc.get(Calendar.MONTH));
      System.out.println("Week of year = " +
         gc.get(Calendar.WEEK_OF_YEAR));
      System.out.println("Week of month = " +
         gc.get(Calendar.WEEK_OF_MONTH));
      System.out.println("Day of year = " +
         gc.get(Calendar.DAY_OF_YEAR));
      System.out.println("Day of week = " +
```

```
        gc.get(Calendar.DAY_OF_WEEK));
    }
}
```

1.
```
import java.util.*;

class RandomDoubleVector {

  public static void main(String args[]) {

    // Create a vector
    Vector v = new Vector();

    // Generate a random int between 10 and 25
    int count = (int)(15 * Math.random() + 10);

    // Generate random double values that
    // have a Gaussian distribution
    Random random = new Random();
    for(int i = 0; i < count; i++) {
      double d = random.nextGaussian();
      v.addElement(new Double(d));
    }

    // Display the elements in the vector
    Enumeration e = v.elements();
    while(e.hasMoreElements())
      System.out.println(e.nextElement());
  }
}
```

2.
```
import java.util.*;

class ReverseVector {

  public static void main(String args[]) {

    // Create a vector
    Vector v = new Vector();

    // Convert the arguments to Double objects
    // and store them in the vector
    for(int i = 0; i < args.length; i++) {
      v.addElement(new Double(args[i]));
    }

    // Display the elements in reverse order
    for(int i = v.size() - 1; i >= 0; i--) {
      System.out.print(v.elementAt(i) + " ");
    }
  }
}
```

10.5 **EXERCISE**

1.
```java
import java.util.*;

class PushPop2 {

  public static void main(String args[]) {

    // Create stack
    Stack stack = new Stack();

    // Push non-duplicate elements onto stack
    for(int i = 0; i < args.length; i++) {
      Object obj = new Integer(args[i]);
      if(stack.search(obj) == -1)
        stack.push(obj);
    }

    // Pop elements from stack and display
    while(!stack.empty()) {
      Object obj = stack.pop();
      System.out.println(obj);
    }
  }
}
```

10.6 **EXERCISE**

1.
```java
import java.util.*;

class Person {
  String name, telephone, fax, email;

  Person(String name, String telephone, String fax, String email) {
    this.name = name;
    this.telephone = telephone;
    this.fax = fax;
    this.email = email;
  }

  public String toString() {
    return name + "; " + telephone + "; " + fax + "; " + email;
  }
}

class PeopleHashtable {

  public static void main(String args[]) {

    // Create a hashtable and populate it
    Hashtable hashtable = new Hashtable();
    Person p1 = new Person("Susan", "5634", "2343", "sue");
    hashtable.put("111111111", p1);
```

```
             Person p2 = new Person("Claire", "4545", "3331", "claire");
             hashtable.put("222222222", p2);
             Person p3 = new Person("Kim", "9821", "9899", "kim");
             hashtable.put("333333333", p3);
             Person p4 = new Person("Viviane", "4689", "2211", "viv");
             hashtable.put("444444444", p4);
             Person p5 = new Person("Barbara", "1212", "6655", "barb");
             hashtable.put("555555555", p5);


             // Display the elements of the hashtable
             Enumeration e = hashtable.keys();
             while(e.hasMoreElements()) {
               Object k = e.nextElement();
               Object v = hashtable.get(k);
               System.out.println("key = " + k + "; value = " + v);
             }
           }
         }
```

10.7 EXERCISE

```
1. import java.util.*;

   class StringTokenizerDemo2 {

     public static void main(String args[]) {

       String str =
         "123/45.6/-11.2/41/-90.1/100/99.99/-50/-20";
       StringTokenizer st = new StringTokenizer(str, "/");
       while(st.hasMoreElements()) {
         String s = (String)st.nextElement();
         System.out.println(s);
       }
     }
   }
```

MASTERY SKILLS CHECK: Chapter 10

1. A vector is a collection of objects that automatically expands in size as more elements are added to it.
2. The **Enumeration** interface allows you to iterate through a collection of objects.
3. A hashtable is a data structure that contains multiple key/values pairs. Both keys and values are objects. The keys must be unique; the values need not be.
4. import java.util.*;

```
class DaysTillChristmas {

  public static void main(String args[]) {

      // Get calendar for today's date
      GregorianCalendar today = new GregorianCalendar();

      // Get today's month
      int todayMonth = today.get(Calendar.MONTH);

      // Get today's day-of-month
      int todayDayOfMonth = today.get(Calendar.DAY_OF_MONTH);

      // Get today's year
      int todayYear = today.get(Calendar.YEAR);

      // Get today's day-of-year
      int todayDayOfYear = today.get(Calendar.DAY_OF_YEAR);

      // Calculate the number of day till Christmas
      int numDays;
      if(todayMonth == 11 && todayDayOfMonth > 25) {
        GregorianCalendar xmas = new GregorianCalendar(todayYear + 1, 11,
          25);
        int xmasDayOfYear = xmas.get(Calendar.DAY_OF_YEAR);
        numDays = xmasDayOfYear + 31 - todayDayOfMonth;
      }
      else {
        GregorianCalendar xmas = new GregorianCalendar(todayYear, 11, 25);
        int xmasDayOfYear = xmas.get(Calendar.DAY_OF_YEAR);
        numDays = xmasDayOfYear - todayDayOfYear;
      }

      // Display the number of days till Christmas
      System.out.println("The number of days till Christmas is " +
          numDays);
  }
}
```

5. ```
import java.util.*;

class CitiesCountries {

  public static void main(String args[]) {

      Hashtable ht = new Hashtable();
      ht.put("Tokyo", "Japan");
      ht.put("Beijing", "China");
      ht.put("Bangkok", "Thailand");
      ht.put("Taipei", "Taiwan");
      ht.put("Shanghai", "China");
      ht.put("Seoul", "South Korea");
      ht.put("Bombay", "India");

      if(args.length == 0) {
        System.out.println("Supply the name of a city as " +
```
```

```
        "a command line argument!");
      return;
    }

    String city = args[0];
    String country = (String)ht.get(city);
    if(country != null)
      System.out.println(city + " is located in " + country);
    else
      System.out.println(city + " is not located in the hashtable");
  }
}
```

CUMULATIVE SKILLS CHECK: Chapter 10

```
1. import java.util.*;

class MonthCalendar {
  static String dayNames[] = { "Sun", "Mon",
    "Tue", "Wed", "Thu", "Fri", "Sat" };
  static String monthNames[] = { "January",
    "February", "March", "April", "May",
    "June", "July", "August", "September",
    "October", "November", "December" };
  static int daysInMonths[] = { 31, 28, 31, 30, 31, 30,
      31, 31, 30, 31, 30, 31 };

  public static void main(String args[]) {

    // Get year, month, date, and day-of-week
    GregorianCalendar gc = new GregorianCalendar();
    int year = gc.get(Calendar.YEAR);
    int month = gc.get(Calendar.MONTH);
    int date = gc.get(Calendar.DATE);
    int dow = gc.get(Calendar.DAY_OF_WEEK);

    // Handle leap years
    daysInMonths[1] +=
      gc.isLeapYear(year) ? 1 : 0;

    // Change to the first day of the month
    gc.add(Calendar.DATE, -date + 1);

    // Determine the day of week
    int fdow = gc.get(Calendar.DAY_OF_WEEK);

    // Compute the variable dom
    // (If necessary, this will be a negative value)
    int dom = 2 - fdow;

    // Display month and year
    System.out.println(monthNames[month] + " " + year + "\n");
```

```
      // Display column headings
      for(int i = 0; i < 7; i++) {
        String s = dayNames[i];
        System.out.print(s + " ");
      }
      System.out.println("");

      // Display dates
      for(int row = 0; row < 6; row++) {
        for(int col = 0; col < 7; col++) {
          if(dom > daysInMonths[month]) {
            break;
          }
          if(dom > 0) {
            // Display date in the grid cell
            if(dom < 10)
              System.out.print("   " + dom + " ");
            else
              System.out.print(" " + dom + " ");
          }
          else {
            System.out.print("      ");
          }
          ++dom;
        }
        System.out.println("");
      }
    }
  }
}
```

2. ```
import java.util.*;

class Task extends Thread {

  ResourceCoordinator rc;
  int id;

  public Task(ResourceCoordinator rc, int id) {
    this.rc = rc;
    this.id = id;
  }

  public void run() {

    try {

      // Establish an infinite loop
      while(true) {

        // Get a resource
        Resource r = rc.getResource();

        // Use the resource
        int t = (int)(10000 * Math.random() + 1000);
        Thread.sleep(t);
```
```

```
          // Release the resource
          rc.releaseResource(r);

          // Sleep before doing more work
          Thread.sleep(8000);
        }
      }
      catch(Exception e) {
      }
    }
}

class Resource {
  int id;

  public Resource(int id) {
    this.id = id;
  }

  public String toString() {
    return "" + id;
  }
}

class ResourceCoordinator {
  Stack resources = new Stack();

  public ResourceCoordinator() {
    for(int i = 0; i < 4; i++) {
      resources.push(new Resource(i));
    }
  }

  public synchronized Resource getResource() {

    while(true) {

      // Check if a resource is available
      if(!resources.empty()) {
        Resource r = (Resource)resources.pop();
        System.out.println("Get resource " + r);
        return r;
      }

      // Wait for an available resource
      try {
        wait();
      }
      catch(InterruptedException ie) {
        ie.printStackTrace();
      }
    }
  }

  public synchronized void releaseResource(Resource r) {
```

```java
      // Push the resource onto the stack
      System.out.println("Release resource " + r);
      resources.push(r);

      // Notify all waiting threads
      notifyAll();
  }
}

class ResourcesTasks {

  public static void main(String args[]) {

    // Create resource coordinator
    ResourceCoordinator rc = new ResourceCoordinator();

    // Create tasks
    for(int i = 0; i < 10; i++) {
      new Task(rc, i).start();
    }
  }
}
```

CHAPTER 11

REVIEW SKILLS CHECK: Chapter 11

```java
1. import java.util.*;

  class DaysTillEndOfYear {

    public static void main(String args[]) {

      // Determine current day-of-year
      Calendar calendar1 = Calendar.getInstance();
      int doy1 = calendar1.get(Calendar.DAY_OF_YEAR);

      // Determine current year
      int year = calendar1.get(Calendar.YEAR);

      // Determine December 31 day-of-year
      Calendar calendar2 = new GregorianCalendar(year, 11, 31);
      int doy2 = calendar2.get(Calendar.DAY_OF_YEAR);

      // Compute days remaining in current year
      int days = doy2 - doy1;
      System.out.println(days +
        " days remain in current year");
    }
  }
```

```
2. import java.util.*;

   class Producer extends Thread {
     Queue queue;

     Producer(Queue queue) {
       this.queue = queue;
     }

     public void run() {
       int i = 0;
       while(true) {
         queue.add(i++);
       }
     }
   }

   class Consumer extends Thread {
     String str;
     Queue queue;

     Consumer(String str, Queue queue) {
       this.str = str;
       this.queue = queue;
     }

     public void run() {
       while(true) {
         System.out.println(str + ": " + queue.remove());
       }
     }
   }

   class Queue {
     private final static int SIZE = 5;
     private Vector queue = new Vector();
     int count = 0;

     synchronized void add(int i) {

       // Wait while the queue is full
       while(count == SIZE) {
         try {
           wait();
         }
         catch(InterruptedException ie) {
           ie.printStackTrace();
           System.exit(0);
         }
       }

       // Add data to queue
       queue.addElement(new Integer(i));

       // Increment count
       ++count;
```

```
      // Notify waiting threads
      notifyAll();
    }

  synchronized int remove() {

      // Wait while the queue is empty
      while(count == 0) {
        try {
          wait();
        }
        catch(InterruptedException ie) {
          ie.printStackTrace();
          System.exit(0);
        }
      }

      // Read data from queue
      Integer iobj = (Integer)queue.firstElement();
      queue.removeElement(iobj);

      // Decrement count
      --count;

      // Notify waiting threads
      notifyAll();

      // Return element from queue
      return iobj.intValue();
    }
  }

  class ProducerConsumers {

    public static void main(String args[]) {
      Queue queue = new Queue();
      new Producer(queue).start();
      new Consumer("ConsumerA", queue).start();
      new Consumer("ConsumerB", queue).start();
      new Consumer("ConsumerC", queue).start();
    }
  }

3. import java.util.*;

  class Worker extends Thread {
    final static int NUMWORKERS = 10;

    Toolbox toolbox;
    int id;

    public Worker(Toolbox toolbox, int id) {
      this.toolbox = toolbox;
      this.id = id;
    }
```

```
        public void run() {

          try {

            // Establish an infinite loop
            while(true) {

              // Get two of the tools
              Tool tools[] = toolbox.getTools();

              // Use the tools
              int t = (int)(10000 * Math.random() + 10000);
              Thread.sleep(t);

              // Release the tools
              toolbox.releaseTools(tools);

              // Sleep before doing more work
              Thread.sleep(20000);
            }
          }
          catch(Exception e) {
          }
        }
      }

      class Tool {
        final static int NUMTOOLS = 4;
        int id;

        public Tool(int id) {
          this.id = id;
        }

        public String toString() {
          return "" + id;
        }
      }

      class Toolbox {
        Stack tools = new Stack();

        public Toolbox() {
          for(int i = 0; i < Tool.NUMTOOLS; i++) {
            tools.push(new Tool(i));
          }
        }

        public synchronized Tool[] getTools() {

          while(true) {

            // Check if two tools are available
            if(tools.size() >= 2) {
              Tool tool0 = (Tool)tools.pop();
```

```
        Tool tool1 = (Tool)tools.pop();
        System.out.println("Get tools " + tool0 + " " + tool1);
        Tool a[] = new Tool[2];
        a[0] = tool0;
        a[1] = tool1;
        return a;
    }

      // Wait for two tools to become available
      try {
        wait();
      }
      catch(InterruptedException ie) {
        ie.printStackTrace();
      }
    }
  }

  public synchronized void releaseTools(Tool a[]) {

    // Put the tools back in the toolbox
    System.out.println("Release tools " + a[0] + " " + a[1]);
    tools.push(a[0]);
    tools.push(a[1]);

    // Notify all waiting threads
    notifyAll();
  }
}

class WorkersTools {

  public static void main(String args[]) {

    // Create Toolbox
    Toolbox toolbox = new Toolbox();

    // Create workers
    for(int i = 0; i < Worker.NUMWORKERS; i++) {
      new Worker(toolbox, i).start();
    }
  }
}
```

11.1 EXERCISE

```
1. import java.io.*;

  class Rename {

    public static void main(String args[]) {

      try {
```

```
                    // Create file object for old file
                    File oldFile = new File(args[0]);

                    // Create file object for new file
                    File newFile = new File(args[1]);

                    // Rename oldFile as newFile
                    boolean result = oldFile.renameTo(newFile);

                    // Display result
                    System.out.println(result);
                }
                catch(Exception e) {
                    e.printStackTrace();
                }
            }
        }
```

11.2 **E**XERCISES

```
1. import java.io.*;

   class DigitCounter {

       public static void main(String args[]) {

           try {

               // Allocate an array to hold digit counts
               int counts[] = new int[10];

               // Create a file reader
               FileReader fr = new FileReader(args[0]);

               // Read characters
               int i;
               while((i = fr.read()) != -1) {
                   char c = (char)i;
                   int k = c - '0';
                   if(k >= 0 && k < 10)
                       ++counts[k];
               }

               // Display digit counts
               for(int j = 0; j < 10; j++) {
                   char c = (char)('0' + j);
                   System.out.print(c + "=");
                   System.out.print(counts[j] + "; ");
               }

               // Close file reader
               fr.close();
           }
           catch(Exception e) {
```

```
            System.out.println("Exception: " + e);
        }
      }
    }

2. import java.io.*;

  class FileCopy {

    public static void main(String args[]) {

      try {

        // Create a file reader
        FileReader fr = new FileReader(args[0]);

        // Create a file writer
        FileWriter fw = new FileWriter(args[1]);

        // Read and copy characters
        int i;
        while((i = fr.read()) != -1) {
          fw.write(i);
        }

        // Close the file writer
        fw.close();

        // Close file reader
        fr.close();
      }
      catch(Exception e) {
        System.out.println("Exception: " + e);
      }
    }
  }
```

11.3   EXERCISES

```
1. import java.io.*;

  class TabFilter {

    public static void main(String args[]) {

      try {

        // Create a buffered reader
        FileReader fr = new FileReader(args[0]);
        BufferedReader br = new BufferedReader(fr);

        // Create a buffered writer
        FileWriter fw = new FileWriter(args[1]);
        BufferedWriter bw = new BufferedWriter(fw);
```

```
                // Convert tab to space characters
                String s;
                while((s = br.readLine()) != null) {
                  StringBuffer sb = new StringBuffer();
                  for(int i = 0; i < s.length(); i++) {
                    char c = s.charAt(i);
                    if(c == '\t')
                      c = ' ';
                    sb.append(c);
                  }
                  s = sb.toString() + "\n";
                  fw.write(s, 0, s.length());
                }

                // Close file reader and writer
                fr.close();
                fw.close();
              }
            catch(Exception e) {
              System.out.println("Exception: " + e);
            }
          }
        }
```

2.
```
   import java.io.*;

   class ReverseConsoleInput {

     public static void main(String args[]) {

       try {

         // Create an input stream reader
         InputStreamReader isr = new InputStreamReader(System.in);

         // Create a buffered reader
         BufferedReader br = new BufferedReader(isr);

         // Read and process lines from console
         String s;
         while((s = br.readLine()) != null) {
           for(int i = s.length() - 1; i >= 0; i--) {
             char c = s.charAt(i);
             System.out.print(c);
           }
           System.out.println("");
         }

         // Close input stream reader
         isr.close();
       }
       catch(Exception e) {
         System.out.println("Exception: " + e);
       }
```

```
        }
    }
```

EXERCISE

```
1. import java.io.*;

   class PrintWriterDemo2 {

       public static void main(String args[]) {

           try {

               // Create a print writer
               FileWriter fw = new FileWriter(args[0]);
               BufferedWriter bw = new BufferedWriter(fw);
               PrintWriter pw = new PrintWriter(bw, false);

               // Experiment with some methods
               pw.println(true);
               pw.println('A');
               pw.println(500);
               pw.println(40000L);
               pw.println(45.67f);
               pw.println(45.67);
               pw.println("Hello");
               pw.println(new Integer("99"));

               // Close print writer
               pw.close();
           }
           catch(Exception e) {
               System.out.println("Exception: " + e);
           }
       }
   }
```

EXERCISES

```
1. // The syntax to use this application is:
   //     java FileSplitter inputfile outputfile filesize
   // Here, inputfile is the name of the file to be split.
   // Bytes are read from inputfile and are written to
   // outputfile0, outputfile1, outputfile2, ...
   // until all of the bytes from inputfile are read.
   // The size of each outputfile is specified by filesize.
   // The inputfile and outputfile arguments are required.
   // If filesize is omitted, a value of 1024 is used.

   import java.io.*;

   class FileSplitter {
```

```
      public static void main(String args[]) {

        try {

          // Create a file input stream
          FileInputStream fis =
            new FileInputStream(args[0]);

          // Determine size of the buffer
          int size = 1024;
          if(args.length > 2) {
            size = Integer.parseInt(args[2]);
          }

          // Create a buffer of the correct size
          byte buffer[] = new byte[size];

          // Initialize the count
          int count = 0;

          // Process data from the file
          while(true) {

            // Read a block from the file
            int i = fis.read(buffer, 0, size);
            if(i == -1)
              break;

            // Create an output file
            String filename = args[1] + count;
            FileOutputStream fos =
              new FileOutputStream(filename);
            fos.write(buffer, 0, i);
            fos.flush();
            fos.close();

            // Increment count
            ++count;
          }
        }
        catch(Exception e) {
          e.printStackTrace();
        }
      }
}
// The syntax to use this application is:
//     java FileMerger inputfile outputfile
// Here, data is read from inputfile0, inputfile1, ...
// and is written to outputfile.  Both of these
// arguments are required.

import java.io.*;

class FileMerger {
  private final static int BUFFERSIZE = 1024;
```

```java
public static void main(String args[]) {

  try {

    // Create a file output stream
    FileOutputStream fos =
      new FileOutputStream(args[1]);

    // Create a buffer
    byte buffer[] = new byte[BUFFERSIZE];

    // Initialize the count
    int count = 0;

    // Process data from the input files
    while(true) {

      // Create a file input stream
      String filename = args[0] + count;
      FileInputStream fis;
      try {
        fis = new FileInputStream(filename);
      }
      catch(FileNotFoundException fnfex) {
        break;
      }

      // Process data from the file
      while(true) {

        // Read a block from the file
        int i = fis.read(buffer, 0, BUFFERSIZE);
        if(i == -1)
          break;

        // Append data to the output file
        fos.write(buffer, 0, i);
        fos.flush();
      }

      // Increment count
      ++count;
    }

    // Close the output file
    fos.close();
  }
  catch(Exception ex) {
    ex.printStackTrace();
  }
}
}
```

```
2. import java.io.*;

   class FibonacciOut {

     public static void main(String args[]) {

       try {

         // Create a file output stream
         FileOutputStream fos =
           new FileOutputStream(args[0]);

         // Create a data output stream
         DataOutputStream dos =
           new DataOutputStream(fos);

         // Write 15 Fibonacci numbers
         int count = 0;
         int i = 0;
         int j = 1;
         do {
           dos.writeShort(j);
           int k = i + j;
           i = j;
           j = k;
         } while(++count < 15);

         // Close file output stream
         fos.close();
       }
       catch(Exception e) {
         System.out.println("Exception: " + e);
       }
     }
   }

   import java.io.*;

   class FibonacciIn {

     public static void main(String args[]) {

       try {

         // Create a file input stream
         FileInputStream fis =
           new FileInputStream(args[0]);

         // Create a data input stream
         DataInputStream dis =
           new DataInputStream(fis);

         // Read and display data
         for(int i = 0; i < 15; i++) {
           System.out.print(dis.readShort() + " ");
         }

         // Close file input stream
```

```
          fis.close();
        }
      catch(Exception e) {
        System.out.println("Exception: " + e);
      }
    }
  }
```

11.6 ▐ *E*XERCISE

1. `import java.io.*;`

```
class ReverseFile {

  public static void main(String args[]) {

    try {

      // Create random access file
      RandomAccessFile raf =
        new RandomAccessFile(args[0], "r");

      // Initialize position in file
      long position = raf.length();

      // Process characters in the file
      while(position > 0) {

        // Update position
        position -= 1;

        // Seek and read character
        raf.seek(position);
        char c = (char)raf.readByte();

        // Display character
        System.out.print(c);
      }
    }
    catch(Exception e) {
      e.printStackTrace();
    }
  }
}
```

11.7 ▐ *E*XERCISES

1. `import java.io.*;`

```
class StreamTokenizerDemo3 {

  public static void main(String args[]) {
```

```java
    try {

      // Create a file reader
      FileReader fr = new FileReader(args[0]);

      // Create a buffered reader
      BufferedReader br = new BufferedReader(fr);

      // Create a stream tokenizer
      StreamTokenizer st = new StreamTokenizer(br);

      // Consider end-of-line as a token
      st.eolIsSignificant(true);

      // Declare variable to count lines
      int lines = 1;

      // Process tokens
      while(st.nextToken() != StreamTokenizer.TT_EOF) {
        switch(st.ttype) {
          case st.TT_EOL:
            ++lines;
          }
        }

      // Display the number of lines
      System.out.println("There are " + lines + " lines");

      // Close file reader
      fr.close();
    }
    catch(Exception e) {
      System.out.println("Exception: " + e);
    }
  }
}
```

2.
```java
import java.io.*;

class StreamTokenizerDemo4 {

  public static void main(String args[]) {

    try {

      // Create a file reader
      FileReader fr = new FileReader(args[0]);

      // Create a buffered reader
      BufferedReader br = new BufferedReader(fr);

      // Create a stream tokenizer
      StreamTokenizer st = new StreamTokenizer(br);

      // Process tokens
```

```
      while(st.nextToken() != StreamTokenizer.TT_EOF) {
        switch(st.ttype) {
          case st.TT_WORD:
            System.out.println(st.lineno() + ") " +
              st.sval);
            break;
          case st.TT_NUMBER:
            System.out.println(st.lineno() + ") " +
              st.nval);
            break;
          default:
            System.out.println(st.lineno() + ") " +
              (char)st.ttype);
        }
      }

      // Close file reader
      fr.close();
    }
    catch(Exception e) {
      System.out.println("Exception: " + e);
    }
  }
}
```

MASTERY SKILLS CHECK: Chapter 11

1. A stream is an abstraction for either a source or destination of data.
2. Both character and byte streams read and write bytes. However, character streams convert between characters and bytes by using character encoding rules that are appropriate for the user's locale.
3. The superclasses for input and output character streams are **Reader** and **Writer**.
4. The superclasses for input and output byte streams are **InputStream** and **OutputStream**.
5.
```
import java.io.*;

class DirectoryTree {

  public static void main(String args[]) {

    // Check if file exists
    File file = new File(args[0]);
    if(!file.exists()) {
      System.out.println(args[0] + " does not exist.");
      return;
    }

    // Display directory tree
    tree(args[0]);
  }
```

```java
    public static void tree(String filename) {

      // Create a file object
      File file = new File(filename);

      // If file is not a directory,
      // display filename and return
      if(!file.isDirectory()) {
        System.out.println(filename);
        return;
      }

      // Process contents of this directory
      String files[] = file.list();
      for(int i = 0; i < files.length; i++) {
        tree(filename + File.separator + files[i]);
      }
    }
  }
```

6. ```java
   import java.io.*;

   class FilteredDirectoryTree {

     public static void main(String args[]) {

       String suffix = null;
       if(args.length > 1) {
         suffix = args[1];
       }
       tree(args[0], suffix);
     }

     public static void tree(String filename, String suffix) {

       // Create a file object
       File file = new File(filename);

       // If file is not a directory,
       // display filename and return
       if(!file.isDirectory()) {
         if(suffix == null || filename.endsWith(suffix))
           System.out.println(filename);
         return;
       }

       // Process contents of this directory
       String files[] = file.list();
   ```
   ```

```
        for(int i = 0; i < files.length; i++) {
          tree(filename + File.separator + files[i], suffix);
        }
      }
    }

7. import java.io.*;

   class FilteredDirectoryTreeSizes {

     public static void main(String args[]) {

       String suffix = null;
       if(args.length > 1) {
         suffix = args[1];
       }
       tree(args[0], suffix);
     }

     public static void tree(String filename, String suffix) {

       // Create a file object
       File file = new File(filename);

       // If file is not a directory,
       // display filename and size and return
       if(!file.isDirectory()) {
         if(suffix == null || filename.endsWith(suffix)) {
           long length = file.length();
           System.out.println(filename + ": " + length);
         }
         return;
       }

       // Proces contents of this directory
       String files[] = file.list();
       for(int i = 0; i < files.length; i++) {
         tree(filename + File.separator + files[i], suffix);
       }
     }
   }
```

CUMULATIVE SKILLS CHECK: *Chapter 11*

```java
1. import java.io.*;

   class CircleArea {
     static BufferedReader br;

     public static void main(String args[]) {

       try {

         // Get a buffered reader for the standard input
         InputStreamReader isr =
           new InputStreamReader(System.in);
         br = new BufferedReader(isr);

         while(true) {

           // Prompt user for radius
           System.out.print("Radius? ");

           // Process user input
           String str = br.readLine();
           double radius;
           try {
             radius = Double.valueOf(str).doubleValue();
           }
           catch(NumberFormatException nfe) {
             System.out.println("Incorrect format!");
             continue;
           }

           // Check that radius is > 0
           if(radius <= 0) {
             System.out.println("Radius must be positive!");
             continue;
           }

           // Display area and return
           double area = Math.PI * radius * radius;
           System.out.println("Area is " + area);
           return;
         }
       }
       catch(Exception e) {
         e.printStackTrace();
       }
     }
   }

2. import java.io.*;

   class DocComments {
```

```java
   public static void main(String args[]) {

      try {

         FileReader fr = new FileReader(args[0]);
         BufferedReader br = new BufferedReader(fr);

         boolean display = false;

         String line;
         while((line = br.readLine()) != null) {
           char array[] = line.toCharArray();
           int length = array.length;
           int i = 0;
           while(true) {
             if(i >= length)
               break;
             if(array[i] == '/') {
               if((i + 1) < length && array[i + 1] == '*') {
                 if((i + 2) < length && array[i + 2] == '*') {
                   display = true;
                   i += 3;
                   continue;
                 }
               }
             }
             else if(array[i] == '*') {
               if((i + 1) < length && array[i + 1] == '/') {
                 display = false;
                 System.out.println("");
                 i += 2;
                 continue;
               }
             }
             if(display)
               System.out.print(array[i]);
             i += 1;
           }
         }
      }
      catch(Exception e) {
        e.printStackTrace();
      }
   }
}
```

```java
3. import java.io.*;
   import java.util.*;

   public class Employees {

     public static void main(String args[]) {

       try {

         // Create a file reader
```

```
        FileReader fr = new FileReader(args[0]);

        // Create a buffered reader
        BufferedReader br = new BufferedReader(fr);

        // Read lines from file
        String s;
        while((s = br.readLine()) != null) {

          // Create string tokenizer
          StringTokenizer st =
            new StringTokenizer(s, ";");

          // Output tokens
          System.out.print("Name: ");
          System.out.println(st.nextToken());
          System.out.print("Location: ");
          System.out.println(st.nextToken());
          System.out.print("Phone: ");
          System.out.println(st.nextToken() + "\n");
        }

        // Close file reader
        fr.close();
      }
      catch(Exception e) {
        e.printStackTrace();
      }
    }
  }
```

CHAPTER 12

REVIEW SKILLS CHECK: Chapter 12

```
1. import java.io.*;

class LetterCounter {

  public static void main(String args[]) {

    try {

      // Allocate an array to hold letter counts
      int counts[] = new int[26];

      // Create a file reader
      FileReader fr = new FileReader(args[0]);

      // Read characters
```

```
          int i;
          while((i = fr.read()) != -1) {
            char c = Character.toLowerCase((char)i);
            int k = c - 'a';
            if(k >= 0 && k < 26)
              ++counts[k];
          }

          // Display character counts
          for(int j = 0; j < 26; j++) {
            char c = (char)('a' + j);
            System.out.print(c + "=");
            System.out.print(counts[j] + "; ");
          }

          // Close file reader
          fr.close();
        }
        catch(Exception e) {
          System.out.println("Exception: " + e);
        }
      }
    }
```

2.
```
import java.io.*;

class ArithmeticQuiz {
  static BufferedReader br;

  public static void main(String args[]) {

    try {

      // Get a buffered reader for the standard input
      InputStreamReader isr =
        new InputStreamReader(System.in);
      br = new BufferedReader(isr);

      while(true) {

        // Create operands and operator
        int i = (int)(12 * Math.random());
        int j = (int)(12 * Math.random());
        int op = (int)(2 * Math.random());

        // Create question
        String q;
        int a;
        if(op < 1) {
          q = i + " + " + j + " ?";
          a = i + j;
          question(q, a);
        }
        else {
          q = i + " - " + j + " ?";
          a = i - j;
```

```
          question(q, a);
        }
      }
    }
    catch(Exception e) {
      e.printStackTrace();
      return;
    }
  }

  static void question(String q, int a)
  throws IOException {

    // Display question
    System.out.println(q);

    // Get user input
    String str = br.readLine();

    // Check answer and provide feedback
    int answer = Integer.parseInt(str);
    if(answer == a)
      System.out.println("Correct!");
    else {
      System.out.print("Incorrect! ");
      System.out.println("The answer is " + a);
    }
  }
}
```

```
3. import java.io.*;
   import java.util.*;

   class FileSlice {

     public static void main(String args[]) {

       try {

         // Create a buffered reader
         FileReader fr = new FileReader(args[0]);
         BufferedReader br = new BufferedReader(fr);

         // Obtain start and end field indexes
         int f1 = Integer.parseInt(args[1]);
         int f2 = Integer.parseInt(args[2]);

         // Create an infinite loop
         while(true) {

           // Read a line from the file
           String line = br.readLine();
           if(line == null)
             break;

           // Create a string tokenizer
```

```
                    StringTokenizer st = new StringTokenizer(line);

                    // Process tokens
                    String output = "";
                    int f = 0;
                    while(st.hasMoreTokens()) {
                      ++f;
                      String token = st.nextToken();
                      if(f >= f1 && f <= f2) {
                        output += token + " ";
                      }
                    }

                    // Display output
                    System.out.println(output);
                }
            }
            catch(Exception e) {
              System.out.println("Exception: " + e);
            }
        }
    }
```

12.1 EXERCISE

```
1. import java.net.*;

   class LocalAddress {

     public static void main(String args[]) {

       try {

         // Get local name and address
         InetAddress ia = InetAddress.getLocalHost();
         String name = ia.getHostName();
         System.out.println(name);
         String address = ia.getHostAddress();
         System.out.println(address);
       }
       catch(Exception e) {
         e.printStackTrace();
       }
     }
   }
```

12.2 EXERCISE

```
1. import java.io.*;
   import java.net.*;

   class SquareClient {
```

```java
      private final static int BUFSIZE = 20;

      public static void main(String args[]) {
        try {

          // Get server, port, and value
          String server = args[0];
          int port = Integer.parseInt(args[1]);
          double value = Double.valueOf(args[2]).doubleValue();

          // Create socket
          Socket s = new Socket(server, port);

          // Write value to server
          OutputStream os = s.getOutputStream();
          DataOutputStream dos = new DataOutputStream(os);
          dos.writeDouble(value);

          // Read result from server
          InputStream is = s.getInputStream();
          DataInputStream dis = new DataInputStream(is);
          value = dis.readDouble();

          // Display result
          System.out.println(value);

          // Close socket
          s.close();
        }
        catch(Exception e) {
          System.out.println("Exception: " + e);
        }
      }
    }

import java.io.*;
import java.net.*;

class SquareServer {
  private final static int BUFSIZE = 20;

  public static void main(String args[]) {
    try {

      // Get port
      int port = Integer.parseInt(args[0]);

      // Create server socket
      ServerSocket ss = new ServerSocket(port);

      // Create infinite loop
      while(true) {

        // Accept incoming requests
        Socket s = ss.accept();
```

```
                    // Read value from client
                    InputStream is = s.getInputStream();
                    DataInputStream dis = new DataInputStream(is);
                    double value = dis.readDouble();

                    // Square the input
                    value *= value;

                    // Write result to client
                    OutputStream os = s.getOutputStream();
                    DataOutputStream dos = new DataOutputStream(os);
                    dos.writeDouble(value);

                    // Close socket
                    s.close();
                }
            }
            catch(Exception e) {
                System.out.println("Exception: " + e);
            }
        }
    }
```

12.3 EXERCISE

```
1. import java.net.*;

   class DatagramReceiver2 {
     private final static int BUFSIZE = 20;

     public static void main(String args[]) {
       try {

         // Obtain port
         int port = Integer.parseInt(args[0]);

         // Create a DatagramSocket object for the port
         DatagramSocket ds = new DatagramSocket(port);

         // Create a buffer to hold incoming data
         byte buffer[] = new byte[BUFSIZE];

         // Create infinite loop
         while(true) {

           // Create a datagram packet
           DatagramPacket dp =
             new DatagramPacket(buffer, buffer.length);

           // Receive data
           ds.receive(dp);

           // Display address from the datagram packet
```

```
              InetAddress ia = dp.getAddress();
              System.out.println(ia);

              // Display port from the datagram packet
              System.out.println(dp.getPort());
          }
      }
      catch(Exception e) {
        e.printStackTrace();
      }
    }
}
```

12.4 **E**XERCISE

```
1. import java.net.*;

class URLDemo2 {
  private final static int BUFSIZE = 20;

  public static void main(String args[]) {
    try {

        // Obtain url
        URL url = new URL(args[0]);

        // Obtain protocol, host, port, file
        String protocol = url.getProtocol();
        String host = url.getHost();
        int port = url.getPort();
        String file = url.getFile();

        // Display data
        System.out.println("url = " + url);
        System.out.println("protocol = " + protocol);
        System.out.println("host = " + host);
        System.out.println("port = " + port);
        System.out.println("file = " + file);
    }
    catch(Exception e) {
      e.printStackTrace();
    }
  }
}
```

MASTERY SKILLS CHECK: Chapter 12

1. Dotted decimal and dotted string.
2. **InetAddress**

3. Server sockets are used by a server to accept incoming requests from a client. A socket is one end of a bi-directional communication path between two machines.

4. **java.net.DatagramPacket**, **java.net.DatagramSocket**

5. protocol://host:port/filename

*C*UMULATIVE SKILLS CHECK: *Chapter 12*

```java
1. import java.io.*;
   import java.net.*;

   class AdderClient {
     private final static int BUFSIZE = 512;

     public static void main(String args[]) {
       try {

           // Get server and port
           String server = args[0];
           int port = Integer.parseInt(args[1]);

           // Create socket
           Socket s = new Socket(server, port);

           // Create input and output streams for socket
           InputStream is = s.getInputStream();
           DataInputStream dis = new DataInputStream(is);
           OutputStream os = s.getOutputStream();
           DataOutputStream dos = new DataOutputStream(os);

           // Create buffered reader for console
           InputStreamReader isr =
             new InputStreamReader(System.in);
           BufferedReader br =
             new BufferedReader(isr);

           // Create infinite loop
           while(true) {

             // Obtain a number from the user
             System.out.print("Input number: ");
             String str = br.readLine();
             double d = Double.valueOf(str).doubleValue();

             // Send the number to the server
             dos.writeDouble(d);

             // Read total from server
             double total = dis.readDouble();

             // Display total
             System.out.println("Current total: " + total);
```

```
      }
    }
    catch(Exception e) {
    }
  }
}

import java.io.*;
import java.net.*;

class ServerThread extends Thread {
  private Socket s;
  private double total = 0;

  public ServerThread(Socket s) {
    this.s = s;
    total = 0;
  }

  public void run() {

    try {

      // Get input and output streams
      InputStream is = s.getInputStream();
      DataInputStream dis = new DataInputStream(is);
      OutputStream os = s.getOutputStream();
      DataOutputStream dos = new DataOutputStream(os);

      // Create an infinite loop
      while(true) {

        // Read value from client
        double value = dis.readDouble();

        // Add the value to the total
        total += value;

        // Write sum to client
        dos.writeDouble(total);
      }
    }
    catch(Exception e) {
    }
  }
}

import java.net.*;

class ThreadedServer {
  private final static int BUFSIZE = 512;

  public static void main(String args[]) {
    try {

      // Get port
```

```
        int port = Integer.parseInt(args[0]);

        // Create server socket
        ServerSocket ss = new ServerSocket(port);

        // Create infinite loop
        while(true) {

          // Accept incoming requests
          Socket s = ss.accept();

          // Start a thread to handle this client
          ServerThread st = new ServerThread(s);
          st.start();
        }
      }
      catch(Exception e) {
        System.out.println("Exception: " + e);
      }
    }
  }
```

2.
```
import java.net.*;

class Sensor {

  public static void main(String args[]) {

    try {

      // Create destination Internet address
      InetAddress ia =
        InetAddress.getByName(args[0]);

      // Obtain destination port
      int port = Integer.parseInt(args[1]);

      // Create a datagram socket
      DatagramSocket ds = new DatagramSocket();

      // Establish an infinite loop
      while(true) {

        // Create a random sensor value
        int value = (int)(20 * Math.random());
        String s = "" + value;
        System.out.println("Sensor value is " + s);

        // Create a datagram packet
        byte buffer[] = s.getBytes();
        DatagramPacket dp =
          new DatagramPacket(buffer, buffer.length, ia, port);

        // Send the datagram packet
        ds.send(dp);
```

```java
          // Sleep for 20 seconds
          Thread.sleep(20000);
        }
      }
      catch(Exception e) {
        e.printStackTrace();
      }
    }
  }


import java.net.*;

class Collector {
  private final static int BUFSIZE = 20;

  public static void main(String args[]) {
    try {

      // Obtain port
      int port = Integer.parseInt(args[0]);

      // Create a DatagramSocket object for the port
      DatagramSocket ds = new DatagramSocket(port);

      // Create infinite loop
      while(true) {

        // Create a buffer to hold incoming data
        byte buffer[] = new byte[BUFSIZE];

        // Create a datagram packet
        DatagramPacket dp =
          new DatagramPacket(buffer, buffer.length);

        // Receive data
        ds.receive(dp);

        // Get data from the datagram packet
        String str = new String(dp.getData());

        // Display the data
        System.out.println(str);
      }
    }
    catch(Exception e) {
      e.printStackTrace();
    }
  }
}
```

CHAPTER 13

REVIEW SKILLS CHECK: Chapter 13

1. The Transmission Control Protocol (TCP) is used to transfer information via sockets.
2. The User Datagram Protocol (UDP) is used to transfer information via datagrams.
3.
```java
// Usage:
//    java TCPRandomNumberServer port
// Here, port is the port on which the server
// accepts incoming client requests

import java.io.*;
import java.net.*;

class TCPRandomNumberServer {
  static TCPBroadcastThread tcpBroadcastThread;

  public static void main(String args[]) {

    // Get port
    int port = Integer.parseInt(args[0]);

    try {

      // Create a separate thread to broadcast
      // the random numbers to the clients
      tcpBroadcastThread = new TCPBroadcastThread();
      tcpBroadcastThread.start();

      // Create server socket
      ServerSocket ss = new ServerSocket(port);

      // Create infinite loop
      while(true) {

        // Accept incoming requests
        Socket s = ss.accept();

        // Get a data output stream for this socket
        OutputStream os = s.getOutputStream();
        DataOutputStream dos = new DataOutputStream(os);

        // Tell the broadcast thread about
        // this output stream
        tcpBroadcastThread.addDataOutputStream(dos);
      }
    }
    catch(Exception e) {
```

```
      System.out.println("Exception: " + e);
    }
  }
}

import java.io.*;
import java.net.*;
import java.util.*;

class TCPBroadcastThread extends Thread {
  Vector dataOutputStreams = new Vector();

  public void run() {

    try {

      // Create an infinite loop
      while(true) {

        // Sleep for 2 seconds
        Thread.sleep(2000);

        // Generate a random integer
        int r = (int)(100 * Math.random());

        // Send value to each output stream
        Enumeration e = dataOutputStreams.elements();
        while(e.hasMoreElements()) {
          try {
            DataOutputStream dos;
            dos = (DataOutputStream)e.nextElement();
            dos.writeInt(r);
          }
          catch(Exception e1) {
          }
        }
      }
    }
    catch(Exception e2) {
    }
  }

  void addDataOutputStream(DataOutputStream dos) {
    dataOutputStreams.addElement(dos);
  }
}

// Usage:
//    java TCPRandomNumberClient server port
// Here, server is the dotted decimal or dotted string
// name of the server and port is the port on which
// that server listens for incoming requests

import java.io.*;
import java.net.*;
```

```
class TCPRandomNumberClient {
  private final static int BUFSIZE = 512;

  public static void main(String args[]) {
    try {

      // Get server and port
      String server = args[0];
      int port = Integer.parseInt(args[1]);

      // Create socket
      Socket s = new Socket(server, port);

      // Create data input stream
      InputStream is = s.getInputStream();
      DataInputStream dis = new DataInputStream(is);

      // Create infinite loop
      while(true) {

        // Read number from server
        int i = dis.readInt();

        // Display number
        System.out.println(i);
      }
    }
    catch(Exception e) {
    }
  }
}
```

13.2 *EXERCISE*

```
2. import java.applet.Applet;
   import java.awt.Graphics;
   /*
     <applet code="DrawLines" width=200 height=200>
     </applet>
   */

   public class DrawLines extends Applet {

     public void paint(Graphics g) {
       g.drawLine(50, 50, 200, 200);
       g.drawLine(0, 0, 100, 200);
       g.drawLine(0, 200, 180, 20);
     }
   }
```

13.3 **E**XERCISE

1. The four methods are **init( )**, **start( )**, **stop( )**, and **destroy( )**. The **stop( )** method is invoked when the applet viewer is minimized, and **start( )** is called when the applet viewer is later maximized. Also, the **stop( )** method is called if the user is viewing a Web page that contains the applet and then goes to another page. The **start( )** method is called if the user returns to the page that contains the applet.

13.4 **E**XERCISES

1.
```java
import java.applet.*;
import java.awt.*;
/*
  <applet code="DrawRectangle" width=500 height=300>
  </applet>
*/

public class DrawRectangle extends Applet {

  public void paint(Graphics g) {
    g.drawRect(100, 50, 300, 200);
  }
}
```

2.
```java
import java.applet.*;
import java.awt.*;
/*
  <applet code="DrawCircle" width=500 height=300>
  </applet>
*/

public class DrawCircle extends Applet {

  public void paint(Graphics g) {
    g.drawOval(150, 50, 200, 200);
  }
}
```

13.5 **E**XERCISE

1.
```java
import java.applet.Applet;
import java.awt.*;
/*
  <applet code="HorizontalColorBars" width=200 height=200>
  </applet>
*/

public class HorizontalColorBars extends Applet {
  Color colors[] = { Color.black, Color.blue, Color.cyan,
```

```
        Color.darkGray, Color.gray, Color.green, Color.lightGray,
        Color.magenta, Color.orange, Color.pink, Color.red,
        Color.white, Color.yellow };

    public void paint(Graphics g) {
      int deltay = 200/colors.length;
      for(int i = 0; i < colors.length; i++) {
        g.setColor(colors[i]);
        g.fillRect(0, i * deltay, 200, (i + 1) * deltay);
      }
    }
  }
```

13.6 EXERCISES

1.
```
import java.applet.*;
import java.awt.*;
/*
  <applet code="FontDemo2" width=250 height=200>
  </applet>
*/

public class FontDemo2 extends Applet {

  public void paint(Graphics g) {

    // Draw baseline
    int baseline = 100;
    g.setColor(Color.lightGray);
    g.drawLine(0, baseline, 250, baseline);

    // Draw string
    g.setFont(new Font("SansSerif", Font.ITALIC, 80));
    g.setColor(Color.black);
    g.drawString("Wxyz", 5, baseline);
  }
}
```

2.
```
import java.applet.*;
import java.awt.*;
/*
  <applet code="FontMetricsDemo2" width=300 height=200>
  </applet>
*/

public class FontMetricsDemo2 extends Applet {

  public void paint(Graphics g) {

    // Draw baseline
    int baseline = 100;
    g.setColor(Color.lightGray);
    g.drawLine(0, baseline, 300, baseline);
```

```
        // Draw string
        Font font = new Font("SansSerif", Font.PLAIN, 18);
        g.setFont(font);
        g.setColor(Color.black);
        g.drawString("Wxyz", 5, baseline);
        g.setColor(Color.lightGray);

        // Get FontMetrics
        FontMetrics fm = g.getFontMetrics(font);

        // Draw line at baseline - ascent
        int ascent = fm.getAscent();
        int y = baseline - ascent;
        g.drawLine(0, y, 300, y);

        // Draw line at baseline + descent
        int descent = fm.getDescent();
        y = baseline + descent;
        g.drawLine(0, y, 300, y);

        // Draw line at baseline + descent + leading
        int leading = fm.getLeading();
        y = baseline + descent + leading;
        g.drawLine(0, y, 300, y);

        // Draw line at baseline + height
        int height = fm.getHeight();
        y = baseline + height;
        g.drawLine(0, y, 300, y);

        // Draw string
        g.setColor(Color.black);
        g.drawString("\"'?/^{9}|[0]*@#", 5, y);
        g.setColor(Color.lightGray);

        // Draw line at baseline + height + descent
        y = baseline + height + descent;
        g.drawLine(0, y, 300, y);
    }
}
```

13.7 *EXERCISES*

```
1. import java.applet.*;
   import java.awt.*;
   /*
     <applet code="X" width=200 height=200>
     </applet>
   */

   public class X extends Applet {

     public void paint(Graphics g) {
       Dimension d = getSize();
```

```
        g.drawLine(0, 0, d.width, d.height);
        g.drawLine(d.width, 0, 0, d.height);
    }
}
```

2.
```
import java.applet.*;
import java.awt.*;
/*
  <applet code="Harmonics" width=400 height=200>
  </applet>
*/

public class Harmonics extends Applet  {

  public void paint(Graphics g) {

    // Draw rectangle around the display area
    Dimension d = getSize();
    int width = d.width;
    int height = d.height;
    g.setColor(Color.blue);
    g.drawRect(0, 0, width - 1, height - 1);

    // Draw lines for x and y axes
    int y = height/2;
    g.drawLine(0, y, width, y);
    g.drawLine(width/2, 0, width/2, height);

    // Compute data values and remember
    // max and min values
    double max = 0;
    double min = 0;
    double deltax = 2 * Math.PI/(width - 1);
    double x = -Math.PI;
    double data[] = new double[width];
    for(int i = 0; i < width; i++) {
      double value = f(x);
      data[i] = value;
      min = (value < min) ? value : min;
      max = (value > max) ? value : max;
      x += deltax;
    }

    // Scale and translate data values
    double scale = height/(max - min);
    for(int i = 0; i < width; i++) {
      double value = data[i];
      double k = (value - min)/(max - min);
      data[i] = height * (1 - k);
    }

    // Draw curve for data values
    g.setColor(Color.black);
    for(int i = 1; i < width; i++) {
      g.drawLine(i - 1, (int)data[i - 1], i, (int)data[i]);
    }
```

```
        }

      private double f(double x) {
        double value = 0;
        for(int i = 0; i < 4; i++) {
            value += ((double)1/(i + 1)) * Math.sin((i+1) * x);
        }
        return value;
      }
    }
```

13.8 EXERCISE

1. Code base is "host4" and document base is "host3". The file **Example2.class** is retrieved from code base. The **.html** and **.jpg** files are retrieved from document base.

13.9 EXERCISES

1.
```
import java.applet.*;
import java.awt.*;
import java.net.*;
/*
  <applet code="Ellipse" width=200 height=200>
  <param name="major" value=140>
  <param name="minor" value=70>
  </applet>
*/

public class Ellipse extends Applet {

  public void paint(Graphics g) {
    String major = getParameter("major");
    String minor = getParameter("minor");
    int majoraxis = Integer.parseInt(major);
    int minoraxis = Integer.parseInt(minor);
    Dimension d = getSize();
    int x = d.width/2 - majoraxis/2;
    int y = d.height/2 - minoraxis/2;
    g.drawOval(x, y, majoraxis, minoraxis);
  }
}
```

2.
```
import java.applet.*;
import java.awt.*;
/*
  <applet code="MagentaCircle" width=120 height=120>
  </applet>
*/

public class MagentaCircle extends Applet {
```

```
      public void paint(Graphics g) {
        setBackground(Color.cyan);
        Dimension d = getSize();
        int xc = d.width/2;
        int yc = d.height/2;
        int radius = 50;
        setForeground(Color.magenta);
        g.fillOval(xc - radius, yc - radius, 2 * radius, 2 * radius);
      }
    }
```

13.10 EXERCISE

```
1. import java.applet.*;
   import java.awt.*;
   import java.util.*;
   /*
     <applet code="ShowDate" width=200 height=200>
     </applet>
   */

   public class ShowDate extends Applet {
     String[] monthNames = {
       "January", "February", "March",
       "April", "May", "June",
       "July", "August", "September",
       "October", "November", "December" };

     public void paint(Graphics g) {

       // Obtain date information
       Calendar calendar = Calendar.getInstance();
       int month = calendar.get(Calendar.MONTH);
       int date = calendar.get(Calendar.DATE);
       int year = calendar.get(Calendar.YEAR);

       // Create string with date information
       String str = monthNames[month] + " " + date + " " + year;

       // Display in center of applet
       Font font = getFont();
       FontMetrics fm = getFontMetrics(font);
       Dimension d = getSize();
       int x = (d.width - fm.stringWidth(str))/2;
       int y = d.height/2;
       g.drawString(str, x, y);

       // Display on status line
       showStatus(str);
     }
   }
```

| 13.11 | ***E**XERCISE* |

```
1. import java.applet.*;
   import java.awt.*;
   /*
     <applet code="DrawRandomImage" width=280 height=280>
     <param name="count" value="8">
     <param name="file0" value="file0.jpg">
     <param name="file1" value="file1.jpg">
     <param name="file2" value="file2.jpg">
     <param name="file3" value="file3.jpg">
     <param name="file4" value="file4.jpg">
     <param name="file5" value="file5.jpg">
     <param name="file6" value="file6.jpg">
     <param name="file7" value="file7.jpg">
     </applet>
   */

   public class DrawRandomImage extends Applet {
     Image image;

     public void init() {

       // Select a random image
       String str = getParameter("count");
       int count = Integer.parseInt(str);
       int n = (int)(count * Math.random());
       String filename = getParameter("file" + n);

       // Get image
       image = getImage(getDocumentBase(),
         filename);
     }

     public void paint(Graphics g) {
       g.drawImage(image, 0, 0, this);
     }
   }
```

| 13.12 | ***E**XERCISES* |

```
1. import java.applet.*;
   import java.awt.*;
   /*
     <applet code="MovingDot" width=250 height=250>
     </applet>
   */

   public class MovingDot extends Applet
   implements Runnable {
     double radians = 0;
     Thread t;
```

```java
      public void init() {

        // Start thread
        t = new Thread(this);
        t.start();
      }

      public void run() {
        try {
          while(true) {

            // Request a repaint
            repaint();

            // Sleep before moving dot
            Thread.sleep(100);
          }
        }
        catch(Exception e) {
        }
      }

      public void paint(Graphics g) {

        // Compute center of applet
        Dimension d = getSize();
        int xcenter = d.width/2;
        int ycenter = d.height/2;

        // Calculate position of dot
        int x = xcenter + (int)(100 * Math.cos(radians));
        int y = ycenter - (int)(100 * Math.sin(radians));

        // Draw dot
        g.fillRect(x - 2, y - 2, 5, 5);

        // Increment radians
        radians += Math.PI/180;
      }
    }
```

```java
2. import java.applet.*;
   import java.awt.*;
   /*
     <applet code="ConnectedDots" width=250 height=100>
     </applet>
   */

   public class ConnectedDots extends Applet
   implements Runnable {
     int xlast, ylast;
     Thread t;

     public void init() {

       // Initialize xlast and ylast
```

```
        xlast = -1;
        ylast = 1;

        // Start thread
        t = new Thread(this);
        t.start();
    }

    public void run() {
      try {
        while(true) {

          // Request a repaint
          repaint();

          // Sleep before displaying next dot
          Thread.sleep(200);
        }
      }
      catch(Exception e) {
      }
    }

    public void update(Graphics g) {
      paint(g);
    }

    public void paint(Graphics g) {

      // Pick a random point in the applet
      Dimension d = getSize();
      int x = (int)(Math.random() * d.width);
      int y = (int)(Math.random() * d.height);

      // Draw dot
      g.fillRect(x - 2, y - 2, 5, 5);

      // Draw a line from the previous dot
      if(xlast != -1) {
        g.drawLine(xlast, ylast, x, y);
      }

      // Update xlast and ylast
      xlast = x;
      ylast = y;
    }
}
```

13.13   *E*XERCISE

```
1. import java.applet.*;
   import java.awt.*;
   /*
     <applet code="BufferedAnalogMeter" width=400 height=200>
```

```
      <param name="amplitude" value="8">
      <param name="frequency" value="0.5">
      <param name="max" value="10">
      <param name="min" value="-10">
    </applet>
*/

public class BufferedAnalogMeter extends Applet
implements Runnable {

  // Declare variables for meter range
  double max, min;

  // Declare variables for sine wave
  double amplitude, frequency;

  // Declare variables
  double value;
  double time;
  Thread t;

  // Declare buffer and graphics
  Image buffer;
  Graphics bufferg;

  public void init() {

    // Read parameters for sine wave
    String samplitude = getParameter("amplitude");
    amplitude = Double.valueOf(samplitude).doubleValue();
    String sfrequency = getParameter("frequency");
    frequency = Double.valueOf(sfrequency).doubleValue();

    // Read parameters for meter range
    String smax = getParameter("max");
    max = Double.valueOf(smax).doubleValue();
    String smin = getParameter("min");
    min = Double.valueOf(smin).doubleValue();

    // Determine size of applet
    Dimension d = getSize();
    int h = d.height;
    int w = d.width;

    // Create background buffer
    buffer = createImage(w, h);

    // Start thread
    t = new Thread(this);
    t.start();
  }

  public void run() {
    try {
      while(true) {
```

```java
      // Compute radians
      double radians = 2 * Math.PI * frequency * time/1000;

      // Compute current value of the sine wave
      value = amplitude * Math.sin(radians);

      // Compute interval between samples
      long interval = (long)(10/frequency);

      // Update time
      time += interval;

      // Request update of screen
      repaint();

      // Sleep until next sample
      Thread.sleep(interval);
    }
  }
  catch(Exception ex) {
    ex.printStackTrace();
  }
}

public void update(Graphics g) {
  paint(g);
}

public void paint(Graphics g) {

  // Determine size of applet
  Dimension d = getSize();
  int h = d.height;
  int w = d.width;

  // Get graphics context for buffer
  if(bufferg == null)
    bufferg = buffer.getGraphics();

  // Clear buffer
  bufferg.clearRect(0, 0, w, h);

  // Compute radius of dial arc
  int r1 = (int)(0.4 * w);
  int r2 = (int)(0.8 * h);
  int radius = (r1 < r2) ? r1 : r2;

  // Draw arc representing the dial
  int centerx = (int)(w * 0.5);
  int centery = (int)(h * 0.9);
  int xa = centerx - radius;
  int ya = centery - radius;
  bufferg.drawArc(xa, ya, 2 * radius, 2 * radius, 0, 180);

  // Draw line representing the base of the meter
  bufferg.drawLine(centerx - radius, centery,
```

```
          centerx + radius, centery);

      // Compute position of needle
      double angle;
      if(value > max) {
        angle = 180;
      }
      else if(value < min) {
        angle = 0;
      }
      else {
        angle = (int)(180 * (value - min)/(max - min));
      }

      // Draw line representing the needle
      double radians = angle * Math.PI/180;
      int x = (int)(centerx - radius * 0.9 * Math.cos(radians));
      int y = (int)(centery - radius * 0.9 * Math.sin(radians));
      bufferg.setColor(Color.blue);
      bufferg.drawLine(centerx, centery, x, y);

      // Copy background buffer to screen
      g.drawImage(buffer, 0, 0, null);
    }
  }
```

*M*ASTERY SKILLS CHECK: Chapter 13

1. Can't read or write local disk, execute native code, or start other applications. Can only open a socket back to the host from which its was downloaded.

2. **java.awt.Graphics**

3. Ascent: pixels above the baseline. Descent: pixels below the baseline. Leading: pixels between the descent of one line and the ascent of the following line. Height: sum of ascent, descent, and leading.

4. **getFont( )**, **getFontMetrics( )**, **getForeground( )**, **getSize( )**, **paint( )**, **repaint( )**, **setBackground( )**, **setFont( )**, **setForeground( )**, **update( )**

5. applet tag

6. Code base: defines where the **.class** file for the applet is located. Document base: defines where the **.html** and other files are located. They have different values when the applet tag explicitly assigns a value to code base.

7. **showDocument( )**, **showStatus( )**

8. **init( )**, **start( )**, **stop( )**, and **destroy( )**

9.
```
import java.applet.*;
import java.awt.*;
/*
  <applet code="Momentum" width=250 height=250>
  </applet>
```

```
*/

public class Momentum extends Applet
implements Runnable {

  // Size of square in pixels
  final static int SIZE = 10;

  // Applet height and width
  int h, w;

  // Position of upper left square position
  int x, y;

  // Square velocity
  int vx, vy;

  // Background buffer
  Image buffer;

  // Graphics context for background buffer
  Graphics bufferg;

  // Reference to thread
  Thread t;

  public void init() {

    // Determine size of applet
    Dimension d = getSize();
    h = d.height;
    w = d.width;

    // Create background buffer
    buffer = createImage(w, h);

    // Initialize x, y
    x = (int)((w - SIZE) * Math.random());
    y = (int)((h - SIZE) * Math.random());

    // Initialize vx, vy
    vx = 1;
    vy = 1;

    // Start thread
    t = new Thread(this);
    t.start();
  }

  public void run() {

    try {

      while(true) {

        // Sleep for 50 msec
```

```
      Thread.sleep(50);

      // Repaint applet
      repaint();
    }
  }
  catch(Exception e) {
  }
}

public void update(Graphics g) {
  paint(g);
}

public void paint(Graphics g) {

  // Get graphics context for buffer
  if(bufferg == null)
    bufferg = buffer.getGraphics();

  // Clear buffer
  bufferg.clearRect(0, 0, w, h);

  // Draw border
  bufferg.setColor(Color.black);
  bufferg.drawRect(0, 0, w - 1, h - 1);

  // Update x, y
  x += vx;
  y += vy;

  // Update x, vx
  if(x + vx > w - SIZE) {
    vx = -vx;
  }
  else if(x + vx < 0) {
    vx = -vx;
  }
  x += vx;

  // Update y, vy
  if(y + vy > w - SIZE) {
    vy = -vy;
  }
  else if(y + vy < 0) {
    vy = -vy;
  }
  y += vy;

  // Draw rectangle
  bufferg.setColor(Color.blue);
  bufferg.fillRect(x, y, SIZE, SIZE);

  // Copy background buffer to screen
  g.drawImage(buffer, 0, 0, null);
```

```
      }
   }

10. import java.applet.*;
    import java.awt.*;
    /*
      <applet code="Banner" width=350 height=100>
      <param name="message" value="This is the message">
      <param name="t1" value="200">
      <param name="t2" value="3000">
      </applet>
    */

    public class Banner extends Applet
    implements Runnable {

      // Message to be displayed
      String message;

      // Msec between characters
      int t1;

      // Msec to display complete message
      int t2;

      // Width and height of applet
      int w, h;

      // Index of next characters to display
      int index;

      // Background buffer
      Image buffer;

      // Graphics context for background buffer
      Graphics bufferg;

      // Reference to thread
      Thread t;

      public void init() {

        // Process parameters
        message = getParameter("message");
        t1 = Integer.parseInt(getParameter("t1"));
        t2 = Integer.parseInt(getParameter("t2"));

        // Determine size of applet
        Dimension d = getSize();
        w = d.width;
        h = d.height;

        // Create background buffer
        buffer = createImage(d.width, d.height);

        // Start thread
```

```
    t = new Thread(this);
    t.start();
  }

  public void update(Graphics g) {
    paint(g);
  }

  public void paint(Graphics g) {

    // Get graphics context for buffer
    if(bufferg == null)
      bufferg = buffer.getGraphics();

    // Clear buffer
    bufferg.clearRect(0, 0, w, h);

    // Set font
    bufferg.setFont(new Font("Serif", Font.BOLD, 36));

    // Display substring
    String str = message.substring(0, index);
    Dimension d = getSize();
    bufferg.drawString(str, 5, d.height/2);

    // Copy background buffer to screen
    g.drawImage(buffer, 0, 0, null);
  }

  public void run() {
    try {
      while(true) {

        // Request a repaint
        repaint();

        // Sleep before displaying next character
        // and update index
        if(index == message.length()) {
          Thread.sleep(t2);
          index = 0;
        }
        else {
          Thread.sleep(t1);
          ++index;
        }
      }
    }
    catch(Exception e) {
    }
  }
}
```

CUMULATIVE SKILLS CHECK: Chapter 13

```java
1. import java.applet.*;
   import java.awt.*;
   /*
     <applet code="ImageAnimation" width=280 height=280>
     <param name="count" value="4">
     <param name="file0" value="slide0.jpg">
     <param name="file1" value="slide1.jpg">
     <param name="file2" value="slide2.jpg">
     <param name="file3" value="slide3.jpg">
     <param name="msec" value="1000">
     </applet>
   */

   public class ImageAnimation extends Applet
   implements Runnable {
     int count;
     Image images[];
     int msec;
     Thread thread;
     int index;

     public void init() {

       // Read the count parameter
       String str = getParameter("count");
       count = Integer.parseInt(str);

       // Allocate and initialize array of images
       images = new Image[count];
       for(int i = 0; i < count; i++) {
         String filename = getParameter("file" + i);
         images[i] = getImage(getDocumentBase(),
           filename);
       }

       // Read msec parameter
       str = getParameter("msec");
       msec = Integer.parseInt(str);

       // Create and start thread
       thread = new Thread(this);
       thread.start();
     }

     public void paint(Graphics g) {
       g.drawImage(images[index], 0, 0, this);
     }

     public void run() {
       try {
         while(true) {
           Thread.sleep(msec);
```

```
              ++index;
              if(index >= count)
                index = 0;
              repaint();
          }
        }
        catch(Exception e) {
        }
      }
    }
```

```
2. import java.applet.*;
   import java.awt.*;
   import java.util.*;
   /*
     <applet code="DailyImage" width=280 height=280>
     <param name="day1" value="sun.jpg">
     <param name="day2" value="mon.jpg">
     <param name="day3" value="tue.jpg">
     <param name="day4" value="wed.jpg">
     <param name="day5" value="thu.jpg">
     <param name="day6" value="fri.jpg">
     <param name="day7" value="sat.jpg">
     </applet>
   */

   public class DailyImage extends Applet {
     Image image;

     public void init() {

       // Determine the current day of the week
       Calendar calendar = Calendar.getInstance();
       int dow = calendar.get(Calendar.DAY_OF_WEEK);

       // Get an image object
       image = getImage(getDocumentBase(),
         getParameter("day" + dow));
     }

     public void paint(Graphics g) {
       g.drawImage(image, 0, 0, this);
     }
   }
```

```
3. import java.applet.*;
   import java.awt.*;
   import java.util.*;
   /*
     <applet code="Clock" width=200 height=200>
     </applet>
   */

   public class Clock extends Applet
   implements Runnable {
     Thread t;
```

```java
public void init() {
  t = new Thread(this);
  t.start();
}

public void run() {
  try {
    while(true) {
      Thread.sleep(60000);
      repaint();
    }
  }
  catch(Exception e) {
  }
}

public void paint(Graphics g) {

  // Draw circle
  Dimension d = getSize();
  int xc = d.width/2;
  int yc = d.height/2;
  int radius = (int)((d.width < d.height) ?
    0.4 * d.width : 0.4 * d.height);
  g.drawOval(xc - radius, yc - radius, 2 * radius, 2 * radius);

  // Draw marks for hours along circle perimeter
  for(int i = 0; i < 12; i++) {
    double degrees = i * 30;
    double radians = degrees * Math.PI/180;
    int xa = xc + (int)(0.9 * radius * Math.cos(radians));
    int ya = yc - (int)(0.9 * radius * Math.sin(radians));
    int xb = xc + (int)(radius * Math.cos(radians));
    int yb = yc - (int)(radius * Math.sin(radians));
    g.drawLine(xa, ya, xb, yb);
  }

  // Get calendar initialized to current date/time
  Calendar calendar = Calendar.getInstance();

  // Draw minute hand
  int minute = calendar.get(Calendar.MINUTE);
  double degrees = 90 - 6 * minute;
  double radians = degrees * Math.PI/180;
  int xh = xc + (int)(0.8 * radius * Math.cos(radians));
  int yh = yc - (int)(0.8 * radius * Math.sin(radians));
  g.drawLine(xc, yc, xh, yh);

  // Draw hour hand
  int hour = calendar.get(Calendar.HOUR_OF_DAY) % 24;
  degrees = 90 - 30 * hour - 30 * (minute/60.0f);
  radians = degrees * Math.PI/180;
  int xm = xc + (int)(0.5 * radius * Math.cos(radians));
  int ym = yc - (int)(0.5 * radius * Math.sin(radians));
  g.drawLine(xc, yc, xm, ym);
```

```
        }
    }
```

CHAPTER 14

REVIEW SKILLS CHECK: Chapter 14

```
1. import java.applet.*;
   import java.awt.*;
   /*
     <applet code="AmplitudeModulation" width=300 height=200>
     </applet>
   */

   public class AmplitudeModulation extends Applet {

     public void paint(Graphics g) {

       // Draw axes
       g.setColor(Color.lightGray);
       Dimension d = getSize();
       int width = d.width;
       int height = d.height;
       g.drawRect(0, 0, width - 1, height - 1);
       g.drawLine(0, height/2, width, height/2);
       g.drawLine(width/2, 0, width/2, height - 1);

       // Draw waveform
       g.setColor(Color.blue);
       double dx = 4 * Math.PI / width;
       double x = -2 * Math.PI;
       for(int i = 0; i < width - 1; i++) {
         double f1 = Math.sin(x) * Math.sin(10 * x);
         double f2 = Math.sin(x + dx) * Math.sin(10 * (x + dx));
         int y1 = (int)((height - height * f1) / 2);
         int y2 = (int)((height - height * f2) / 2);
         g.drawLine(i, y1, i + 1, y2);
         x += dx;
       }
     }
   }

2. import java.applet.*;
   import java.awt.*;
   /*
     <applet code="ProgressBar" width=400 height=100>
     <param name="w" value="200">
     <param name="h" value="50">
     <param name="time" value="10000">
     <param name="color" value="0x0000ff">
     </applet>
```

```
*/
public class ProgressBar extends Applet
implements Runnable {
  int w, h, time;
  int count;

  // Declare buffer and graphics
  Image buffer;
  Graphics bufferg;

  public void init() {

    // Get applet parameters
    w = Integer.parseInt(getParameter("w"));
    h = Integer.parseInt(getParameter("h"));
    time = Integer.parseInt(getParameter("time"));
    Color color = Color.decode(getParameter("color"));

    // Set foreground color
    setForeground(color);

    // Determine size of applet
    Dimension d = getSize();

    // Create background buffer
    buffer = createImage(d.width, d.height);

    // Start thread
    Thread thread = new Thread(this);
    thread.start();
  }

  public void run() {

    try {

      for(count = 1; count <= w; count++) {
        Thread.sleep(time/w);
        repaint();
      }
    }
    catch(Exception e) {
    }
  }

  public void update(Graphics g) {
    paint(g);
  }

  public void paint(Graphics g) {

    // Get graphics context for buffer
    if(bufferg == null)
      bufferg = buffer.getGraphics();
```

```
      // Draw rectangle
      Dimension d = getSize();
      int x = (d.width - w)/2;
      int y = (d.height - h)/2;
      bufferg.drawRect(x, y, w, h);
      bufferg.fillRect(x, y, count, h);

      // Copy background buffer to screen
      g.drawImage(buffer, 0, 0, null);
   }
}
```

3.
```
import java.applet.*;
import java.awt.*;
import java.util.*;
/*
  <applet code="GaussianDots" width=300 height=300>
  </applet>
*/

public class GaussianDots extends Applet
implements Runnable {
  int x, y;

  public void init() {
    x = y = -1;
    Thread thread = new Thread(this);
    thread.start();
  }

  public void run() {
    Random random = new Random();
    try {
      while(true) {
        Dimension d = getSize();
        Thread.sleep(100);
        x = (int)(d.width/2 + d.width * random.nextGaussian()/8);
        y = (int)(d.height/2 + d.height * random.nextGaussian()/8);
        repaint();
      }
    }
    catch(Exception e) {
    }
  }

  public void update(Graphics g) {
    paint(g);
  }

  public void paint(Graphics g) {
    g.fillRect(x, y, 1, 1);
  }
}
```

14.1 EXERCISES

1. Event sources provide registration/unregistration methods, generate events, and send events to registered listeners.
2. Event listeners register for notifications, implement a listener interface, and unregister for notifications.
3.
```
public void add TypeListener(TypeListener el)
public void add TypeListener(TypeListener el)
   throws TooManyListenersException
public void removeTypeListener(TypeListener el)
```

14.2 EXERCISES

1. **java.util.EventObject**
2. Mouse clicked, dragged, entered, exited, moved, pressed, or released
3. **java.util.EventObject**, **java.awt.AWTEvent**, **java.awt.event.ComponentEvent**, **java.awt.event.InputEvent**

14.3 EXERCISES

1. **java.util.EventListener**
2. **java.awt.event.MouseListener**, **java.awt.event.MouseMotionListener**
3.
```java
import java.applet.*;
import java.awt.*;
import java.awt.event.*;
/*
  <applet code="TrackMouse" width=300 height=300>
  </applet>
*/

public class TrackMouse extends Applet
implements MouseMotionListener {
  Point p;

  public void init() {
    addMouseMotionListener(this);
  }

  public void mouseDragged(MouseEvent me) {
    p = me.getPoint();
    repaint();
  }

  public void mouseMoved(MouseEvent me) {
    p = me.getPoint();
    repaint();
  }
```

```
      public void paint(Graphics g) {
        if(p != null) {
          g.fillRect(p.x - 10, p.y - 10, 10, 10);
        }
      }
    }
```

14.4 **E**XERCISES

1. An adapter class provides empty implementations of all methods in a particular listener interface. It can be useful if you want to override only some of the methods defined by that interface.

2.
```
import java.applet.*;
import java.awt.*;
import java.awt.event.*;
/*
  <applet code="MouseMotionAdapterDemo" width=100 height=100>
  </applet>
*/

public class MouseMotionAdapterDemo extends Applet {

  public void init() {
    setBackground(Color.white);
    addMouseListener(new Adapter1(this));
    addMouseMotionListener(new Adapter2(this));
  }
}

class Adapter1 extends MouseAdapter {
  MouseMotionAdapterDemo mmad;

  public Adapter1(MouseMotionAdapterDemo mmad) {
    this.mmad = mmad;
  }

  public void mouseReleased(MouseEvent me) {
    mmad.setBackground(Color.white);
    mmad.repaint();
  }
}

class Adapter2 extends MouseMotionAdapter {
  MouseMotionAdapterDemo mmad;

  public Adapter2(MouseMotionAdapterDemo mmad) {
    this.mmad = mmad;
  }

  public void mouseDragged(MouseEvent me) {
    mmad.setBackground(Color.cyan);
    mmad.repaint();
```

```
    }
  }
```

EXERCISES

1. An inner class exists within the scope of an expression or another class. Therefore, it has access to the variables and methods in that scope.

2.
```
import java.applet.*;
import java.awt.*;
import java.awt.event.*;
/*
  <applet code="MouseMotionAdapterInner" width=100 height=100>
  </applet>
*/

public class MouseMotionAdapterInner extends Applet {

  public void init() {
    setBackground(Color.white);
    addMouseListener(new Adapter1());
    addMouseMotionListener(new Adapter2());
  }

  class Adapter1 extends MouseAdapter {

    public void mouseReleased(MouseEvent me) {
      setBackground(Color.white);
      repaint();
    }
  }

  class Adapter2 extends MouseMotionAdapter {

    public void mouseDragged(MouseEvent me) {
      setBackground(Color.cyan);
      repaint();
    }
  }
}
```

EXERCISE

1.
```
import java.applet.*;
import java.awt.*;
import java.awt.event.*;
/*
  <applet code="MouseMotionAnonymous" width=100 height=100>
  </applet>
*/

public class MouseMotionAnonymous extends Applet {
```

```
public void init() {
  setBackground(Color.white);
  addMouseListener(new MouseAdapter() {
    public void mouseReleased(MouseEvent me) {
      setBackground(Color.white);
      repaint();
    }
  });
  addMouseMotionListener(new MouseMotionAdapter() {
    public void mouseDragged(MouseEvent me) {
      setBackground(Color.cyan);
      repaint();
    }
  });
}
}
```

M ASTERY SKILLS CHECK: *Chapter 14*

1. Sources provide registration/unregistration methods, generate events, and unicast/multicast events to listeners. Listeners register to receive event notifications, implement an interface to receive events, and unregister when they no longer want to receive events of that type. In effect, the source delegates event processing to one or more listeners.
2. **java.util.EventObject**
3. **java.util.EventListener**
4. **java.awt.event.MouseListener, java.awt.event.MouseMotionListener**
5. An adapter class provides empty implementations of all methods in a particular listener interface.
6. An inner class is one that can be defined within the scope of an expression or another class. It has access to the variables and methods of its enclosing class. Therefore, it does not need to save a reference to that class.
7. An anonymous inner class does not have a name. It can be used to further simplify the development of event handlers.

C UMULATIVE SKILLS CHECK: *Chapter 14*

```
1. import java.applet.*;
   import java.awt.*;
   import java.awt.event.*;
   /*
     <applet code="Brighter" width=300 height=300>
     </applet>
   */

   public class Brighter extends Applet
```

```
      implements MouseListener {
        int i;
        Color color;

        public void init() {
          color = new Color(i, i, i);
          setBackground(color);
          addMouseListener(this);
        }

        public void mouseClicked(MouseEvent me) {
          i += 10;
          if(i > 255)
            i = 255;
          color = new Color(i, i, i);
          setBackground(color);
          repaint();
        }

        public void mouseEntered(MouseEvent me) {
        }

        public void mouseExited(MouseEvent me) {
        }

        public void mousePressed(MouseEvent me) {
        }

        public void mouseReleased(MouseEvent me) {
        }
      }

2. import java.applet.*;
   import java.awt.*;
   import java.awt.event.*;
   /*
     <applet code="CircleMaker" width=300 height=300>
     </applet>
   */

   public class CircleMaker extends Applet {
     int xc, yc, x, y;
     boolean down;
     int radius;

     public void init() {

       // Set background color
       setBackground(Color.white);

       // Define anonymous inner class for
       // mouse events
       addMouseListener(new MouseAdapter() {
         public void mousePressed(MouseEvent me) {
           xc = me.getX();
           yc = me.getY();
```

```
        down = true;
      }
      public void mouseReleased(MouseEvent me) {
        down = false;
      }
    });

    // Define anonymous inner class for
    // mouse motion events
    addMouseMotionListener(new MouseMotionAdapter() {
      public void mouseDragged(MouseEvent me) {
        int dx = Math.abs(xc - me.getX());
        int dy = Math.abs(yc - me.getY());
        radius = (dx > dy) ? dx : dy;
        repaint();
      }
    });
  }

  public void paint(Graphics g) {
    if(down)
      g.drawOval(xc - radius, yc - radius, 2 * radius, 2 * radius);
  }
}
```

3.
```
import java.applet.*;
import java.awt.*;
import java.awt.event.*;
/*
  <applet code="ColorChanger" width=120 height=120>
  </applet>
*/

public class ColorChanger extends Applet
implements MouseListener, Runnable {
  boolean down;

  public void init() {
    Thread thread = new Thread(this);
    thread.start();
    addMouseListener(this);
  }

  public void mouseClicked(MouseEvent me) {
  }

  public void mouseEntered(MouseEvent me) {
  }

  public void mouseExited(MouseEvent me) {
  }

  public void mousePressed(MouseEvent me) {
    down = true;
  }
```

```
    public void mouseReleased(MouseEvent me) {
      down = false;
    }

    public void update(Graphics g) {
      paint(g);
    }

    public void run() {
      try {
        int angle = 0;
        while(true) {
          Thread.sleep(200);
          if(!down) {
            double radians = angle * Math.PI / 180;
            int r = (int)(127 * Math.sin(radians) + 127);
            int g = (int)(127 * Math.sin(2 * radians) + 127);
            int b = (int)(127 * Math.sin(3 * radians) + 127);
            Color color = new Color(r, g, b);
            setBackground(color);
            repaint();
            ++angle;
            if(angle > 360)
              angle = 0;
          }
        }
      }
      catch(Exception e) {
      }
    }
  }
```

CHAPTER 15

REVIEW SKILLS CHECK: Chapter 15

```
1. import java.applet.*;
   import java.awt.*;
   import java.awt.event.*;
   /*
     <applet code="SuspendImageAnimation" width=280 height=280>
     <param name="count" value="4">
     <param name="file0" value="slide0.jpg">
     <param name="file1" value="slide1.jpg">
     <param name="file2" value="slide2.jpg">
     <param name="file3" value="slide3.jpg">
     <param name="msec" value="1000">
     </applet>
   */
```

```
public class SuspendImageAnimation extends Applet
implements Runnable {
  int count;
  Image images[];
  int msec;
  int index;
  boolean suspendFlag;

  public void init() {

    // Read the count parameter
    String str = getParameter("count");
    count = Integer.parseInt(str);

    // Allocate and initialize array of images
    images = new Image[count];
    for(int i = 0; i < count; i++) {
      String filename = getParameter("file" + i);
      images[i] = getImage(getDocumentBase(),
        filename);
    }

    // Read msec parameter
    str = getParameter("msec");
    msec = Integer.parseInt(str);

    // Create and start thread
    Thread thread = new Thread(this);
    thread.start();

    // Register to process mouse clicks
    addMouseListener(new MouseAdapter() {
      public void mouseClicked(MouseEvent me) {
        suspendFlag = !suspendFlag;
      }
    });
  }

  public void paint(Graphics g) {
    g.drawImage(images[index], 0, 0, this);
  }

  public void run() {
    try {
      while(true)  {
        Thread.sleep(msec);
        if(suspendFlag)
          continue;
        ++index;
        if(index >= count)
          index = 0;
        repaint();
      }
    }
    catch(Exception e) {
    }
```

```
      }
    }

2. import java.applet.*;
   import java.awt.*;
   import java.awt.event.*;
   /*
     <applet code="Windmill" width=300 height=300>
     </applet>
   */

   public class Windmill extends Applet
   implements Runnable {
     double radians;
     boolean operate;

     public void init() {

       // Create thread to animate windmill
       Thread thread = new Thread(this);
       thread.start();

       // Anonymous inner class for mouse drags
       addMouseMotionListener(new MouseMotionAdapter() {
         public void mouseDragged(MouseEvent me) {
           operate = true;
         }
       });

       // Anonymous inner class for mouse clicks
       addMouseListener(new MouseAdapter() {
         public void mouseClicked(MouseEvent me) {
           operate = false;
         }
       });
     }

     public void run() {
       try {
         while(true) {
           Thread.sleep(100);
           if(operate)
             repaint();
         }
       }
       catch(Exception e) {
       }
     }

     public void paint(Graphics g) {

       // Calculate length of a windmill arm
       Dimension d = getSize();
       int r = (d.width > d.height) ? d.width : d.height;
       r = (int)(0.3 * r);
```

```
      // Calculate center of display area
      int xc = d.width/2;
      int yc = d.height/2;

      // Draw vertical tower
      g.drawLine(xc, d.height, xc, yc);

      // Draw 1st arm
      int x = xc + (int)(r * Math.cos(radians));
      int y = yc - (int)(r * Math.sin(radians));
      g.drawLine(xc, yc, x, y);

      // Draw 2d arm
      x = xc + (int)(r * Math.cos(radians + Math.PI/2));
      y = yc - (int)(r * Math.sin(radians + Math.PI/2));
      g.drawLine(xc, yc, x, y);

      // Draw 3d arm
      x = xc + (int)(r * Math.cos(radians + Math.PI));
      y = yc - (int)(r * Math.sin(radians + Math.PI));
      g.drawLine(xc, yc, x, y);

      // Draw 4th arm
      x = xc + (int)(r * Math.cos(radians + 1.5 * Math.PI));
      y = yc - (int)(r * Math.sin(radians + 1.5 * Math.PI));
      g.drawLine(xc, yc, x, y);

      // Increment radians
      radians += Math.PI/180;
    }
  }
```

15.2 *E*XERCISE

```
1. import java.applet.*;
   import java.awt.*;
   import java.util.*;
   /*
     <applet code="Greeting" width=250 height=60>
     </applet>
   */

   public class Greeting extends Applet {

     public void init() {
       Label label = new Label();
       Calendar calendar = Calendar.getInstance();
       int hours = calendar.get(Calendar.HOUR_OF_DAY);
       if(hours < 12) {
         label.setText("Good morning");
       }
       else if(hours < 18) {
         label.setText("Good afternoon");
       }
```

```
      else {
        label.setText("Good evening");
      }
      add(label);
    }
  }
```

15.3 EXERCISE

```
1. import java.applet.*;
   import java.awt.*;
   import java.awt.event.*;
   /*
     <applet code="ToggleButton" width=200 height=60>
     </applet>
   */

   public class ToggleButton extends Applet
   implements ActionListener {
     Button b;

     public void init() {
       b = new Button("Start");
       b.addActionListener(this);
       add(b);
     }

     public void actionPerformed(ActionEvent ae) {
       if(b.getLabel().equals("Start"))
         b.setLabel("Stop");
       else
         b.setLabel("Start");
     }
   }
```

15.4 EXERCISE

```
1. import java.applet.*;
   import java.awt.*;
   /*
     <applet code="CanvasDemo2" width=501 height=200>
     </applet>
   */

   class MyCanvas2 extends Canvas {

     public void paint(Graphics g) {

       // Draw axes
       g.setColor(Color.lightGray);
       Dimension d = getSize();
       g.drawRect(0, 0, d.width - 1, d.height - 1);
```

```
      g.drawLine(0, d.height/2, d.width, d.height/2);
      g.drawLine(d.width/2, 0, d.width/2, d.height - 1);

      // Draw waveform
      g.setColor(Color.blue);
      double dx = 4 * Math.PI / d.width;
      double x = -2 * Math.PI;
      int h = d.height;
      for(int i = 0; i < d.width - 1; i++) {
        double f1 = Math.sin(10 * x) * Math.sin(x);
        double f2 = Math.sin(10 * (x + dx)) * Math.sin(x + dx);
        int y1 = (int)((h - h * f1) / 2);
        int y2 = (int)((h - h * f2) / 2);
        g.drawLine(i, y1, i + 1, y2);
        x += dx;
      }
    }
}

public class CanvasDemo2 extends Applet {

  public void init() {
    MyCanvas2 myCanvas2 = new MyCanvas2();
    myCanvas2.setSize(401, 150);
    add(myCanvas2);
  }
}
```

15.5   *E*XERCISE

```
1. import java.applet.*;
   import java.awt.*;
   import java.awt.event.*;
   /*
     <applet code="AddColors" width=400 height=60>
     </applet>
   */

   public class AddColors extends Applet
   implements ItemListener {
     Checkbox red, green, blue;
     Canvas canvas;

     public void init() {
       red = new Checkbox("Red");
       red.addItemListener(this);
       add(red);
       green = new Checkbox("Green");
       green.addItemListener(this);
       add(green);
       blue = new Checkbox("Blue");
       blue.addItemListener(this);
       add(blue);
       canvas = new Canvas();
```

```
        canvas.setBackground(Color.black);
        canvas.setSize(30, 30);
        add(canvas);
    }

    public void itemStateChanged(ItemEvent ie) {
      int rgb = 0;
      if(red.getState())
        rgb = 0xff0000;
      if(green.getState())
        rgb |= 0x00ff00;
      if(blue.getState())
        rgb |= 0x0000ff;
      Color color = new Color(rgb);
      canvas.setBackground(color);
      canvas.repaint();
    }
}
```

15.6 *EXERCISE*

```
1. import java.applet.*;
   import java.awt.*;
   import java.awt.event.*;
   /*
     <applet code="SelectColor" width=400 height=60>
     </applet>
   */

   public class SelectColor extends Applet
   implements ItemListener {
     CheckboxGroup cbg;
     Checkbox red, green, blue;
     Canvas canvas;

     public void init() {
       cbg = new CheckboxGroup();
       red = new Checkbox("Red", cbg, true);
       red.addItemListener(this);
       add(red);
       green = new Checkbox("Green", cbg, false);
       green.addItemListener(this);
       add(green);
       blue = new Checkbox("Blue", cbg, false);
       blue.addItemListener(this);
       add(blue);
       canvas = new Canvas();
       canvas.setBackground(Color.red);
       canvas.setSize(30, 30);
       add(canvas);
     }

     public void itemStateChanged(ItemEvent ie) {
       Color color;
```

```
      Checkbox cb = cbg.getSelectedCheckbox();
      if(cb == red)
        color = Color.red;
      else if(cb == green)
        color = Color.green;
      else
        color = Color.blue;
      canvas.setBackground(color);
      canvas.repaint();
    }
  }
```

15.7 EXERCISE

```
1. import java.applet.*;
   import java.awt.*;
   import java.awt.event.*;
   /*
     <applet code="ColorChoice" width=200 height=60>
     </applet>
   */

   public class ColorChoice extends Applet
   implements ItemListener {
     Choice c1;
     Canvas canvas;

     public void init() {
       c1 = new Choice();
       c1.addItem("Red");
       c1.addItem("Green");
       c1.addItem("Blue");
       c1.addItemListener(this);
       add(c1);
       canvas = new Canvas();
       canvas.setBackground(Color.red);
       canvas.setSize(30, 30);
       add(canvas);
     }

     public void itemStateChanged(ItemEvent ie) {
       Color color;
       if(c1.getSelectedItem().equals("Red"))
         color = Color.red;
       else if(c1.getSelectedItem().equals("Green"))
         color = Color.green;
       else
         color = Color.blue;
       canvas.setBackground(color);
       canvas.repaint();
     }
   }
```

15.8	**E**XERCISE

```
1. import java.applet.*;
   import java.awt.*;
   /*
     <applet code="NamePassword" width=500 height=60>
     </applet>
   */

   public class NamePassword extends Applet {

     public void init() {
       Label l1 = new Label("Name: ", Label.RIGHT);
       add(l1);
       TextField tf1 = new TextField("Joe O'Neil", 20);
       add(tf1);
       Label l2 = new Label("Password: ", Label.RIGHT);
       add(l2);
       TextField tf2 = new TextField("", 20);
       add(tf2);
       tf2.setEchoChar('*');
     }
   }
```

15.9	**E**XERCISE

```
1. import java.applet.*;
   import java.awt.*;
   import java.awt.event.*;
   import java.util.Enumeration;
   import java.util.Hashtable;
   /*
     <applet code="ColorList" width=400 height=100>
     </applet>
   */

   public class ColorList extends Applet
   implements ItemListener {
     Hashtable ht;
     List list;
     Canvas canvas;

     public void init() {

       // Create hash table
       ht = new Hashtable();
       ht.put("Black", Color.black);
       ht.put("Blue", Color.blue);
       ht.put("Cyan", Color.cyan);
       ht.put("Dark Gray", Color.darkGray);
       ht.put("Gray", Color.gray);
       ht.put("Green", Color.green);
       ht.put("Light Gray", Color.lightGray);
```

```
        ht.put("Magenta", Color.magenta);
        ht.put("Orange", Color.orange);
        ht.put("Pink", Color.pink);
        ht.put("Red", Color.red);
        ht.put("White", Color.white);
        ht.put("Yellow", Color.yellow);

        // Create list
        list = new List();
        Enumeration keys = ht.keys();
        while(keys.hasMoreElements()) {
          list.add((String)keys.nextElement());
        }
        list.addItemListener(this);
        add(list);

        // Create canvas
        canvas = new Canvas();
        canvas.setBackground(Color.black);
        canvas.setSize(30, 30);
        add(canvas);
    }

    public void itemStateChanged(ItemEvent ie) {
      String str = list.getSelectedItem();
      canvas.setBackground((Color)ht.get(str));
      canvas.repaint();
    }
}
```

<hr>

15.10 EXERCISE

```
1. import java.applet.*;
   import java.awt.*;
   import java.awt.event.*;
   /*
     <applet code="ColorScrollbars" width=400 height=60>
     </applet>
   */

   public class ColorScrollbars extends Applet
   implements AdjustmentListener {
     Scrollbar rsb, gsb, bsb;
     Canvas canvas;

     public void init() {
       Label rl = new Label("Red", Label.RIGHT);
       add(rl);
       rsb = new Scrollbar(Scrollbar.HORIZONTAL, 255, 5, 0, 255);
       rsb.addAdjustmentListener(this);
       add(rsb);
       Label gl = new Label("Green", Label.RIGHT);
       add(gl);
       gsb = new Scrollbar(Scrollbar.HORIZONTAL, 0, 5, 0, 255);
```

```
        gsb.addAdjustmentListener(this);
        add(gsb);
        Label bl = new Label("Blue", Label.RIGHT);
        add(bl);
        bsb = new Scrollbar(Scrollbar.HORIZONTAL, 0, 5, 0, 255);
        bsb.addAdjustmentListener(this);
        add(bsb);
        canvas = new Canvas();
        canvas.setSize(30, 30);
        canvas.setBackground(new Color(255, 0, 0));
        add(canvas);
    }

    public void adjustmentValueChanged(AdjustmentEvent ae) {
      int r = rsb.getValue();
      int g = gsb.getValue();
      int b = bsb.getValue();
      Color color = new Color(r, g, b);
      canvas.setBackground(color);
      canvas.repaint();
    }
  }
```

15.14 ***E*XERCISE**

```
1. import java.applet.*;
   import java.awt.*;
   /*
     <applet code="PanelDemo2" width=200 height=250>
     </applet>
   */

   public class PanelDemo2 extends Applet {

     public void init() {

       // Set layout manager
       setLayout(new GridLayout(1, 2));

       // Create panel for entry 1, 1
       Panel p11 = new Panel();
       p11.setLayout(new GridLayout(3, 1));
       CheckboxGroup cbg = new CheckboxGroup();
       Checkbox red = new Checkbox("Red", cbg, true);
       p11.add(red);
       Checkbox green = new Checkbox("Green", cbg, false);
       p11.add(green);
       Checkbox blue = new Checkbox("Blue", cbg, false);
       p11.add(blue);
       add(p11);

       // Create panel for entry 1, 2
       Panel p12 = new Panel();
       p12.setLayout(new GridLayout(4, 1));
```

```
      Checkbox annuities = new Checkbox("Annuities");
      p12.add(annuities);
      Checkbox bonds = new Checkbox("Bonds");
      p12.add(bonds);
      Checkbox options = new Checkbox("Options");
      p12.add(options);
      Checkbox stocks = new Checkbox("Stocks");
      p12.add(stocks);
      add(p12);
    }

    public Insets getInsets() {
      return new Insets(5, 5, 5, 5);
    }
  }
```

15.15   EXERCISE

```
1. import java.applet.*;
   import java.awt.*;
   import java.awt.event.*;
   /*
     <applet code="FrameCounterApplet" width=200 height=200>
     </applet>
   */

   class MyCounterFrame extends Frame {

     MyCounterFrame(String title, String count) {
       super(title);
       addWindowListener(new WindowAdapter() {
         public void windowClosing(WindowEvent we) {
           setVisible(false);
           dispose();
         }
       });
       Label label = new Label(count, Label.CENTER);
       add(label, "Center");
     }
   }

   public class FrameCounterApplet extends Applet
   implements ActionListener {
     int count;

     public void init() {
       Button b = new Button("Create Frame");
       b.addActionListener(this);
       add(b);
     }

     public void actionPerformed(ActionEvent ae) {
       ++count;
       MyCounterFrame mcf =
```

```
      new MyCounterFrame("MyCounterFrame", "" + count);
    mcf.show();
    mcf.setSize(200, 200);
  }
}
```

15.16 EXERCISE

1.

```
import java.awt.*;
import java.awt.event.*;

class MenuFrame2 extends Frame
implements ActionListener, ItemListener {
  TextArea ta;

  public static void main(String args[]) {
    MenuFrame2 mf2 = new MenuFrame2("MyFrame");
    mf2.show();
    mf2.setSize(200, 200);
  }

  MenuFrame2(String title) {

    // Invoke the superclass constructor
    super(title);

    // Register to receive window events
    addWindowListener(new WindowAdapter() {
      public void windowClosing(WindowEvent we) {
        System.exit(0);
      }
    });

    // Create and set manu bar
    MenuBar mb = new MenuBar();
    setMenuBar(mb);

    // Create menu A
    Menu a = new Menu("A");
    mb.add(a);
    MenuItem a1 = new MenuItem("A1");
    a1.addActionListener(this);
    a.add(a1);
    MenuItem a2 = new MenuItem("A2");
    a2.addActionListener(this);
    a.add(a2);
    MenuItem a3 = new MenuItem("A3");
    a3.addActionListener(this);
    a.add(a3);

    // Create menu B
    Menu b = new Menu("B");
    mb.add(b);
```

```
          MenuItem b1 = new MenuItem("B1");
          b1.addActionListener(this);
          b.add(b1);
          MenuItem b2 = new MenuItem("B2");
          b2.addActionListener(this);
          b.add(b2);

          // Create sub-menu for B3
          Menu b3 = new Menu("B3");
          b.add(b3);
          MenuItem b31 = new MenuItem("B31");
          b31.addActionListener(this);
          b3.add(b31);
          MenuItem b32 = new MenuItem("B32");
          b32.addActionListener(this);
          b3.add(b32);
          MenuItem b33 = new MenuItem("B33");
          b33.addActionListener(this);
          b3.add(b33);

          // Create menu C
          Menu c = new Menu("C");
          mb.add(c);
          MenuItem c1 = new MenuItem("C1");
          c1.addActionListener(this);
          c.add(c1);
          MenuItem c2 = new MenuItem("C2");
          c2.addActionListener(this);
          c.add(c2);

          // Create menu D
          Menu d = new Menu("D");
          mb.add(d);
          CheckboxMenuItem d1 = new CheckboxMenuItem("D1");
          d1.addItemListener(this);
          d.add(d1);
          CheckboxMenuItem d2 = new CheckboxMenuItem("D2");
          d2.addItemListener(this);
          d.add(d2);

          // Create a text area and add it to the frame
          ta = new TextArea(10, 20);
          add(ta, "Center");
      }

    public void actionPerformed(ActionEvent ae) {
        ta.append("ActionEvent: " +
          ae.getActionCommand() + "\n");
    }

    public void itemStateChanged(ItemEvent ie) {
        CheckboxMenuItem cbmi = (CheckboxMenuItem)ie.getSource();
        ta.append("ItemEvent: " +
          cbmi.getLabel() + "\n");
    }
}
```

15.17	**E** *XERCISE*

1.
```java
import java.awt.*;
import java.awt.event.*;

public class RandomColorDialogDemo extends Frame
implements ActionListener {

  public static void main(String args[]) {
    RandomColorDialogDemo rcdd = new RandomColorDialogDemo();
    rcdd.setVisible(true);
    rcdd.setSize(200, 100);
  }

  RandomColorDialogDemo() {
    super("Random Color Dialog Demo");

    // Set layout manager
    setLayout(new FlowLayout());

    // Create button
    Button b = new Button("Random Color Dialog");
    b.addActionListener(this);
    add(b);

    // Anonymous inner class handles window events
    addWindowListener(new WindowAdapter() {
      public void windowClosing(WindowEvent we) {
        System.exit(0);
      }
    });
  }

  public void actionPerformed(ActionEvent ae) {
    RandomColorDialog rcd =
      new RandomColorDialog(this, "Random Color Dialog", true);
    rcd.show();
  }
}

class RandomColorDialog extends Dialog
implements ActionListener {

  RandomColorDialog(Frame parent, String title, boolean mode) {
    super(parent, title, mode);

    // Create and add "Center" panel
    Panel pc = new Panel();
    Canvas canvas = new Canvas();
    canvas.setSize(100, 100);
    int red = (int)(255 * Math.random());
    int green = (int)(255 * Math.random());
    int blue = (int)(255 * Math.random());
    Color color = new Color(red, green, blue);
    canvas.setBackground(color);
```

```
      pc.add(canvas);
      add(pc, "Center");

      // Create and add "South" panel
      Panel ps = new Panel();
      Button ok = new Button("OK");
      ok.addActionListener(this);
      ps.add(ok);
      add(ps, "South");

      // Lay out components and set the initial size
      // of this dialog box
      pack();

      // Anonymous inner class handles window events
      addWindowListener(new WindowAdapter() {
        public void windowClosing(WindowEvent we) {
          dispose();
        }
      });
    }

    public Insets getInsets() {
      return new Insets(40, 20, 20, 20);
    }

    public void actionPerformed(ActionEvent ae) {
      dispose();
    }
  }
```

*M*ASTERY SKILLS CHECK: *Chapter 15*

1. Button: action events. Canvas: mouse and mouse motion events. Check box: item events. Choice: item events. Text field: action and text events. Text area: text events. List: action and item events. Scrollbars: adjustment events

2. Flow: centers elements in a row. Border: positions elements in five "geographic" regions. Grid: positions elements in a grid

3. Window activated, closed, closing, deactivated, deiconified, iconified, opened

4. Menu items: action events. Checkbox menu items: item events

5.
```
import java.awt.*;
import java.awt.event.*;

public class ColorDialogDemo extends Frame
implements ActionListener {
  Canvas canvas;

  public static void main(String args[]) {
    ColorDialogDemo cdd = new ColorDialogDemo();
```

```
        cdd.setVisible(true);
        cdd.setSize(200, 100);
      }

    ColorDialogDemo() {
      super("Color Dialog Demo");

      // Set layout manager for dialog
      setLayout(new FlowLayout());

      // Add button
      Button b = new Button("Color Dialog");
      b.addActionListener(this);
      add(b);

      // Add canvas
      canvas = new Canvas();
      canvas.setSize(50, 50);
      canvas.setBackground(Color.red);
      add(canvas);

      // Handle window events
      addWindowListener(new WindowAdapter() {
        public void windowClosing(WindowEvent we) {
          System.exit(0);
        }
      });
    }

   public void actionPerformed(ActionEvent ae) {

      // Create and show color dialog
      ColorDialog cd =
        new ColorDialog(this, "Color Dialog", true);
      cd.show();
   }
}

class ColorDialog extends Dialog
implements ActionListener, AdjustmentListener {
  ColorDialogDemo parent;
  Scrollbar sr, sg, sb;

  ColorDialog(ColorDialogDemo parent, String title, boolean mode) {
    super(parent, title, mode);
    this.parent = parent;

    // Get red, green, and blue components of canvas color
    Color color = parent.canvas.getBackground();
    int r = color.getRed();
    int g = color.getGreen();
    int b = color.getBlue();

    // Create and add "Center" panel
    Panel pc = new Panel();
    pc.setLayout(new GridLayout(3, 2, 5, 5));
```

```
      Label lr = new Label("Red");
      lr.setAlignment(Label.RIGHT);
      pc.add(lr);
      sr = new Scrollbar(Scrollbar.HORIZONTAL, r, 10, 0, 255);
      pc.add(sr);
      sr.addAdjustmentListener(this);
      Label lg = new Label("Green");
      lg.setAlignment(Label.RIGHT);
      pc.add(lg);
      sg = new Scrollbar(Scrollbar.HORIZONTAL, g, 10, 0, 255);
      pc.add(sg);
      sg.addAdjustmentListener(this);
      Label lb = new Label("Blue");
      lb.setAlignment(Label.RIGHT);
      pc.add(lb);
      sb = new Scrollbar(Scrollbar.HORIZONTAL, b, 10, 0, 255);
      pc.add(sb);
      sb.addAdjustmentListener(this);
      add(pc, "Center");

      // Create and add "South" panel
      Panel ps = new Panel();
      Button ok = new Button("OK");
      ok.addActionListener(this);
      ps.add(ok);
      add(ps, "South");

      // Handle window events
      addWindowListener(new WindowAdapter() {
        public void windowClosing(WindowEvent we) {
          System.exit(0);
        }
      });

      // Lay out components and set the initial size
      // of this dialog box
      pack();
    }

    public Insets getInsets() {
      return new Insets(40, 20, 20, 20);
    }

    public void actionPerformed(ActionEvent ae) {
      dispose();
    }

    public void adjustmentValueChanged(AdjustmentEvent ae) {

      // Get scroll bar values
      int r = sr.getValue();
      int g = sg.getValue();
      int b = sb.getValue();

      // Set background color of canvas
      parent.canvas.setBackground(new Color(r, g, b));
```

```
        // Repaint canvas
        parent.canvas.repaint();
    }
}
```

▰▰ CUMULATIVE SKILLS CHECK: Chapter 15

```
1. import java.awt.*;
   import java.awt.event.*;
   import java.util.*;

   public class DateDialogDemo extends Frame
   implements ActionListener {

     public static void main(String args[]) {
       DateDialogDemo ddd = new DateDialogDemo();
       ddd.setVisible(true);
       ddd.setSize(200, 100);
     }

     DateDialogDemo() {
       super("Date Dialog Demo");

       // Set layout manager
       setLayout(new FlowLayout());

       // Create button
       Button b = new Button("Date Dialog");
       b.addActionListener(this);
       add(b);

       // Anonymous inner class handles window events
       addWindowListener(new WindowAdapter() {
         public void windowClosing(WindowEvent we) {
           System.exit(0);
         }
       });
     }

     public void actionPerformed(ActionEvent ae) {
       DateDialog dd =
         new DateDialog(this, "Date Dialog", true);
       dd.show();
     }
   }

   class DateDialog extends Dialog
   implements ActionListener {
     static String monthNames[] = { "January",
       "February", "March", "April", "May",
       "June", "July", "August", "September",
       "October", "November", "December" };
```

```
      DateDialog(Frame parent, String title, boolean mode) {
        super(parent, title, mode);

        // Create string with date information
        Calendar calendar = Calendar.getInstance();
        int month = calendar.get(Calendar.MONTH);
        int date = calendar.get(Calendar.DAY_OF_MONTH);
        int year = calendar.get(Calendar.YEAR);
        String str = monthNames[month] + " ";
        str += date + " ";
        str += year;

        // Create and add "Center" panel
        Panel pc = new Panel();
        Label label = new Label(str, Label.CENTER);
        pc.add(label);
        add(pc, "Center");

        // Create and add "South" panel
        Panel ps = new Panel();
        Button ok = new Button("OK");
        ok.addActionListener(this);
        ps.add(ok);
        add(ps, "South");

        // Lay out components and set the initial size
        // of this dialog box
        pack();

        // Anonymous inner class handles window events
        addWindowListener(new WindowAdapter() {
          public void windowClosing(WindowEvent we) {
            dispose();
          }
        });
      }

      public Insets getInsets() {
        return new Insets(40, 20, 20, 20);
      }

      public void actionPerformed(ActionEvent ae) {
        dispose();
      }
    }

2. // Usage:
   //    java ChatServer
   // There are no command line arguments.
   // The server listens for incoming requests
   // on port 2000.

   import java.net.*;
   import java.util.*;
```

```
class ChatServer {
  static Vector serverThreads;

  public static void main(String args[]) {
    try {

      // Create vector to hold server threads
      serverThreads = new Vector();

      // Create server socket
      ServerSocket ss = new ServerSocket(2000);

      // Create infinite loop
      while(true) {

        // Accept incoming requests
        Socket s = ss.accept();

        // Start a thread to handle this client
        ServerThread st = new ServerThread(s);
        st.start();

        // Add thread to vector
        serverThreads.addElement(st);
      }
    }
    catch(Exception e) {
      System.out.println("Exception: " + e);
    }
  }

  public synchronized static void echoAll(String str) {
    Enumeration e = serverThreads.elements();
    while(e.hasMoreElements()) {
      try {
        ServerThread st = (ServerThread)e.nextElement();
        st.echo(str);
      }
      catch(Exception ex) {
        // Ignore any problems communicating with a client
      }
    }
  }
}

import java.io.*;
import java.net.*;

class ServerThread extends Thread {
  private BufferedReader br;
  private PrintWriter pw;

  public ServerThread(Socket socket) {

    try {
```

```
        // Get buffered reader and writer for socket
        InputStream is = socket.getInputStream();
        InputStreamReader isr = new InputStreamReader(is);
        br = new BufferedReader(isr);
        OutputStream os = socket.getOutputStream();
        pw = new PrintWriter(os, true);
      }
      catch(Exception e) {
        // Ignore any problems communicating with client
      }
    }

  public void run() {

      try {

        // Create an infinite loop
        while(true) {

          // Read string from a client
          String str = br.readLine();

          // Echo this string to all clients
          ChatServer.echoAll(str);
        }
      }
      catch(Exception e) {
        // Ignore any problems communicating with client
      }
    }

  public void echo(String str) {

      try {

        // Write string to client
        pw.println(str);
      }
      catch(Exception e) {
        // Ignore any problems communicating with client
      }
    }
  }
}

// Usage:
//    java ChatClient address
// Here, address is the dotted decimal or
// dotted string form of the IP address for
// the machine that executes the ChatServer.

import java.awt.*;
import java.awt.event.*;
import java.io.*;
import java.net.*;

class ChatClient extends Frame
```

```
implements ActionListener, Runnable {
  TextArea ta;
  TextField tf;
  BufferedReader br;
  PrintWriter pw;

  public static void main(String args[]) {

    // Create chat client
    ChatClient cc =
      new ChatClient("ChatClient", args[0], 2000);
    cc.show();
    cc.setSize(200, 200);
  }

  ChatClient(String title, String address, int port) {

    // Invoke the superclass constructor
    super(title);

    // Handle window closing event
    addWindowListener(new WindowAdapter() {
      public void windowClosing(WindowEvent we) {
        System.exit(0);
      }
    });

    // Create a text area and add it to the frame
    ta = new TextArea(10, 20);
    ta.setEditable(false);
    add(ta, "Center");

    // Create a text field and add it to the frame
    tf = new TextField("", 25);
    tf.addActionListener(this);
    add(tf, "South");

    try {

      // Create socket
      Socket s = new Socket(address, port);

      // Create buffered reader and writer for that socket
      InputStream is = s.getInputStream();
      InputStreamReader isr = new InputStreamReader(is);
      br = new BufferedReader(isr);
      OutputStream os = s.getOutputStream();
      pw = new PrintWriter(os, true);
    }
    catch(Exception e) {
    }

    // Create a thread to listen for messages from server
    Thread thread = new Thread(this);
    thread.start();
  }
```

```
    public void actionPerformed(ActionEvent ae) {

      try {

        // Write contents of text field to server
        String str = tf.getText();
        pw.println(str);

        // Clear text field
        tf.setText("");
      }
      catch(Exception e) {
      }
    }

    public void run() {

      try {

        while(true) {

          // Read a string from the server
          String str = br.readLine();

          // Append that string to the text area
          ta.append(str + "\n");
        }
      }
      catch(Exception e) {
      }
    }
  }

3. import java.applet.*;
   import java.awt.*;
   import java.util.*;
   /*
     <applet code="CalendarApplet" width=500 height=250>
     </applet>
   */

   public class CalendarApplet extends Applet {

     static String dayNames[] = { "Sun", "Mon",
       "Tue", "Wed", "Thu", "Fri", "Sat" };
     static String monthNames[] = { "January",
       "February", "March", "April", "May",
       "June", "July", "August", "September",
       "October", "November", "December" };
     static int daysInMonths[] = { 31, 28, 31, 30, 31, 30,
         31, 31, 30, 31, 30, 31 };

     public void init() {

       // Create a calendar initialized with the
```

```java
    // current date/time
    GregorianCalendar gc = new GregorianCalendar();

    // Adjust the date of this calendar to the 1st
    // of the current month
    int date = gc.get(Calendar.DATE);
    gc.add(Calendar.DATE, -(date - 1));

    // Get year, month, and day-of-week components
    int year = gc.get(Calendar.YEAR);
    int month = gc.get(Calendar.MONTH);
    int dow = gc.get(Calendar.DAY_OF_WEEK);

    // Adjust for leap year
    daysInMonths[1] += gc.isLeapYear(year) ? 1 : 0;

    // Create GUI
    setLayout(new BorderLayout());
    String s = monthNames[month] + " " + year;
    Label calendarLabel = new Label(s, Label.CENTER);
    add(calendarLabel, "North");
    CalendarCanvas calendarCanvas = new CalendarCanvas(year, month, dow);
    add(calendarCanvas, "Center");
  }
}

class CalendarCanvas extends Canvas {
  int year, month, dow;

  public CalendarCanvas(int year, int month, int dow) {
    this.year = year;
    this.month = month;
    this.dow = dow;
  }

  public void paint(Graphics g) {

    // Draw rectangle around the canvas boundaries
    Dimension d = getSize();
    int h = d.height;
    int w = d.width;
    g.drawRect(0, 0, w - 1, h - 1);

    // Draw lines for the grid columns
    int c = w/7;
    for(int i = 1; i < 7; i++) {
      g.drawLine(i * c, 0, i * c, h);
    }

    // Draw lines for the grid rows
    int r = h/13;
    for(int i = 1; i <= 11; i = i + 2) {
      g.drawLine(0, i * r, w, i * r);
    }

    // Draw the names of the days on the grid
```

```
for(int i = 0; i < 7; i++) {
  String s = CalendarApplet.dayNames[i];
  FontMetrics fm = g.getFontMetrics();
  int ascent = fm.getAscent();
  int width = fm.stringWidth(s);
  int x = i * c + (c - width)/2;
  int y = (r - ascent)/2 + ascent;
  g.drawString(s, x, y);
}

// Compute the variable dom (day-of-month)
// (If necessary, this will be a negative value)
int dom = (1 <= dow) ? 1 - dow + 1 :  1 - 8 + dow;

// Draw numbers into the grid cells
for(int row = 0; row < 6; row++) {
  for(int col = 0; col < 7; col++) {
    if(dom > CalendarApplet.daysInMonths[month]) {
      break;
    }
    if(dom > 0) {
      // Display date in the grid cell
      String s = "" + dom;
      FontMetrics fm = g.getFontMetrics();
      int ascent = fm.getAscent();
      int width = fm.stringWidth(s);
      int x = c * col + (c - width)/2;
      int y = 2 * r * row +
        (2 * r - ascent)/2 + ascent + r;
      g.drawString(s, x, y);
    }
    ++dom;
  }
}
}
}
```

CHAPTER 16

REVIEW SKILLS CHECK: Chapter 16

1. Title and menu bars
2. **show( )**
3. **BorderLayout**
4. **FlowLayout**
5.
```
import java.applet.*;
import java.awt.*;
import java.awt.event.*;
import java.util.*;
```

```
/*
  <applet code=Calculator width=250 height=250>
  </applet>
*/

public class Calculator extends Applet
implements ActionListener {
  private final static int NBUTTONS = 18;
  String buttonLabels[] = { "0", "1", "2", "3", "4", "5",
    "6", "7", "8", "9", ".", "+/-", "+", "-", "=", "*", "/", "C" };
  Button buttons[];
  TextField tf;
  String operator;
  double register1, register2;
  boolean overwriteDisplay;

  public void init() {

    // Initialize operator
    operator = "";

    // Set Layout manager for the applet
    setLayout(new BorderLayout());

    // Create panel to hold the text field
    Panel pn = new Panel();
    tf = new TextField(20);
    tf.setEditable(false);
    pn.add(tf);
    add("North", pn);

    // Create buttons
    buttons = new Button[NBUTTONS];
    for(int i = 0; i < NBUTTONS; i++) {
      buttons[i] = new Button(buttonLabels[i]);
      buttons[i].addActionListener(this);
    }

    // Create panel to hold the buttons
    // Use a grid layout manager for that panel
    Panel pc = new Panel();
    pc.setLayout(new GridLayout(6, 3));

    // Add buttons to the grid
    for(int i = 0; i < NBUTTONS; i++) {
      pc.add(buttons[i]);
    }

    // Add the grid to the applet
    add("Center", pc);
  }

  public void actionPerformed(ActionEvent ae) {

    // Determine which button was pressed
    String ac = ae.getActionCommand();
```

```java
// Check if the "C" key was pressed
if(ac.equals("C")) {
  tf.setText("");
  operator = "";
  register1 = 0;
  register2 = 0;
  return;
}

// Check if the "+/-" key was pressed
if(ac.equals("+/-")) {
  String s = tf.getText();
  if(s.startsWith("-")) {
    tf.setText(s.substring(1));
  }
  else {
    tf.setText("-" + s);
  }
  return;
}

// Process decimal point.
if(ac.equals(".")) {
  if(overwriteDisplay) {
    tf.setText(ac);
    overwriteDisplay = false;
    return;
  }
  String s = tf.getText();
  if(s.indexOf('.') != -1)
    return;
  s += '.';
  tf.setText(s);
  return;
}

// Process digits
if(ac.equals("0") || ac.equals("1") || ac.equals("2") ||
ac.equals("3") || ac.equals("4") || ac.equals("5") ||
ac.equals("6") || ac.equals("7") || ac.equals("8") ||
ac.equals("9")) {
  if(overwriteDisplay)
    tf.setText(ac);
  else
    tf.setText(tf.getText() + ac);
  overwriteDisplay = false;
}

// Process operators
if(ac.equals("+") || ac.equals("-") ||
ac.equals("*") || ac.equals("/") ||
ac.equals("=")) {
  register2 = Double.valueOf(tf.getText()).doubleValue();
  register1 = calculate(operator, register1, register2);
  tf.setText("" + register1);
```

```
          operator = ac;
          overwriteDisplay = true;
      }
    }

    public double calculate(String operator, double r1, double r2) {
      if(operator.equals("+")) r1 += r2;
      else if(operator.equals("-")) r1 -= r2;
      else if(operator.equals("*")) r1 *= r2;
      else if(operator.equals("/")) r1 /= r2;
      else r1 = r2;
      return r1;
    }

    public Insets getInsets() {
      return new Insets(10, 10, 20, 10);
    }
  }
```

```
6. import java.applet.*;
   import java.awt.*;
   import java.awt.event.*;
   /*
     <applet code="Gradient" width=250 height=250>
     </applet>
   */

   public class Gradient extends Applet
   implements ItemListener {
     Checkbox cb1, cb2;
     MyCanvas myCanvas;

     public void init() {

       // Set layout manager
       setLayout(new BorderLayout());

       // Create panel for "North"
       Panel pn = new Panel();
       CheckboxGroup cbg = new CheckboxGroup();
       cb1 = new Checkbox("Horizontal", cbg, true);
       cb1.addItemListener(this);
       pn.add(cb1);
       cb2 = new Checkbox("Vertical", cbg, false);
       cb2.addItemListener(this);
       pn.add(cb2);
       add(pn, "North");

       // Create panel for "Center"
       Panel pc = new Panel();
       myCanvas = new MyCanvas(this);
       myCanvas.setSize(200, 200);
       pc.add(myCanvas);
       add(pc, "Center");
     }
```

```java
    public void itemStateChanged(ItemEvent ie) {
      myCanvas.repaint();
    }
}

class MyCanvas extends Canvas {
  Gradient gradient;

  public MyCanvas(Gradient gradient) {
    this.gradient = gradient;
  }

  public void paint(Graphics g) {

    // Select horizontal or vertical gradient
    if(gradient.cb1.getState())
      hgradient(g);
    else
      vgradient(g);
  }

  public void hgradient(Graphics g) {
    Dimension d = getSize();
    float delta = (float)(255/d.width);
    for(int i = 0; i < d.width; i++) {
      int c = (int)(delta * i);
      g.setColor(new Color(c, c, c));
      g.drawLine(i, 0, i, d.height);
    }
  }

  public void vgradient(Graphics g) {
    Dimension d = getSize();
    float delta = (float)(255/d.height);
    for(int i = 0; i < d.height; i++) {
      int c = (int)(delta * i);
      g.setColor(new Color(c, c, c));
      g.drawLine(0, i, d.width, i);
    }
  }
}
```

Index

& (bitwise AND), 119
& (Boolean logical AND), 96
&& (short-circuit AND), 96-97
*, 20
\, 17, 18, 93
| (bitwise OR), 119
| (Boolean logical OR), 96
|| (short-circuit OR), 96-97
^ (bitwise exclusive OR), 119
^ (Boolean logical exclusive OR), 96
{ }, 84
=, 13
= = (Boolean logical operator), 96
= = (relational operator), 81
!, 96
! = (Boolean logical operator), 96
! = (relational operator), 81
/, 20
//, 27
/* */, 28
/** */, 27
<, 81
< <, 119-120, 121
< =, 81
-, 19, 20, 21
—, 20, 90-92
( ), 20, 21
%, 20, 21
+ (addition operator), 20
+ (concatenation operator), 15, 17, 18, 19
+ +, 20, 90-92
? :, 99
>, 81
> >, 119-120, 121
> > >, 119-120
> =, 81
; (semicolon), 10, 13
[ ], 30
~, 119

A

abstract
    class modifier, 183-184
    method modifier, 189, 190-191
Abstract Window Toolkit (AWT), 8, 368, 418, 442
accept( ), 352, 353
ActionEvent class, 421, 424, 448
ActionListener interface, 421, 449, 466, 469
actionPerformed( ), 421, 449, 467, 469, 490, 495, 500, 503
Activation frame, 231-232
Adapter classes, 432-433
    and inner classes, 434-437
add( ), 443, 445
    for border layout managers, 479
    for Menu objects, 492